An Oral History of Development Cooperation

"In this era when development cooperation undergoes drastic transformation, it is crucial for us to learn from past experience to inform future strategies. Japan's approach has focused on teaching people how to fish rather than giving them fish, thereby fostering unbreakable bonds of trust with local people. This book vividly depicts how these trusting relationships enabled development projects to overcome unforeseen challenges and crises. By sharing narratives of those involved, the book also reveals their expectation, frustration, and a shared sense of accomplishment. This book is a must read for anyone interested in the future direction of global efforts in development cooperation."

—Tanaka Akihiko, *President, Japan International Cooperation Agency (JICA)*

Yoichi Mine

An Oral History of Development Cooperation

Experiences of Japan and its Partners

Springer

Yoichi Mine
JICA Ogata Sadako Research Institute for
Peace and Development
Tokyo, Japan

ISBN 978-981-95-5478-2 ISBN 978-981-95-5479-9 (eBook)
https://doi.org/10.1007/978-981-95-5479-9

This work was supported by JICA Ogata Research Institute.

Translation from the Japanese language edition: "Kaihatsu kyōryoku no ōraru historī: Kiki wo koete" by Yoichi Mine, © The JICA Ogata Sadako Research Institute for Peace and Development 2023. Published by University of Tokyo Press. All Rights Reserved.

This Springer imprint is published by the registered company Springer Nature Singapore Pte Ltd.
The registered company address is: 152 Beach Road, #21-01/04 Gateway East, Singapore 189721, Singapore

Preface

In her essay titled 'Milky Currents', Ishimure Michiko, a poet and storyteller based in Minamata, a quiet fishing town devastated by mercury pollution during the rapid industrialisation of post-war Japan (see Chapter 6), wrote,

> .... the folks who reside in my landscape are not persons unconcerned with literacy, but they themselves are the undeciphered existence waiting to be read. If such an existence is still alive and stays within us, I believe one should read these human persons as if one were reading fragments of oracle bone scripts, as if one were deciphering Incan pictographs. For we have now entered an era in which the soil and our people are being weathered and destroyed alive, more drastically than the relics buried underground. (Ishimure 1988: 138)

People's knowledge is 'being weathered and destroyed alive', indeed. If we do not collect people's memories now and carefully interpret what they recount, it will become impossible to preserve their lived experiences as part of historical records and pass them on to future generations. In the world of development cooperation, where visitors and locals, the drifters and the settled, have interacted and shared diverse emotions, myriad events and experiences are waiting to be documented.

To write this book, I listened to the voices of nearly 300 people, whether renowned or unknown, although I am not very good at talking to living people. In order to interact effectively with the interviewees, I undertook thorough preparatory desk research. I downloaded reports on the projects from electronic libraries, read them beforehand, and met Japanese informants to understand the projects as much as possible. I also read academic literature, travel guides, and sometimes novels about the places. In virtual reality, I used Google Street View to walk around the streets of the places I would visit. However, preparation was rarely complete. I stuffed copies of documents into my hand luggage and skimmed through them on the flight, only to reassure myself.

The meetings could have been equally stressful for interviewees. A professor was coming all the way to write a book about a project to which they had devoted half their lifetime. As they recalled one critical event after another from the past, some may have found it difficult to sleep on the eve of the interview, like me.

Then comes the meeting day. I met interviewees in small coffee shops, living rooms of their homes, hotel lobbies, office conference rooms, empty school classrooms, farms, factories, and laboratories. I began by saying, 'I am writing an oral history of Japan's development cooperation. This project is important, so I've come here to talk with you about the project you engaged in.' The introductions were similar, so they came out quickly. In the meantime, I could see that the interviewee was watching me. I also observed his or her countenance as we started exchanging words. While writing this, I no longer remember what language we spoke. Instead, I can more easily recall their smile, bewildered expression, and tone of voice.

The main questions had already been communicated to the interviewees. There labouredwere three main questions: How do you evaluate the project? What kind of difficulties did the project encounter? And how were the relationships between the Japanese experts and your people? Far from being illiterate, most of my interviewees were those who had received artisanal training in their professions and with unwavering devotion for the sake of people around them and for their home country. Typically, they might not have been ordinary common folk, yet they were definitely not among the power elites.

Those whom I spoke to were the so-called 'counterparts' of Japanese development cooperation experts. They were the local professionals who received technology transfer from Japanese experts, worked together, and made their project sustainable after the Japanese assistance was terminated. They were local agricultural extension workers, civil engineers, high school teachers, medical doctors and nurses, and civil servants taking charge of particular development projects; all were supposed to be the peers of Japanese experts. Some might argue that, if one intends to write a history of development cooperation, one should first listen to the voices of ordinary people, the ultimate beneficiaries of development projects. However, I deliberately chose to foreground the perspectives of the local counterparts, rather than the so-called end users. The reason I focused on this group of locals will be explained in Chapter 1. I hope the reader will fully grasp my intention while engaging with the theoretical part that precedes the case studies.

More precisely, from June 2018 to August 2024 (when my fieldwork was resumed after the long hiatus due to COVID-19), I interviewed 288 people (including participants in group interviews) involved in 16 projects in 13 countries (including Japan). Although I also conducted interviews with Japanese experts and officers of the Japan International Cooperation Agency (JICA), I seldom cite interview narratives obtained from these people on the donor side. This is because the voices of Japanese aid workers and officers have already been strongly represented in numerous publications. This book attempts to restore balance by amplifying the voices on the side of the developing countries.

As the title indicates, this book presents an oral history of Japan's development cooperation. As the reader will see in the case study chapters, the description in this book is based not only on oral sources but also on documentary sources. I have used published papers and reports mainly to provide the background to the projects, and then attempted to use oral information extensively in the sections that discuss the projects' dynamics on the ground. Discovering new documentary materials for historical research is challenging, but if such documents have already been classified and stored, we can access them by visiting archives. By contrast, conducting interviews to write an oral history is an act by historians of creating historical resources that have not existed. This is where the pleasure of oral history lies, and I leave it to the reader to judge the extent to which this work is successful. Oral history can only be reconstructed based on the memories of living people. The memories of adult people living today are of events in the recent past, not a century but typically several decades ago. Therefore, this book mainly deals with projects from the 1980s onwards, with a few exceptional cases dating back to the 1960s and 1970s.

On different occasions, not a few interviewees asked me, 'In what language will you write the book?' I answered, 'Well, I will write it in Japanese.' Then they would reply, 'Please write your book in English, too. I would love to know how you describe me and our project.' Now, I am glad to present this version of the history to an international audience, including those who joined conversations with me. In the long run, however, I wish the local people who grew the projects to write their own history in whatever language they prefer. Until that time, this book will serve as a makeshift.

The counterparts, as the main source of information in this book, were not chosen at random. They were the people who were approached by JICA and agreed to be interviewed. Readers who think that research that is not scientifically representative is worthless should refer to the results of public opinion surveys rather than reading this kind of book, which is full of selection bias; the majority of the interviewees are those who participated in development projects and spoke passionately about their own experiences. There were also cases where I missed the chance to interview knowledgeable key figures, because they happened to be away when I visited. This book is the result of purely qualitative researches to supplement quantitative ones. Yet, when I discovered similarities in the patterns of interviewees' responses under starkly different circumstances, I felt that I might have reached a kind of 'saturation', which represents some sort of robustness in qualitative investigation (Bertaux 1997).

The book is not structured to follow the flow of time in chronological order. Chapter 1 will provide a detailed description of the methodology underlying this book. The main discussion from Chapters 2 to 6 is organised by sector—agriculture and fisheries, manufacturing, education, health, and human security—and these are all arranged thematically. However, within each section of these chapters, the content traces a similar time sequence from the conception of a project and visits by Japanese experts to their collaboration with local people, so-called graduation, and the discussion of the prospect for future scaling-up, though they mostly had to follow bumpy gravel roads. While designing this book's structure, I happened to read a fascinating work, *The Periodic Table*, by Primo Levi, a collection of short autobiographical stories inspired by the characteristics of 21 elements from argon to carbon (Levi 1982). In that book, the individual stories have their own self-contained worlds and are arranged in a particular order. Although no one can compare my prosaic book to such a literary masterpiece, when I was describing the connections between the autonomous projects, I was reminded of the world of the *Table.* The logic behind the arrangement of the chapters in this book will be explained in Chapter 1.

* * *

This book is an outcome of collaboration with countless people. First of all, I want to express my sincere gratitude to all the counterparts who agreed to be interviewed and took the time to read the parts of the manuscript that concerned them—draft versions of this book were widely circulated and discussed among them. Those contributors are listed at the end of the book. JICA's president, Dr. Tanaka Akihiko, warmly encouraged the publication of this English version. Members of the ambitious research project initiated by JICA's former President Dr. Kitaoka Schinichi, 'Japan's Development Cooperation: A Historical Perspective', carefully read my Japanese manuscript and provided invaluable comments. Mr. Goto Kensuke of University of Tokyo Press gave professional guidance to the research members. Various departments and overseas offices of JICA supported the fieldwork and provided excellent feedback. Several JICA colleagues aided me beyond the scope of their duties. Among many, I thank Ms. Yanagihara Makiko, who skilfully and selflessly arranged field research in various parts of Asia, Africa, and Latin America and now works in Peru. Ms. Asano Keiko meticulously helped me prepare the English edition.

I hope this book will be read with a critical mind, especially by practitioners of development and scholars of development studies outside Japan, be they working in the Global South, Western traditional donors, or emerging donor countries.

July 2025

Yoichi Mine
Executive Director
JICA (Japan International Cooperation Agency) Ogata Sadako Research Institute for Peace and Development
Ichigaya, Tokyo, Japan

Contents

About the Author

Yoichi Mine is Executive Director of the JICA Ogata Sadako Research Institute for Peace and Development. He is also Extraordinary Professor, the Department of Political Science, University of Stellenbosch in South Africa. His research interests include human security, international development, and African area study. His English publications include *Connecting Africa and Asia: Afrasia As a Benign Community* (Routledge, 2022), *Human Security Norms in East Asia* (co-edited, Palgrave, 2019), *Human Security and Cross-Border Cooperation in East Asia* (co-edited, Palgrave, 2019), *Migration and Agency in a Globalizing World* (co-edited, Palgrave, 2018), and *Preventing Violent Conflict in Africa* (co-edited, Palgrave, 2013).

Abbreviations

AAR, Japan	Association for Aid and Relief, Japan
ACFOD	Asian Cultural Forum on Development
ADB	Asian Development Bank
ADEA	Association for the Development of Education in Africa
ADTEC	Advanced Technology Training Centre
AICAD	African Institute for Capacity Development
ASEAN	Association of Southeast Asian Nations
BBWS	Brantas River Basin Management Office
BKD	bacterial kidney disease
CECAPRO	Centro de Calidad y Productividad (Quality and Productivity Centre)
CEFOF	Centro de Formación de Formadores y de Personal Técnico para el Desarrollo Industrial de Centroamérica (Training Centre for Trainers and Technical Personnel for the Industrial Development of Central America)
CEMASTEA	Centre for Mathematics, Science and Technology Education in Africa
CETEM	Centro de Tecnologia Mineral (Mineral Technology Research Centre)
CIAST	Centre for Instructor and Advanced Skill Training
CIDA	Canadian International Development Agency
COVAX	COVID-19 Vaccines Global Access
CUNA	Colegio Universitario de Alajuela (Alajuela University College)
DA	development agency
DFID	Department for International Development
EEC	Eastern Economic Corridor
FAJE	Federation of Associations for Japanese Emigration
FAO	Food and Agriculture Organization
FDI	foreign direct investment
GRIPS	National Graduate Institute for Policy Studies

GTZ	Deutsche Gesellschaft für Technische Zusammenarbeit (German Agency for Technical Cooperation)
HDI	Human Development Index
HPC	Higher Population Council
HUCZCZ	Hokkaido University Center for Zoonosis Control in Zambia
ICT	information and communication technology
IDB	Inter-American Development Bank
ILO	International Labour Organization
ISA	infectious salmon anaemia
IT	information technology
IUD	intrauterine device
JBIC	Japan Bank for International Cooperation
JEMIS	Japan Emigration Service
JEPC	Japan Emigration Promotion Co., Ltd
JICA	Japan International Cooperation Agency
JICE	Japan International Cooperation Center
JKCAT	Jomo Kenyatta College of Agriculture and Technology
JKUAT	Jomo Kenyatta University of Agriculture and Technology
JKUCAT	Jomo Kenyatta University College of Agriculture and Technology
JMTI	Japan Malaysia Technological Institute
JOCV	Japan Overseas Cooperation Volunteers
JOHUD	Jordanian Hashemite Fund for Human Development
JPC	Japan Productivity Center
JST	Japan Science and Technology Agency
JVC	Japan International Volunteer Center
KADC	Kilimanjaro Agricultural Development Centre
KADP	Kilimanjaro Agricultural Development Project
KATC	Kilimanjaro Agricultural Training Centre
KEMRI	Kenya Medical Research Institute
KOICA	Korea International Cooperation Agency
KSTC	Kenya Science Teachers College
LARA	Licensed Agencies for Relief in Asia
LDP	Liberal Democratic Party
MJIIT	Malaysia-Japan International Institute of Technology
MoW	Memory of the World
NC	numerical control
NEP	New Economic Policy
NGO	non-governmental organisation
NIES	Newly Industrialising Economies
NIH	National Institutes of Health
NIMD	National Institute for Minamata Disease
NMIMR	Noguchi Memorial Institute for Medical Research
NPF	narrative policy framework
ODA	official development assistance

OECD	Organisation for Economic Co-operation and Development
OECF	Overseas Economic Cooperation Fund
OHP	overhead projector
OJT	on-the-job training
OPAC	Okinawa Peace Assistance Center
OTCA	Overseas Technology Cooperation Agency
PDM	project design matrix
PKI	Partai Komunis Indonesia (Indonesian Communist Party)
PLN	Perusahaan Listrik Negara (State Electricity Company)
RIHN	Research Institute of Humanity and Nature
SADC	Southern African Development Community
SADCC	Southern African Development Coordination Conference
SAP	structural adjustment programme
SATREPS	Science and Technology Research Partnership for Sustainable Development
SERNAP	Servicio Nacional de Pesca y Acuicultura (Chilean National Fisheries and Aquaculture Service)
SMASE	Strengthening Mathematics and Science Education
SMASE-WECSA	Strengthening of Mathematics and Science Education in Western, Eastern, Central and Southern Africa
SMASSE	Strengthening Mathematics and Science in Secondary Education
SME	small and medium-sized enterprise
TANU	Tanganyika African National Union
TCTP	third-country training programme
TQC	Total Quality Control
TRC	Truth and Reconciliation Commission
TVA	Tennessee Valley Authority
TVET	technical and vocational education and training
UNDP	United Nations Development Programme
UNEP	United Nations Environment Programme
UNESCO	United Nations Educational, Scientific and Cultural Organization
UNICEF	United Nations Children's Fund
UNZA	University of Zambia
USAID	United States Agency for International Development
UTN	Universidad Técnica Nacional (National Technical University)
WHO	World Health Organization

List of Figures

Chapter 1
Voices from the Receiving Side: Writing an Oral History of Development Cooperation

1.1 One Fact, Many Truths

1.1.1 Putting the Receiving Side on the Central Stage

Let me begin by asking a question. Is it worth writing about Japan's development cooperation today? The days when Japan was the largest donor in the world have been gone for decades. Although Japan has not entirely lost its economic power, emerging countries such as China, India, Brazil, and Indonesia are catching up. The United States and Europe are becoming increasingly inward-looking and somehow losing their normative lustre as leading providers of global public goods. Can we learn anything from declining nations, including Japan?

Let me answer. One of the reasons I wanted to discuss Japan's development cooperation is simply that I am not a citizen of any other country. I happened to be born and raised in Japan, and I am acquainted with Japan's experience. Had I been Chinese, I would probably have written a book on the Chinese development experience.

The other reason is more of my own choice and perspective. Historically, Japan was the first non-Western nation that crossed the North–South divide and joined the group of developed nations in terms of material prosperity. In this process, Japan acted shamefully when emulating the Western powers in expanding its colonies in the Asia–Pacific region, yet it is undeniable that the country has accumulated national wealth at an astonishing pace throughout the past century. The goal of the social transformation known as development is to move from chronic indigence to sustainable well-being, and being part of the West is not a condition for this transformative process, as demonstrated by Japan's experience. Development is always a process of hybrid 'translative adaptation', which 'involves selectively adopting and adapting foreign knowledge and technologies to the specific conditions of the home society' (Ohno 2024: 5).

Y. Mine, *An Oral History of Development Cooperation*,
https://doi.org/10.1007/978-981-95-5479-9_1

I believe that Japan can provide a unique model for so-called 'late developers', precisely because it has struggled to 'selectively adopt and apply' dominant foreign knowledge in uncharted waters and tried to replicate such endeavours with other developing nations. In my view, here lies the most significant utility in learning from Japan's development cooperation: Japan has been a pioneering, intermediary translator of development.

In this regard, it becomes crucial to inquire how this Japanese way of 'doing development' appeared in the eyes of those who worked with Japanese in the Global South. This study therefore seeks to reconstruct the history of Japan's development cooperation through extensive use of oral evidence on the receiving side of the assistance. A large amount of official documentary materials is kept at the JICA Library, the Ministry of Foreign Affairs, and other public offices and agencies, and is being digitalised. There is also a considerable volume of Japanese articles and commercial books written by Japanese experts and policy-makers involved in development cooperation. However, these are materials left by the giving side, and we seldom see documents based on the voices of the receiving end of the assistance. One of the chief objectives of this book is to fill that lacuna and better understand the chemistry, whether successful or not, at the interface between the giving nation, Japan, and the receiving nations.

In the post-war decades, Japan intended to provide assistance to the newly independent countries in the Global South so that they could succeed in nation-building through the development of human resources and infrastructure.[1] A long-standing Japanese slogan captured this philosophy: 'contributing to national development (*kuni-zukuri*) through human development (*hito-zukuri*)'.[2] A brochure published by JICA in 1994 to mark the 20th anniversary of the agency was entitled 'Human Development, National Development, and Heart-to-Heart Communications', and the back page of the brochure reads 'Beyond States, Beyond Nations, Creating Wisdom

---

[1] Technical cooperation focuses on supporting national development through human (resources) development, while yen loans aim to support national development through infrastructure development. Yamada Junichi's *History of Infrastructure Cooperation* (2021) discusses the latter cycle (in Japanese), while my book focuses on the former. However, the two are not mutually exclusive: the integration of the yen loan section of the Japan Bank for International Cooperation (JBIC) and JICA in 2008 was intended to achieve synergies by combining technical cooperation, yen loans, and the provision of grants. As for the birth of the Global South discourses in the light of human security, see Mine (2023).

[2] Literally, the translation of *hito-zukuri* (人づくり) and *kuni-zukuri* (国づくり) is 'human-making and nation-making'. In practice, the meaning of *hito-zukuri* is close to, but broader than, human resources development. In this book, I choose the term 'human development', though this is not the same as the concept of human development that has its own definition laid by the United Nations Development Programme (UNDP) (UNDP 1990; Fukuda-Parr and Kumar 2009). On the other hand, I choose the term 'national development' for the term *kuni-zukuri,* though it can also be translated as 'nation-building.' *Kuni* may refer to a nation, a state, or a country. This combination of terms appeared for the first time, perhaps, in Matsunaga Yasuzaemon's *Hito-zukuri, Kuni-zukuri,* a collection of essays on the challenge of nation-building in post-war Japan (Matsunaga 1965). Matsunaga led the electronic power industry in Japan and is known as a designer of the Numata Dam on the Tone River system.

for Tomorrow'[3] (JICA 1994d). The underlying aspiration was to provide dedicated support for development projects with a banal and yet universal objective of satisfying what Adam Smith called 'the desire to better one's condition' (Smith 1999: 358). It was hoped that national wealth would be augmented in developing countries as the collective outcomes of development projects that capitalise on the potentially rich human resources. Japan has achieved such an objective in the process of rapid modernisation, albeit with much pain and regression (as discussed later in Chap. 6).

In the all too famous words of the historian E. H. Carr, history is 'an unending dialogue between the present and the past' (Carr 1987: 30). We interpret the past on the basis of the conditions, values, and preoccupations of our present times. However, fabricating facts, neglecting critical events, or pretending that what our forerunners dreamt of did not exist is to abdicate scholarly responsibility. History is a process of interaction between the historian and the historical facts, and 'the historian without his facts is rootless and futile; the facts without their historian are dead and meaningless' (ibid.). Many Japanese actors of development cooperation in the twentieth century cherished the aspirations of contributing to nation-building in the South. Whether those aspirations were realised remains a subject for critical inquiry, but I think their existence is itself a historical fact.

Who, then, are the main actors of 'national development through human development'? In the Japanese media, the activities of experts in human resources development and Japan Overseas Cooperation Volunteers (JOCV, or JICA Volunteers) struggling in developing countries are widely documented and publicised.[4] By contrast, the recipients of assistance who think and act on their own initiative rarely attract the attention they deserve.[5] The local beneficiaries of international cooperation are generally portrayed as those who are needy or grateful for the assistance. While their images are sometimes vividly captured in photographs, they are rarely represented as people with agency who evaluate and may criticise the Japanese practice of development assistance. Perhaps the best-known project in the field of development studies that has attempted to shed light on the agency of ordinary people by collecting their lively narratives is the World Bank's three-volume publication, *The Voices of the Poor* (Narayan Patel et al. 2000, Narayan Chambers et al. 2000; Narayan and Petesch 2002). However, as the focus of that research was not on 'cooperation' per se, I wanted to adopt a somewhat different approach.

[3] For readers who can read Japanese, the original phrase is: 「国を超え，民族を超え，英知を，明日のために」. See also JICA (1999b).

[4] A series of public relations magazines in Japanese such as *Overseas Technical Cooperation* (1962–74), *International Cooperation* (1974–2005), *Monthly JICA* (2005–08), *Jica's World* (2008–13), *mundi* (2013–2021), *JICA Magazine* (2021–), *Young Power* (1965–78), and *Crossroads* (1978–) communicate the activities of professionals and volunteers. Magazines such as the Overseas Economic Cooperation Fund's *OECF Newsletter* (1993–1999) and the Japan Bank for International Cooperation's *JBIC Today* (2003–) also portray Japanese actors mainly in the private sector.

[5] The recent monographs of JICA's project history series (launched in 2010) have been focusing more on presenting the voices of their counterparts. Some titles are translated into English and other languages. https://www.jica.go.jp/english/jica_ri/publication/projecthistory/index.html (English); https://www.jica.go.jp/jica-ri/ja/publication/projecthistory/index.html (Japanese).

The narratives of the givers are often thick, while those of the recipients tend to appear thin. The former may be angsty and perceptive, while the latter appear to be sanguine and innocent. Several factors account for this asymmetry; the Japanese public, the taxpayers, want to see the Japanese working hard, their efforts bearing fruit, and the local people being thankful to Japan—the public pressure to prove that tax money has been spent appropriately is imperative. In addition, in order to motivate Japanese experts, officers, and JICA Volunteers, it is instrumental to show that their seniors have accomplished meaningful tasks after hardships. It is also essential for project reports to communicate how the stated goals have been achieved. For the purpose of measurement, objective figures would be more effective than subjective perceptions of beneficiaries. Human joys and sorrows are not easy to measure.

However, the basic philosophy of Japan's development cooperation has been to 'support people's self-help effort', and this means that development projects are to be 'owned' by local people. According to this philosophy, local people should help themselves and take the initiative in designing and implementing projects for themselves. The role of donors should be no more than standing by and lending a helping hand. Given the ownership of the recipient side, it must be the local people, not the donors, who ultimately judge whether a project has succeeded or failed. Critical questions therefore arise: What did the local people expect from their counterparts who hailed from the islands in East Asia? How did the former evaluate the quality of the latter's collaboration? What problems did they encounter? Where and how did they stumble and succeed? Answering these questions would contribute to having a fuller, more balanced picture of the history of development cooperation.

Then, an idea popped into my head. In order to give a better historical outlook of development cooperation, we need to record and present the voices of the people on the receiving end of assistance. If so, simply, let us do it now. Why not visit the sites of development projects around the world, find the people involved in them, listen to their stories, and record them? Officially documented materials will be stored almost permanently in the public domain. Future researchers and practitioners will be able to read them. However, the stories that are not documented but remain only in people's personal memories will not last unless they are recorded in some form. Someone who was involved in the project in 1980 at the age of 30 is already almost 75 at the time of writing this book.

Let us give it a try. The sooner, the better.

1.1.2 Project Sites I Visited

Thus, my journey to visit development projects began. I took up JICA's large and small projects as examples. In this section, I will explain how I selected the projects for fieldwork.

At the outset, I discussed my intentions and preferences with the staff of the JICA Ogata Research Institute.[6] The majority of development projects are small ones. Some are carried out by individual JICA Volunteers, while others disappear after preliminary feasibility studies. For this research, I selected a set of projects that were relatively large in scale in terms of budget and duration of time. One reason for this choice was a practical one. If a chosen project were not big enough, the people involved would have dispersed and disappeared, rendering it almost impractical to trace and find interviewees. The other reason was more substantial. A relatively large and enduring project may have become a norm for subsequent projects, thereby generating broader ripple effects. Such a big project may have started as a small experimental project and gradually scaled up.

On the other hand, I thought it would be better not to select only the successful projects—most readers interested in this subject are likely to have discerning eyes, so self-congratulation would alienate them. Instead, I wanted to include projects that were on the verge of collapse at some point in the past, even though they are now regarded as successful ventures. I also wanted to visit projects that have not yet produced a dazzling impact or are in the shadow of past glories.[7]

With these considerations in mind, I selected the projects one by one with the staff of the Institute. Since 2014 marked the 60th anniversary of Japan's Official development assistance (ODA), the contents of major projects of the past were presented on a special website of JICA, which I found resourceful. After seeking the opinions of JICA's departments in charge of the shortlisted projects, the final selection was made. Five countries in Asia (Indonesia, Malaysia, Cambodia, Thailand, and Jordan), four in Africa (Kenya, Tanzania, Zambia, and Ghana), three in Latin America (Costa Rica, Brazil, and Chile), and two places in Japan (Minamata and Okinawa) were chosen (Fig. 1.1). The 16 projects in these countries were classified into the following categories: agriculture and fisheries, manufacturing, education, health, and human security, corresponding to the chapters structured in this book.

We also considered including in case studies other projects such as the construction of Delhi Metro in India, reforestation in Nepal, emergency relief following the 2008 Sichuan earthquake in China, the construction and the maintenance of the Matadi Bridge in the Democratic Republic of the Congo, and the infrastructure development for elementary schools in the Philippines. However, due to the unexpected outbreak of the COVID-19 pandemic, these case studies had to be cancelled. In retrospect, including all of them would have resulted in a book of unmanageable length.

---

[6] The JICA Research Institute was established in October 2008 to conduct research on development issues. The research component was legally included in JICA's official mission when JICA merged with JBIC that year. In April 2020, the institute was renamed the JICA Ogata Sadako Research Institute for Peace and Development (JICA Ogata Research Institute).

[7] Sato (2021: Chaps. 6 and 9) (in Japanese) investigated the current state of the 'problematic projects' in Southeast Asia that were the targets of ODA bashing in the 1980s. The fact is that ten out of 12 projects he visited were (to Sato's own surprise) well received by local people. Sato argued that this perverse outcome did not mean that the project was carefully designed but was realised through local dynamics and the passage of time.

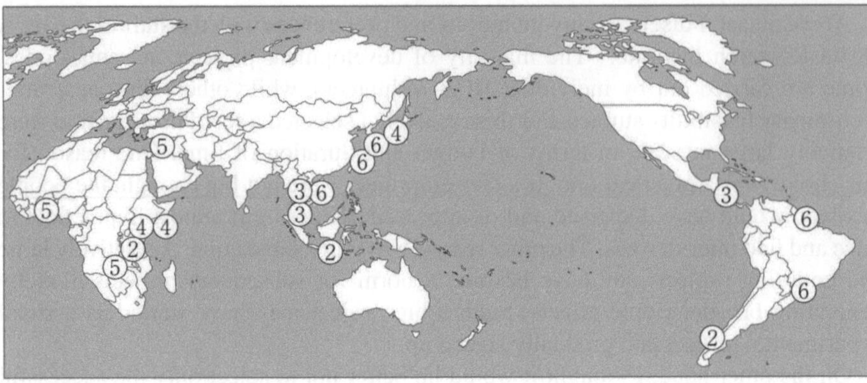

Fig. 1.1 Distribution of case studies. Note: Numbers are chapter numbers. Source: Author

1.1.3 Focus on Counterparts

A total of 288 interviews were conducted with counterparts in these 16 projects. The time spent on each interview varied but averaged approximately one hour. The interviews took place in meeting rooms in public offices, school classrooms, laboratories, interviewees' homes, coffee shops, hotel lobbies, etc. Whenever possible, I sought to situate conversations within the ordinary spaces of people's professional and personal lives.

When approaching interviewees, we prioritised a category of people known in the international development lexicon as 'counterparts'.[8] Unlike civil society cooperation, ODA is based on the transfer of resources from government to government. Therefore, the main interviewees were selected from those who worked for public organisations and directly managed projects at the receiving end (the significance of having counterparts as the main interviewees will be discussed in Sect. 1.2 of this chapter). They were the people who utilised the skills they had acquired on the frontline of development cooperation, such as agricultural extension workers in rural development, teachers in schools and universities, engineers in charge of the maintenance of industrial infrastructure, doctors and nurses in medical institutions, etc. They were sometimes invited to Japan for training and worked face-to-face with Japanese professionals.

While the core interviewees were professionals in the aid recipient country, I also sought to expand the range of informants. For example, so-called 'technologists' or 'assistants', the staff in research institutions and universities who engage

[8] A counterpart is a person who performs the same function in a partner organisation, and in technical cooperation, the dispatched experts and their local counterparts form a temporary team as colleagues. Although the term represents equal positions of two sides, it is sometimes used to conceal the implicit or explicit power relations between those who teach (have more resources) and those who are taught (have less resources). Some people do not like the term because of such opacifying connotations. I use the term an aid recipient country and a partner country interchangeably, and the choice of the term depends on the contexts.

in the daily management of laboratories, may have impartially observed project dynamics. Furthermore, we also improvised additional interviews with local people like farmers working in the paddy fields, patients in medical facilities, students in schools, etc. Although the interviews with this category of people were not conducted systematically, they provided invaluable contextual information.

Before the interviews, I prepared common questions and asked the interviewees to think of them in advance. For instance, in the study of the Brantas River basin in Indonesia (Chap. 2), the following questions were posed.

Question A: What advantages and disadvantages did this project bring to your community, your country, and yourself?

Intention: The aid givers and the aid receivers may understand the same thing in different ways. I want to know how people evaluate the project. Please do not hesitate to mention any negative aspects of the project.

Question B-1: Was a sense of mutual trust nurtured in the course of the implementation of the project? Did you notice any change in the relationships among local people during the project? If so, why and how did these changes occur?

Question B-2: How about your relationships with (and your perceptions of) Japanese development workers? Do you have any suggestions for improving Japan's aid practice?

Intention: Development projects always have side effects. Sometimes, these effects can be more important than the intended outcomes. I would like to know how the project changed human relations.

Question C: If possible, please tell me some of the challenges this project encountered in the past. When and why did these challenges happen? How were they resolved?

Intention: Development projects always attempt to bring about changes on the ground, thereby inducing specific local reactions. I want to know how the challenges were addressed by the local side as well as by the Japanese side. Honest and critical observations are much appreciated.

To avoid misinterpretation, I explained the intentions before asking the questions. Question A is about the general evaluation of the project. Although I was a full-time professor at a private Japanese university at the time of the interviews, I was doing research for JICA and did not want to pretend to be neutral. Some people made practical suggestions to JICA, hoping that the donor would hear their voices. Question B asks how relationships between people have been transformed as a side effect of the project. Many counterparts were keen to express their views on their relationships with Japanese experts. Question C concerns the difficulties encountered by the projects, on which some people gave intriguing opinions that were sometimes at odds with the statements in official reports.

While some may be concerned that respondents felt pressured by the donor (the presence of JICA) and were not inclined to say what they really thought, I think most were honest in expressing their views. When someone is a member of a certain organisation, the person will be under pressure not to disclose personal opinions that go against the organisation's interests. However, for most of the people I met, JICA was outside their group hierarchy, and their projects had already been completed by the time of the interviews (which means no more major funding was expected from JICA immediately). While there might be some cognitive bias due to their perceptions of past events, the incentive to please the interviewer by glorifying the projects seemed weak, if not non-existent.

The interviews were primarily conducted in English, with the assistance of Indonesian interpreters in Indonesia and Spanish and Portuguese interpreters in Latin America. Interviews with Japanese Brazilians and Japanese citizens were conducted in Japanese. Very few of the interviewees spoke English as their home language. All the interview narratives were transcribed into Japanese within a few days, and the book was published in Japanese. As this edition is an English translation of that book, the details of the wording of the quoted narratives are likely to be somewhat different from those of the original spoken narratives, though I endeavoured to remain faithful to the original narratives.

1.1.4 Objectivity of Narratives

Although key academic literature on the history of Japan's development cooperation is already available,[9] oral histories that capture the perspectives of people in the aid recipient countries remain limited. Why has this not been done, given its palpable significance?

I think there are two reasons. First, it is challenging to identify appropriate interviewees. If interviews with local counterparts and beneficiaries were regularly conducted and recorded as part of future project evaluations, they could be used directly as sources for historical research. However, this has not become routine yet. Time has passed, and people have scattered, so the writers have to start from scratch, using the limited information left on documents or gathered from various informants to find out where key persons are. Since this experimental study was part of the official project of the JICA Ogata Research Institute, the JICA staff laboriously helped me locate the people involved.

Second, and more fundamentally, in both history and development studies, subjective narratives tend to be discredited as factual evidence when compared to written records. There are always misconceptions on the part of those giving evidence, and even if people remember events accurately, they are not inclined to say something against themselves to strangers. In fact, if you asked me to share with you what happened in my workplace 20 years ago, I would probably be at a loss. Memories fade very quickly. It must be even more challenging to explain the experience in a foreign language to a foreign researcher.

The epistemological tension between fact and memory has long been recognised. The Japanese novelist Akutagawa Ryunosuke wrote a short historical fiction, *In a Bamboo Grove* (藪の中), in 1922.[10] The story juxtaposes the conflicting narratives

[9] As for a classic English volume on the history of Japan's development cooperation, see Kato et al. (2016). See also Shimomura (2020, 2022) for an authoritative account of the history written in Japanese.

[10] English translation is in Akutagawa (2006). In writing *In a Bamboo Grove,* Akutagawa was inspired by American novelist Ambrose Bierce's *The Moonlit Road* (1907) (in Bierce 1970). While

given by three parties and four witnesses to an armed robbery in the suburb of Kyoto about a millennium ago. Since all narratives appear half-true, the reader is left to ponder what the conflicting narratives mean. While Kurosawa Akira adapted this story in his acclaimed 1950 film *Rashomon* (羅生門), in which the truth is revealed at the end, Akutagawa's original novel presented only a set of seven entangled hypotheses without offering any judgement.

Furthermore, we may distinguish truth from fact. Let me take the example of South Africa, where the Truth and Reconciliation Commission (TRC) was set up to seek restorative justice in post-apartheid South Africa. Since 1996, public hearings have been held in various locations where victims of human rights violations, such as torture and abduction, were given opportunities to share their stories. Occasionally, this was done in the presence of the perpetrators, accompanied by an outpouring of emotion. As those hearings were not judicial proceedings, it was practically impossible to verify whether the details of the narratives were objectively correct, though each testimony should contain certain existential truth. In 1998, the TRC published comprehensive reports in seven volumes.[11]

One of the famous cases scrutinised by the TRC was the Sharpeville massacre that occurred in March 1960, when 69 people were killed when police opened fire indiscriminately on a peaceful gathering. While collecting people's narratives on that incident, a South African political historian, Tom Lodge, met an interviewee who recounted a story of helicopters firing at innocent people. The sound he heard 'was the rat-a-tat-a-tat of machine guns and the wailing of ambulance sirens, and a red helicopter which flew surprisingly low' (Lodge 2011: 280). The fact is that this statement is ungrounded because helicopters were not used by the security forces until the 1970s. However, given the gradual intensification of political repression since 1960, which led to the brutal use of helicopters, such a conflation of memories should not be seen as a 'lie'. The overall recollections of the witness were 'sufficiently precise to be persuasive.... He definitely heard and saw helicopters' on other occasions (ibid. 280–281).[12]

In collecting narratives, I wanted to capture people's thoughts and perceptions rather than extract detailed facts from what they said. Personal memories about the amount of a farm's harvest, for example, may not be accurate, even if the interviewees

Bierce's work is a gothic fantasy of parents and a child, Akutagawa's is more of an Asian allegory about the fates of selfish individuals.

[11] The report is downloadable from https://www.justice.gov.za/trc/report/ There is a huge corpus of literature on the Truth and Reconciliation Commissions. See Hayner (2001) for a comprehensive work that chronicled the experiences of truth commissions in the world and Wison (2001) for a detailed legal and anthropological analysis of the South African experience. As for the political limitation of the TRC, see Mamdani (2002).

[12] As will be discussed in Chap. 6, similarly conflated (but contextually genuine) memories are found in the narratives of survivors of the war in Okinawa. At the same time, a historian's personal experience can even be the subject of professional inquiry. For example, the French historian Ivan Jablonka gave a painstakingly detailed account of the events leading to the death of his grandparents in Auschwitz (Jablonka 2012).

are honest and serious, while the descriptions in the JICA reports are meticulous—if often insipid in their presentation[13]—in recording factual data. I have used the information in such reports to describe 'when, where, who, what, and how much'. Oral history is not just about collecting voices based on which facts are investigated but also relates to the silence, the deception, and the unexpected (Santhiago and Hermeto 2022).

I think of my memories of past events; feelings of joy, anger, and sadness stay long. Subjective evaluations of the practical aspects of the project, such as 'this part went well' or 'that part fell short of the expectation', remain along with memories of accomplishment and failure. While conducting interviews for this book, I encountered local counterparts who did not attach importance to the events highlighted in the JICA reports. On the other hand, I found some events seldom mentioned in the reports, which local people talk about with enthusiasm. We may assume that those who were committed to a project and frustrated by its downfall would vividly remember what happened. Conversely, those who were half-heartedly involved in the project would not remember much. I thought that the possible subjective distortion of the information could be rectified by increasing the number of interviews and by supplementing the narratives with factual descriptions in the JICA reports.

I do not pretend to have treated the narratives of the givers and those of the receivers equally, but am deliberately biased towards amplifying the latter. The donors' narratives are 'strong' in that they are already well recorded and archived, while the recipients' narratives are 'weak' in that they are scarcely documented. The strategy of this book is therefore to restore the balance between the two by bringing the narratives of the counterparts to the fore, with the expectation that hundreds of individual narratives will join together to form a powerful current.

Preliminary discussions were held with Japanese professionals and JICA officers to contextualise the fieldwork and refine interview selection. While I am sincerely grateful to those who helped me, their testimonies are cited sparingly in this book, with the exception of former JICA volunteers and grassroots citizens (Chaps. 5 and 6).

1.1.5 History and Narratives

The ancient Greek word *historia* denoted knowledge acquired through inquiry, particularly, an intellectual effort to find causal links between events. From this comes the modern English term 'history', which means a series of past events that occurred over time and the study thereof. The word 'story', which describes how events happened, also descends from the same *historia.* In French, the word *histoire* has two meanings:

[13] Honestly speaking, JICA's reports up to the mid-1980s tended to be more enjoyable reads than recent ones, as the authors expressed their honest feelings more freely. This is at least partly because the experts at that time did not have to worry about public criticism of ODA and to use various templates of reporting.

history and story (the German word for history, *Geschichte,* originally referred only to events that happened in the past, not the stories about them). Where a written language system does not exist, stories are transmitted orally. The Gospel of St John in the New Testament begins with the line, 'In the beginning was the word', but the word (*logos*) here did not mean the written word. Unlike the European terminology, the word 'history' in Chinese characters (歴史) signifies written records. 歴 means events that occur at regular intervals (as in rows of rice plants), and 史 means the person who makes the calendar, namely, the officials in charge of public records.

Given the title of this book, *An Oral History of Development Cooperation,* let us pose and consider the layered meanings of 'oral history' a little further. Since this book is based on Japanese historiography, I would like to explain it bearing the Japanese context in mind.

The term oral history has a dual meaning. First, oral history denotes collective memories accumulated by generations of memory keepers or storytellers in a given community. This is a history 'owned' by people and verbally sustained and carried on as participatory history practice. The Japanese legendary folklorist Yanagita Kunio identified such practice with oral traditions, folklore, or *littérature orale,* which existed long before professional researchers began to probe them academically (Yanagita 1976: 15–16). The body of oral history in this sense consists of shared narratives that describe historical sequences of events and encode symbolic meanings and communal affects. The leading Japanese anthropologist Kawada Junzo, a student of Claude Lévi-Strauss, presented a lively account of oral history in West Africa, paying attention to the historical structures that emerged through popular narration (Kawada 1998).

In his *Gurindji Journey* (titled *Radical Oral History* in the Japanese version), Hokari Minoru, a young historian, presented a fresh approach to oral history, pondering on his experience in indigenous Australian outback settlements, where he was 'conducting the same kind of fieldwork as that of an anthropologist: entering a community with permission, learning the language, and living among the people' (Hokari 2011: 32). For Hokari, 'doing history' is an act of people's interacting or connecting with the past in their day-to-day lives. History is told, shared, and maintained by people. History is 'everywhere around us. We need to listen carefully to what it is telling us' (ibid. 41–42). Hokari challenges the privileged position of historians and suggests that indigenous narratives such as 'US President Kennedy visited the Gurindji country' and 'the earth punished the white man' may well be accepted as part of authentic historical analysis. Provocatively, he invites us to believe people's seemingly irrational narratives rather than making them the objects of mythology. As the philosopher Charles Taylor notes, humanity has long been embedded in mythological worlds, and it is only a modern phenomenon that our society is disciplined on the basis of secularity (Taylor 2004). Today, historians from indigenous communities have begun to write about 'our' oral histories (Mahuika 2019), while Hokari's contribution affirms the authenticity of 'their' oral histories within plural epistemologies.

The second meaning of oral history refers to a history written by professional historians who use oral evidence as primary historical materials. This is not an intimate history/story told by a respected old person by the fireside but a history written by scholars affiliated with universities and institutions including libraries. The works are published in the form of academic monographs or articles instead of being shared in communities. The origin of oral history understood in this way can be traced back to the establishment of court historians in ancient kingdoms and empires, where historians were accountable to the rulers. While I am not strictly a 'professional' historian myself—I have not worked for a department of history—this book belongs to this scholarly category.

Professional oral history can be further divided into two sub-categories: popular history and policy history. The beginning of contemporary oral history as popular history was marked by Paul Thompson's landmark work, *The Voice of the Past* (Thompson 2000), which drew on the rich tradition of British social history. Nowadays, we have plenty of English-language guides, handbooks, and readers for scholars who practice oral history in this sense (e.g., Hoopes 1979; Charlton et al. 2006; Ritchie 2011, 2015; Perks and Thomson 2016; Smith 2017), and substantial series of oral history monographs are published by major academic presses.[14]

In Japanese academia, this genre was recognised as an emerging branch of historiography in the 1980s based on an intensive dialogue between historians and journalists. Honda Katsuichi, known for his books on the Nanjing Massacre and the Vietnam War, remarked that his work was akin to 'collecting evidence for a trial' (Historical Science Society of Japan 1988a, 1988b). He distanced his work on Nanjing from the 'truth', which is 'often emotional and cannot escape a sense of ambiguity' and instead sought to establish the 'facts' (Honda 1984). In other words, Honda attempted to reconstruct people's history not by using the strength of human empathy but by removing subjectivity as much as possible when he assembled historical evidence. He tried to reconfigure the processes of the Nanjing Massacre by scrutinising the facts, which occurred at the level of individuals, based on what historians would have called rigorous source criticism. With regard to oral history as popular history in Japan, Okado Masakatsu underscored the importance of *gemba* (現場),[15] the place where historians engage in the real life and livelihood of people, and sought to liberate

[14] To get an idea of the themes of contemporary oral history in the world, it is worth looking at the new and old titles of oral history series published by Oxford University Press, https://global.oup.com/academic/content/series/o/oxford-oral-history-series-oralhis/?cc=us&lang=en&, Palgrave https://link.springer.com/series/14606, and Routledge https://www.routledge.com/Practicing-Oral-History/book-series/POHLCP?srsltid=AfmBOoqfP21lFZ1d6mnzCUBg4UBZx1sLXXACVPRH3HYGFXVnll1pFuME. There are also research fields similar to oral history, such as life history and life story, but these are often classified as part of qualitative research in the social sciences rather than the humanities. See *Sage Handbook of Qualitative Research* (Denzin et al. 2024).

[15] *Gemba* (that literally means 'site', 'field' or 'ground') is a Japanese term that is often used but difficult to translate into English. Okado uses this term as a counterpoint to deskwork theories, as a place where grassroots people live their lives and where grounded historians immerse themselves in fieldwork. The term was also used as the main title of a book written by Imai Masaaki, which describes the originally Japanese-style (and now applied worldwide) business/factory management

historical research from the insulated academic spaces and make it more grounded (Okado 2017). There is a need for sustained work rather than one-off experiments in such attempts.

In parallel, oral history as a part of policy studies has also rapidly enhanced its presence in Japan. At the end of the 1990s, on the initiative of political scientist Mikuriya Takashi, a substantial research project was launched at the National Graduate Institute for Policy Studies (GRIPS) to produce the 'oral history of public figures by professionals for the public'. Mikuriya and his colleagues attracted keen attention by publishing a series of oral histories based on interviews with policy-makers, including former prime ministers such as Miyazawa Kiichi (Mikuriya and Nakamura 2015). In Japanese contexts, there are reasons why this branch of oral history is pertinent. Public figures tend not to detail decision-making processes, and paradoxically, the quantity of information in the public records is shrinking due to the recent information disclosure legislation. There is a widespread practice in Japan of not committing crucial matters in writing to avoid criticism when they are made public in the future—they prefer carrying the facts to their graves (Mikuriya 2002; Japanese Political Science Association 2005).[16]

How does this book fit into these classifications? If the choice is either popular history or policy history, this book falls somewhere in between. Some of the interviewees are public figures involved in policy-making, while others are ordinary people living in towns and villages. In fact, most interviewees belong to the intermediary social stratum. They are local professionals, the counterparts of Japanese professionals, responsible for implementing specific development projects. As we will see in the following chapters, they are the people who encountered difficulties in the projects and struggled to resolve them sometimes with the support of foreign experts. I thought that by assembling the narratives of local counterparts, it would become possible to trace the dynamic trajectories of the development of projects.

During the interviews, I did not use tape or digital recorders but scribbled the conversations in my notebook.[17] After the interviews, back in the hotel, I tried to transcribe what people told me on the same day (or in a few days in case the narratives were too thick) while my memory was still fresh. If I had put off the job, the pothooks on my fieldnotes would have become illegible even to me. Over time, these transcribed narratives have totalled nearly 300 pages. Miyamoto Tsuneichi, the author of the classic Japanese ethnography written in 1960, *The Forgotten Japanese: Encounters with Rural Life and Folklore* (Miyamoto 2020), is said to have used a similar method: after careful preparation for fieldwork, he would 'speak casually

called *Kaizen* (Iamai 1997). See Chap. 3. The late Ogata Sadako advocated *Gembashugi* (*gemba*-ism), the field-oriented approach, as a renewed keyword of Japanese development cooperation.

[16] Independently of Japanese circumstances, policy research based on the narrative policy framework (NPF) is burgeoning globally (Roe 1994; Shanahan et al. 2018; Jones et al. 2020; Schlaufer et al. 2022).

[17] As for a classic guide for taking fieldnotes, see Emerson, Fretz, and Shaw (1995). 'Audio and video recordings, which seemingly catch and preserve almost everything occurring within an interaction, actually capture but a slice of ongoing social life' (ibid. 9). As for the criticality of what is *not* recorded, see Sheftel and Zembrzycki (2013).

[with local people], as if having a gossip talk, without recorders or even notes, and then write it down on a notebook after returning to his inn' (Suzuki 1988: 62).

My sources, however, are not exclusively oral. As presented in the case studies in the subsequent chapters, I also made substantial use of print sources including JICA's reports written by experts. The interview narratives are cited from the transcription and embedded in the text. A Japanese historian, Yoshizawa Minami, argued that oral history must also be subject to rigorous verification in the same way as we do when writing a history based on documentary sources (though the delight of experimental oral history practice lies in the fact that the interviewer and the interviewees work together to create a historical record that did not exist) (Historical Science Society of Japan 1988a: 16–22). In my research, while the information in most narratives appeared to be correct, I noticed subjective misunderstanding or exaggeration to varying degrees. When citing narratives in this book, I tried to set aside unreliable information, while respecting unique interpretations of an event by individual interviewees.

During the interviews, my colleague took pictures of those who were sitting in front of me with a digital camera on condition that these would be used only for the purpose of internal records and would never be circulated in public.[18] When I read the narrative scripts several months later, the pictures of interviewees' faces attached to the documents always had a curious effect: every time I saw them, memories of the interview scenes popped up to the surface and flooded back to me. I could even recall nuances such as their tone of voice, countenances, gestures, and even lighting in the room. Photographs, I discovered, could function as powerful indices or codes, unlocking layers of recollection beyond the textual record.

1.2 Making Democracy Work

1.2.1 Teaching How to Fish

The major part of the narratives derives from the middle layer of development cooperation, namely, the local counterparts of Japanese experts. Is this focus appropriate? Development cooperation is supposed to help improve the lives of ordinary people in developing countries. If so, shouldn't we listen first and foremost to the voices of people in villages and towns, the ultimate beneficiaries of development projects? In this book, however, I wanted to take a modest detour from a purely 'people-centred' approach. As mentioned several times, the main interviewees were engineers, agricultural extension workers, government officers, teachers, doctors, nurses, and others who worked directly with the Japanese professionals. The rationale for this approach requires some elaboration.

[18] It was Ms. Yanagihara Makiko of JICA who arranged my interviews behind the scenes by making appointments and taking photographs.

During the 1980s and the 1990s, Japanese ODA was subject to intense criticism both domestically and internationally (Japan was pushed up to the position of the world's top donor in 1989 and from 1991 to 2000). Detractors argued that the peaceful lives of local villagers were disturbed, that the funds were appropriated to prop up authoritarian regimes, and that the ultimate beneficiaries of the aid were Japanese private companies. Dissident scholars such as Murai Yoshinori and Sumi Kazuo established a style of argumentation demanding 'No More ODA' by examining the cases of conspicuous failures of yen loans and technology transfer projects especially in Asia. While it is impossible to make a scientific judgement on the success or failure of the entire aid system by selectively highlighting cases—the same limitations apply to this book—these critics established the method of critical inquiry based on fieldwork.[19]

At the time, criticism of development assistance was hardly unique to Japan. Perhaps the most influential was *Lords of Poverty*, written by a British journalist, Graham Hancock, which exposed how every big project ended in dismal failure while the elites of the World Bank and other donors were attending lavish cocktail parties (Hancock 1989). Hancock's argument in the 1980s not only previsioned grassroots criticism of ODA but also a neoliberal critique of interventionist aid. At the turn of the century, in response to Jeffrey Sachs's new 'big push' theory to eradicate poverty, William Easterly elaborated a counterargument that emphasised the role of 'searchers' who experiment to find practical solutions tailored to local conditions (Sachs 2005; Easterly 2006).

In this context, the role of non-governmental organisations (NGOs) also came into the limelight. David Korten (1990) distinguished between the first-generation NGOs involved in emergency relief and charity and the second-generation NGOs working directly with the poor in grassroots development projects, and he shed light upon the emerging third-generation NGOs that sought global justice through advocacy. In Japan, new NGOs mushroomed in the late 1980s when the bubble economy coincided with the global call for famine relief in Ethiopia. Most of the criticism of ODA in Japan was written in Japanese, and as such, the campaign was aimed at raising awareness among the Japanese public. It is worth noting, however, that in Southeast Asia, networks of NGOs such as the Asian Cultural Forum on Development (ACFOD) have been organised since the 1970s. The possibility of collaboration

[19] While a postgraduate student, I read numerous books critical of Japanese ODA in Japanese, such as Nagai (1983), Murai (1988), and Sumi (1989), with much interest. Hoshino Masako, who was dispatched to Laos in 1965 as a member of the first batch of JOCV, recalled her experience of pre-deployment training in Kyoto. 'A group of Kyoto University students stormed into our accommodation and said, "This is Japan's top-down government policy. Such thing as Japanese language education has no benefit to other countries. It is taught only to make people feel closer to Japan. Why are you going to teach development submissive to the government policy? You are arrogant, and you are wrong." They attacked us furiously, saying those things. While it didn't escalate into violence, I thought what they were saying made sense' [VOL 10]. The contexts of the domestic criticism of ODA at the time are discussed in Shimomura (2022: Chap. 7) and Sato (2021: Chap. 6) in Japanese. Prior to the closure of the United States Agency for International Development (USAID) by the Trump Administration, there have also been decades of sober academic debates and advocacy for the abolition of foreign aid. See Bauer (1981, 1984, 2004), for example.

between Japanese NGOs and their counterparts in aid recipient countries began to be pursued (Ohashi 2016: 327).

Although the advocacy of 'No More ODA' did not lead to an immediate reduction in the amount of development assistance, it decisively inaugurated an era of heightened scrutiny of donor-recipient relations, both governmental and non-governmental. Gone were the days when good intentions were enough.

There is a famous adage that describes an ideal attitude that a donor should take towards a recipient: 'Don't give them a fish, but teach them how to fish.' This means that, if you give a man a fish, you will feed him for a day, and if you teach a man how to fish, he will feed himself for a lifetime. This adage, a reminiscence of Samuel Smiles's philosophy of self-help (2002), is supposed to be originally Chinese, though its exact origin is not very clear. If the man depends on the charity of others, he will starve soon after the goodwill of others disappears. Instead, he should learn how to work with his hands and stand on his feet. If he is willing to learn, and if you are capable of teaching, why don't you teach him how to fish?

This primordial 'self-help' philosophy pertaining to technology transfer was criticised by James Ferguson, an anthropologist known for his political anatomy of development aid in Southern Africa (Ferguson 2015). First, fishermen are always assumed to be men (teach a 'man' how to fish), which is palpable gender discrimination. Second, local people may already know how to fish, and it may not be necessary for outsiders to teach them such a skill; they may simply want to acquire adequate means to fish, such as repaired boats, nets, and access to fishing grounds. Third (theoretically, this is the most important), according to Ferguson, this saying bears an implicit bias for production. The idea is to mobilise underutilised human resources into productive activities (fishing in this case) to promote economic development. In reality, however, nearly half of the world's fishery products are based on aquaculture (see the case of salmon farming in Chap. 2, Sect. 2.3). It is better to consider ways to distribute resources fairly than to add to unemployment by teaching skills for jobs that are not in demand. Breaking away from the obsession with production, we should remember that everyone has the right to access basic goods that are already abundantly produced. The focus should be switched from production to consumption and redistribution.

While Ferguson's argument contains some truth, I think the maxim, 'teaching how to fish', still retains heuristic value. For every fisher, fishing can be both a livelihood and *ludus* (play) (Huizinga 1955). If there is a woman who is interested in fishing, you should teach her as well. If somebody knows the skill better than you, you can ask her or him to teach you. In the first place, we should note that 'fishing' in the adage is an analogy, for fishing is just an example of a vocation that is part of the social division of labour. A group of fishers go out to catch fish to sell them to villagers, and likewise, a group of teachers teach children to read and write in the village community. As Ferguson argues, fair redistribution is important, and this means that we need skills for the efficient redistribution of goods and services as well. In any vocation, people who want to acquire professional skills have to be taught these skills by someone.

1.2.2 Principals and Agents

While acquiring hands-on experience is invaluable, it is unrealistic for an individual to work as an all-round generalist and do every task alone. In a world where the social division of labour has evolved, individuals perform specific work for others, whether through market relations or in the public sector. If the service is complex and of a public nature, the contractual relationship between service providers and receivers often extends over the long term. Professionals entrusted with such responsibilities strive to achieve success, yet outcomes may or may not be satisfactory to the clients. Then, how can the quality of professional performance best be secured?

Principal-agent theory is an influential organisational theory originally proposed by Michael C. Jensen and others (Jensen and Meckling 1976; Jensen 1998). Their discussion concerned the separation between ownership and management of private firms; the principals are the owners of the company (shareholders), and the agents are its managers. Although the principals delegate power to the agents to achieve what the principals want in the longer term, it is not guaranteed that the agents will achieve the best results as desired by the principals. The principals select suitable and capable agents and then try to manage and monitor the agents' activities. If shareholders are not satisfied with the company's performance, they can remove the management team. It is also necessary for the principals to provide appropriate incentives and boost the morale of the agents so that they can perform to the best of their ability.

The principal-agent framework illustrates the logic of so-called shareholder democracy in management studies. The destructive nature of stock market capitalism has been widely critiqued in Keynesian, Marxist, critical, and communitarian perspectives.[20] Generally speaking, however, the principal-agent approach can be extended to describe the mechanisms that make democracy work better in terms not only of business accountability but also of the quality of public services. To date, several studies have applied the principal-agent framework in the field of development cooperation, but in most cases, the providers of development assistance are considered the principals, while their executors the agents, as discussed in Azam and Laffont (2003), Martens et al. (2002), Hawkins et al. (2006), and Bourguignon and Sundberg (2007).[21] In this section, I take up a unique work, Francis Fukuyama's *State-Building: Governance and World Order in the Twenty-First Century* (2004), which assumes that the principal-agent relationship should ultimately work within the framework of a nation in the context of post-conflict state-building (the practical aspect of nation-building, *kuni-zukuri*, which I mentioned at the beginning of this

[20] It is impractical to show a comprehensive list of criticisms of shareholder capitalism, which seeks to maximize returns to company owners. See Dore (2000) as an eloquent defence of Japanese-style welfare capitalism, and Stiglitz (2024) as the latest, forceful advocacy of a 'good society'.

[21] The political economy of development assistance presented in Ferguson (1990) can also be seen as an example of the failure of the North-South principal-agent function. As for the review of the application of principal-agent theory to the analysis of the control of politicians through elections (and the control of bureaucracies by the government branches), see Gailmard (2014). Case studies of the principal-agent relationship may be useful to unravel the mechanism of substitution between democracy and state capacity *vis-à-vis* development outcomes. See Hanson (2015).

chapter). 'In the public sector, the principals are the public at large. In a democracy their first-level agents are their elected representatives; the legislators act as principals with regard to the executive branch agents delegated to carry out the policies they have legislated' (Fukuyama 2004: 66).

The principal-agent framework works within the executive. For example, Japan's international cooperation policy is laid out by the Ministry of Foreign Affairs as the principal and implemented by JICA as the agent, which then outsources much of its work to individual experts and organisations, including private firms, through tender. In societies, the system of representation is multi-layered, and the work of the agents is highly specialised and sophisticated. A non-professional citizen cannot draft the texts of a legislative bill. A client of a law firm does not understand the details of the law, but a legal practitioner does.

In the public space, it is ultimately the principal, the sovereign collective of citizens of a nation, which evaluates the work of the agents. The agents, the civil servants, are accountable to the citizenry, which is the principal and the ultimate beneficiary. On the premise that state capacity in developing countries is still very weak, Fukuyama discusses the challenges in securing functioning public institutions in the following three aspects (ibid. 68–69).

First, the goals are often unclear (ibid. 69–74). Principals are not a homogeneous entity seeking to maximise their own clearly defined interests—if public opinion were monolithic, there would be no need for competitive elections. As what the principals want is ambiguous, there is room for multiple agents to assert themselves as representing the will of the principals. In fact, all players act under the condition of bounded rationality (Simon 1997); Fukuyama offers an example. Suppose a school administrator intends to hire an innovative but unqualified teacher to improve student performance. The teachers may resist, saying that if such teachers were hired, they would not be able to maintain the basic standard of education. Both the school administrator and the teachers claim that their aim is to promote the interests of the parents and students, who are the principals. In reality, the school administrator may be driven by nepotism and want to hire his relatives, while the unionised teachers may just want to maintain their job status and privileges. In the first place, the principals may not know exactly what they want the agents to do. If parents (and children) have the opportunity to discuss the problem among themselves and interact with the administrator and teachers, the outcomes may be different.

Second, even if the goals are clear, it may not be easy to measure the extent to which the agents have achieved such goals (Fukuyama 2004: 74–91). Here, Fukuyama introduces the concept of *specificity* based on Pritchett and Woolcock (2004) and Israel (1987). Services such as aircraft maintenance—any country needs qualified mechanics for international airports—are highly specific. There are precise manuals on the procedures to maintain the huge and delicate machines. If an aircraft had an accident, there would be a rigorous investigation into who failed to follow the procedure and where the manuals were flawed. The operation of institutions such as a central bank is also highly specific. On the other hand, the specificity of schoolteachers' work in career counselling for students is relatively weak. Although such guidance has a significant, sometimes decisive impact on students' future life courses, it takes years for the results to be obvious, and it is almost impossible to determine exactly which part of the counselling has caused students' success or failure. Road maintenance is also a less specific area where many people are involved as agents and transaction volumes are high; the result may be the same even when some workers slack off. This difference in the nature of work explains at least partly the coexistence in some developing countries of the diffusion of sophisticated information technology in urban enclaves and the persistence of poverty in vast rural areas.

At this point, Fukuyama emphasises the role of trust and teamwork, given the fact that informal norms followed by agents can supplement formal incentive structures and play a critical role in determining performance levels. As a country modernises, kinship and village relations are gradually replaced by new identities based on the workplace, where pieces of work are specified and closely monitored, and incentives are offered. However, the professionals may work as diligently as possible, even when the material incentives are feeble, if they take pride in their jobs, enjoy camaraderie, and have respectable leaders. If this is the case, the best performance of agents' work can be guaranteed not necessarily by offering a good salary but by nurturing trustful relationships in the individual workplace—if 'loyalty' to the organisation is augmented as described by Hirschman (1970). The attempt of *kaizen* in manufacturing, as shown in Chap. 3, is a case in point.

Third, despite the advantage of decentralised decision-making, it is not easy to decide how much authority should be delegated to different levels of agents (Fukuyama 2004: 91–103). Fukuyama refers to the concept of subsidiarity, which is one of the founding principles of the European Union (Føllesdal 1998, 2025; Estella 2002; Syrpis 2004): local problems should be solved locally, while higher authorities decide only on issues that cannot be solved locally. The decision to solve problems specific to factory lines can be based on the empirical knowledge accumulated in the factory, even though the company management decides where to build a new factory. Indeed, 'local agents need to be empowered to act on local knowledge' (Fukuyama 2004: 94). As power is dispersed, however, the risk of autonomous units deviating from generally accepted norms also increases. Southern states of the US justified slavery against the idea of equal dignity of human persons, resulting in the Civil War, as indicated by Fukuyama (ibid. 97). In the context of development cooperation, while the best practice of a unit of a government may be emulated by other units voluntarily, the corruption rampant in a small unit may be contagious across hierarchies. In brief, there is no general theory of optimality of decentralisation.[22]

While the above three aspects all address critical issues, the second aspect, ensuring effective performance of the agents, seems to be the most important in development cooperation. Regarding the first aspect, the donor is supposed not to shape but to respect people's demands in the aid recipient country; concerning the

---

[22] Principal-agent relationships may also work properly at the level of sub-national communities rather than in a larger nation-state. See Mine et al. (2013) and Murotani and Mine (2015) on the merit of decentralised governance in preventing conflict and strengthening state legitimacy in fragile states.

third, in the sovereign state system, the donor country is not allowed to interfere in the institutional design, such as constitutional decentralisation of the governance of the recipient country. Nevertheless, the donor is expected outright to contribute to improving the performance of the agents of the sovereign people of the aided country, which is to address the second aspect. The counterparts of development cooperation may not serve central governments but local ones. Although many engage in jobs with high specificities, such as agricultural extension, civil engineering, vocational training, mathematics teaching, and epidemic control, a host of developing countries still lack professionals in those fields.

Then, how should foreign experts, who are supposed to have useful skills, teach future fishers how to fish? Relationships can be complicated because local people may not want to be told what to do by foreigners. In fact, the locals are usually the ones most familiar with the unique contexts of the place of cooperation.

1.2.3 The Spaces in Which Learning Takes Place

Let me summarise what has been discussed so far and illustrate the spaces in which 'teaching (and learning) how to fish' occurs in development cooperation. While P refers to the principals (the people as the sovereign), A refers to the agents (the government). In Fig. 1.2, P-*α* represents the principals of country α, A-α represents the agents of country *α*, P-*β* represents the principals (the emergent sovereign) of country *β*, and A-*β* represents the agents (the government in the making) of country *β*. DA is the development agency of country *α*. The horizontal arrow via DA indicates the transfer of resources (technology, commodities, or money) from country α to country *β*; the sovereign citizens and the government of country α entrust the DA, as their agents, with the task of providing benefits to the people (possibly the former subject) of country *β*.

The chief role expected of the DA in this figure is not to give fish directly to P-*β*. Normatively, in a developing country, the act of 'catching and distributing fish' should occur within the feedback loop between P-*β* and A-*β*. If external actors continue

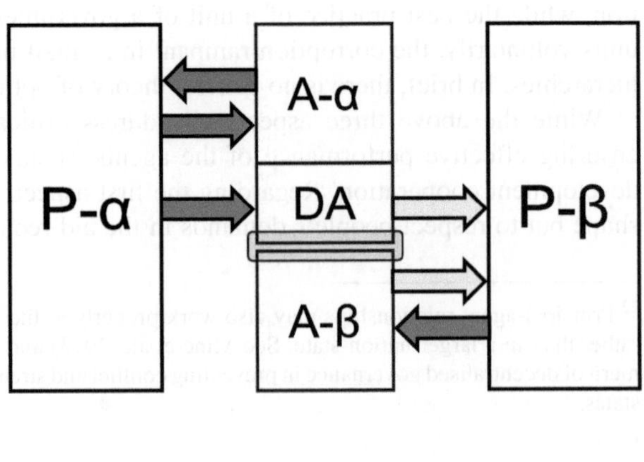

Fig. 1.2 Principals, agents, and development cooperation. Source: Author

giving fish without due respect for the functioning of the democratic loop in the locality, the growth of the principal-agent relationship in country β will be hampered. Yet, the function of governments as agents may still be weak in emerging nations that have just been freed from colonial rule, fragile nations that have gone through violent conflicts, and impoverished nations disadvantaged in resource endowments. The DA is, therefore, expected to assist in improving the quality of democracy and service delivery in country β, which is represented by the arrows connecting A-β and P-β.

As noted at the beginning of this chapter, the goal of Japanese ODA has long been national development (*kuni-zukuri*) through human (resources) development (*hito-zukuri*). Figure 1.2 visualises the space for technology transfer where DA and A-β interact in the shaded area, on the right side of which the arrows from DA to P-β and from A-β to P-β are running in parallel. Experts from the DA demonstrate how to catch fish, and those experts and their counterparts fish together in the context of country β. Finally, the counterparts do it by themselves, and foreign experts withdraw. This is how technology transfer ideally works. However, as the case studies in this book reveal, it is often challenging to determine the most appropriate timing for withdrawal. There are different, conflicting views on both sides as to whether it is 'about time' or 'too early.'[23]

To fully understand the meaning of Fig. 1.2, it is of use to compare it with Fig. 1.3 and Fig. 1.4. In terms of sequence, Fig. 1.2 can be considered a snapshot of the transition from Fig. 1.3 to Fig. 1.4. The initial condition, namely, the colonial situation, is illustrated by Fig. 1.3. Note the absence of an arrow from P-β and hence the absence of A-β. In colonies, representative governments did not exist or were placed under the strict supervision of the imperial metropolis, whose institutions and languages were imposed from the top down. At the same time, the DA was expected to provide services to the colonial subjects. In the British Empire, the Colonial Development and Welfare Acts of 1940 and 1945 recognised that Britain should take responsibility for the social development and welfare of people in the colonies. Thus, the arrow flows from left to right, and the relationship remains unilateral. It is not permissible for the P-β to select their own agents, as long as the sovereignty of the people of country β is negated. Kwame Nkrumah, Ghana's first prime minister, declared in the vortex of the independence campaign, "Seek ye first the political kingdom and all else shall be added onto you" (Nkrumah 1957, 164). Dozens of Asian and African countries that achieved independence after World War II, including Ghana, patiently sought to build up the administrative capacity necessary to serve the principals of sovereign nations. Against this background, as illustrated in Fig. 1.2, the contribution of the DA to nation-building was much appreciated in post-independent countries in the Global South.

In *Rural Development: Putting the Last First*, Robert Chambers called on urban outsiders to take a careful approach to understanding the reality of rural poverty. It

[23] In the case of yen loans, Japanese experts are employed by the recipient government and therefore institutionally embedded in the P-β and A-β loop in country β.

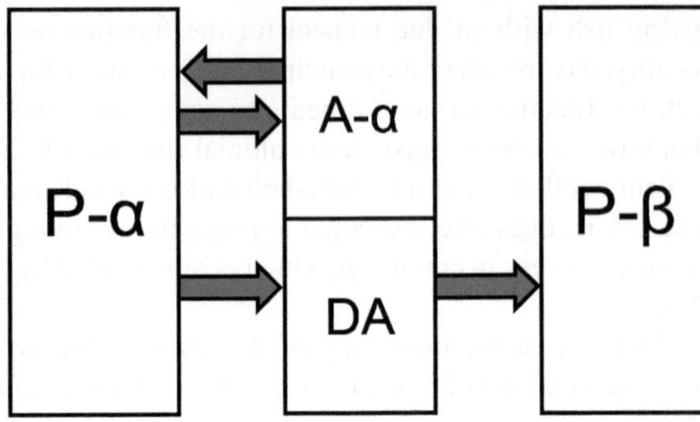

Fig. 1.3 Absence of A-β (colonial situation). Source: Author

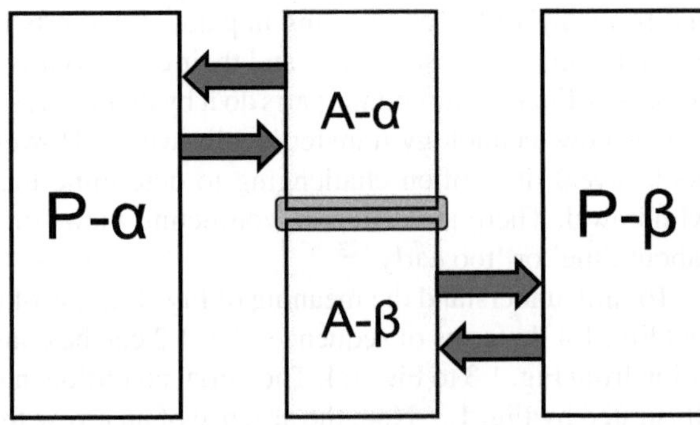

Fig. 1.4 Coexistence of Sovereign nations. Source: Author

is worrisome, however, that the government factor was almost invisible in Chambers' work. Government officers loathed working in rural areas, because they were blinded by their 'urban bias' to the realities of rural life. In this respect, civil servants were outsiders like 'us' (Chambers 1983: 8–9, 11). Although his willingness to empathise with impoverished farmers is admirable, local agricultural extension workers remained sidelined, while foreign scholars and local farmers eagerly discussed the future of the village. The pattern somehow resembles the colonial situation described in Fig. 1.3.

This book does not place much emphasis on examining how much ODA directly benefits local people. If the Japanese are serving the local people with great success in the absence of local governments, this could be both the cause and the result of a failure of nation-building. Instead, we want to see the circles of arrows spinning successfully within country β, which depends largely on the quality of technology transfer that takes place through the collaboration between the DA and A-β (the horizontally shaded area in Fig. 1.2). In order to assess the quality of the DA's work, it is necessary to listen to the voices of their counterparts, namely, A-β.

When development cooperation succeeds, internal feedback between the principals and the agents in country β begins to work, and consequently, DA withdraws: the configuration transits from a composite relationship of Fig. 1.2 to a symmetric, simpler one of Fig. 1.4, and this means that country β now becomes fully independent and self-sustaining as a sovereign state not only formally but also substantially. Development projects evolved at the stage of Fig. 1.2 are now embedded in the loop of P-β and A-β in Fig. 1.4. It is at this point that the mission of support for nation-building is complete.

However, it must be noted that, even in the state depicted in Fig. 1.4, the agents of country α and country β are not completely disconnected: the shaded area between A-α and A-β indicates cooperation between equals. International cooperation will continue even after a developing country has 'graduated' from the position of an aided country and does not receive ODA anymore. For instance, JICA still has an office in China, the second-largest economy in the world, where cooperation continues on issues such as environmental degradation, food safety, pandemic control, and ageing. Japan's relationships with key countries of the Association of Southeast Asian Nations (ASEAN) and emerging nations like Brazil, Turkey, and South Africa are also entering this phase of 'international cooperation' between peers rather than 'development cooperation' between the donor and the recipients.

So far, the principal-agent relationship has been described as the relationship between the sovereign people and their representative government. However, it should also be noted that, as can be seen from the fact that the theory of principal-agent originally emerged from the theory of business corporation and shareholder democracy, its scope is not limited to the relationship between people and their national government. Principal-agent relationships can be established, for example, between citizen funders and NGOs, between local people and local governments, and between parents/students and schools. Professional cooperation can broadly be established between agents to teach each other 'how to fish'. For instance, I supervised a PhD student from Zimbabwe who wrote his dissertation on agricultural cooperatives in Africa and Asia. He visited Japanese villages and interviewed farmers while tending cattle, participating in rice planting, and helping harvest vegetables to craft policy recommendations. Not only do Japanese students conduct participatory observation in African villages, but also African students do similar activities in Japan. The kind of equal learning exchange seen between A-α and A-β in Fig. 1.4 could work between developed countries, between developing countries, and between developing and developed countries.

The development of this form of cross-border, horizontal cooperation shows that we can imagine another model beyond the one shown in Fig. 1.4. In addition to the collaboration between their agents, we can expect the spread of voluntary cooperation between citizens of country α and country β as equal sovereign nations, as illustrated in Fig. 1.5 and discussed later in Chap. 4 (Sect. 4.4) in regard to JICA Volunteers (Okabe 2024). Grassroots cooperation can take the form of cultural exchange, volunteering, and study abroad, but when we face serious global challenges (climate change, natural disasters, pandemics, economic crises, refugees, etc.), the call for emergency relief becomes urgent. At the time of the COVID-19 pandemic, while progress was made in coordinating national policies and institutionalising COVID-19 Vaccines Global Access (COVAX) to supply vaccines to developing countries, the private sector also propelled the global responses by operating the supply chain for

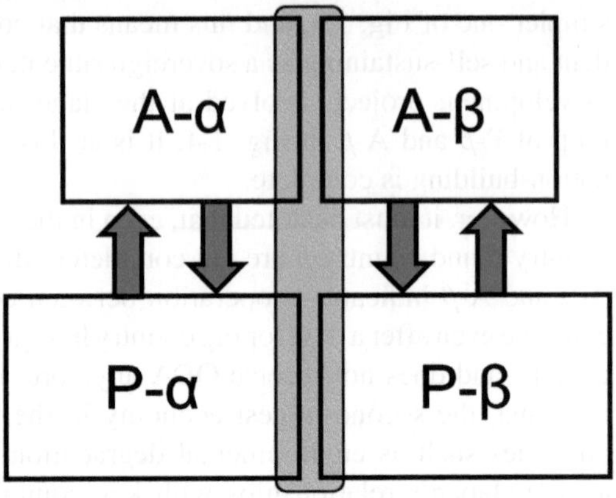

Fig. 1.5 Horizontal cooperation. Source: Author

masks and other critical equipment. This dimension of horizontal cooperation also highlights the limitations of the original principal-agent theory. While shareholder democracy remains important, business corporations need to be accountable not only to their company members but also to their customers and society at large.

In today's context, the absence of A-*β*, as in Fig. 1.3, can be present in situations other than colonial rule. For example, the government of country β may collapse or substantially be weakened due to civil war, military aggression, or a massive natural disaster. In such a case, principals and agents around the world may have to provide quick and direct support to P-*β*. This was the case in Japan after the Great East Japan Earthquake in 2011. In addition to international NGOs, 23 countries dispatched relief and medical teams to the tsunami-affected areas in the Tohoku region of Japan. These included teams from Indonesia, Thailand, and Jordan, which are the subject of the case studies in this book.[24]

This book is not a historical study of colonial policies but of post-war Japanese development cooperation. Therefore, the main subject of this book's description corresponds to Fig. 1.2: the effort of national development through human (resources) development. Many countries in the Global South still need assistance with nation-building, and it should be noted that most development cooperation projects still fall into this category. However, even in the era of nation-building assistance, there are moments when horizontal cooperation based on genuine empathy emerges between peoples. Voluntary cooperation in 'civic community' makes democracy work in a country, for example Italy (Putnam 1993), strengthening the principal-agent cycle in

[24] The US has provided a massive amount of aid to post-conflict countries as well as to those affected by humanitarian disasters and emerging infectious diseases, and this focus seems to correspond to the modern version of Fig. 1.3. However, USAID that has long been responsible for US bilateral aid was abruptly shut down by an executive order issued by President Donald Trump in January 2025. On the other hand, Japan's assistance, which has prioritised the capacity development of public institutions (Fukuda-Parr et al. 2002; JICA 2004a) rather than humanitarian resource transfer, has worked more in line with the situation depicted in Fig. 1.2. Despite the use of the same term 'international cooperation', the nature and modalities of collaboration vary considerably across donor countries.

a nation, and such trustful relationships between independent citizens can be forged across national boundaries, which will be demonstrated in case studies especially in the latter part of this book.

In addition to the narratives of the counterparts, I conducted interviews with local people, the ultimate beneficiaries of development cooperation, sometimes by jumping in at the fieldwork site. On the Japanese side, I also collected the voices of Japanese citizens, rather than experts, involved in participatory development cooperation. In Chap. 4 (Sect. 4.4), I attempt to trace the significance of teaching and learning by presenting the reflection on their field experiences in Africa by former members of JICA Volunteers. Furthermore, in Chap. 6, I discuss the perspective of broadly defined human security, describing the experiences of Japanese Brazilians who visited Japan for youth training and citizens in Minamata and Okinawa who hosted the trainees from Brazil and Cambodia, respectively. These sections aim to depict the dynamics of transnational and horizontal learning at the citizen level between countries α and β. The collaborative spirit of Fig. 1.5 (the vertically shaded area) emerges in every state of development cooperation.

1.3 Blessings in Disguise

1.3.1 Overcoming Crises

It is indispensable to teach and learn 'how to fish' to make the principal-agent relationship work in the public space. Yet, we know that our learning trajectories are seldom linear. The learning of foreign languages often proceeds by incremental memorisation of words and phrases until, in an unforeseen conversational encounter, comprehension and fluency "click." Athletic performance also depends on routine training, yet team capability may undergo a discontinuous leap after a single, evenly matched contest. We may have an abrupt leap in learning processes in these ways. To capture such dynamics, I also consciously tried to collect narratives about critical junctures of project histories.

A classic precursor of such an approach is Albert O. Hirschman's *Development Projects Observed* (Hirschman 1967). As a study for the World Bank and the Brookings Institution, Hirschman travelled and visited development projects in 11 countries—El Salvador, Ecuador, Peru, Uruguay, India, Pakistan, Thailand, Italy, Uganda, Ethiopia, and Nigeria—between 1964 and 1965 and examined the factors of success and failure of development projects, mostly large-scale projects concerning irrigation, power generation, and railways financed by the World Bank.

In that work, Hirschman paid attention to the role of the psychology of project implementers in addition to financial and technical factors. He presented the principle of the 'Hiding Hand' as the central mechanism of a project achieving unexpected success against adversity. The first episode of the book concerned a paper mill in Pakistan, which began to operate in 1953. The project counted on the abundant bamboo resources of the Chittagong Hill Tracts, but unfortunately all the local bamboo bloomed and died at once (a situation that only occurs every 50–70 years). Forced to react to the crisis, the mill imported pulp, sourced bamboo from other places, and even experimented with growing different types of material to tide it over the crisis. As a result, the diversification of raw materials in the paper industry was accomplished unintentionally (Hirschman 1967: 9–10).

The mere fact that a difficulty has arisen is not enough to generate a creative response. The paper mill could have simply been shut down. This is where Hirschman emphasises people's mindset. If we knew that we were going to encounter difficulties in advance, we would make necessary preparations or just cancel the project. In reality, however, people launch risky projects without knowing what will happen next; they are blindfolded, luckily, by the 'Hiding Hand' from behind. By the time the crisis occurs, a certain amount of investment has already been made in the project, and we can no longer turn back. 'Creativity always comes as a surprise to us; therefore, we can never count on it and we dare not believe in it until it has happened' (ibid. 13).

In *The Strategy of Economic Development* (1958), Hirschman had given an example of demographic transition and elucidated the critical conditions under which innovation occurred. As the population grows, per capita income falls. People may not react if the decline in income is marginal and gradual, but when its fall is regarded as a sudden shock, people are likely to exert a distinctive effort to maintain their income levels by working harder or raising productivity; they will find themselves in a situation of 'going up the descending escalator'. However, there is no qualitative distinction between the skill of going up a descending escalator to stay at the same point and that of going up stairs to reach a higher point. Hardships train people. A society that has faced adversities will be more likely to adapt to the next crisis with relative ease (Hirschman 1958: 176–182).

We assume that development projects evolve step by step to achieve a prescribed goal. The PDCA (Plan, Do, Check, Act) cycle, a key element of *kaizen,* is palpably helpful in the project implementation stage; as a rule of thumb, 90% of difficulties are likely to be solved or addressed by regular check-ups using the PDCA cycle.[25] However, like in our individual lives, a development project may face serious contingencies in its lifespan. The PDCA cycle cannot be applied when the very project design is fundamentally shaken. Nassim Nicholas Taleb called such a contingency a 'black swan', an event that most people assume will never happen, but when it occurs, it has a huge, lasting impact (black swans are very rare, but they do exist). Real change in human society takes place not through predictable events but as a result of unpredictable, highly improbable deviations (Taleb 2001, 2007).

The word 'crisis' comes from the Greek word *Krinein,* which means 'to separate' and 'to decide': a person standing at a bifurcation point is about to make a clear

[25] See Imai (1986: 60–65) as a classic work that situated the PDCA cycle at the heart of *kaizen* practice. A precondition for the PDCA cycle to work smoothly is the standardisation of procedures (ibid. 121–127).

decision. The Chinese word for crisis is 危機 (危机). The first character危 illustrates a state where a person is cowering in fear on a cliff, and the second character 機 means a critical moment. On the other hand, the possibility of something unfavourable happening in the future is called risk. 'The word "risk" derives from the early Italian *risicare,* which means "to dare." In this sense, risk is a choice rather than a fate' (Bernstein 1998, 8). In Chinese, the risk is translated as 風険 (风险), which implies the difficulty (険) pertaining to the unpredictability of future wind (風). Sailors listen carefully to weather forecasts and 'read the wind' through decades of experiences and intuition.

When a crisis is a purely humanitarian disaster, a donor as a member of the international community is expected to provide a big dollop of relief aid to the affected country. However, if a crisis occurred due to site-specific, human-made factors, a donor may decide not to disrupt local dynamics by intervening half-heartedly. While the projects with relatively short histories may not (yet) have faced any crisis, other major projects with longer histories may have already experienced adversities, which I classify roughly into three types: political crises, environmental crises, and crises of financial sustainability. We may draw useful lessons from how the projects encountered, and responded to, these challenges in the past.

1.3.2 Classification of Development Projects

A development project presented in this book is regarded as a semi-autonomous unit. In this section, let me try to present an orderly classification of those projects.

The regional distribution of projects was presented in the world map, Fig. 1.1. In addition to geography, the selection of cases was also based on the sectors: agriculture and fisheries, the primordial human activities; manufacturing, a driver of economic development; education, activities for the cultivation of humanity; healthcare, an enabler of the reproduction of life; and human security, a precursor of future transnational cooperation. Then, every chapter is designed to accommodate three stories about projects that can be grouped in a specific sector, sequenced from the oldest to the newest. Figure 1.6 illustrates this arrangement (the actual sequence of projects is not necessarily the 1970s, the 1980s, and the 1990s).

Now the dimension of crises is overlaid onto the configuration of projects. Table 1.1 shows the mapping of the 15 projects (three projects by five chapters). Political crises concern violent ruptures in political regimes, such as *coups d'état* and civil wars; environmental crises are related to water conflict and pollution; and crises of financial sustainability generally refer to situations where the projects cannot make both ends meet. Typically, all these crises arise during the period of project implementation, though several projects designed against the backdrop of devastating crises such as war and chemical pollution are also included in Table 1.1.

Some political crises (caused by human society) and environmental crises (caused by the interaction between humans and nature) can be considered 'black swans' that nobody anticipated. The crisis of institutional and financial sustainability could

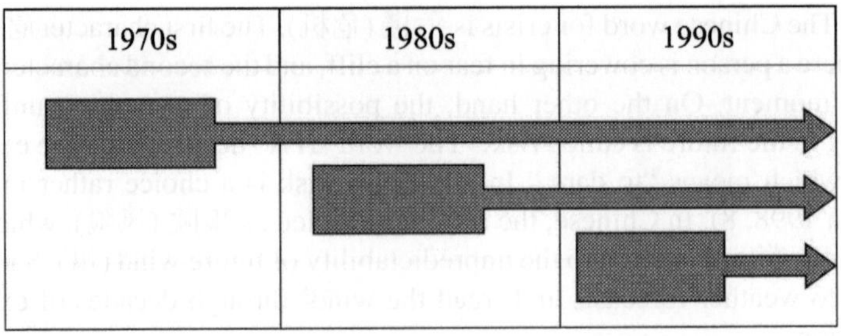

Fig. 1.6 Example of chronological arrangement of projects. Source: Author

Table 1.1 Crises Development Projects Faced

	Project	Politics	Environment	Autonomy
Agriculture and Fisheries (Chap. 2)	Water management (Indonesia)	○		
	Salmon farming (Chile)		○	
	Rice cultivation (Tanzania)		○	
Manufacturing (Chap. 3)	Vocational training (Malaysia)	[○]		○
	Industrial complex (Thailand)	[○]	○	
	Kaizen (Costa Rica)			○
Education (Chap. 4)	University education (Kenya)			○
	Mathematics and science in secondary education (Kenya)			○
	Japan overseas cooperation volunteers (Kenya)	–	–	–
Healthcare (Chap. 5)	Medical research (Ghana)	○		
	Veterinary medicine (Zambia)			○
	Family planning (Jordan)	○		
Human Security (Chap. 6)	*Nikkei* Brazilians (Brazil)	[○]	–	–
	Mercury pollution (Minamata/Brazil)		[○]	
	Peace (Okinawa/Cambodia) and water management (Cambodia)	[○]		

Note [○] indicates that the project was designed to *respond* to a crisis
Source Author

be caused by various factors including gaps in expectations between the local and Japanese stakeholders, which may occur in any project. Let me explain these three categories of crises a little more.[26]

[26] Given the complex, cascading, and cross-border nature of contemporary crises, the development agencies are required to nurture holistic views and explore multi-sectoral, multi-stakeholder approaches. See Tanaka (2015) and Ogata Sadako Research Institute (2024).

[A] Political Crisis

Political turmoil in an aid recipient country may shake the very foundations of a project. The project for integrated development of the Brantas River basin in Indonesia was interrupted by the military coup in 1965 and subsequent political repression. The army led by Commander Suharto, who later replaced Sukarno as the state president, and vigilante groups slaughtered communists and their sympathisers. The Brantas region was a stronghold of the Indonesian communist party, and the construction of the dams had to be suspended (Chap. 2, Sect. 2.2). The Noguchi Memorial Institute for Medical Research (NMIMR) in Ghana set sail amid the heavy storm as a military *coup d'état* broke out in 1979, the same year the construction of the facility was completed (Chap. 5, Sect. 5.2). Regardless of their quantity and quality of resources spent in the past, large-scale projects may be seen as a legacy of the former enemy regime and deliberately neglected.

The family planning project in Jordan grew successfully and took root in the country's institutions gradually. However, just as the prospect of disseminating its achievements regionwide was discussed, civil war broke out in Syria in 2011. Unexpectedly, the project implemented by the Jordanian government had to take into account the needs of the Syrian refugees in Jordan. Once a major violent conflict breaks out in one's neighbourhood, attempts at scaling up face serious challenges (Chap. 5, Sect. 5.4).

The projects in Malaysia and Thailand were launched not least to take historical responsibility, rather than to respond to their contemporary political crises. The memories of World War II and the rise of anti-Japanese sentiment in Southeast Asia in the 1970s profoundly impacted how Japanese experts worked with their counterparts. Examples of technology transfer and yen loans are examined to illustrate how the projects took shape in Southeast Asia (Chap. 3, Sect. 3.2 and 3.3). One of the predecessors of today's JICA is the Japan Emigration Service (JEMIS). After World War II, ethnic-Japanese (*Nikkei*) Brazilians were divided into the 'victorious' group, who continued believing that Japan won the war, and the 'defeated' group, who accepted the fact of Japan's defeat, and the two camps engaged in violent confrontation. While half a century has passed, the identities of the descendants of Japanese migrants in Latin America continue to waver between full integration into local society and the preservation of *Nikkei* consciousness. Japanese Brazilian youth joined training in Japan to rediscover their dual home (Chap. 6, Sect. 6.2).

Okinawa was a site of fierce ground battles during the final stage of World War II, while Cambodia saw genocide in the late 1970s; in contrast to the massacre in Indonesia, it was self-claimed communists who tortured and killed people in Cambodia. At the end of the book, it is demonstrated that horizontal international cooperation based on human security and infrastructure development plays a substantial role in securing peace in places haunted by the memories of extreme forms of violence (Chap. 6, Sect. 6.4).[27]

[27] Oral history is an appropriate method for recording the extraordinary suffering of ordinary people in times of war and war-like situations. The approach of 'crisis oral history' is emerging (Cave and

[B] Environmental Crisis

Agriculture, forestry and fisheries are based on the metabolism between nature and human society. While production may dramatically increase by enlarging facilities, obtaining more raw materials, and organising all-day shifts in the manufacturing industry, this principle does not apply to primary sectors that engage with living creatures. One cannot harvest rice in the middle of winter or grow cassava in the desert. In the case of Chile's salmon industry, the proliferation of fish pens on the coast led to a large-scale fish epidemic (called the sanitary crisis) in 2009, and salmon aquaculture suffered a severe blow (Chap. 2, Sect. 2.3). In Kilimanjaro, Tanzania, an exemplary project for extending rice cultivation faced a water conflict in the 1990s, as more farmers voluntarily joined profitable rice production, causing tensions in villages. Working with local communities and helping them manage the commons is a new challenge for development cooperation targeting the countryside (Chap. 2, Sect. 2.4).

Industrialisation brings about rapid economic development, as exemplified in the Eastern Seaboard Development Plan in Thailand, where air and water pollution raised concerns among the local and urban citizens (actually, there was also a 'political' crisis: the project was suspended in 1985, not least due to pressure from the World Bank) (Chap. 3, Sect. 3.3). The Minamata disease caused by the organic mercury pollution in the Shiranui Sea, Kumamoto Prefecture, Japan, is well documented, but local people continue suffering. Now, communities in Minamata are being regenerated through *moyai naoshi*,[28] involving multiple stakeholders including the municipality. Less known is that the lessons of the Minamata disease have been shared with Brazilian professional chemists, who play a significant role in preventing mercury poisoning in the Amazon River basin (Chap. 6, Sect. 6.3).[29]

[C] Crisis of Institutional and Financial Sustainability

The category of probably the most commonly observed crises, which every project may face at a certain point, is the crisis of institutional sustainability. Projects initiated to serve the donor's interest may not continue after the cooperation period. Buildings and facilities are constructed, but the project runs short of funds and personnel, and their institutional survival becomes at risk. Otherwise, circumstances may have changed, and the initial high priority given by the aid recipient country may have disappeared. In these cases, when the government of the recipient country stops

Sloan 2014). Iokibe (2020) vividly describes the dedication of Japanese government officers in coping with major earthquakes.

[28] In the local language, *moyai* means bonding fishing boats by rope, while *naoshi* means mending/repairing. *Moyai naoshi* therefore refers to local attempts at rehabilitating trust and social relationships in the communities of Minamata torn apart by the deadly mercury pollution.

[29] There can be a branch of oral history that records the interaction between humans and the environment (Sloan and Cave 2022). Furthermore, we may think of an oral history that tries to 'listen to the land' (Lee and Newfont 2017).

funding, the project may disappear quietly without leaving a trace. This is the problem of sustainability, which is one of the main criteria in project evaluation.[30]

Given that the rationale of development cooperation is to teach people how to fish, a project can be considered successful when local fishers can fish on their own after their foreign teachers leave. But things are not that easy in practice. Transfer of vocational training skills and management skills in Malaysia and Costa Rica was generally successful, but former cutting-edge technologies became obsolete (Chap. 3, Sect. 3.2 and 3.4). Whether traditional manufacturing industries can make a successful transition to higher value-added ones remains a significant challenge for the contemporary Japanese and developing economies.

The three projects in Africa that went through sustainability crises all relate to education. There was an option for the management of the Jomo Kenyatta University of Agriculture and Technology (JKUAT) in Kenya to survive as a relatively small practice-oriented college rather than to take a risk to transform into a full-scale university, and the latter path was eventually chosen (Chap. 4, Sect. 4.2). The project to develop science and mathematics education in Kenya counted on teachers' voluntary collaboration but met with strong resistance. However, this training method was eventually accepted as a norm in Kenya's educational settings and became self-sustaining (Chap. 4, Sect. 4.3). The School of Veterinary Medicine at the University of Zambia was on the verge of collapse with a paucity of qualified teaching staff, but it managed to take off as Zambian students who took PhD degrees returned one after another (Chap. 5, Sect. 5.3). In these cases, bold experiments paid off against the odds. In retrospect, it might seem that success was assured from the beginning, but in the middle of the crisis, everyone involved in the projects was not very confident about their future prospects.

Development projects are like living organisms and show complex, semi-autonomous, evolutionary trajectories through interaction with the external environment, even though each project is embedded in the whole of the international cooperation regime. In a sense, development projects can be considered Janus-faced holons, which, 'relative to their sub-ordinates in the hierarchy, function as self-contained wholes; relative to their superordinates as dependent parts. As such, they represent both wholeness and partness' (Koestler 1967: 58). In the following chapters, I will examine how development projects overcame crises in individual circumstances in the post-war world. With the rise of China and other non-Western donors, the relative advantage of Japanese development cooperation in terms of the abundance of resources and the superiority of technology seems to be waning, even though its presence is still substantial. For elderly counterparts, the memory of working with Japan may have been evoked as a memory of their good old days. However, after conducting a series of intensive interviews, I have come to believe that the experiences of the project counterparts contain a wealth of lessons and wisdom that should

[30] Sustainability (Will the benefits last?) is the sixth of the six evaluation criteria of the Organisation for Economic Co-operation and Development (OECD) to evaluate development projects. https://www.oecd.org/en/topics/sub-issues/development-co-operation-evaluation-and-effectiveness/evaluation-criteria.html.

be widely shared by the new generations of development practitioners and thinkers across the Global South and North.

Each case study has its own passage of time and presents a self-contained story. Readers are now welcome to start reading from any of the following chapters.

Chapter 2
Blessings of Water, Blessings of People: Farming and Fishing Industries

2.1 Managing the Commons

2.1.1 Water and People's Livelihoods

From space, the Earth looks blue. The seas, lakes, and white clouds are of water. The Earth is dubbed as a water planet. Water management has always been linked to the configuration of political power, although the history of water is much longer than the history of human civilisations (Wittfogel 1957; Boccaletti 2021).

Without water on the Earth, life could not have been created. Without enough water, humans cannot sustain life. In ancient India, China, and Greece, water was considered one of the basic elements that made up the world.[1] On land, animals and people congregate where water is available. Crops grow with water, and settlements are built along rivers. People worship water sources, and oases are resting places for travellers. The oceans, which cover 70% of the Earth's surface, provide a rich source of protein in the form of fish and shellfish and allow people to travel long distances by boat. On the other hand, water can also be violent, swamping people and their property. River basins are subject to flooding, and coastlines to tsunami and storm surges. Water washes away dirt and cools down hot things, but it can also carry poisons from one place to another.

The Human Development Report 2006, published by the United Nations Development Programme (UNDP), featured water issues. The report highlighted the importance of water to ordinary people from two perspectives: its biological indispensability for human life and its usefulness as a means of livelihood. The report distanced itself from the Malthusian view that population growth would lead to a gradual depletion of water resources, resulting in a catastrophe for human society. In fact,

[1] In the 1940s, Carl Schmitt (1997) vividly described the evolution of geopolitics in terms of land, water, fire, and air, referring to Leviathan as the sea beast and predicting the age of air raids.

Y. Mine, *An Oral History of Development Cooperation*,
https://doi.org/10.1007/978-981-95-5479-9_2

the question facing humanity is not general scarcity but the inequitable distribution of water resources. At the time of its publication, 'some 1.1 billion people in developing countries had inadequate access to water, and 2.6 billion lacked basic sanitation.' The report argued that this was not so much the question of the physical availability of water as one of 'institutions and political choices'. Water shortages place a disproportionate burden on certain groups of people, especially women and children, who sacrifice enormous amounts of time and educational opportunities just to fetch water (UNDP 2006: 2–3). As water is linked to all aspects of human life, it is difficult to conceive of a development agency dedicated solely to the question of water. In 2003, the UN established UN-Water, which is not a specialised agency but coordinates the activities of more than 30 UN agencies whose activities are related to water management.

Water resources are a finite public good that should be shared by all living creatures. The ecologist scholar Garrett Hardin illustrated the difficulty of managing commons in his article 'The Tragedy of the Commons' (Hardin 1968). Suppose that there are open pastures available to everyone. A cattle keeper, a greedy but rational man, would calculate the utility to himself of adding a new animal to his herd. If all cattle keepers increase the number of cattle in order to maximise their utility, the cattle will eat up all the grass, the commons will collapse, and no one will be able to continue herding. As a result of all carrying out the natural act of promoting their self-interests, everyone's welfare will eventually be destroyed.

How can the tragedy of the commons be avoided? If pastures are divided up as private property, individual herders may try to prevent overgrazing and use their pieces of land sustainably, though poor herders (who are likely to be the majority) may lose their land entitlements and be evicted. If pastures are made state property, all herders could continue herding, but it is not easy for the state to exercise adequate control over the local environment. Human societies have developed a third way, which is neither total market laissez-faire nor state control: the voluntary management of resources by local communities. Elinor Ostrom, the first woman to win the Nobel Prize in Economics in 2009, has carefully documented cases from around the world, where users of the commons have developed cooperative strategies and crafted optimal rules and institutions from the bottom up (Ostrom 1990). In light of such discussions, Hardin summarised that what we faced was not a tragedy of the commons but a tragedy of the *unmanaged* commons (Hardin 1994).

2.1.2 Beyond the Crises

All three projects this chapter takes up are embedded in the water cycle, first in the river basin (flood control), then from the river to the sea (fish stocking and aquaculture), and finally back to the water sources (irrigated agriculture). As explained at the end of Chap. 1, all development projects presented in this book went through some sort of crisis. Here, I will outline the main points regarding the projects this chapter is going to deal with.

Section 2.2, the first case study of this chapter, looks at the integrated development of the Brantas River basin in East Java, Indonesia. This long-standing comprehensive project began in the late 1950s as part of Japan's post-war reparations for Indonesia, though its roots can be traced back to the times of Dutch colonial rule and the Japanese military occupation. It was an ambitious project to manage a raging, violent river and utilise water resources effectively. When the reparations started as in-kind provisions of goods and services (Shimomura 2020: 40–41), the Japanese workers arrived and operated heavy machinery to build the dams. However, construction came to a complete halt when a political cataclysm occurred in Indonesia in September 1965. After the political crisis, construction resumed under President Suharto with the substantial provision of yen loans from the Japanese government. Even under the decades-long development dictatorship of Suharto, some degree of local autonomy appears to have developed in eastern Java. Nowadays, Perum Jasa Tirta I (Water Management Corporation) officers wear uniforms and maintain all dams in the Brantas River basin as a single public asset. During interviews, local counterparts often talked about the imperishable 'Brantas Spirit'.

Section 2.3, the second case study, discusses the fisheries industry in Chile. In this field, Japan's original cooperation was conducted not in aquaculture but in the stocking of salmon. Since 1969, for almost 20 years, a team of Japanese and Chilean experts struggled to develop a hatchery in a town bordering Argentina where they released juvenile salmon into the river in the hope that fishers could catch adult fish when they returned home. If successful, it would have significantly benefited small-scale fishing families. Although technology transfer for stocking advanced in the 1970s and 80s, this attempt eventually failed to produce significant returns of salmon, and the project was terminated. Nevertheless, having acquired extensive knowledge of salmon's ecology, the Chilean counterparts ventured to move into private aquaculture enterprises where they would play a pivotal role. Then, the so-called sanitary crisis erupted in 2007, with a large quantity of farmed salmon succumbing to an infectious disease. The experts who spent time in salmon stocking decades ago are sceptical about bringing the logic of engineering to the fishing industry.

Finally, Sect. 2.4, the third case study, is about rice farming in Kilimanjaro, Tanzania. In the 1980s, a large expanse of paddy fields was constructed with a provision of yen loans, and rice production was augmented. In the mid-1990s, however, a conflict over water resources among local farmers emerged. Farmers outside the project area, who witnessed the success of rice cultivation, started to divert water to their paddy fields upstream, and as a result, farmers downstream in the project area began to suffer severe water shortages. In Kilimanjaro villages, the cooperation concentrated on constructing irrigation canals and paddy fields, but the need to nurture a cooperative system to manage local commons has become widely recognised. Tanzanian and Japanese stakeholders are now attempting to develop farmers' organisations.

2.1.3 The Local Ownership in the Management of Commons

When evaluating a development project, it is essential not to categorise it simply as a roaring success or a total failure. For commercial projects, it is sufficient to calculate the benefits against the costs in monetary terms, but the objectives of development cooperation are much broader, and the criteria for evaluation cannot but be complex and composite. If local counterparts who participated in a project acquired skills, left the project that eventually dissolved with no vestige of collaboration, and transferred their experiences extensively to other projects, such a process could also be considered a success if not of the initial project but of the technology transfer at large.

The three projects described in this chapter have one thing in common. The Japanese did not give up on waiting for their counterparts to become self-reliant, which is hard to imagine in today's world of yearly performance evaluation. In the development of the Brantas River basin, through decades of cooperation since the late 1950s, the local counterparts observed the behaviour of the Japanese, worked with them, and gradually moved to a stage where they could manage everything and expand the projects by themselves. The flow of 'see, learn, try, and do' formulated by the Indonesians is not a short-term project cycle like PDCA (discussed to some extent in Chap. 3) but a transition over time from dependence to independence (i.e., from Fig. 1.3 through Figs. 1.2 to 1.4 in Chap. 1). Such a process requires great patience and commitment on the part of the donors. In Chile, the period of waiting for the adult salmon to return lasted for more than 20 years. Even though the fish did not return in large numbers, Chileans who received technology transfer moved into the private sector and became key players in the aquaculture industry. Rice cultivation in Kilimanjaro is another long-standing project that has continued to evolve for decades, now addressing the challenges of institution-building.

Human resources nurtured in this way are not mere groups of skilful individuals but dynamic teams bound together by mutual trust. While Japanese experts eventually return home, local counterparts remain in the same place more often than not. Whether in Indonesia, Chile or Tanzania, the counterparts maintain close networks among themselves. In Chile, some professionals moved into the private sector, and they called in their former colleagues to lead the salmon farming industry together.

In Chap. 1, it was assumed that the principal-agent relationship would function primarily at the national government level. Prima facie, ODA is a form of intergovernmental transfer of resources, but the logic of sub-national locality may work more forcefully, especially when the project involves primary industries that rely on specific local environments. A nation-state is too large as a framework for collective action to take shape to manage the local commons. Volcano Kelud erupts recurrently, around which the Brantas River carries abundant water; the clear water springs out of the Patagonian plateau and flows into the South Pacific; the coffee fields on the side of the gigantic Mount Kilimanjaro overlook the vast rice paddies spreading at its foot. Each has a unique natural landscape and is home to the people who continue living there. Each configuration of human and natural environments requires locally tailored policies that are different from those in big cities like Jakarta, Santiago, and

Dar es Salaam. Retaining the sense of locality, the skills and lessons accumulated in the individual projects may expand outwards through mechanisms such as the third-country training programme (TCTP) (Kato 2012; Chandy 2013).

Now, let me begin with the story of the Brantas River in Indonesia as the first of the case studies.

2.2 Dams Nurturing People: The Development of the Brantas River Basin (Indonesia)

2.2.1 The Beginning of Cooperation

Indonesia is an archipelagic state consisting of almost 15,000 islands of various sizes. The population is approximately 280 million, and the total area of the islands is 1.9 million square kilometres. Compared to Japan, Indonesia has almost twice the population and is 3.7 times the size. The most densely populated island is Java, home to several big cities like Jakarta, the capital; Bandung, the highland city; Yogyakarta, the ancient capital; and Surabaya, the major commercial and industrial city. 140 million people, more than half of Indonesia's population, reside in Java, where intensive rice cultivation has been practised and a variety of new and old industries have developed.

Historically, Indonesian society was highly decentralised, with local kingdoms and chiefdoms ruling their own territories, and there had never been a consolidated political power to unite the place covering today's Indonesia. In 1602, however, with the establishment of the Dutch East India Company, the Netherlands attempted to rule the entire islands from the sea. In the nineteenth and twentieth centuries, the Netherlands administered Indonesia as the Dutch East Indies. After the Japanese occupation during World War II, Indonesia declared its independence in August 1945 and officially broke away from the Netherlands in 1949.[2]

The Brantas River,[3] which flows around the eastern part of Java, has an unusual whirlpool shape. The active volcano, Mount Kelud, is located at the centre and encircled by lowlands, which are surrounded further by highlands and mountains. The Brantas River, therefore, cannot flow directly to the sea but instead flows clockwise through the lowlands, reaching the sea at Surabaya in the north (Fig. 2.1). The total length of the river is 320 km, making it the second longest river in Java after the Solo River (540 km).

---

[2] As for a comprehensive history of Indonesia throughout pre-colonial and post-colonial times, see Taylor (2003).

[3] While both 川 and 河 mean rivers, many Japanese project documents used 河 instead of 川 to refer to the Brantas River. The character 可 means right-angled bend, and the term 河 originally referred to the winding Yellow River. The shape of the Brantas fits perfectly with this character. When we visited Nippon Koei before conducting the fieldwork, Mr Hatao Shigemichi and Ms Hashimoto Mayumi explained in detail the significance of the Brantas River project for the development of Nippon Koei and provided us with information materials.

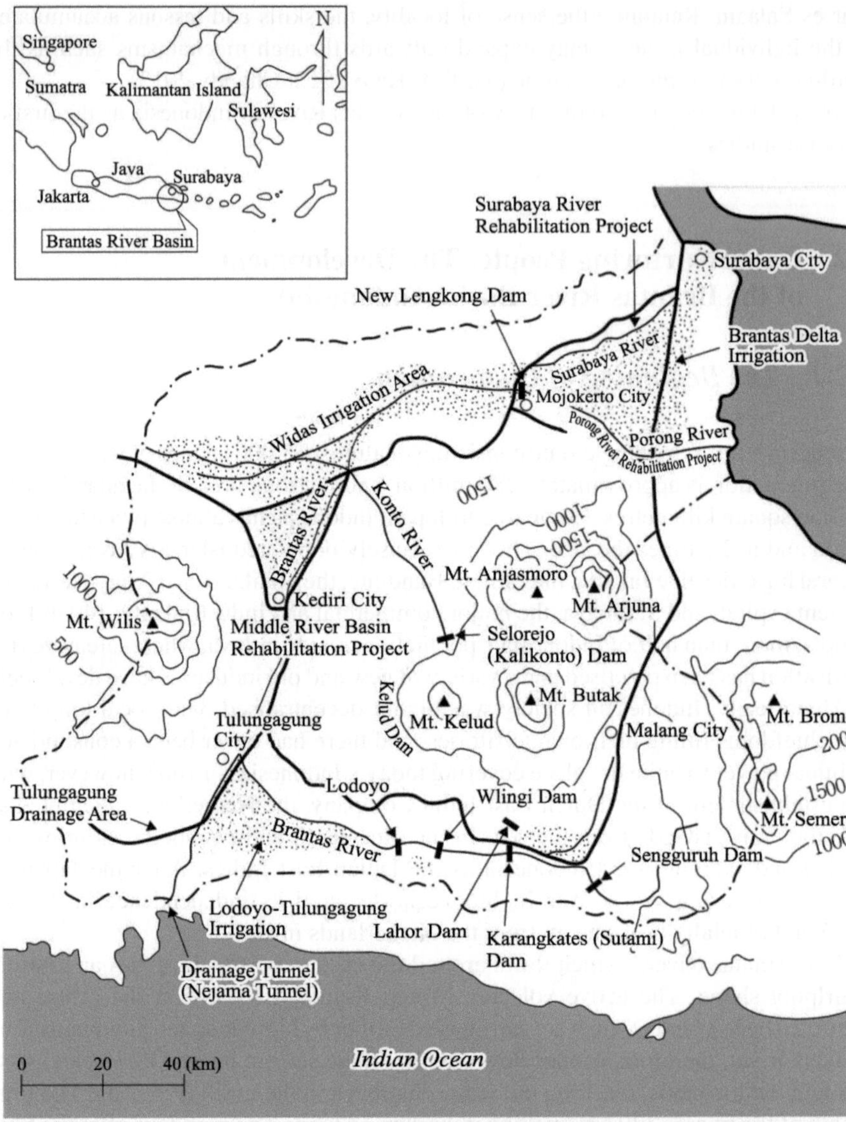

Fig. 2.1 Dam complex in the Brantas River Basin. Source: Adapted from Yamada (2021: 74)

The nature of the Brantas River basin is far from benign. Explosive eruptions of Kelud periodically generated thermal mudflows that reshaped the outlook of the basin. The risk of flooding increases as the riverbed rises due to the fall of volcanic ash and debris, which means that flood control in the basin has always been a pressing issue. The Japanese term 'sabo dam' (check dam), intended to hold back sediment and control erosion, has become an everyday term for Indonesian water engineers.

On the other hand, the water resources of the Brantas River have great industrial potential. The volcanic ash soil is fertile and suitable for agriculture. As Indonesia's population grew after independence, there was a strong need to expand the irrigated farmland to increase food production and to develop hydroelectric power plants and water supply systems.

In 1958, with Japanese assistance, the development of the Brantas River basin gained momentum and eventually became an exemplary model representing Japanese ODA in terms of scale and duration. To date, eight large dams, eight water gates and 20 water intakes have been constructed in the river basin, with a significant portion of the assistance being provided by Japan.[4] Concurrently, at the time of the commencement of cooperation, the construction of two large infrastructure development projects, the Kurobe Dam and the Aichi Irrigation Canals, started in Japan by utilising the World Bank loan (in 1956 and 1957, respectively). These and the Brantas projects were cascading global projects, so to speak.[5]

The solid Indonesian commitment to the project was evidenced by the ways local officers in their 80s looked back on those days. The development of the Brantas River basin evolved in three phases. Rusfandi Usman, former president director of Jasa Tirta I (Water Management Corporation), explained:

> When the temporary partition dam was constructed at Karangkates, the Indonesian experts and workers mostly just observed how the teams from Nippon Koei and Kajima Corporation handled everything. But in the second phase, when the main dam was constructed, the Indonesians started to do the job, with guidance from the Japanese experts. Then, in the third phase, the Indonesians took over and built the dam on their own. It was just like the saying goes, 'People make dams, and dams make people.' A lot of people who gained experience in Brantas went on to work all over Indonesia as government officers, consultants, or contractors. They contributed to water resources development across Indonesia. Yes, it was a huge transformation. [IDN 13]

In a similar vein, Tjoek Walujo Subijanto, former president director of Jasa Tirta I, said that the project gradually became owned by Indonesians through the stages of 'observe,' 'learn', 'try' and 'do' (Almizan 2004a; Subijanto et al. 2013; Subijanto 2015). Tracing these stages, the rest of this section describes the history of the integrated development of the Brantas River basin since the 1950s.

---

[4] Of the 103.7 billion yen in financial assistance to the Brantas River basin (excluding the city of Surabaya) up to 1995, 75.7 billion yen came from Japan (including 600 million yen as post-war reparations), 11.2 billion yen from the Asian Development Bank (ADB), 800 million yen from the World Bank, and 16 billion yen from other donors. Japan's presence was overwhelming, though not exclusive. The bulk of Japanese aid, excluding the reparations, was provided through the Overseas Economic Cooperation Fund (OECF) (Nippon Koei and Koei Research Institute 1997: 49). The resources from the Indonesian side were the equivalent of 113.3 billion yen (ibid. 120).

[5] The construction of the Kurobe Dam was a clear indication of the shift in Japan's engineering technology from a military to a civilian orientation, even though the narrative style of *The Sun of Kurobe* (Kimoto 1964), which was later adapted into a popular film, is almost like a war chronicle. For the Aichi irrigation project, see Nakayama and Fujikura (2013) (in English).

2.2.2 *Post-War Reparations (1958–1965)*

The initiative for the development of the Brantas River basin was taken by Kubota Yutaka, who founded Nippon Koei, a leading Japanese development consulting company, in 1946. Kubota was born in 1890 in a village north of the Aso volcanic caldera field in Kumamoto. After studying civil engineering at Tokyo Imperial University, he orchestrated colonial development projects in northern Korea to construct dams. Several large hydroelectric plants built by Kubota and others, known retrospectively as 'imperial consultants', continued to operate in North Korea after its independence. During World War II, Kubota was also involved in surveys of water resources development in the Asia–Pacific, including French Indochina (today's Vietnam, Laos, Cambodia) and Dutch East Indies (today's Indonesia). After the war, in 1953, Kubota travelled around the world searching for opportunities to set up new construction businesses (Yamada 2021: 11–15).[6]

The Netherlands, which took pride in its advanced water management technology, carried out development projects in the Brantas River basin in the nineteenth century. However, without substantial projects after Indonesia achieved independence in 1949, the basin faced frequent volcanic eruptions and flooding. Kubota, who visited the Brantas River basin and saw the Tulungagung area that suffered chronic flooding, conjectured that the construction of a drainage tunnel for the area 'can be completed in one year' (Koizumi 2008; Nippon Koei and Koei Research Institute 1997: 51–54).

Currently, three drainage tunnels are in operation south of Tulungagung. Nippon Koei secured an order for the first tunnel in 1958. Construction began in 1959 by Kajima Construction and finished in 1961. There was a big cave-in during the construction, but fortunately, there were no casualties as the day happened to be a holiday, and the 1,000-m tunnel was completed really in about a year (Nippon Koei and Koei Research Institute 1997: 281). The construction of the second tunnel was finished in 1986 (funded by the Asian Development Bank), making the regular swamp almost disappear. The third tunnel was completed in 1991 (funded by Austria), and its water was to be used to generate hydroelectric power on the Indian Ocean side. Sutomo, a former engineer who once managed the tunnel's water gates, explained:

> I remember when Tulungagung was completely flooded. People had to build their houses on stilts, and during the rainy season, we couldn't even tell whose paddy field was whose! There was no proper education, and everyone was really, really poor. Back then, the villagers had nowhere to go, since it was before the government started relocating people to other islands. [IDN 11]

Thanks to a series of construction works, the swamps of Tulungagung were transformed into farmland, and paddy fields were allocated to the villagers. Malaria and skin diseases have all but disappeared. The Japanese named the first tunnel 'Nejama Tunnel' because the meaning of the Indonesian name of that area was 'root (*ne*) and mountain (*yama*)'. The local people somehow liked the Japanese pronunciation of

[6] For the continuity from the pre-war colonial engineering to the post-war development activities of Kubota and others, see Moore (2013; 2020). See also the Nippon Koei website. https://www.n-koei.co.jp/consulting/english/aboutus/history/founder/.

'Nejama (pronounced as Neyama or Niama)', which is the tunnel's nickname even today.

There was another tunnel in South Tulungagung that was rarely mentioned in documents. Known locally as a '*romusha* tunnel', it was a drainage tunnel that the Japanese army attempted to construct by mobilising local villagers during World War II but was abandoned after the war. Mujianto, an announcer for Tulungagung's municipal radio station, told us about his family: 'During the war, my grandmother was mobilised to construction work, but she caught malaria and got a very high fever. She came back home, but the fever never went away, and eventually, she passed away' [IDN 10]. It is calculated that about 10% of the local population was forcibly mobilised to construct this tunnel under Japanese military rule (Sato 1994: 198).

Even though a specific infrastructure project was not intended as a reparation for specific damage, these projects did begin as parts of Japan's post-war reparations for Indonesia. A former engineer, Setyo Adiwidjono, said, 'The development of Brantas started as reparations. But I wonder how Japan could develop so quickly that reparations could be offered only a decade after the war was over' [IDN 16]. For sure, he looked like he did not understand it.

In 1961, when the first tunnel of the South Tulungagung Drainage was opened, Nippon Koei finalised the first master plan for the integrated development of the Brantas River basin and submitted it to the Indonesian Ministry of Public Works (Nippon Koei 1961). At that time, the experience of the Tennessee Valley Authority (TVA) in the United States was a shining example for both Japanese and Indonesian engineers (Lilienthal 1944). With flood control engineering at its core, the project would work comprehensively to promote the local economy and improve the well-being of villagers in the region.

In this master plan, two multi-purpose dams were given high priority, and their construction began promptly: the Karangkates Dam (commenced in 1962), located between Malang and Tulungagung, and the Selorejo Dam (commenced in 1963) in the highlands near the summit of Mount Kelud.[7] A former worker who grew up in a village near the Selorejo Dam recalled. 'I remember that during the construction of the Selorejo Dam, there was a lot of hustle and bustle with the big heavy machinery brought in from Japan. It was easy to find a job thanks to the project' [IDN 06].

During this period, large Japanese general contractors such as Kajima Corporation took charge of the construction. At that time, the Japanese surveyed the place and designed and built the dams, while the Indonesians watched and performed auxiliary work. It was in the late 1960s that this attitude of 'observing' changed dramatically to a 'learning', 'trying' and 'doing' style.

[7] Selorejo is the name of the village where the dam is located. Karangkates Dam was later called Sutami Dam after the Minister of Water Resources.

2.2.3 *Political Crisis (1965–67)*

During World War II, the Japanese freed Sukarno, a hero of the Indonesian independence movement who had been imprisoned by the Dutch authorities, and gave support to him. After the defeat of Japan, Sukarno and his movement fought a war of independence against the Dutch military, resulting in the formal transfer of sovereignty in 1949. After independence, President Sukarno was running a government on a delicate balance between the military, nationalists, and the Indonesian Communist Party (PKI: Partai Komunis Indonesia), while on the diplomatic front, he chaired the Asian-African Conference (Bandung Conference) in 1955 and became a leader of the Non-Aligned Movement. Although Sukarno was very active and respected externally and also enjoyed popular support internally, Indonesia's economy remained stagnant, and his political base among the elite was insecure. Sukarno was born in Surabaya, and the Brantas River basin was his home region. It is undeniable that giving leverage to the Sukarno regime was one of the reasons why this region was chosen as a major site for Japan's post-war reparations and development assistance to Indonesia.

However, Sukarno's 'Bonapartiste' style of politics was unstable, and the balance between strange bedfellows finally collapsed with the aborted coup on 30 September 1965. On that day, the left-wing presidential security forces, led by Lt. Col. Untung, attacked right-wing army generals, killing seven of them in an attempt to seize state power. In response, Army Maj. Gen. Suharto launched an immediate counter-attack. Suharto crushed the left forces and, claiming that the PKI was behind the coup attempt, took the army's lead in controlling the media, mobilising landlord militias, and crushing all PKI cells throughout Indonesia. At least half a million communists and their sympathisers were mercilessly killed in the years that followed, with some estimates putting the figure at between one and two million. For a long time, it was taboo in Indonesia to speak openly about this incident, and the truth has been disclosed gradually only in recent years.[8]

As remembered by Nippon Koei's Japanese employees, the PKI was influential in Malang, where their business office was located, and many towns and villages upstream of the dams were also the strongholds of the PKI. These were surrounded by army troops and Muslim militias that crushed them one by one. A large number of soldiers came to the construction site of the Karangkates Dam. They captured PKI cadres, who would not return. There were also PKI members and sympathisers among the construction workers, and about 1,000 workers were gathered in a square and forced to pledge to break off their relationship with the party (Nippon Koei and Koei Research Institute 1997: 252). By the time of this incident, the organisation of

[8] Details of the process were revealed after the fall of the Suharto regime in 1998. The English literature includes Anderson and McVey (1971) and Roosa (2006). Hearman (2018) discusses the communist resistance in Blitar, and Bevins (2020) focuses on the implications for the US. According to Kurasawa, 15,000 people were executed in Kediri in the middle reaches of the Brantas River, whose water is said to have been stained red with the blood of headless corpses (Kurasawa 2014: Chap. 6) (in Japanese).

the PKI became vulnerable through the open, legal activities its members carried out under the Sukarno regime. There was little resistance, partly because the PKI cadres had vainly hoped for Sukarno's mediation. In March 1968, Suharto was officially inaugurated as Indonesia's president. Sukarno was stripped of real power and, after imprisonment, died in June 1970.

An Indonesian engineer who was in charge of the quarrying department at the Karangkates Dam recalls that the 'chaos' that emerged after the 30 September incident lasted until 1968. 'Discipline broke down everywhere. The worst was in 1967, when employees sometimes lost their reason, became careless and industrial accidents followed daily.' To restore order, rituals were held to drive away the evil spirit, known locally as the 'white tiger' (Madjid 2004: 52). Nippon Koei was baffled. The incident was followed by 'weeks of fear and chaos that made it impossible for us to work', and the Japanese Embassy recommended they leave the country temporarily (Nippon Koei and Koei Research Institute 1997: 252). If it was today, Japanese aid workers would have quickly evacuated from the country on the grounds of risk management, but the decision was made to remain in the area at the time. Yet it was not certain whether the development project of the Brantas River basin would continue after such a huge political upheaval. Once in power, Suharto steadily entrenched a 'developmental dictatorship' (Olson 1993). However, it would have required a political decision to reinvest substantial resources in the home region of his predecessor, who could endanger the legitimacy of the new regime.

The person who set the flow in motion was Suryono, who had been appointed as general manager of the Brantas River Integrated Development Office established in Malang in 1965, affectionately remembered in both Indonesia and Japan as Professor Suryono. At this juncture, in 1966, the eruption of Mount Kelud caused a massive flow of thermal mud and a fall of volcanic ash, which raised the bed of the Brantas River. Mizuhara Yoshio, an engineer at Nippon Koei, noted that 'the behaviour of Mount Kelud was often associated with President Sukarno, and there were local expectations of the return of Bung Karno [Sukarno's nickname]' (Mizuhara 1997: 96). Almizan Abdullah, head of the Karangkates Dam construction office, recalled, 'The Karangkates Dam was a temporary partition dam, so there was a risk that it would collapse during heavy rainfall. I think Professor Suryono used this as a weapon to persuade the government to continue the project' [IDN 05]. The possibility of a dangerous flood, which was real, was used to put pressure on the regime from the bottom up.

After confirming that Suharto had seized real power in the Indonesian government, Japan decided to grant yen loans to Indonesia through the Overseas Economic Cooperation Fund (OECF) in March 1966, and the construction work of the Karangkates and Selorejo Dams restarted in the following year. After the regime change, the Brantas River project, which had been half-completed with post-war reparations, was resumed with the formal provision of ODA loans.[9] The dams could not just be

[9] Japan, which was close to Sukarno, veered to support the Suharto regime after a period of hesitation in the immediate aftermath of the nationwide violence. For the circumstances and consequences discussed by Japanese scholars, see, for example, Miyagi (2004: Chap. 6) and Sato (2021: Chap. 5).

left under construction. Suryono was at pains to coordinate with the Suharto administration in Jakarta, and eventually the regional development project was getting larger and larger.

2.2.4 The Era of Cooperation (1967–1970)

A total of 318 Japanese engineers were deployed for the construction of the Karangkates Dam from 1962 to 1973, and 99 for the construction of the Selorejo Dam from 1963 to 1972. In the late 1960s, the site of the Karangkates Dam attracted more than a hundred engineers at once, strengthening their presence significantly (Nippon Koei and Koei Research Institute, 1997: 114–117). Almizan Abdullah, who actively engaged in the construction of the Karangkates Dam, was 84 years old at the time of the interview. He described the situation as follows:

> When we were building the main dam, as many as 150 Japanese came to Brantas and trained us. We all worked together, so we were like a team. Yes, it was one big team. We didn't understand each other's language very well, but we could understand it with gestures. Indonesians are flexible people, and the Japanese respect local ways of doing things. No one was arrogant. When I was a student, I learnt Japanese military songs at school. When I sang *Kimigayo* [the Japanese national anthem] and other songs in front of them, the Japanese apologised and said, 'Sorry, sorry.' Then I replied, 'OK, OK.' [IDN 05]

A dam cannot be built halfway and abandoned. Only through the provision of yen loans did Nippon Koei and Kajima Construction resume work on the dams. However, Indonesia's enthusiasm for technology transfer went far beyond business transactions. On the local side, Indonesians may have needed something to concentrate upon in order to overcome the extraordinary tragedy of the mass killings of Indonesians by Indonesians, and it was also effective for social rehabilitation that the project brought tangible benefits to people's everyday lives. As Rusfandi Usman, former president director of Jasa Tirta I, explained, 'the local people welcomed the dam construction not only because of the material benefits but also because they were employed as workers. People who were originally farmers became drivers, welders, and construction workers. Many regarded their Japanese counterparts as their teachers' [IDN 13].

In the old days, 'we used the abacus and the slide rule' [IDN 16], not the computer. Hardiono, a former worker at the Karangkates Dam and now a teacher at a vocational high school, remembered:

> Mr Furuya of Nippon Koei taught me how to work since 1974. He was strict with time. He tried to speak Indonesian, but when that was not effective, he taught me with gestures. Mr Furuya scolded us severely when we did not follow safety procedures. [IDN 08]

A former worker at the Selorejo Dam recalled:

> A Japanese man called Puita-san taught me details about electrical stuff. He was a short, fat man. He spoke Indonesian a little. I remember he brought bananas, telling me to share them with friends. He also took us on trips to Yogyakarta and Bali. [IDN 06]

This person nicknamed ‘Puita’ by his Japanese colleagues would probably have brought the Japanese custom of company outings to Indonesia. Time after work also seemed to be important. Rusfandi recalls with nostalgia, ‘On the site of Karangkates, we used to cook and eat together in the canteen once a week. We also played football’ [IDN 13]. Interestingly, the Japanese tried to speak Indonesian and had their children learn Indonesian, whereas today most Japanese expatriates prefer English teaching.

Bedjo Siswojo, a local primary school teacher, was hired around 1967 to teach Indonesian at a primary school set up for workers’ families at the Karangkates Dam. ‘In those days, many Japanese brought their families, so I think about one in four school children was Japanese. Children should be able to speak Indonesian if their parents want them to keep up with their studies at school. So, I also gave Indonesian lessons to children in Japanese homes. The children’s progress was so rapid that some spoke not only Indonesian but also Javanese [not Japanese]’ [IDN 09].

For professional engineers engaging in the construction of dams, it was a cinch to clear the land and open an impromptu golf course near the site. While the Japanese and Indonesian husbands enjoyed playing golf, their wives socialised. Rusfandi’s wife said of those days:

> In Karangkates, we had a good relationship with Kiyora-san’s family. Madam gave me nice clothes and accessories, and in return, I gave her batiks. When they left Indonesia, they left behind some very nice furniture. We still use it today…. Kiyora-san’s baby died here. Alas, I think it was a premature birth, and the baby was cremated here. It must have been a very painful experience for her. I wonder how she is now. I would love to see Kiyora-san again. [IDN 14]

2.2.5 One River, One Plan, One Management (1970-)

The 1970s saw a radical shift in the modality of development cooperation in the Brantas region. The Overseas Technical Cooperation Agency (OTCA) released the second master plan in 1972, and JICA the third in 1985.[10] In the meantime, the Indonesian side started to take responsibility for implementing the projects on the construction sites. ‘Only about three Japanese were assigned to the management job, and about two to the supervision, and the Indonesian side took charge of the main construction work’ (Nippon Koei and Koei Research Institute 1997: 116). In addition to Nippon Koei, companies such as Sanyu, Nikken, and Pacific Consultants participated in the project. Based on the experience of the South Tulungagung Drainage, the Karangkates Dam, and the Selorejo Dam, donors’ assistance was extended to

[10] In 1974, OTCA and JEMIS (Japan Emigration Service) merged to form JICA. OTCA (1972; 1973a), drafted by Nippon Koei, is a compilation of comprehensive development research based on hydrological survey analysis. Nippon Koei and Koei Research Institute (1997) reviewed the progress of past projects in light of these master plans. JICA (1998a) and JICA and Bureau of Water Resources (1998), which contained the fourth master plan, recognised the priority of maintaining existing facilities and developing human resources rather than constructing new dams. Indonesia (2017) emphasises the importance of quantitative research on the impact of climate change on the basin.

other new dams in the basin and also to the urban development in Surabaya (Nippon Koei and Koei Research Institute, 1997: 122–123).

By the 1970s, livelihoods in the Brantas River basin had largely stabilised. Indonesia achieved rice self-sufficiency in 1980, as a result of a steady increase in unit yields. In the Brantas region, the rice harvest increased dramatically from 1.11 million tonnes (1965) to 2.67 million tonnes (1993) in almost the same area of paddy fields (the area of farmland is now shrinking due to the expansion of urban residential areas). This is thanks to the development of irrigation canals, which allowed rice cultivation to continue during the dry season, and the spread of double cropping.

Hydroelectric power generation meets the peak electricity demands at night (6–11 pm). The maximum output of electricity generated by the dams is 105,000 kW at the Karangkates Dam, 54,000 kW at the Wlingi Dam (completed in 1978), 29,000 kW at the Sengguruh Dam (completed in 1988) and 36,000 kW at Tulungagung Power Station (completed in 1991). In the 1960s, the electrification rate in the Brantas region was less than 10%, but by 1993 it exceeded 85% (ibid. 125, 148). Furthermore, thanks to the fine-tuned water flow regulation of upstream to downstream dams, there have been no major floods during the wet season in recent years.

A former worker employed at the Selorejo dam from 1969 obtained the job in compensation for providing his land for the construction. He recalls, 'Ordinary people could see the change. Before the dams started serving people, most houses in villages were made of bamboo. There were just a few brick-made houses. There was hardly any electricity. Very few people had motorbikes. But after the dams were constructed, all the houses became brick-made, electricity reached almost all houses, and everyone started riding Honda CBs. Every house enjoyed the fruit of development' [IDN 07].

A former president director of Jasa Tirta I, Subijanto, sums up the achievements of the Brantas River project: 'The important thing is that people's security has improved so much. This includes food security. We no longer have to worry about the future' [IDN 17]. As the age of developmental dictatorships was over, Subijanto stressed the need to strengthen feedback between people and the government. The development of the Brantas region contributed not only to the development of physical infrastructure but also to the development of institutions. One of the challenges since the 1990s has been to change the way civil servants work. Subijanto continues: 'Civil servants used to think they were the "kings" who were served by people, but they now need to realise that they are no longer the "kings". They must be the servants of people. We have to change our mindset. It is essential to listen to the voices of the people' [IDN 17].

The Brantas River Integrated Development Office was established in 1965. Until then, the South Tulungagung Drainage had been operated under the Irrigation Department of the Ministry of Public Works, while the Karangkates and Selorejo Dams were under the management of the State Electricity Company (PLN). However, the first master plan for the Brantas region accommodated the idea that development projects were comprehensive multi-purpose projects and, therefore, should be managed by a single entity in all phases, from planning to construction and operation. Such an idea was behind the launch of the Integrated Development Office.

With the TVA model in mind, it seems that both the Indonesian and Japanese sides wanted to develop an autonomous, basin-wide public agency. It was the dream of Brantas officers to abolish the vertically divided centralised national bureaucracy and to realise a more decentralised mechanism of 'One River, One Plan, One Management'. Although there are slight discrepancies between different narratives as to when this slogan was established [IDN 05; IDN 17; IDN 18], all agreed that Prof. Suryono's philosophy was to create an autonomous organ in the basin [IDN 17; IDN 19; IDN 20; IDN 21; IDN 22].[11] However, nowadays, the Brantas River Basin Development Office has been split into three entities (Almizan 2004b).

The first is the consulting firm called Indra Karya (established in 1980), which means the 'work of the god of water' in Hinduism. The second is the construction company Brantas Abipraya (established in the same year), which is now engaged not only in water resources infrastructure projects but also in road construction. The third is Jasa Tirta (established in 1990), which is responsible for operation and maintenance of the infrastructure once construction is completed. The mission includes serving water to the beneficiaries, flood control, infrastructure maintenance, and small rehabilitation. The task of the Brantas River Basin Management Office (BBWS) is to coordinate overall activities from the office in Surabaya as an outpost agency of the Ministry of Water Resources in Jakarta.

While Indra Karya and Brantas Abipraya have become self-sustaining private firms at the national level, Jasa Tirta I functions as the public agency that maintains and manages the water resources infrastructure in the Brantas region. Roedjito Dwidjomustopo, former president director of Jasa Tirta I, wondered:

> Why was Jasa Tirta set up? Here is my view. Professor Suryono, Mr Almizan and other leaders were aware of the experience of state-owned electricity projects. I think they knew very well that, even if you create a government department, it will remain just a small *bonsai* tree embedded in the big structure. Instead, they wanted to plant a single independent tree and let it grow. [IDN 18]

Educational institutions also grew as part of the regionwide institution. University-educated hydraulic engineers were trained in Indonesia so that the dams could be maintained only by the Indonesians after the Japanese engineers left. The University of Brawijaya, founded in Malang in 1961, established the only Department of Water Resources Engineering in Indonesia in 1963 under the leadership of Dean of Engineering Suryono himself. A veteran faculty member, Abdul Aziz Hoesein, explained, 'In the beginning, we didn't have our own facilities, so we used the Sutami Dam and the Selorejo Dam as our laboratories. About 1,300 graduates specialising in water resources management are scattered across the country. Whenever I use the Nakayasu formula (Nakayasu Synthetic Unit Hydrograph), it reminds me of Japanese engineers. Now, girl students have a big presence in engineering. This year

[11] The Aichi Irrigation Canal Project was heavily influenced by the spirit of the TVA, which was hailed as an ideal by the Japanese engineers involved in the development of the Brantas River basin (Shimomura and Wang 2015). Almizan noted, 'We created the slogan, "One River, One Plan, One Management" in the period from 1962 to 65. It is Professor Suryono who added "One Management" to the idea of the TVA' [IDN 05].

[2018], we have 110 new students in the Department of Water Resources: 55 are men, and 55 are women, exactly half and half' [IDN 12]. The division of labour, with husbands being civil engineers and their wives being housewives, is breaking down very quickly in Indonesia. A vocational high school named after Prof. Suryono has opened just next to the Karangkates Dam.

Ultimately, the project was successful not only because it was one of the national flagship projects in Indonesia but also because it met the needs of local livelihoods. The emotional attachment of local stakeholders to the Brantas River basin was revealed in some interviews. As Fauzi Idris, director of the Water Resources Management Directorate in Jakarta, described: 'The Brantas project always involved local human resources, which had a very positive impact. Local people felt that the project belonged to them because the dam was constructed in a place where people lived. And the dam brought them real economic benefits' [IDN 03].

The project not only strengthened trust among the people in the Brantas River basin but also made a far-reaching impact throughout Indonesia. Rusfandi remarks, 'Things really went like the slogan, "people make dams, and dams make people." Professional people who grew up in Brantas are now dispersed all over Indonesia, working in water resources development as government officers, consultants, and contractors' [IDN 13]. Many of those involved in the development of the Brantas region are now in retirement. Rusfandi, who was 77 at the time of the interview, has high hopes for the future: 'We regularly hold alumni reunions of the former Brantas project staff in Malang. About 300 people, including their wives, come together. Some are in wheelchairs. We want to organise a big reunion with the Japanese people before long' [IDN 13].

2.2.6 Local Ownership Beyond the Developmental Dictatorship

See, learn, try, and do. The project for the Brantas River basin development has been an extraordinary venture to mobilise the Indonesians' power of self-reliance over several decades. Both Sukarno and Suharto had strong links with water management. Sukarno studied water resources management at the Bandung Institute of Technology. He is buried in the grave in Blitar, close to the Brantas River and a little upstream of Tulungagung, also known for the anti-Japanese uprising in 1945. On the other hand, Suharto came from a humbler background: his father was a village water management officer.

Dams are typical of hard infrastructure. However, as early as the 1960s, the construction of dams on the Brantas River became closely linked to the support for human resources development. It was Japanese private companies, such as Nippon Koei and the Kajima Corporation, rather than a government agency, such as OTCA, that played a pivotal role in the technology transfer on the ground. Local Indonesians vividly remember the humility of the Japanese engineers and their families and their efforts to integrate into the local community in the 1960s. An officer of the Ministry of Water Resources, who worked with Japanese counterparts, commented, 'Japanese are polite and disciplined people' [IDN 01].

What about future challenges? The city of Malang, with a population of nearly one million, lies upstream of the spiral-shaped Brantas River. The water usage in Malang may affect the lives of people living downstream, and the problem of water conflicts with Surabaya, a large city of nearly three million, could become serious. There is also the problem of maintenance. Muhammad Amir Hamzah from the Ministry of Public Works and Housing in Jakarta said, 'Some of the dams have already reached the end of their useful life. The Indonesian side can practice routine maintenance, but in the long term, we may have to secure loans from abroad' [IDN 04]. Airlangga Mardjono, a Malang-born Jakarta administrator, pointed out, 'From now, the rehabilitation of the dams will become necessary. We are also working with the Chinese and Koreans. I think their ideas about development are basically the same as those of the Japanese' [IDN 02].

Interviewees all agreed that development projects in the Brantas River basin greatly benefited local people. The impact of development is evident when one sees that every part of farmland in the basin is utilised and that vehicles owned by locals cause traffic jams. However, one would also see disparities between those who have become very rich and those who have become only slightly rich. Hasan Bisri, former president of Indra Karya, said:

> I am from Malang. So, I have seen the effects of the Brantas development with my own eyes. Electricity supply has stabilised, floods have been under control, wetlands have disappeared, rice cultivation has expanded, and people's incomes have increased. But, as you see, many young people now want to go to big cities. They stay in their hometown until they finish high school, then go to Malang, Surabaya and other cities. They don't want to go back to their original places. [IDN 15]

In 1998, after the outbreak of the Asian financial crisis, the Suharto regime collapsed, and Indonesia entered an era of popular democracy. As Hamzah emphasised, the resettlement of villagers and intervention in natural environments should be made only in line with the principle of 'deliberative democracy', and fair compensation must be provided to residents affected by the construction work [IDN 04]. As a former worker at the Selorejo Dam put it: 'At the time of President Suharto, there was no need for obtaining an agreement of residents. Everyone followed orders coming from above' [IDN 07].

In the parallel case of dam construction in Indonesia, the Kota Panjang Dam in Sumatra was vehemently opposed by local people resentful of the relocation and insufficient compensation, and a court case began in 2002 to hold the Japanese government responsible (Yamada 2021: 75–78; Sato 2021: 167–169, 247–248). The reason why such criticism did not surface in Brantas could be a combination of factors. The Brantas River was a raging river in a densely populated area, and the residents themselves wanted to tame the water flow; a group of local engineers led by Prof. Suryono emerged and took responsibility for the regional development endeavour; and the presence of Japanese workers, who looked very perceptive about historical contexts, was appreciated by their local counterparts.

The institutional development of the Brantas River basin was fostered by the 'tripartite trust' between the Japanese, their Indonesian counterparts, and the residents of the Brantas region (Fujimoto 2013). After the Japanese left, it is now essential to keep the principal-agent cycle working smoothly within Indonesia.

2.3 When Will They Come Back?: Fish Stocking and Aquaculture Project (Chile)

2.3.1 Salmon Across the Pacific

Seen from Japan, Chile is located on the opposite side of the Pacific Ocean and almost the furthest place on the globe. The two countries are separated by 17,000 km at the shortest distance. However, the fact that they share the Pacific Ocean binds the two countries together. A big earthquake in either of these volcanic countries would trigger a tsunami that will reach the other place almost in a day. When the Chilean earthquake hit in May 1960, Japan, particularly along the Sanriku coast, was seriously affected. A Moai statue donated by Chile and transported from Easter Island was erected in Miyagi Prefecture to remember the 41 casualties in Shizugawa Town (now part of Minami Sanriku). This statue was washed away during the 2011 Great East Japan Earthquake, and Chile donated a new Moai statue. At the time of this earthquake, a tsunami reached the Chilean coast, and many houses were washed away (Uchio 2019).

It is not only disasters but also the production and consumption of salmon that link the two countries. In Japan, salmon is an essential part of the everyday diet. Moreover, Japanese *sushi* has become globally popular, and salmon *sashimi,* which is tender and nicely fatty, is consumed worldwide. Wild salmon swim from rivers to the sea, return to the same rivers to spawn, and live out their lives. However, most of today's commercial salmon is farmed at sea. Full-scale sea farming of salmon in Japan began in 1975 in the sea off Shizugawa Town, where the Moai statue is located. The farming of salmon for export from Chile to Japan started a little later, in 1979. In both ventures, the initiative was taken by the Japanese fisheries company Nichiro (now Maruha Nichiro).[12]

According to fisheries statistics of the Food and Agriculture Organization (FAO), in 2021, 79.9% of the global salmon production was based on aquafarming, while 20.1% was captured from the sea. Norway was the world's top producer of Atlantic salmon with 1,563,000 tonnes, followed by Chile with 725,000 tonnes (FAO 2024). The largest exporter of salmon to the Japanese market in the same year was Chile,

---

[12] For more information on the origins of salmon farming in Japan, see: https://www.maruha-nichiro.co.jp/salmon/fishery/08.html (Japanese). In general, salmon is classified as saltwater fish and trout as freshwater fish, but biologically they are the same. Norwegian salmon is almost exclusively Atlantic salmon, while Chilean salmon also includes coho salmon and rainbow trout. Chum salmon was originally the mainstay of Japanese cuisine but has now been overtaken by farmed coho salmon.

with a value of 125.5 billion yen (57%), followed by Norway's 55.1 billion yen (25%).[13] The presence of Chilean salmon is significant worldwide, particularly in the Japanese markets.

Originally, salmon occurred only in the northern hemisphere and could not be found in South America; salmon cannot naturally migrate across the equator, where the water temperature is too high. Historically, it is the activities of Japanese fisheries companies and the cooperation between Japanese experts and their Chilean counterparts that made the salmon industry take root in Chile, especially around the island of Chiloé and in the fjords further south (Fig. 2.2). Salmon products accounted for 6.5% of Chile's total exports in 2023, and jobs and income have been created in impoverished villages of southern Chile. Although not as large as copper, which accounts for half of total exports, they contribute, along with fruits and wine, to export diversification. The salmon industry has a strong presence as an engine of economic development, particularly in the southern region of Chile.[14]

The close collaboration between Japanese experts and their Chilean counterparts in the early years of the salmon industry in Chile has already been extensively documented in Hosono (2010) in Japanese and in Hosono, Iizuka, and Katz (2016) in English. When I conducted the interviews, the Chilean counterparts reflected on the history of the salmon industry over the past 50 years and contemplated the future direction. In this section, I present the narratives of retired 'adventurers' (Infante Varas et al. n.a.: 11) to trace the history of international cooperation across the Pacific Ocean.

2.3.2 *First Encounters (1969–1976)*

The cooperation that eventually gave rise to the Chilean salmon industry was initiated by a field survey conducted by the Japan Fisheries Association, a federation of Japanese fishing companies founded in 1882. In the late 1960s, as the negotiation between Japan and the Soviet Union on fishing quotas in the North Pacific reached a deadlock, the Japanese fishing industry wanted to explore new fishing grounds where it had never set foot. Against this background, the association sent a mission to southern Chile in 1969 (Shirahata 2015).

Jorge Katz, an economist from Argentina at the University of Chile, attributes cooperation in this field to the combination of the relative backwardness of Chilean aquaculture technology and Japan's strong demand for seafood. Many farmers in southern Chile who grew maize, wheat, and potatoes had maintained a half-farming, half-fishing lifestyle. 'Spain and Portugal had nurtured family fishing traditions, but there was no such practice in Chile. Knowledge of fishing was not disseminated in

[13] Ministry of Agriculture, Forestry and Fisheries Agricultural and Marine Products Import and Export Statistics: https://www.maff.go.jp/j/tokei/kouhyou/kokusai/#l.

[14] See the export statistics provided by the Central Bank of Chile. https://www.bcentral.cl/en/web/banco-central/areas/statistics/external-sector/foreign-trade-of-goods.

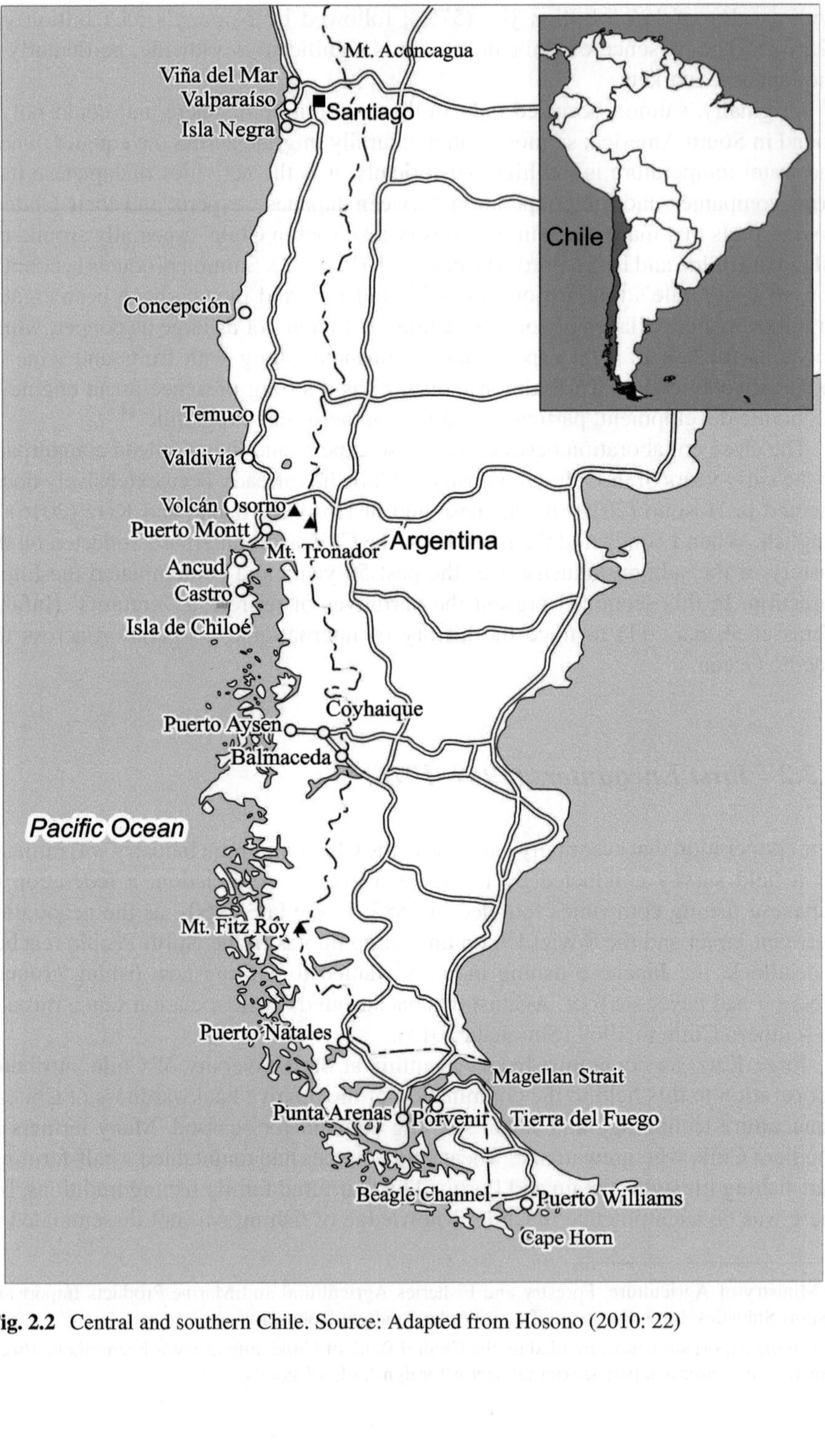

Fig. 2.2 Central and southern Chile. Source: Adapted from Hosono (2010: 22)

remote villages' [CHL 03]. Chile had a demand for technology, and Japan had a market for the products. Katz, after commenting that his knowledge of the salmon industry was limited to the last decade, noted:

> I noticed that the local people appreciated the help they got from the Japanese. People in Santiago don't seem to fully understand it, and honestly, I used to think Fundación Chile was the only major player in developing Chile's industries. But when I went down south and talked to the locals, I realised how much of an impact Japan had made. It might have started just as technical support, but the Japanese took the time to understand and respect the local culture. You can't talk about Chile's salmon industry without recognizing their contribution. It's a big problem that people in Santiago don't know about it. [CHL 03]

At the end of 1969, Pablo Aguilera, a young man in his twenties, was serving for a field mission of the Japan Fisheries Association in Chile. After studying fisheries at the Catholic University of Valparaiso, he was posted to Coyhaique as an officer of the Ministry of Agriculture and Livestock. Coyhaique, the administrative capital of the Aysén region (11th Region), is a small town surrounded by mountains and streams. The rivers around Coyhaique have long been popular for sport fishing, where trout were bred and released into ponds. After guiding a research team, Aguilera was invited by OTCA to Japan in the following year to receive training in Nakashibetsu, Hokkaido. Aguilera learnt the importance of water. 'If the water is close to the spring, the temperature and quality are constant, and it is easy to make a plan. In contrast, the water in the middle of rivers is not clean enough and not suitable for release' [CHL 04]. In Hokkaido, the young Aguilera seemed much appreciated due to his serious attitude, willingly taking on tasks such as shovelling snow and pushing a stalled car (Infante Varas et al. n.a.: 25).

In November 1970, Salvador Allende of the Socialist Party of Chile was elected president of Chile with the support of communists, trade unions, and the Christian left and initiated radical political change, including nationalisation, land reform, and pro-poor policies. The following year, 1971, the new government welcomed the second mission of the Japan Fisheries Association. At the time, Aguilera happened to work in Coyhaique in the Aysén region, Allende's electoral stronghold. President Allende even suggested that the national army could be used to survey Chilean fisheries if necessary (Shirahata 2015).

The technician in charge of Aguilera in Hokkaido was Nagasawa Aliaky (Ariaki). Nagasawa was the only person at the Nakashibetsu hatchery who spoke English, a foreign language. While in Japan, Aguilera also met fisheries scientist Shiraishi Yoshikazu at the Nikko Aquaculture Research Institute, and their visit to Chile in 1972 marked the beginning of full cooperation. However, Shiraishi died suddenly of a brain haemorrhage after he arrived in Chile. After various potential sites were weighed and compared, Coyhaique was eventually selected as the place of a hatchery (Hosono 2010: 25–28). It is reported that the decision was based on 'the natural conditions of the Simpson River that flows through Coyhaique, which are very similar to those in Hokkaido, and the social conditions for maintaining experimental environments' (JICA 1979: 1). Located in Patagonia, Coyhaique is close to the border region with Argentina, where a military base was also located. There may have been security considerations on the Chilean side.

However, Allende's regime was overthrown in a *coup d'état* in September 1973, and Gen. Augusto Pinochet and his allies installed a military regime. The salmon project was suspended but resumed the following year. In 1976, a full-scale hatchery was constructed on a bank of the Simpson River in Coyhaique, with the Chilean government providing land and buildings and the Japanese side providing equipment. The facility was named the Shiraishi Hatchery in memory of the late Dr Shiraishi.

2.3.3 Waiting for Their Return (1976–1988)

In Coyhaique, the salmon were hatched from eggs and released: cherry salmon from 1973 and chum salmon from 1974. 'I heard the Japanese released salmon to a river with sake. In Chile, they did it with wine' [CHL 13]. At that time, Coyhaique was a remote, isolated place. 'I think life must have been hard for the Japanese because it was freezing in winter. For some periods, planes could not land at the airport. There was no television signal, and we could barely hear the local radio' [CHL 07].[15]

Teamwork was indispensable for the small group working at the Shiraishi Hatchery. Mario Puchi, who was born in Coyhaique, was dispatched to his hometown in 1974 as an employee of the Ministry of Agriculture and Livestock. He worked alongside Aguilera and Nagasawa. 'It was hard work, but we were dealing with living creatures. I think everyone was fascinated by the work and loved it' [CHL 06]. The Shiraishi Hatchery was equipped with the latest technology of the time, with quality laboratory equipment and fish dissection facilities. 'Up until then, in aquaculture, they had been feeding the fish raw food by hand. In Chile, the dry pellet feeding started here' [CHL 15].

However, the salmon did not return. In 1980, the Coyhaique staff began to rear and release the fry in Ensenada Baja, close to the mouth of Aysén River (JICA 1981a). If the fry were raised to a larger size at this bay hatchery before being released, they would not be eaten by other big fish but able to produce their eggs (Hosono 2010: 53). Puchi took charge of the research voyage on a vessel called *Alevin* (French for 'fry') to track the released salmon. 'Following the salmon in the waters around the Aysén region was possible, but exact tracking was practically impossible once the salmon went out to the ocean' [CHL 06]. Tulio Zuñiga, a member of the Coyhaique staff, also began working with Puchi on the research vessel. 'Sometimes, we gave nets to local fishermen and asked them to keep the salmon they caught. But we had no way of knowing where the salmon was from, so we didn't know if they were originally from our hatchery or not' [CHL 02].

During this period, the Japanese experts and their Chilean counterparts continued to work together in the hatchery, the fish pens, the offices, the laboratories, and on board the vessels. The counterparts acquired the full range of skills from egg

[15] I visited Coyhaique in July 2019. It was already winter, but very warm with only a little snow visible on top of the surrounding mountains. Local people told me that the climate had notably changed, with no heavy snowfall in recent years.

collection, stocking, aquaculture, and processing to export. As JICA's institutional counterpart was the Chilean National Fisheries and Aquaculture Service (SERNAP), all the Chileans were civil servants. A large-scale project-type technical cooperation was carried out for five years from 1979.[16] Carlos Conley Milo, who had worked with JICA since 1979 as SERNAP's deputy director-general, brought a photo of the plate of a chum salmon he had caught to the hotel cafe where we met.[17] He said:

> Chilean experts got skilled thanks to working together with Japanese experts. Later, when sea farming started to grow, private companies could use the knowledge those Chilean experts had gained. Honestly, without that knowledge, the Chilean salmon industry wouldn't have taken off the way it did. It was Mr Nagasawa and his team who set everything in motion. I think Nagasawa-san truly came to love Chile while putting so much effort into his work here. [CHL 01]

Mario Vargas, a veterinary scientist trained in Hokkaido, said he was taught to observe salmon carefully and understand how fish feel. Salmon play and try to protect their territory. When they stay still, there is some reason. Vargas said he learnt to recognise when salmon were sick, uncomfortable or stressed. In Hokkaido, Puchi was also told by an expert who spoke little English or Spanish that 'it is important to talk with the fish' (Infante Varas et al. n.a.: 12, 25). For Puchi, the memory of working with Japanese experts was still fresh. He recalled:

> What I've gained from working with Japanese experts goes beyond just knowledge. It's about setting goals, staying committed to them, achieving them, and taking responsibility for the outcomes. In other words, working with the Japanese taught me not just technical skills but also important lessons about being human – about attitudes and ways of thinking. [CHL 06]

Héctor Novoa, who had been involved in the project since 1972, visited Nagasawa after he moved to Argentina.

> The Japanese experts I worked with were cheerful and incredibly friendly. Many of them even brought their families along. Those with kids often made friends with Chileans who were outside the group. Some of their children even became fluent in Spanish. I remember one expert whose son was born in Coyhaique! [CHL 07]

However, not all memories of the Japanese are positive. Rodolfo Aguirrebeña, who studied veterinary medicine and worked in the laboratory in Coyhaique, said that the experts constantly berated him over trivial matters. At the time of the interview, he still could not forget the humiliation he received in those days. 'There seem to be two types of experts: those who are too strict and those who manage to connect with the locals. Some Chileans tend to look up to the Japanese almost like gods, but since I'm from Spain, I didn't see them that way' [CHL 13].

In a more recent example, Javier Valencia Camp from the Chinquihue Foundation, which works on community development on the island of Chiloé, shared his

---

[16] 'Project-type technical cooperation' combines three sorts of inputs—dispatching experts, receiving trainees, and providing equipment—into a single project. It started in 1957 and was reorganised into 'technical cooperation projects' in 2002.

[17] The nameplate reads, 'One of the first 68 fish to return to Chile in April 1982. Chum salmon. Ensenada Baja, Aysén State.' However, only a few salmon returned [CHL 01].

assessment of the Japanese experts who came to assist with shellfish farming. The Japanese are punctual, but the Chileans are more laid back. However, 'Japanese who stay in Chile for a long time and spend much time with Chileans gradually become more like Chileans.' But newcomers are not like that.

> Honestly, the adaptability of these experts should probably be assessed in Japan before they are sent to Chile. I remember one expert who tried to enforce weekly and monthly targets, something that just doesn't work with fishermen. Others would tell them to choose between farming and fishing and focus on one, but honestly, again, that's not realistic either. [CHL 12]

Overall, in the 1970s and 1980s, technology transfer seemed to be successful. However, the released salmon rarely returned, and reports at that time always included a minority opinion that the project should be discontinued. The introduction to the 1981 annual report contains the following words from the Chilean director of Fisheries: 'They will come back….they should come back….they must come back….we will stand there forever, hand in hand, to receive the wonderful fish that have been on their great migration for many years and will return to their mother river to rest' (JICA 1981a: 1). The project-type technical cooperation was extended in 1984, and follow-up cooperation was carried out in 1988, but the project was finally terminated in 1989.[18] The project could be regarded as a 'failure' in light of its stated objectives.

Reflecting on the project, one of the last-generation experts, Sakai Mitsuo, wrote, 'When we returned to Japan after the end of the project, our team was treated like Vietnam War veterans [in the US]. The project was like a taboo, which JICA and the Fisheries Agency, the government agency concerned, wanted to forget as soon as possible.' Sakai argued that the project was a complex mixture of chance and necessity and that there was little point in determining whether it was a success or a failure (Sakai 1999: 14–15).

In 1986, large, mature salmon were discovered in Puerto Natales, much further south. The released fry are supposed to have migrated towards the Antarctic Circle. The released fish may not have disappeared but now freely circulate in the South Pacific without being noticed. They may even swim up and down the rivers in the frigid southern tip of the South American continent.[19]

---

[18] Cooperation was extended when a return was confirmed in 1982, but it was 'a return of parent salmon, only on a very small scale'. Finally, project-type technical cooperation was terminated in 1989, 'with significant results in technology transfer in various areas, including technique for hatching seed eggs, rearing and stocking, methods for various research activities, fish disease control, and feed development' (JICA 1991a: iv). Since 1988, the counterpart has changed from SERNAP to the Fisheries Development Institute (Instituto de Fomento Pesquero: IFOP). SERNAP would not be involved directly in aquaculture projects but concentrate on regulation and supervision.

[19] Puchi said, 'I believe coho salmon and Atlantic salmon are migrating and spawning in the south. It would not be impossible to develop the release method, but if we released non-native species, we would face strong opposition from environmental activists, so it is not easy to make this happen' [CHL06]. Releasing cherry salmon into inland lakes and swamps has been successful (Hosono 2010: 73).

2.3.4 Moving to the Private Sector (1988–2009)

The development of Chile's salmon aquaculture industry was ignited in a different place than the stocking practice. In 1979, the Japanese fisheries company Nichiro started the sea-farming of coho salmon near Puerto Montt. The first harvest was made in 1980. The Chilean company Mytilus (later Mares Australes) followed up the aquaculture attempt.

More importantly, the Fundación Chile was about to get engaged. This semi-private foundation was known for mobilising venture capital to invest in new start-ups and selling them when they become profitable, thereby driving the development of promising industrial sectors (Meissner 1988; Katz 2006; Agosin et al. 2010). In 1981, Fundación Chile bought the aquaculture facilities of Domsea Farms on the island of Chiloé, established the new company Salmones Antártica, and expanded its sea farming to grow coho salmon. In 1988, the annual production reached 1,000 tonnes, making Chile's largest aquaculture company. An international tender was immediately offered, and it was decided that Nippon Suisan (Nissui) would take over the firm (Hosono 2010: 48–68).[20] As we have seen, SERNAP had an aquaculture farm in Ensenada Baja to raise juvenile salmon. The farm of Fundación Chile was set up just next to it, and the two facilities closely collaborated.

Although the released fry did not return, sea farming expanded thanks to the substantial entry of private companies. By the end of the 1980s, as JICA's cooperation was closing, the Chilean counterparts left one after another, heading for the private sector. Aguilera was the first to leave. Puchi said, 'I moved in 1987. I don't know what the Japanese thought about our departure. I remember an expert saying, "The salmon industry will grow in Chile, but it lacks the basic knowledge. You've got it, so please use it"' [CHL 06]. Indeed, in Coyhaique and Ensenada Baja, these counterparts had acquired the critical know-how of salmon farming.

Aguilera became a production manager at Mytilus. Aguilera and Puchi discussed the idea of establishing a new firm, and Puchi's brother Victor joined to start the new aquaculture company, AquaChile. At the time, some small family businesses were entering into salmon farming. 'It was a gradual, slow process. But in the 1990s, the small family businesses were swallowed up by larger companies' [CHL 03]. AquaChile, run by Aguilera and Puchi, survived the competition and grew to become the largest Chilean salmon farming company. The 1990s also saw Norwegian companies beginning to be active in Chile. The share of Atlantic salmon increased, and the facilities became more extensive, automated, and efficient. The size of fish tanks expanded, and feeding was automated (Hosono 2010: 107–113).

Some people who remember the days of traditional cooperation cannot accept the modern way of mechanised aquaculture. 'Back in the day, we fed the salmon

[20] It did not mean that Japanese companies dominated the Chilean salmon industry. According to the ranking of major firms by salmon export value in 2001, the Dutch company Marine Harvest ranked first, and the Chilean company AquaChile ranked second. Salmones Antártica, which the Japan-based Nissui Corporation acquired from Fundación Chile, ranked seventh (Iizuka, Roje and Vera 2016: 82). Corporate mergers and acquisitions are always active in Chile.

by hand, not with machines. When you fed them in one spot, they got all excited, and somehow, that energy would spread to the salmon in other areas. It was one of those things you could only notice when you were there, feeling it for yourself. That was not written in manuals. It was romantic' [CHL 02]. Marcelo Guerra, who supervises the aquaculture farm at AquaChile, has been working in aquaculture with his wife for 25 years. 'Aquaculture is a beautiful job. It is a romantic job. I feel like the water has bewitched us.' But these days, with mechanisation, 'generations like us are disappearing. Young people say, "Do you have Wi-Fi? If not, I'm leaving."' Guerra was grateful to the company for not firing them during the sanitary crisis that I will discuss in the next section, saying that his company regarded the employees as an asset [CHL 09].

In 1990, the rule of Gen. Pinochet was over, and Chile entered an era of civilian government again. According to Miro, who stepped down as SERNAP's deputy director general, 'politics does not necessarily affect the private sector. I think there is continuity no matter what happens with the government' [CHL 01]. The Chilean counterparts moved to various companies and organisations. Pablo Martens, who had worked in Coyhaique to make food for salmon, returned to Santiago and took a job in the giant grocery supermarket, Jumbo. Once, when lobsters for sale died in a pond, he used the knowledge he obtained in Coyhaique to solve the problem. 'There weren't many salmon on the shelves' during the sanitary crisis [CHL 05].

2.3.5 Sanitary Crisis and Beyond (2009-)

With numerous fish pens spreading in southern Chile and its farmed salmon exports approaching those of Norway, catching up seemed to be well underway. Many of the Chilean experts of the Coyhaique generation played a significant role in this process.[21] At this very moment, the Chilean salmon industry was hit hard by the spread of an infectious salmon disease: the sanitary crisis. The Infectious Salmon Anaemia (ISA) virus was detected in 2007, and an explosive outbreak devastated Atlantic salmon (coho salmon and rainbow trout were relatively intact) in 2009. Chilean salmon production plummeted from a peak of 700,000 tonnes in 2006 to 200,000 tonnes in 2010, and 60% of salmon farms were forced to close in 2009. The immediate trigger is thought to have been contamination of imported eggs (Iizuka and Zanlungo 2016: 111). While nearly 20,000 jobs were instantly lost, the crisis led to rapid institutional reorganisation, such as closer cooperation between aquaculture farms and new government regulations (Iizuka 2016: 159).

---

[21] Short-sighted laissez-faire policies cannot bring about dynamic industrial development. On the supply side, it is necessary to break down technological constraints and secure investment in new industrial ventures, while on the demand side, it is essential to develop institutions to make the market mechanism function. During the start-up phase of the Chilean salmon industry, the technical cooperation between JICA and SERNAP, the activities of Fundación Chile and the strong demand from the Japanese market all played critical roles (Hosono 2010: 77–87, 154–162) (in Japanese).

Puchi said he could have predicted this crisis because he had lost many salmon to bacterial kidney disease (BKD) before. When the salmon in the pens of Fundación Chile in Ensenada Baja were infected with the BKD, the disease spread to the adjoining pens operated by SERNAP, where most salmons were killed. This was due to the failure to stop the importation of contaminated eggs and the lack of space between the pens. 'There were times when we had to shut everything down – the farms and the processing plants. We had to empty all the big tanks, scrub them clean, and filter the water. A lot of investment was required' [CHL 06].

The sanitary crisis caused by the ISA virus resulted in mass salmon mortality and seriously impacted human livelihoods; employment in the salmon industry plummeted. Jobs were lost, especially in Los Lagos (10th region), as the centre of aquaculture began to move down to the Aysén region (11th region) to avoid the high concentration of salmon pens (Katz 2016: 180–182). There were also major labour disputes. Katz indicated, 'rheumatism and other illnesses are common because of the cold temperatures in the factory. The workers are willing to make their voices heard, even if the firm is eventually forced to move elsewhere. I think discontent is fermenting under the surface' [CHL 03].

Miriam Chávez, the union chair at AquaChile's salmon processing plant, is a single mother raising three children. We listened to her story in a cafe near the factory.

> The work at the factory is demanding—cleaning, gutting, deboning, and packing. Back in 2007, there were about 1,300 workers, but now it's down by a third. The winter weather is brutal. The temperature drops to minus 5 degrees, and the freezers are even colder at minus 45 degrees. It's hard work, but we only earn minimum wage. Most of the union members are women, about 60%, and the men respect what we say as the woman union leaders. [CHL 08]

In 2008, there was a major industrial dispute in the company. Many people lost their income and homes and got divorced. 'There was a time we couldn't even afford to give our children salmon, even though we worked with it every day. But now, the union members can buy export-quality salmon at half-price and give our family a taste of what we process. We can even bring our kids to the factory and show them what their parents do' [CHL 08].

Although there is a strong trend towards mechanisation and automation in the aquaculture industry, not all operations can be mechanised. One of the major differences between the Norwegian and Chilean salmon industries is that the former often exports dressed salmon, which is just gutted, while Chile usually exports carefully processed salmon products. Chile's strength lies in its ability to carry out detailed work, such as removing small bones from the salmon flesh, but its low wages make it profitable. The working conditions for the women who do such work are still inadequate.[22]

But why did the sanitary crisis happen? Many of the counterparts from the Coyhaique generation, who worked at the heart of the salmon industry and are now retired, speak of their discomfort with the 'engineering mindset' prevalent in

[22] Puchi, one of the founders of AquaChile, introduced the union leaders to us, saying, 'I want you to understand both the positive and negative aspects' [CHL 06].

the industry. Aguirrebeña lamented, 'People who studied engineering and business management now dominate the salmon industry and make decisions. They are not people who majored in biology at universities. But salmon are living creatures' [CHL 13]. Mario Vargas, who was responsible for the research in the project, said:

> I left the salmon industry partly because it became all about business efficiency. Engineers were under pressure to put more fish in the pens. Well, the harvest was 5 tonnes. They say, why not 15 tonnes? Then, the fish would get stressed, diseases would spread, and things would go downhill. They're living creatures, after all. Can you imagine? How do you feel if you are crammed into a fish tank like them? [CHL 15]

A situation in which the quality of public goods deteriorates and the harvest diminishes as a result of micro-actors rationally seeking to maximise their self-interest is called the 'tragedy of the commons' (Sect. 2.1.1). Suppose that a shepherd considers only the short-term utility to himself of having one more sheep. All shepherds will want to have as many sheep as possible, the grass in the pasture will be eaten up, and there will be nothing left for the sheep to eat. Any engineer should understand this logic (Iizuka and Katz 2011). In Chile, the aquaculture companies' competitive pursuit of self-interest may not have caused diminishing returns but disrupted the equilibrium of fish life and their environment. Manufacturing and fishing require different approaches. The Chilean counterparts of the Coyhaique generation, who used to release their fry carefully by hand, blew a whistle about the future of the salmon industry.

The island of Chiloé, famous for its World Heritage churches, is home to a number of small-scale farmers who grow cholito and oysters, but they have been involved in a conflict with the large aquaculture farms. A member of the fishers' union I met nurtured and sold *ogonori,* which was used to make agar, and was worried about the recent expansion of nearby salmon pens. They used the same bay, but the seawater did not move much, so the place was contaminated [CHL 10]. Another union member who used to work as a diver for an aquaculture company knew what the seabed was like. In the cold rain, he showed me around his small aquaculture farm, close to the big company's large pens. 'We can't farm near those fish pens because the sediment of salmon feed has made the seabed like mud' [CHL 11].

Is there a future in which large-scale aquaculture, with its high environmental impact, can coexist with small-scale ventures operated by fishers' associations? A local anonymous journalist commented that transparency in aquaculture companies is crucial.

> Once, there was a big problem. Salmon carcasses were dumped at sea, and not long after, a red tide surfaced. People protested, blaming the dumping for the red tide. It got so intense that the island of Chiloé was locked down. We never know the real cause – perhaps, because of climate change. However, the community didn't trust the companies, and the companies didn't share substantial information. So, the real problem is that local people cannot make an informed judgement. [CHL 16]

This is not to say that the criticism of the salmon industry is dominant in the local community. In the past, people from Chiloé 'had to leave the island and migrate to Argentina to find work. Many worked in oil fields or on cattle ranches, but that's not necessarily the case anymore. Thanks to the salmon industry, a family can stay together' [CHL 07]. An anonymous journalist also emphasised that the impact of the salmon industry on Chiloé was significant. 'Forty years ago, it was unimaginable that people would buy private cars' [CHL 16]. What is needed is continuous improvement in the governance of companies so that the whole industry can be sustainable.[23]

2.3.6 Returning Home

Javier Valencia Camp of the Chinquihue Foundation on the island of Chiloé advocates ecotourism to overcome environmental crises and underdevelopment. The Chinquihue Foundation supports small-scale aquaculture of shellfish and other species operated by fishers' associations. From 1997 to 2002, the foundation engaged in JICA's project-type technical cooperation. JICA supported experimental sustainable aquaculture that was developing in parallel with large-scale salmon farming (JICA Chile Office and UNICO International 2006). According to Camp, life on islands is potentially more prosperous than life in cities, and absolute poverty is manifest only in cities. He noted that people's values are changing gradually for the better, even though young people who migrated to big cities tend not to return to their hometowns. He explained:

> Now, people are looking for more sustainable ways of consumption and small-scale industries. They prefer eating fish locally in places close to the sea where fish is caught. There's also a growing interest in eco-tourism, like birdwatching, fly fishing, and working with local fishermen. Many foreign companies offer these services, but I think they should involve local people. We're considering training young fishermen and selling fish at better prices by keeping the quantity of catches under control. [CHL 12]

The SERNAP counterparts who worked with the Japanese in the 1970s and 1980s also had their own dreams. Some of them not only learnt skills but were also pulled out of poverty by the subsequent development of the salmon industry. Novoa, born in Coyhaique, recalled his childhood:

> When I was small, life was very tough. Our house was far from town, so in winter, I went to school on horseback. We didn't have electricity. We lived off what we could catch, like birds, rabbits, or whatever. My father left when I was two, so my mother worked very hard, doing laundry for other families to make ends meet. She didn't have an education but did everything she could do for me and my brothers. [CHL 07]

Novoa says he now returns to Coyhaique often.

> I bought a house there. Things are much better now. There are roads, so we can drive to Coyhaique, even if it takes four or five days. When I was a child, I dreamed of becoming a pilot, but we were very poor, so I thought it was impossible. But I made it! I got a license to

[23] For information on controversial issues regarding salmon farming in Chile, see Japanese reports such as Sakuma (2007). Kitano Koichi pointed out that, while stocking is beneficial to a wide range of small-scale fishers, vertically integrated firms will monopolise the profits as large-scale aquaculture becomes mainstream (Kitano 2011).

> fly small planes. Once, I flew a single-engine propeller plane from Chile to Argentina. [CHL 07]

If Novoa was a 'man of the mountain', Eduardo Cárdenas, born and raised in Chiloé and working in the salmon industry before returning to the island, would be a 'man of the sea'. He studied Japanese hard while tending the fish pens in Ensenada Baja. Reflecting on his experiences, he suggested, 'I think the only solution is to develop ecotourism,' given the island's ageing population and environmental problems. He added:

> I think there are two types of people on the island. Some go out, explore the world, and then come back with new experiences. Others stay and never leave the island. But if you don't get out, your horizon remains narrow. For me, working with the Japanese opened up my world in ways I never imagined. [CHL 14]

It is not necessary for their collaboration partners to be Japanese, but there is no doubt that the range of the choices of the islanders was expanded as a result of the long-term development cooperation.

During the 1970s and 1980s, the Chileans who were dedicated to developing the salmon industry stayed in touch with each other as 'alumni' of the cooperation with JICA and utilised their knowledge and experiences in the private sector. Interviewees often mentioned that they had been 'called' and 'invited' by their former colleagues. Networked social capital seems to have been in place, and the 'principle of conservation and mutation of social energy' has been at work (Hirschman 1984). On the other hand, some observe that 'Chilean people respect the attitude of taking risks and making a fortune. Thanks to these people, the salmon and wine industries have developed in this country' (CHL 13).

Activities in the private sector can be considered part of development cooperation (Shimomura 2020: 3–4). The case of Chile was ahead of the curve, as human resources developed in a specific field in the public sector were relocated to another field in the private sector to make a big difference—a similar case will be discussed in Chap. 3 (Sect. 3.4), which deals with the experience in Costa Rica. Today, universities are also called upon to develop business strategies in collaboration with the private sector. The Shiraishi Hatchery in Coyhaique is now part of the University of Los Lagos and is used as an aquaculture farm for sturgeon whose eggs are prized as caviar. When I visited, there was no sign of the old laboratory actively used, but the experimental tools were carefully maintained and preserved, perhaps as a tribute to the past cooperation.

2.4 Coming Down from the Mountains to Grow Rice: Agricultural Development in Kilimanjaro (Tanzania)

2.4.1 Ujamaa Socialism

The United Republic of Tanzania, located in East Africa facing the Indian Ocean, has unique historical features. The country was formed in 1964 as a united republic consisting of the continental Tanganyika (achieved independence in 1961) and the island state of Zanzibar (achieved independence in 1963), which had long served as a trading post between Asia and Africa. Tanzania's national language is Kiswahili, a blend of the Bantu language in continental Africa and Arabic from the maritime world, instead of a language of the former European colonial power. The first president, Julius Nyerere, was known as a Pan-Africanist political leader along with President Kwame Nkrumah of Ghana. While President Nkrumah looked to the Soviet Union and called for rapid African unification, Nyerere looked to China and called for a gradual approach to regional integration. By adding Jomo Kenyatta of Kenya to make a triangle (Assensoh 1998), we can understand the post-independence political leadership of Africa from a more balanced perspective (see also Sects. 4.2. and 5.2). One of the most famous Chinese-assisted projects in Tanzania during this period was the TAZARA Railway, which connected Dar es Salaam in Tanzania with Lusaka in Zambia (the project began in 1970 and was completed in 1975). It was a pioneering large-scale Asian-supported infrastructure development in Africa, which is still in operation today (Monson 2009).

Tanzania's ideal of post-independence society was called *Ujamaa* socialism. *Ujamaa,* which literally means 'family-style love and collaboration', was a key concept introduced by President Nyerere in a speech in 1962. For Nyerere, socialism was not a heartless institution but an attitude of the mind. The realisation of socialism in Tanzania required not only the removal of the parasitic capitalist classes but also a return to the principles of sympathy and mutual help, which was thought to be inherent in traditional agrarian societies in Africa before Western colonial rule (Nyerere 1968: Chap. 1). As the Arusha Declaration was adopted by the ruling Tanganyika African National Union (TANU) in 1967, Tanzania embarked on a village-oriented socialist experiment.

Ujamaa socialism was to create what did not exist rather than to return to the past. There had been little tradition of village-based collective work in East African peasant societies. Nyerere's government sought to unite farmers scattered over vast tracts of land into villages (villagisation), encouraging them to work together while giving them access to basic infrastructure such as water supplies, schools, hospitals and agricultural extension services. Ujamaa socialism was an experiment on a scale unprecedented in the history of Tanzania, drawing on a forceful slogan of Ujamaa as an invented tradition to mobilise people and modernise the country (Hyden 1980; Hobsbawm 1983; Scott 1998). Reading a series of reports by Japanese experts who went into the field in the 1980s, I found numerous expressions such as 'teach them [villagers]' and 'train them hard'. Such an attitude seems consistent with, and embedded in, Tanzania's top-down approach to modernisation, though unconsciously perhaps.

In the Cold War context, several Western countries, including Scandinavian countries and Israel, were interested in the idea and practice of Ujamaa socialism. An intriguing fact is that Japan's development assistance has not been greatly affected by the ideological inclinations of the aid-recipient country. A project is worth supporting if a country is geopolitically important and the project design is 'good' enough. This approach can be regarded as a 'client-oriented' rather than a 'philosophy-driven' approach to development cooperation. Looking at development outcomes in Asia, the former approach has often been more successful than the latter (Shimomura 2020: 198–200).

When the three projects discussed in this chapter were launched, Indonesia was governed by President Sukarno, Chile by President Allende, and Tanzania by President Nyerere, with all governments being more or less left-leaning. Then, Sukarno and Allende were overthrown in bloody military action, and Nyerere eventually gave up his doctrine of village collectivism. The projects in these places were to go through political ups and downs and evolved over time at their own paces.

2.4.2 *Ujamaa Villages (1970–1980)*

In 1970, a Japanese mission dispatched to Tanzania, led by Kono Fumihiko, vice chairman of the Japan Federation of Economic Organizations (Keidanren) and chairman of Mitsubishi Heavy Industries, was requested by President Nyerere to undertake a comprehensive development project for the Kilimanjaro region. At the time, Tanzania attempted to allocate certain regions to Western donors to avoid duplication. The ruling party, the Tanganyika African National Union, considered collaborating with Japan through Kilimanjaro's regional administration (OTCA 1970). Subsequently, the Japanese side prepared a comprehensive development plan that included not only agriculture but also small and medium-sized industries, tourism, and infrastructure development, which was the first attempt to offer a full-fledged development plan to a collaborating country after JICA was established in 1974 (JICA 1975).[24] In 1978, an agreement was reached with Tanzania on a project to develop the Kilimanjaro region with a focus on supporting irrigated agriculture, and construction of the Kilimanjaro Agricultural Development Centre (KADC) began in Chekereni village in Lower Moshi (Inoue 1984).

The Kilimanjaro region lies on the border with neighbouring Kenya. Mount Kilimanjaro is a majestic 5,895-m mountain,[25] and high-quality coffee has been grown on its foothills, taking advantage of the cool and rainy climate. The coffee producers'

[24] A study in the Moshi area, where the rice project was later developed, recommended that the use of groundwater for irrigation should be avoided to maintain the water balance of the entire region (JICA 1976a: 78–79). It was then decided to use surface water for rice production.

[25] The glaciers, not the snow, visible on the summit of Kilimanjaro appear to be shrinking due to climate change. Hemingway's short story 'The Snows of Kilimanjaro' (Hemingway 1987), written

Kilimanjaro Native Co-operative Union, the oldest cooperative in Africa,[26] was established in 1930 under British colonial rule. The farmers here belong to an ethnic group known as Chagga, who, given the good incomes from coffee exports, were well educated and secured a solid position in Tanzania's post-independence government. As of 1961, Chagga people accounted for 11.6% of Tanzania's government leadership (compared to a 3.7% share in the population) (Yoshida 1997: 219).

Despite their relative wealth, the Chagga apparently did not oppose egalitarian Ujamaa socialism. The arable land suitable for coffee cultivation in the Kilimanjaro highlands was already occupied by Chagga farmers, and population density was very high, so there was little room for socialist land redistribution. Coffee exports were a valuable source of foreign exchange for Tanzania, so it was unlikely that the government would ever want to hamper the growth of coffee production (ibid. 220–221). Rather, a more serious challenge for the Chagga people was overpopulation. Coffee and bananas were already densely planted on the highland, and the land inherited by farmers' children would only get smaller and smaller; they might as well start new livelihoods as settlers downhill on the newly reclaimed land. Eusebio Mlay of the Ministry of Agriculture said, 'The growing population in the highlands has pushed young people to relocate from the highlands to the lowlands. In principle, it wasn't a forced mobilisation but a voluntary migration. Once they got to the lowlands, they discovered that people were growing rice with help from the Japanese' [TAN 04].

Moshi, the regional capital, lies at the foot of Mount Kilimanjaro, and the plain stretching down from the town is called Lower Moshi. Accustomed to living in the cooler highlands, the Chagga were initially hesitant to settle in the lowland because of possible malaria infections, but an increasing number of people moved down there due to overpopulation. There were several waves of migration. The first was voluntary. Maiko Marindo was 84 years old when he came down from the mountains during British colonial rule. 'I was from Uru and came down to the lowlands in 1953. I made a living from forestry and maize cultivation, gradually buying land from other farmers' [TAN 05]. Marindo is now a successful rice farmer who employs workers.

Then, under Ujamaa socialism, a new village, Chekereni, was established in Lower Moshi. During the colonial period, a railway was constructed in that area to transport sisal, and the name Chekereni was from people's saying, 'check the train' (Lerise 2005: 5). In 1973, at the TANU national conference, it was decided to extend the village collectivisation policy to all regions; Kilimanjaro Region ranked last in the country, with only 1% of the region's population living in Ujamaa villages. Mamangina, aged 78, belonged to a generation of migrants mobilised in Kilimanjaro to keep up with the trend. 'I came down from Marangu in 1971. When I settled in Chekereni village in 1973, there were only ten families. When President Nyerere visited the village, he came to this house' [TAN 06].

---

in 1936, shows that safaris as a pastime for the wealthy were established in the region (mainly on the Kenyan side) before World War II.

[26] Tanzanian scholars now conduct comprehensive research on cooperatives at Moshi Co-operative University. https://www.mocu.ac.tz/.

The Lower Moshi area, where rice cultivation began with Japanese assistance, is a fan-shaped region that extends from the foot of the Kilimanjaro volcano. The area has an abundance of spring water, so the terrain seemed suitable for the development of rice paddies.[27] As many of the inhabitants were migrants from the mountain region, it was assumed there would be little resistance to ground levelling and land reallocation. Full-scale irrigated agriculture requires farmers to work together to maintain the infrastructure, and the Chagga people, who make up the majority of settlers in the area, were known for their political status and hard-working habit. Given such a background, the Tanzanian government may have hoped that the project would serve as a model for the Ujamaa policy and, by extension, for future Tanzanian agriculture. However, for the Japanese experts at the time, the fact that many of the farmers in Lower Moshi were of a migrant nature could mean 'the lack of disciplined society based on customary water management practice. Mutual solidarity and a sense of community are rare, and enforcing the Japanese style of scrupulous water management is not easy' (JICA 1989a).

2.4.3 Expansion of Paddy Fields (1981–1993)

In 1981, when the construction of the building of the KADC, the centre for technology transfer in Chekereni village, was completed, JICA dispatched the experts and started training their Tanzanian counterparts. With the provision of yen loans, large-scale civil engineering work also began. The construction plan was designed by Nippon Koei and implemented by Konoike Construction. At first, farmers in Lower Moshi did not welcome the project. A farmer who spoke out in front of his fellows maintained that the locals 'were afraid that the government would lie and take away our land to create a state-owned farm.' Some resisted surrendering their land because they thought they would not get it back when the construction was over [TAN 11]. Beatus Nicolaus Macha, a field staff member, recalled, 'Lower Moshi is an arid place, so we could grow only maize. The farmers were totally surprised when heavy machinery showed up to clear the land and build water channels. Honestly, it would've been much better if they had communicated more with the farmers. There wasn't much explanation, and we had no idea what on earth they were building' [TAN 10].[28]

Soon, vast paddy fields heaved into sight (Fig. 2.3). The area of irrigated land in Lower Moshi was paddy fields of 1,100 ha and farmland for other purposes of

[27] Mount Kilimanjaro resembles Mount Fuji, and the landscape of rice paddies against the mountain backdrop, with women busily planting rice, is enough to evoke nostalgia for a 'lost Japan'. However, Africa has its own history of the cultivation of indigenous rice originally from West Africa (Fields-Black 2008). In recent years, there has been a strong demand for rice in Africa. During the fieldwork, I frequently heard, 'Our children somehow love rice.' Along with the global sushi boom, japonica rice has also become available in African cities, but the demand for it is still limited to the urban middle class.

[28] Lerise (2005) argues that the Japanese actor failed to fully involve local people in the project, leading to later water conflict.

1,200 ha. Technology transfer was also underway. Festus Joachim Kimaryo, a local staff member, spent time in Tsukuba when young and learnt how to operate tractors and combines. He proudly said he could even repair the machinery [TAN 14]. At the experimental farm in Chekereni, Japanese experts gave training on how to prepare nursery beds and plant rice. Mamangina, an old lady living in Chekereni, said, 'I think the Japanese were very good in training. It was practical, and they taught better than local staff' [TAN 06]. On the maize farm, local farmers were sceptical about what the Japanese experts explained about the benefits of new farming methods. When the experts demonstrated the difference in harvest between a field using the conventional rain-fed method and another field based on irrigation and herbicide side by side, the Ujamaa village leaders accepted the idea of transformation. Seeing it from a different angle, the local farmers 'tested' the Japanese experts, and the new method 'won' in front of them, so they decided to accept the new one (JICA 1984a: 20–21).

In 1987, the construction work was completed, the paddy fields outside the experimental farm were filled with water, and full-scale rice cultivation began. Since 1986,

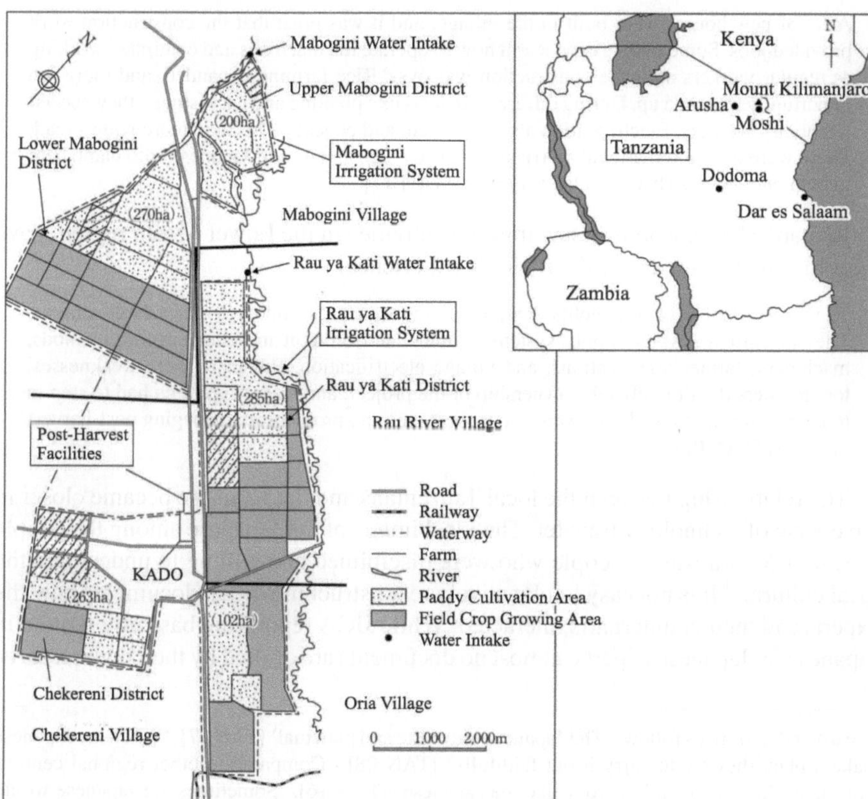

Fig. 2.3 Project area of lower Moshi. Source: Adapted from JICA (1994a: 38)

the Kilimanjaro Agricultural Development Project (KADP) has been responsible for the activities of KADC. According to an evaluation report on KADP conducted jointly by JICA and the Canadian International Development Agency (CIDA), the rice harvest in the region increased steadily from 789 tonnes in 1985 to 10,660 tonnes in 1990 (JICA 1998b: 17). Because agricultural land is owned by the state in Tanzania, individual farmers could not officially buy or sell land. As paddy fields were demarcated by *azemichi* (footpaths), farmers' usufruct became pronounced. Some farmers complained that their farmland was smaller than before the construction. However, after it was explained that the slight reduction of the size of individual land was because of the construction of roads and other public facilities, and as the farmers could see the dramatically increased harvest with their own eyes, they no longer complained [TAN 10]. Marindo, who had been living in Lower Moshi before Ujamaa village was established, said, 'Thanks to the project, we improved our lives by extending our houses, having three meals a day, getting electricity, and buying cars and tractors' [TAN 05]. The benefits were not limited to the increased harvest. I often heard that people could now buy local rice at a lower price, their houses were made of bricks, and their children could go to school [TAN 02].

> A lot of new houses were built in the village, and it was great that the construction work provided jobs. Some people even learnt how to operate the machines and continued working as regular workers after the construction was over. Rice farming expanded, and more job opportunities opened up. During different stages – like planting and harvesting – they needed temporary workers. Electrification also improved, and education became more widespread. There were even international marriages between Tanzanians and Japanese who came here to help out people. That was also very nice. [TAN 11]

Richard Shayo, who oversaw training activities in the Lower Moshi region, gave a cool-headed summary of the region's experience.

> The project had a lot of benefits. People's living standards improved. They built schools. They constructed water supply systems, clinics, and brought in better farming methods, machinery, farmer organizations, and village electrification. But there were weaknesses, too. Farmers didn't really take ownership of the project, and leadership often had to step in to keep things moving. There were water shortages and problems in managing post-harvest facilities. [TAN 09]

The relationship between the local Tanzanians and the Japanese became closer in the course of technology transfer. The ideal image of the Japanese among the people of Lower Moshi was of people who were disciplined and willing to understand the local culture.[29] It is not easy to objectively reconstruct in written documents how the experts and their counterparts interacted. While JICA reports are basically written in Japanese by Japanese experts, almost no documents are drafted by their counterparts.

[29] Farmers' narratives follow: 'The Japanese are polite and punctual' [TAN 07]. 'When the Japanese make a plan, they try to carry it out faithfully' [TAN 08]. 'Compared to other regional centres, Tanzanians here also tend to work like the Japanese' [TAN 16]. 'Sometimes the Japanese would get very angry if our behaviour did not meet their expectations. But I think they were very good at technology transfer. They also knew the Tanzanian culture well' [TAN 15]. 'The Japanese are friendly and modest people. They drink tea with us and eat ugali together' [TAN 05].

Tomitaka Motonori, a JICA expert in Kilimanjaro, wrote nearly 150 pages of the report in English and attached a 12-page summary in Japanese, stating, 'A report written in Japanese by a Japanese expert should be regarded only as a supplement. A report in Japanese that Tanzanian staff cannot read is of little value' (JICA 1991b: 135). This attempt by Tomitaka is highly commendable because most counterparts in developing countries have little way of knowing formally how their activities are being evaluated by the Japanese side.[30]

I heard of the story of the Japanese being punctual not only in Tanzania but also worldwide. The practice may sound intrinsically Japanese but historically speaking, it was not the case. Japanese workers in the Meiji era did not keep time at all, and Europeans who visited Japan were embarrassed by their easygoing attitudes. It was commonplace for a person not to show up at a particular time or not to return after visiting someone. Originally in Japan, until the Edo period, the time of the day was divided into twelve parts: six parts for the daytime and six parts for the night, and the length of these parts varied greatly with the change of seasons. The notion of an objective, regular, and strictly measurable flow of time is a product of modern times. The clock-dominated world of the military, factories, railways and schools captured the Japanese way of life only in the Meiji period, not before.[31]

The lifetime of a project may be short. When donors leave, the project may disappear without being noticed.[32] In this light, the Kilimanjaro rice project has been an exemplary success, which is attributable to the fact that many farmers outside the project area started growing rice after seeing the remarkable harvest in the project area. The rice cultivation technique was spontaneously copied by outside farmers and spread to the surrounding areas [TAN 01]. President Nyerere, who visited Chekereni village, is said to have noted, 'Agriculture should develop both within and without the Ujamaa village' [TAN 07]. Eusebio Mlay, in charge of training at the Ministry of Agriculture, commented, 'At the moment, rice farmers in the lowlands are wealthier than coffee farmers in the highlands, partly because coffee prices are low and coffee farmers sometimes neglect their crops. In the past, people in the highlands were richer than in the lowlands, so the position has been reversed' [TAN 04]. A household survey conducted in 1999 revealed that 98% (79 out of 81 households) of those surveyed in Lower Moshi answered that their standard of living had improved (Katsuki 2001).

---

[30] Asai (2025) is the definitive history of the Kilimanjaro Project written by a Japanese expert in English.

[31] For some counterparts, the Japanese experts, who were extremely strict about time management, might have been like the *Men in Grey* in Ende (1984). Detailed case studies of time and the modernity of Japan are found in Hashimoto and Kuriyama (2001). As for historical evidence translated into English, see Watanabe (2020: Chap. 6), which argued that the charm of Japanese civilisation with an organic individuality that early Western travellers witnessed was completely lost with the advent of modernisation in the late nineteenth century.

[32] A large post-harvest processing facility for rice was built with grant aid in 1987 but was not operational at the time of my visit in 2018.

2.4.4 Water Conflict

If the story had ended here, the Kilimanjaro rice project would have been a simple success story. The process may have been somewhat top-down, but the benefits to farmers were overwhelming. However, the fact is that in Kilimanjaro, the very success of the project led to severe tensions within local agrarian communities. As a result of the expansion of rice cultivation both inside and outside the project area, the shortage of irrigation water gradually rose to the surface.[33] New paddy fields were developed in upstream areas closer to the springs, and water was diverted to these sites before canalising into the project area. Within the project area, as the upstream section consumed much of the coming water, the downstream section started to suffer. The rice harvest within the project area declined from a peak of 10,660 tonnes in 1990 only to 2,884 tonnes in 1995 (JICA 1998b: 17).

When JICA's support for the KADP ended in 1993, resulting in the weakening of Japanese supervision, social tension between local farmers quickly intensified. Disgruntled people even used dynamite to blow up water intakes. Some practised witchcraft, and others were arrested and sentenced (Tsujimura 1999: 178–180; Lerise 2005: 125–129, 136–141). Chekereni was a Ujamaa village, where the training of rice farmers was implemented for the first time; the expectation for rice cultivation was particularly high. Mamangina lamented, 'During droughts, the water stops flowing. The rice paddies dry out completely, leaving no harvest. When years like this go on, I lose hope and feel deeply sad. Even when there is some water, it doesn't reach this far' [TAN 06]. Richard Kimicho, a senior project leader, described the current situation:

> In Chekereni, villagers are furious. Every time government officials come, people in Chekereni complain about water, saying, 'Why do they have water, and we don't?' It's causing jealousy among residents, and the leadership quality was also in question. Leaders should be humble and treat people equally. A big problem is that upstream water does not flow according to a fixed schedule. When someone prioritizes water for certain rice fields owned by certain people who have connections, it creates a lot of jealousy. [TAN 07]

Returning to the discussion at the beginning of this chapter (Sect. 2.1.1), we can argue that this is typical of the tragedy of the 'unmanaged' commons. It is not that if irrigation facilities are built with yen loans and if rice cultivation technology is transferred, the project takes off automatically like 'wind-up toys' (Hirschman 1981: 24). The sustainability of the project can only be guaranteed when farmers' organisation takes root to manage the commons effectively. If there was insufficient water, the intake could have been reduced so that water was distributed equally to all the villages, but such measures did not work in Lower Moshi. Godliving Moshi,

---

[33] During the interviews, I often heard that the only way to solve the problem of water shortage was to find a new source of water [TAN 02][TAN 07][TAN 08][TAN 11]. Before the conflict among the locals came to the surface, it was already known that the main cause of the water shortage was the diversion of irrigation water (JICA 1985a). In addition to this, JICA (1989a) acknowledged problems such as leakage, high fluctuations in river flow, erosion of irrigation canals, ravages of facilities by some locals and livestock, theft, and sabotage.

who oversaw the technology transfer, recalls, 'While JICA's experts were there, we were very disciplined, but after they left, we became less efficient. The infrastructure is deteriorating, and farmers don't care even if cattle encroach on their paddy fields' [TAN 08].

Richard Shayo summarised what had happened so far and gave a straightforward assessment of the attitudes of both the local farmers and the Japanese experts:

> Another challenge is that the culture of sharing is not very strong, and neither is the culture of maintenance. Farmers only care about their fields. They don't work with other villagers to maintain roads or waterways. Some don't even care if their cattle damage the irrigation banks. In other words, there is a lack of ownership.... Some locals stole the project's property, but the way Japanese experts scolded them seemed too harsh. Perhaps, a pre-training course should be developed, so that aid workers understand and respect the local culture. [TAN 09]

When neighbourhood relationships sour to a certain extent, a temporary 'ceasefire' consensus may emerge, even if the underlying contradictions do not disappear. At the time of writing this book, the water conflict in Lower Moshi appears to be under control. Mary Augustine Mtika and Frederick Solomon Mawolle, who provide close guidance to the farmers' organisation, said, 'There is conflict potential, but they compromise.' Chagga people who moved from a village in the highlands are scattered in different villages in Lower Moshi. Then, a villager may have his or her relatives in a village on the other side of the water conflict line [TAN 16]. Kilimanjaro, the centre of coffee production, has a long history of producers' cooperatives. There have also been attempts to organise rice producers' cooperatives in Lower Moshi, but because they remained voluntary, the organisations have not been able to cope with water theft. Kimicho argued that it was time to organise water users' associations in which all farmers who use irrigation water participate compulsorily [TAN 07].

Why did some farmers in Lower Moshi try to monopolise water? In principle, Ujamaa socialism forbade farmers from pursuing their self-interest to grow rich; it was a top-down attempt by the government to nurture unity among farmers. However, when the era of market-oriented structural adjustment arrived in the early 1980s, with the World Bank's Berg Report (World Bank 1981) as a milestone publication, institutions such as marketing boards were eliminated in most African countries. The transformation of rural Kilimanjaro coincided with this period of adjustment. The water conflict in Kilimanjaro may have been at least partly a by-product of adjustment thinking that was to weaken the state functions and encourage individual farmers to run their businesses. However, setting aside ideological orientations, irrigated agriculture and other forms of intensive farming require collective efforts of all local stakeholders, from maintaining water channels to securing inputs and expanding markets for increased outputs. Farmers in the Lower Moshi region began to 'realise that a collective response is indispensable' (Ikegami 2012: 111). Rice farmers in Kilimanjaro are probably learning through experience, rather than being taught by someone else, about the need to maintain public goods from the bottom up in sustainable agriculture.[34]

---

[34] Katsuki (1988) observed that the inherited land was becoming smaller as the population grew in Lower Moshi as in the highlands. A large number of small subsistence rice farmers would emerge.

2.4.5 School of Rice Cultivation (1994-)

The space of development cooperation has different profiles. Lower Moshi was not only an arena for experimentation in agricultural production and water conflicts but also a place for people to meet and exchange their experiences. Godwin Wilfred Chonjo recalled,

> In the past, Lower Moshi was an isolated place. Actually, the local people had no idea what the Japanese were doing. They suddenly showed up and started something strange. But over time, people in Lower Moshi learnt new skills and spread them to other places, even starting rice farming in new areas. Farmers from all over the country, and even from Kenya, came to settle here in Lower Moshi, especially during the peak of rice cultivation. The Japanese were very helpful. Some of them even learnt Swahili, and everyone laughed when a Japanese word accidentally meant something funny in Swahili. [TAN 13]

The success of rice cultivation made Lower Moshi a learning town where serious farmers assemble [TAN 01]. As a successor to KADC and KADP, the stakeholders established the Kilimanjaro Agricultural Training Centre (KATC) in Lower Moshi in 1994. The aim was to use this centre as a base for spreading rice cultivation from Kilimanjaro to all parts of Tanzania. Phase 2 started in 2001, and Phase 3 in 2007. As Anne Assenga of the Ministry of Agriculture noted, in the 2010s, JICA compensated for the decline in Tanzanian government support for the training so that the project could keep floating [TAN 03]. Nicodemus Shauritanga, the current principal of KATC, said:

> Coming from Njombe in the west, I found this project quite unique. Farmers outside Kilimanjaro discovered the value of rice farming. Planting seedlings in straight rows with equal spacing is now common all over Tanzania, but this practice started here in Lower Moshi. The Japanese adapted to our way of life. They ate the same food and did the same things we did. It was a good surprise for me to see how they helped each other. If someone is busy, someone else steps in and takes over the job. [TAN 12]

Mtika and Mawolle, a lovebird couple engaged in organising farmers, draw attention to entrepreneurship and gender to learn lessons from the Kilimanjaro rice project.

> Originally, women engaged in agricultural work and domestic chores, but they didn't get cash income. As rice cultivation spread, women started working for wages in planting and harvesting. Now, they can save money, and some even use it to buy land. Women were not allowed to own land before, but now, more and more women officially own land for farming. The TANRICE project [a national project to disseminate rice production technology launched in 2007] encourages equal participation of men and women in training. They even provide babysitters, and men take care of children, so that women can actively join the activities. [TAN 16]

Ikegami (2001) (in English) observed that traditional social customs such as 'poverty sharing' were breaking down as a result of the creation of wage labour for large-scale farms. Kimicho made an interesting comment: 'I feel that the birth rate in the area is getting down because everyone is working harder. In the coming 50 years, the area of the municipality may expand, and Kaloleni [an upstream rice-growing area outside the project] may become a residential area, where people may grow more vegetables' [TAN 07].

Goodwill activists tend to portray African women as passive victims of patriarchy who face the double burden of poverty and gender discrimination, but this is not always true. As a Danish development economist, Ester Boserup, argued, women in rural communities in sub-Saharan Africa often carry out substantial agricultural work, and their social status is relatively high compared to their counterparts in South Asia (Boserup 1970). Even in the rice-growing areas of Kilimanjaro, men are responsible for occasional physical labour such as ploughing and transport, while women are often responsible for core production activities such as nurturing seedlings, planting, weeding, watering, and harvesting.[35] Gender equality in Kilimanjaro is not a progressive idea brought from an outside society but rather an indigenous practice of local women and men, which can be facilitated by actors from the outside.

President Nyerere's attempt to transform rural African society from the top down, based on the Ujamaa principle of family ties, failed in the face of internal and external resistance. Rather than 'development as freedom', Nyerere may have sought 'development as rebellion', as described in his recent biography (Shivji et al. 2020: Book 3). Initially, the farmers distanced themselves from Nyerere's rebellion and adopted a seemingly domicile attitude towards Ujamaa's ideals, but over time, they began to internalise the need to work together. Development projects can be a catalyst for change and make dormant issues visible.

[35] Women in rural Tanzania are taking advantage of various institutional changes, including land reform, to achieve what is of value to them (Tanaka 2016) (in Japanese).

Chapter 3
The Quest for Human Resources Development: Manufacturing Industry

3.1 *Homo Faber* in the Twentieth Century

3.1.1 Industrialisation and Human Society

In Chapter 2, I examined the development of cooperation in agriculture and fisheries under the underlying theme of water circulation. The primary industry is premised on the direct metabolism between nature and humans. Although gigantic infrastructure projects such as the development of the Brantas River basin mobilised human activities to subdue raging waters, we still cannot prevent the occurrence of natural phenomena such as cyclones and volcanic eruptions. Chileans criticised engineers who were 'trained in engineering and business management' and squeezed too many fish pens into a small sea [CHL 13; CHL 15]. If we can catch 5 tonnes of salmon in one pen, why don't we catch 15 tonnes by adding two more pens? Such attempts caused an imbalance between fish life and the environment on the Chilean coast and eventually led to the spread of infectious diseases among salmon. The same is true for agriculture. The harvest will decline when rice is planted without enough space between seedlings.

However, the activities of the manufacturing industry follow a different logic from that of the primary sector. In manufacturing, if one increases inputs tenfold, one can increase outputs tenfold. As long as land and capital are available, factories can be expanded as much as you want. In service industries involving information technology (IT), one may even expect increasing returns when sales multiply while inputs remain constant. In the twentieth century, nations sought material abundance through industrialisation, and Western capitalism and Eastern socialism vied with each other to prove their superiority in the same playing field. In his 1927 posthumously published short essays, Akutagawa Ryunosuke, a Japanese writer who did not often express political opinions, praised Vladimir Lenin as 'what our Eastern world has bred – an electric locomotive that smells of flowering grasses' (Akutagawa 2006: 198–199). After World War II, in *The Stages of Economic Growth:*

Y. Mine, *An Oral History of Development Cooperation*,
https://doi.org/10.1007/978-981-95-5479-9_3

A Non-Communist Manifesto (Rostow 1960), American economist W. W. Rostow argued that every national economy develops from the stage of traditional society to that of take-off and then drive for maturity, and eventually, it reaches the age of high mass consumption like in the United States, rather than in the Soviet-style controlled economy. By the end of that century, we all learnt about the result of this inter-regime competition.

In a world with advanced industry, citizens would enjoy material abundance, and the potential of human intelligence would prevail far and wide. The Chinese character for engineering, '工', represents a tool, a chisel with a gripping hand. It may be more appropriate to define humans as *homo faber* (man of craft) rather than *homo sapiens* (man of wisdom), if what distinguishes humans from other species is 'the faculty of manufacturing artificial objects, especially tools to make tools, and of indefinitely varying the manufacture' (Bergson 1911: 139). Works in historical philosophy such as those by Henri de Saint-Simon (1817), Auguste Comte (1822) and Herbert Spencer (1876) envisioned modern industrial society as the antithesis of feudal warlord politics. Ironically, however, we now know that popular cutting-edge technologies such as the internet and drones have emerged from the military.

If we look back in human history, manufacturing was associated with a change in human behaviour that went beyond the rise in mere productivity and rationality. In the apprenticeship system, the master would not use voluminous instruction manuals to explain the work process. Instead, the apprentice would learn the procedure by watching and imitating what the master did, acquiring the necessary discipline, sophistication, and aesthetics. Tacit knowledge (Polanyi 1966) and the sense of perseverance and achievement are passed on over generations of workers. In Japan's technical cooperation, many Japanese experts regarded their everyday relations with their counterparts as analogous to traditional master-apprentice relationships, even though what they practised was primarily based on the modern on-the-job training (OJT) that was diffused in private companies in post-war, rather than pre-war, Japan.[1]

3.1.2 Beyond the Anti-Japanese Movement

Industrial development is a process of making consumers' lives more convenient, liberating people from their animal limitations, and awakening them to the joy of unlimited creativity. The development of manufacturing would be at the very heart of the process of modernisation of society. We then face a challenge: it has not always been easy to narrow the gap between the early starters and the later starters of industrialisation, despite the putative benefit of the latter (Gerschenkron 1962). Since the Meiji era, Japan has proactively adopted Western technology and promoted industrialisation and militarisation in a top-down, state-centric way. Later, as Japan transitioned from a militaristic to a peaceful state, civilian manufacturing expanded

[1] Nonaka and Takeuchi (1995) demonstrated how Japanese firms transformed tacit knowledge to explicit knowledge to keep up innovation.

remarkably, and Japanese products such as household appliances and automobiles once conquered not only the Western but also the Asian markets. In Asian countries, questions arose. Why is it only Japan that makes them? Japan was defeated in the war. Yet, why is it that we, also Asians, only end up buying their products?

In this context, anti-Japanese sentiment flared throughout Southeast Asia. In October 1972, the Thai Student Centre called for a boycott of Japanese-made commodities. In January 1974, when Prime Minister Tanaka Kakuei visited the ASEAN countries, students organised a mass protest in Bangkok where they set fire to puppets of Tanaka (Anderson 1998: Chap. 7). In Jakarta, he faced mass opposition and was forced to evacuate, as Indonesians were concerned that Japanese investment would relegate Indonesia into a peripheral position in the regional economy (Robinson 1985). Anti-Japanese public opinion was also manifested in Singapore and Malaysia, while the anger in the Philippines lay dormant under martial law (Suzuki 1991). The anti-Japanese sentiment in Southeast Asia persisted throughout the 1970s and 1980s. Tsurumi Yoshiyuki, one of the Japanese pioneers of contemporary Asian studies based on extensive fieldwork, pointed out three factors behind the anti-Japanese campaign in the early 1970s: the movement emerged at the intersection of bitter memories of the war (history), the arrogant behaviour of some Japanese people (culture), and the rapid inroads of Japanese businesses into local markets (economy) (Tsurumi 1974).[2]

Shimomura Yasutami agreed in principle with Tsurumi's view and emphasised the role of the third factor, the skewed economic relationship between Japan and Southeast Asian countries (Shimomura 2020: Chap. 4). In August 1977, in Manila, Prime Minister Fukuda Takeo announced the so-called Fukuda Doctrine, which conveyed a message that Japan would never become a military power but would build trustful, heart-to-heart relations with Southeast Asians and support the initiative of regional cooperation (including Indochina). The doctrine was warmly welcomed by the Southeast Asian countries, and it was the moment when Japan's proactive and independent diplomacy bore fruit (Sudo 1997; Sudo 2002: 35–37; Iokibe 2021: 561–572). Shimomura pointed out, however, that despite these excellent statements of principle, it took ten years after the announcement of the doctrine for criticism of Japan to subside—on the contrary, at least in Thailand, by the 1980s, anti-Japanese sentiment had spread to farmers and workers and had become a mass movement. It was not until the late 1980s that the Thai grievances began to recede, when the export of industrial products from Southeast Asia to the world market markedly increased.

In light of this trend, this chapter will highlight two micro and macro responses to the crisis Japan faced. First, as a micro response, I take up the ASEAN Human Resources Development (*Hito-zukuri*) Project, announced by Prime Minister Suzuki Zenko during his visit to Southeast Asia in 1981, which aimed to establish centres for this purpose in the Philippines, Thailand, Malaysia, Indonesia, and Singapore and eventually to expand activities throughout ASEAN in order to provide skilled

[2] The fourth factor, a political element, could be added: Japan was regarded as a supporter of the authoritarian political elite of some Southeast Asian countries. See discussions in Japan Culture Forum (1975).

human resources for regionwide industrialisation.[3] Japan constructed buildings, provided equipment, dispatched experts, and conducted training for local counterparts. Section 3.2 of this chapter reviews the work of the Centre for Instructor and Advanced Skill Training (CIAST), established in Malaysia in 1982.

Japanese technical cooperation in this field began in 1960 with the establishment of a centre in West Bengal, India (JICA 1984b: 68). While training in basic skills for young workers became widespread in the 1970s, the focus shifted to 'training and retraining trainers' in the 1980s. CIAST in Malaysia was a flagship project in this new area of cooperation. Adapting the phrase 'teach people how to fish' discussed in Chap. 1 (Sect. 1.2.1), we may say that what CIAST aimed to do was 'teach teachers how to teach.' If this technology transfer was successful, the cycle of self-help would be set in motion, and vocational training would be self-contained within Malaysia. In the 1980s and 1990s, CIAST boasted a solid presence as Malaysia's national centre for human resources development for manufacturing industries. In Section 3.2, I will describe how the relationship between Japanese experts and their Malaysian counterparts developed in specific historical and cultural contexts.

Micro attempts of technology transfer alone are not enough to support full-fledged industrialisation. Section 3.3, the second case study of this chapter, looks at the Eastern Seaboard Development Plan in Thailand, a gigantic macro project that mobilised yen loans. Based on Alfred Marshall's conception of the external economy, economic geography established itself as a unique branch of development studies (Krugman 1991). In the eastern seaboard region, a virtuous cycle of concentration and expansion of production was created through the construction of large-scale infrastructure such as ports, roads, and industrial estates. In addition, the rapid appreciation of the yen following the Plaza Accord in 1985 led to a surge in direct investment from Japan. The industrial parks in the eastern seaboard region weathered the Asian currency crisis of 1997, serving as a strong hub for the Thai export of higher-value-added commodities such as motor vehicles.

Shimomura (2017) carefully discussed the process by which, during the reign of King Bhumibol (Rama IX), a solid consensus was formed among Thai technocrats to promote the industrialisation of the eastern seaboard region. The first half of Sect. 3 of this chapter describes this process, while the second half presents the voices of local people on how they perceived the development project. As I was not able to conduct fieldwork in Thailand due to the COVID-19 pandemic, I entrusted my Japanese friend, who had settled in Thailand, to conduct interviews with local citizens on my behalf.

[3] Indonesia's Centre for Vocational and Extension Service Training (CEVEST) aimed to double the number of vocational trainers in five years, a plan that appeared to be too ambitious to be successfully implemented (Kasahara 1998: 95–98).

3.1.3 *The Ripple Effect of* Kaizen

Although Southeast Asians were critical of Japan's post-war economic expansion, it was not the case that the recipients of the Japanese aid viewed the donor always in a negative light. In places geographically distant from Asia, Japan tended to be regarded as an object of curiosity. By way of comparison, the small Central American country Costa Rica could be kin to post-war Japan, which took pride in its pacifist constitution. The Central American region consists of mainly Spanish-speaking countries with diverse historical and cultural traits. Among them, Costa Rica, a relatively prosperous and politically stable country, has taken a leading role in bringing peace to the region. The country's posture as an altruistic global Good Samaritan has contributed not only to the peace in the region but also to its national interests (Brysk 2005; Lipton and Barash 2019).

As discussed in Section 3.4, the third case study of this chapter, Japan attempted to diffuse the *kaizen* method in Costa Rica. In workplaces that have adopted *kaizen,* workers are not expected merely to follow the instructions of their supervisors but encouraged to identify problems (especially habitual inefficiency) by themselves and propose specific measures to improve and streamline production. Such a system of worker participation is organised in the form of flow charts and slogans and is constantly practised on the shop floor. When such a campaign reaches all the factories, the norm of the workers will change nationwide. Section 2.4 in Chap. 2 discussed the dynamics of rice production in Tanzania and concluded that the development of farmers' organisations to maintain irrigation facilities was crucial. In the late twentieth century, the focus of development cooperation shifted from conventional technology transfer to investment in institutions, whether in primary industry or in other sectors.

In 1992, the Training Centre for Trainers and Technical Personnel for the Industrial Development of Central America (CEFOF: Centro de Formación de Formadores y de Personal Técnico para el Desarrollo Industrial de Centroamérica) was established in Alajuela, adjacent to the main international airport. Japanese experts arrived and trained Costa Rican consultants to diffuse supervisory techniques, including *kaizen,* to local companies. Although some may regard *kaizen* as an attempt to siphon off the voluntary commitment of workers for profit maximisation,[4] it may also bring an unintended consequence of acting as an extraneous catalyst for a process of creative destruction (Schumpeter 1942: 81–86) of the hierarchical relations prevalent in the workplaces in a developing country.

Statistical quality control, one of the sources of *kaizen,* was introduced to Japan in 1950 by the American management scholar W. E. Deming in a lecture in Japan (Imai 1986: 5, 10). Costa Rica is a country strongly influenced by the US management style, so the spread of *kaizen* in Central America can be considered a sort of reverse import. In terms of training of trainers, the work of CEFOF was similar to that

[4] Nakaoka (1970) (in Japanese) cautioned that 'controlled spontaneity' in the workplace where the Taylor system is experimented to its limits will deprive people of the joy of work and eventually make them even less efficient.

of CIAST, but CIAST was not very active in advising companies on management methods. By the time of CEFOF's heyday, the book *Japan as Number One* (Vogel 1979) had become globally popular (its Spanish translation was published in 1981), and corporate managers worldwide began to pay close attention to the so-called Japanese model.[5] Section 3.4.6 concludes the story of Costa Rica by indicating further challenges after the adoption of the *kaizen* method.

3.2 Human Resources Development in ASEAN: The Centre for Instructor and Advanced Skills Training (Malaysia)

3.2.1 Seeking Coexistence

Toba Kinichiro, a management scholar who had lived in the US for many years, was in Malaysia in 1971–72 as a visiting professor at the University of Malaya. One day, a New Zealander, 'Mr Routledge', arrived late for a meeting. Apparently, he was hung up in a dimly lit corridor of the campus, surrounded by local students. It seemed that the exchange went something like this:

> 'How long have you been teaching here?'
>
> 'Five years, I think.'
>
> 'Then why don't you teach in Malay? You've been here for five years and still cannot speak Malay?'
>
> '...'
>
> 'Such people should leave the country immediately. We don't need you.'

As Toba explained, it was not the fault of Mr. Routledge that he gave classes in English, because he was an English language teacher. 'I'm white, so I stand out,' he said, but Toba wondered, 'What if it had been me? Wouldn't they have noticed me because I am a yellow person? Would they have condoned my presence because I had just arrived?' And he realised: if he did not assimilate with the Malays, he would be in the same position as Mr. Routledge in a few years (Toba 1973: 10). Toba argued that a Japanese person conveniently switched 'two faces', a white face and a yellow face, depending on the circumstances. When the Japanese were aware of the presence of Westerners, they might behave like Asians, but in front of Asians, they might identify with Westerners and look down on their fellow Asians. Toba's paperback written in Japanese, published one year before Prime Minister Tanaka's

[5] At the time, Japanese-style work ethics attracted worldwide attention, mixed with suspicion in the West, but the collectivist ethos in the workplace might be a general feature of late development rather than an idiosyncratic trait of Japanese culture (Dore 1990). On the other hand, as the perspective of *Industrious Revolution* suggests, the work ethics of diligence originating in rural areas may be a feature of the East Asian labour-intensive development path (Sugihara 2003).

visit to Southeast Asia and circulated widely in Japan, provided the Japanese public with a hand mirror for self-reflection.[6]

Setting aside the question of Japan's historical position, Malaysia (Fig. 3.1) faced its own domestic problems. In the mid-nineteenth century, Chinese workers were brought into the British Malay Colony for the development of tin mines, and in the late nineteenth century, Indian workers were mobilised for the development of rubber plantations and railway networks. Both groups gradually adapted to urban life in the British colony. The majority Malays, who were predominantly Muslim, continued to live in farming and fishing villages with relatively little contact with the British and later the Japanese colonial authorities. It was mainly the urban Chinese who resisted Japanese militarism and were brutally repressed during World War II. After the Federation of Malaya's independence from Britain in 1957 and the foundation of Malaysia in 1963, Singapore, whose citizens were predominantly ethnic Chinese, seceded from Malaysia in 1965. In Malaysia, Malay, Chinese and Indian citizens remained relatively divided under the single umbrella of the nation-state.[7] As Mahathir bin Mohamad, who became prime minister in 1981, once wrote:

> There was tolerance. There was a certain amount of give and take. But there was no harmony. There was, in fact, cacophony, muted but still audible. And periodically the discordant notes rose and erupted into isolated or widespread racial fights…. The Malays and the Chinese may live as neighbours. They may meet each other in their daily business and even socially. But when they retire, they retire into their respective ethnic and cultural sanctum, neither of which has ever been truly breached by the other. And in their own world, their values are not merely different but are often conflicting. (Mahathir bin Mohamad 1970: 14)

Although there were multiple causes of the conflict, the disparity in living conditions between Malays and other ethnic groups was palpable. In 1971, under the New Economic Policy (NEP), a set of policy measures called the Bumiputra Policy was introduced to address inequalities, but its effects were slow to emerge. In 1979, the average household income of the Chinese was 938 ringgit and that of the Indians 756 ringgit, while that of the Malays was only 492 ringgit, according to a book on human resources in Malaysia read widely by Japanese experts at the time (Kasahara 1991: 21–22). In addition to education, the Bumiputra Policy emphasised employment reforms aimed at upgrading the skills of Malay urban workers and bringing Malay incomes closer to those of ethnic Chinese and Indians. The new Malaysia needs to narrow the gaps in occupation and skills between ethnic groups so that everyone can live a better life. This was the background of CIAST.[8]

[6] The economist Iida Tsuneo who worked for JICA occasionally described Japan's uncomfortable position as the historical 'destiny of Japan' and wrote he was not sure whether Asia 'wanted to become like Japan' (Iida 1998: 87).

[7] Okabe (1976), who analysed the background to the anti-Japanese movement in Southeast Asia, devoted the second half of his Japanese book to an analysis of the 'Chinese factor'. He made a point that the key to nation-building in Southeast Asia in the 1970s was how to deal with the ethnic Chinese population, and this depended to a large extent on the bilateral relations between Southeast Asian countries and China.

[8] The reports on CIAST written in Japanese made little direct reference to the need for affirmative action. In a preliminary investigation report written in Japanese, I have found an exceptionally

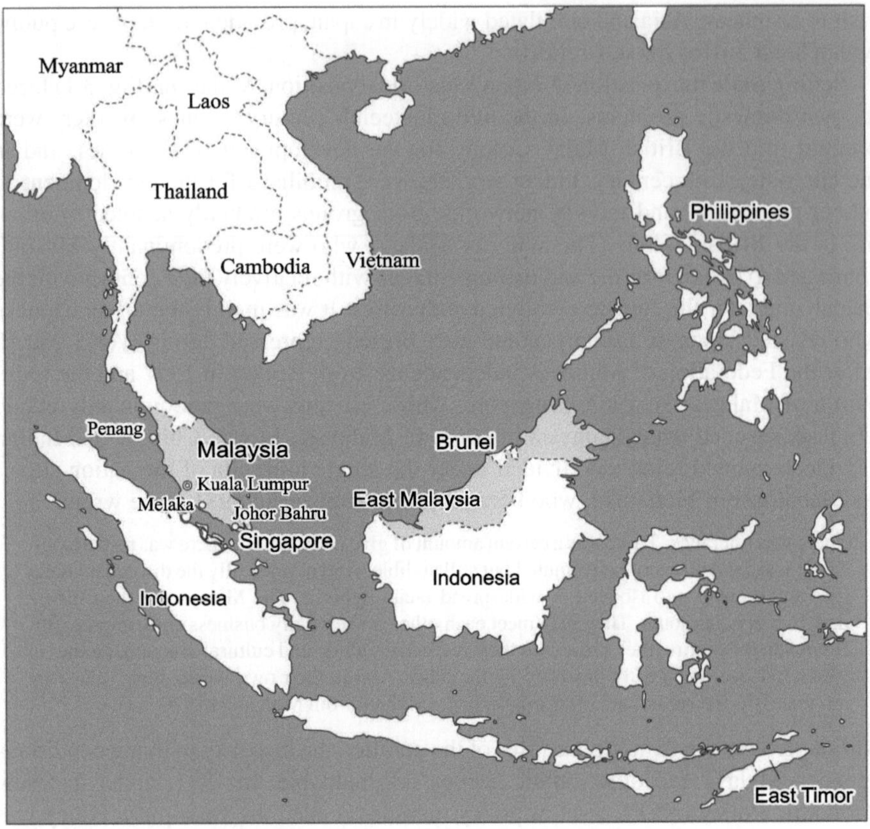

Fig. 3.1 Malaysia in Southeast Asia. Source: Author

The CIAST project was formally launched in 1982. The following year, Kasahara Shohei was appointed as the head of the expert team. Having graduated from the Faculty of Law, the University of Tokyo, Kasahara joined the Ministry of Labour, where he worked for the Employment Promotion Corporation and other institutions before becoming Deputy President of the Vocational Training College (now Polytechnic University).[9] In shaping the direction of CIAST, Kasahara supervised Japanese experts with diverse backgrounds and opinions. In 1984, the construction of the building was completed, and the training of Malaysian vocational instructors began. At the time, Malaysian Prime Minister Mahathir called for the 'Look East' policy so that Malaysians could learn from the development experiences of Japan and South Korea. Then, what did the Mahathir government expect from CIAST?

straightforward passage: 'Malaysia has high expectations for assistance from Japan, which is a leading industrial country and a fellow Asian nation. Malaysia intends to shift its orientation from pro-West, especially pro-British, to pro-Japanese' (JICA 1982b: 8).

[9] This is called 職業能力開発総合大学校 in Japanese. https://www.uitec.jeed.go.jp/english/.

Suraya Wang binti Abdullah, who, as head of the Economic Planning Board at the Malaysian Prime Minister's Office, had coordinated the ministries involved in vocational training, said that Western donors and Japan had different attitudes.[10] She took it that Japan understood the subtlety of the problems Malaysians faced.

> Malaysia tried to learn from Japan, partly because of Japan's advanced technology but also because Japan did not want to impose conditionality. Affirmative action is a very sensitive issue in Malaysia. Any conditionality that will force a change in this [Bumiputra] policy is not acceptable. When Prime Minister Miyazawa proposed solutions for the Asian financial crisis, he did not mention conditionality at all. [MYS 01]

Addressing inequality can be a challenging and sensitive issue in the workplace, especially when foreign stakeholders are involved. Kasahara noted that Japanese residents sometimes gossiped about Malaysians, comparing the characters of ethnic groups. However, as the CIAST team leader, Kasahara tried to build a consensus among the experts so as not to make irresponsible comments on historically complex issues. He noted that the CIAST experts respected the Malaysian constitution and 'agreed not to discuss ethnic matters in front of counterparts' (Kasahara 1991: 84).[11]

3.2.2 Preparation for Take-off (1982–1984)

In CIAST, C stands for 'Centre,' I for 'Instructor,' AS for 'Advanced Skill' and T for 'Training.' According to a calculation cited by Kasahara, in the early 1980s, 60,000 new production workers entered the Malaysian labour market each year. Of these, 12,000 were graduates of public vocational training institutions, and the plan was to increase this number to 20,000. This would require the training of new instructors and the retraining of existing instructors. Building such a chain of training trainers for public institutions, therefore, became the main task of CIAST.[12] In addition, 40,000 people—the difference between 60,000 and 20,000—would enter the private

[10] By the time the NEP was replaced by the New Development Policy (NDP) in 1991, ethnic tensions in Malaysia had been dramatically reduced (Heng 1997). Brown (2005) acknowledged the importance of avoiding a political backlash from wealthy minorities and emphasised that it was important to reduce inequalities while the economy was upbeat and expanding. Gomez (2012) argued that the Bumiputra Policy was losing its effectiveness as free enterprises were being discouraged.

[11] The voices of the experts are quoted mainly from Kasahara's two books. The comprehensive report on the project (JICA 1987b) contains detailed descriptions of the experiences of individual experts. By the time the project opened in 1985, 15 long-term experts had been dispatched to the project.

[12] Vocational training institutions in Malaysia are divided into vocational high schools and polytechnics (technical colleges) in the charge of the Ministry of Education, training institutions in the charge of the MARA Corporation that specialise in vocational training for Malays, youth institutions in the charge of the Ministry of Youth and Sports, and training institutions in the charge of the Ministry of Labour. CIAST is under the jurisdiction of the Manpower Department of the Ministry of Labour but has been positioned as the national centre for the training of all trainers, including those trained in institutions under other ministries.

labour market without vocational training. Since these people would receive on-the-job training in their workplaces, it was considered necessary to train supervisors in the private sector to familiarise them with new technologies and improve their training skills. This was the second task of CIAST. Neither of these tasks involved workers directly but were broadly concerned with the training of public or private trainers. In Malaysia, there was already an instructor training institution operated by the International Labour Organization (ILO), and CIAST was established as its successor (Kasahara 1991: 8–10) [MYS 02; MYS 04; MYS 08].[13]

The courses offered by CIAST were divided into three categories: training methodology, supervisory skills training, and advanced skills training. The courses on training methodology were those about 'how to teach', offering subjects such as skills analysis, audio-visual material production, and the management of training designed particularly for instructors in public training schools. The supervisory skills training courses were for supervisors in the private firms to learn management engineering through subjects such as quality management, safety management and workplace discipline.[14] The courses on advanced skills training consisted of automotive, machine tools and moulds, metalworking, heavy industry, electrical and electronics, and instrumentation and automatic control (JICA 1985b). The subject of advanced skills was particularly popular among Malaysians because the 'advanced Japanese technology' such as NC (numerical control) machine tools was demonstrated on the premises (Kasahara 1991: 104–124).

For the Malaysian manufacturing sector to move beyond simply assembling imported components, it was necessary to acquire advanced skills for its own benefit—for example, Malaysians needed to be able to repair machine tools or at least to know where they broke down. Vocational instructors in Malaysia were usually high school graduates, but those instructors who could handle mechatronics had to be university graduates or at least diploma holders (JICA 1984c: 32). Japanese experts felt that this could potentially be a problem, as university graduates were generally unwilling to get their hands dirty on the work site (JICA 1986: 9). Kasahara was aware that some counterparts at CIAST preferred engaging in management jobs and did not want to go to the classrooms and to stay in direct contact with the trainees. He wrote that there was a perception that professional engineers—even though the majority of those employed at CIAST at the time of its opening were originally from farming and fishing families and were the first generation to settle down in cities—were not the ones to wear work clothes (Kasahara 1991: 66–68).

As the opening of CIAST scheduled for 1984 approached (the full opening was in 1985), the question arose as to who would write the syllabus and the teaching materials. Originally, the Malaysian side had requested Japanese assistance in developing teaching materials, but the Japanese side did not respond positively, making

[13] Here, Kasahara criticised his counterparts for clinging to the ILO method, but the Malaysian counterparts said that while they appreciated Japan's contribution in terms of advanced technology and supervisory skills, the ILO's method was ultimately more influential.

[14] This area of management engineering would eventually be systematised as *kaizen*. See also the case study on Costa Rica in Section 3.4.

excuses that there were few experts in that field (JICA 1982a: 52–53). On arrival, Kasahara and his colleagues insisted that their Malaysian counterparts should write the teaching materials. Partly to encourage self-help efforts on the part of Malaysians, but also because the most advanced area of engineering was rapidly evolving and changing, Kasahara and others thought it would be better for their counterparts to write and rewrite the teaching materials to accommodate Malaysian needs.

However, the Malaysian side assumed that the teaching materials should be included in the support package, and a game of chicken began (Kasahara 1991: 43). In the end, of the 88 module materials produced after the opening of CIAST, 22 were written by Malaysian counterparts, 15 by Japanese experts, and 51 were written jointly by counterparts and experts. Prior to the writing process, counterparts and experts visited a number of local factories together. The preparation of teaching materials turned out to be an excellent rehearsal for collaborative work.

3.2.3 The 'Spirit of Sanzu' (Three ZUs)

Take your time. But do not compromise on what you have to say. 'If you give up, there will be no heart-to-heart communication. Without heart-to-heart communication, effective technology transfer cannot be expected' (Kasahara 1991: 85). To avoid unnecessary friction with counterparts, CIAST experts agreed on the principle of 'no hurry (isoga*zu*), no anger (okora*zu*), no giving up (akirame*zu*). It was called the 'Spirit of Sanzu (three *zu*s: "zu" is a negative suffix in Japanese),' which was a pun on the 'Sanzu River' (the Japanese Buddhist version of River Styx) (Kasahara 1998: 109). Apart from the element that should always be emphasised (such as the principle of self-help), Kasahara encouraged Japanese experts to respect the context of their workplace. Before criticising the Malaysians, the Japanese should try to understand what they feel, how they think, and why it is so.

> One of the driving forces that can further motivate your counterparts is the trusting relationships that evolve with the [Japanese] professionals engaged in technical cooperation. This trust is created and strengthened by respecting the customs of your counterparts. In this sense, the 'respect for local customs' underpins the 'promotion of self-help'. (Kasahara 1991: 99)

In Malaysia, this practically meant that the Japanese should respect Muslim practices of prayer, fasting, and dietary restrictions (some experts tried fasting with their Malaysian colleagues just to get the same feeling). Japanese experts should avoid drinking alcohol and going wild in the presence of Muslims. Do not ask a Muslim woman to shake hands with you. Not only is it a human courtesy not to do anything that makes others feel uncomfortable, but it is also essential for a development project to move forward. Local counterparts may find it difficult to get along with Japanese experts who work non-stop from morning to night. Chatting during working hours and covering up the mistakes of their colleagues are part of the legacy of everyday life in farming and fishing villages, and you cannot change the attitudes of others only by showing your discontent (Kasahara 1991: 130–172; 1998: 111–120).

Some Japanese staff who worked hard to support the Malaysians complained about a 'lack of appreciation' on the Malaysian side. However, as Kasahara indicated, Japan was not the only country involved in technical cooperation with Malaysia, and if Japan disappeared, Canada, Germany, France and other countries would fill the gap. Locally, Japanese companies were regarded as benefiting from economic cooperation (in fact, there is no doubt that private companies were operating in Malaysia because they could make a profit). In addition, the behaviour of the Japanese military during the war was still vividly remembered. We should understand that there are reasons for the attitudes of the counterparts (Kasahara 1991: 87; 1998: 65–67). One of the trainees came up to Kasahara during a tea party at the end of the training course and told him that his father had been killed by the Japanese military during the war. The trainee said, 'I would like to express my gratitude to a Japanese for the first time in my life,' holding tears and asking for a handshake with Kasahara (Kasahara 1991: 169).

3.2.4 Development of Cooperation (1984–1990)

So how did the Malaysian counterparts perceive the CIAST project? Kasahara pointed out that university graduates were not necessarily willing to sweat in workshop activities. Suimi bin Abd Majid, who was in charge of training methodology, admitted that there were such problems among Malaysian trainers. However, this was not due to their elitism. He said:

> Indeed, university graduates were hesitant about teaching hands-on techniques. I don't think it was a matter of individuals' lack of willingness. They were just scared! They might find what they had to do quite embarrassing because they had only learnt theory at university. But, at CIAST, they had to show their skills to trainees who were more experienced than the trainers. I think such a relationship still exists today. [MYS 08]

Roslinda binti Daud, who worked in the electrical and electronics department, said she was also scared of teaching the trainees in the classrooms. She had just graduated from university, but many of the trainees had already gained experience on the factory floor. It was after she received training in Japan that she gained confidence [MYS 09]. Ghazlan bin Ghazali, the second director of CIAST, obtained his degree at a university in Canada, where he learnt a lot about theory.

> I studied mechanical engineering, but my general knowledge was not useful in the practical field. I had only a few chances to use machines when I studied at university, but at CIAST, everything was practical, so I was at a loss. I was fortunate to acquire skills from the experts through one-to-one coaching. Thanks to that, I became able to teach the trainees confidently. [MYS 04]

Zaihan bin Shukri, deputy director general of the Manpower Department, Ministry of Human Resources, recalled that the main factor that contributed to the success of CIAST was that it 'constantly changed its training contents and methods in response to the emergence of new technologies' [MYS 02]. He noted that CIAST was always flexible enough to transform itself in line with the demands of the industry. Shamsida binti Zainal Abdin, who studied electronics, also stressed that CIAST was always ready to change. She remembered that the expert in charge of her was a very quiet person but eager to help her. In Malaysia today, more and more women like her major in electronics and information technology [MYS 03].

Human communication is essential for technology transfer. 'We encouraged the trainees to ask questions of the Japanese experts from the trainees' side, because few Japanese spoke English fluently. Once they asked questions, the Japanese made efforts and tried to answer all the questions' [MYS 04]. Then, some counterparts 'visited Japan for training, stayed there for a certain period, and became fluent in Japanese' [MYS 02]. On the other hand, several Japanese experts could speak Malay thanks to their previous assignment in Indonesia. In this way, communication turned out to be smoother in both directions. Rahmat bin Ayop learnt Japanese in Ichigaya, worked at Showa Rubber in Kashiwa, and met his wife at the Kinokuniya Bookshop in Shinjuku. His counterpart, Mr. Takahashi, whom he called 'father' because he was about the same age as his own father, was eventually dispatched to CIAST as an expert from Showa Rubber, and thus their relationship continued in Malaysia [MYS 05].

Deputy Director General Zaihan said that when he worked at CIAST, his relationship with Japanese experts was 'not like between a master and a henchman, but like among members of a family':

> I came to CIAST after studying in the US but had never had much practical experience. Then, Mr Kasahara and his colleagues taught me practical skills in the classroom. I remember a very effective room arrangement for learning. There was a workshop area and a desk-chair area in the same room, and we moved back and forth between the two areas as questions arose. [MYS 02]

Azmi bin Ali had rich experience in the practical field before joining CIAST in 1983. He had worked for Malayawata Steel (affiliated to Yawata Steel) in Penang, a Japanese-Malaysian joint venture. He recalled:

> Islam remains at the heart of Malaysian values. The Japanese work ethic was very new to Malaysia. It was interesting to see how the Japanese dealt with various issues we faced. The Japanese hold free discussions every morning to reach a consensus. Younger staff members were also asked for their opinions, but that was not practised here in Malaysia. Mr Kasahara took the time to visit the workplaces and ask if there was any problem, if everything was going well. I think the good personal relationships between the Malaysian and Japanese colleagues helped us coordinate the work well. [MYS 06]

In interviews for other projects, I heard that some Japanese experts were too strict or did not respect local culture carefully, but I did not encounter such negative comments from the CIAST staff. Perhaps, the ideas brought in by Kasahara had changed the course of collaboration in Malaysia. However, Suimi bin Abd Majid said, 'I think the depth of our relationship with the Japanese depended on personal characters, as there were no tools like social media at that time' [MYS 08]. The relationships between Japanese experts and their Malaysian counterparts in Malaysia may have been principled but a little aloof. As indicated by interview research comparing job relationships in the US and Japanese companies in Malaysia, the respondents perceived that the Japanese tended to keep their social distance from local staff, in contrast with the friendly Americans who called Malaysian colleagues by their first names (O'Brien 1994). The general image of 'less talkative' Japanese experts might be simply due to the fact that many were not very fluent in English.

Many counterparts were amazed at the Japanese sense of time control. Sayed Salim bin Sayed Mohd Nor, who worked in the electrics and electronics department, laughed, 'I was punctual in Japan, but back in Malaysia, things have gone back to the way they used to be.' It was the experience of video production with a SONY team that he remembers the most fondly from his training experience in Japan. When the trainees sent their short films to Sony, they would evaluate them and give advice. Then, the Malaysians would use them as teaching materials. In those days, they used Beta videotapes instead of VHS. During his stay in Japan, 'the people at SONY spoke English, but English was rarely used in Japan outside that company' [MYS 10].

3.2.5 *End of Assistance (1991)*

In 1991, CIAST 'graduated' from the status of the recipient of Japan's assistance and became managed fully by the Malaysian side. By then, the number of trainees who had attended some CIAST courses reached 6538 (JICA 1992). By 1997, the instructor training course was transformed into an educational programme, and CIAST graduates began to be awarded diploma degrees (Kasahara 1998: 22–23).

At the end of my interviews, eight graduates of CIAST were requested to assemble at their alma mater to share their experiences in a roundtable discussion. They were young engineers in their thirties who taught automotive engineering and welding at vocational schools. When they enrolled in CIAST, none of them knew that the institution had been founded with Japanese assistance. One of them, who grew up in the neighbourhood, said he often passed by CIAST but assumed that the building was a factory. At that time, not many institutions offered diplomas in specific fields of engineering, so the curriculum of CIAST appeared attractive to them. After their enrolment, they found that the practical training was carried out using equipment provided by JICA, which was of excellent quality and the latest model, not available in ordinary factories. They said it was a nice experience to use real machines in the workshop for study. They remembered the instructors used overhead projectors (OHPs) rather than PowerPoint. They all stayed together in a dormitory on the premises, which fostered a strong sense of community. Now, they were all on the teaching side. When one complained that it was difficult to get young students to concentrate on the lessons because they were addicted to electronic games, everyone nodded in agreement. Some of the discussion participants expressed their willingness to study again and obtain university degrees, while others said they did not want to study theory at university again because they loved the practice of manufacturing on the factory floor [MYS 14].

While the diploma courses were running, a plan was tabled to transform CIAST into a university. It was considered practical to turn CIAST into a higher education institution so that the training of trainers could be institutionalised and sustained. At the same time, courses in advanced skills and supervisory skills training for company employees were also popular at CIAST in the 1990s. The flexibility of course materials at CIAST, which could be reviewed in response to changing industrial needs, was highly regarded. There was also a system whereby employers with 50 or more employees contributed 1% of the total wages to a fund, which was then used to supplement skills development projects for the staff, such as retraining at CIAST. Particularly popular in the advanced skills department were automobile maintenance, machine and mould making, welding, electrics and machine control. CIAST's training departments were reorganised to meet the demands for such fields (Kasahara 1998: 24–29, 77–78, 87).

Eventually, the plan to transform CIAST into a university was abandoned because the Ministry of Higher Education disagreed, as CIAST was under the supervision of the Ministry of Human Resources. So educational collaboration in engineering was expanded in other forms. The Japan Malaysia Technological Institute (JMTI) opened at a temporary campus within CIAST to provide vocational training in advanced industrial fields such as production, electronics, information and mechatronics. The operation continued from January 1998 to January 2004. In addition to JMTI, which was eventually relocated to Penang and became fully operational, four Advanced Technology Training Centres (ADTECs) have been established in different places in Malaysia. In 2011, the Malaysia-Japan International Institute of Technology (MJIIT) was established as part of Universiti Teknologi Malaysia to provide advanced engineering education, including postgraduate studies. As JMTI and ADTEC, both run by the Ministry of Human Resources, began to grant diplomas, CIAST ceased to offer diploma courses in 2008 and shifted to non-degree instructor training.[15]

In Japan, there are educational institutions known as 'government ministry universities' (省庁大学校) or civil service colleges. They are not universities or colleges in the narrow sense of the terms specified in the School Education Act, but a separate law has approved their establishment as higher-level educational institutions. The graduates of the National Defence Academy, the National Defence Medical College, the National Fisheries University, the Japan Coast Guard Academy, the Meteorological College, the Polytechnic University, and the National College of Nursing are granted bachelor's, master's and doctoral degrees certified by the National Institution for Academic Degrees and Quality Enhancement of Higher Education, which is under the jurisdiction of the Ministry of Education. On the other hand, other civil colleges do not award degrees to graduates (for example, the Local Autonomy College only trains local government officers and does not provide school education). In Malaysia, CIAST has lost its function as a degree-granting institution and has reverted to an

[15] An evaluation of CIAST and Indonesia's CEVEST concluded that the impact of CIAST was significant particularly when spillover effects were taken into account. It recommended increased collaboration with the private sector (JICA 1995a). There was a discussion in the 1990s about privatising CIAST, but 'the Manpower Department protested and defended CIAST' [MYS 08].

institute focusing on the training of vocational instructors. It has become a less conspicuous institution, not equipped with the latest machinery and equipment as it used to be. Azhari bin Ibrahim lamented that, after the Japanese experts left, advanced technology was no longer taught, the budget shrank due to the presence of competing institutions, and private companies became less responsive [MYS 11].[16] Nevertheless, the CIAST premises are still clean, tidy and well-maintained. Welding expert Mohd Noor bin Menhad said, 'The current machines are not the latest, but if they are only used by the trainees to prove their skills for qualification, they are good enough as they are' [MYS 12].

Isrami bin Ismail, who studied at Iwate University and Nagaoka University of Technology, speaks perfect Japanese. He practices consultancy in Kuala Lumpur and is one of the core members of the Alumni Look East Policy Society (ALEPS), an alumni association of Malaysians who studied at Japanese universities on Malaysian Government scholarships. Having closely observed Malaysian-Japanese cooperation, Isrami referred to several problems remaining in Malaysian vocational training institutions (he did not specifically mention CIAST). For instance, certain skills are lost immediately after the Japanese experts return to Japan. There are various reasons for this, including personnel changes, particularly among those who have been trained by Japanese experts at the training institution. In addition, in some cases, trainees are more skilled than the instructors, due to a lack of real industrial experience among some of the instructors. The pros and cons of the Japanese approach should be examined; one notable characteristic of the Japanese is their tendency to take time and plan meticulously. While this thoroughness is admirable, according to Isrami, it can also result in slower responses [MYS 13].

3.2.6 Flying Geese

CIAST may have ceased to be a cutting-edge technology centre in Malaysia. Yet its name resounds in other Asian countries through 'third-country training', a form of bilateral technology transfer involving another country [MYS 12]. For instance, it may not be efficient for Japan to invite Cambodian trainees directly to Japan in a specific field of technology transfer. Then Malaysia (a third, pivotal country that is neither Japan nor Cambodia) provides such activities (Malaysia's technology level is high enough), and trainees not only from Cambodia but also from Laos, Vietnam and other Southeast Asian countries are to gather in Malaysia and be trained by Malaysian experts (regional cooperation and economy of scale will be enhanced). Third-country training in Malaysia has been conducted since 1983 on a half-Malaysian, half-Japanese cost-sharing basis (JICA 2018). This kind of training

[16] Sayed Salim bin Sayed Mohd Nor was very candid. 'When there were Japanese in CIAST, we had advanced technology and were respected, but now, not many companies recognise us. CIAST is dead' [MYS 10].

is considered a practical form of triangular cooperation to promote South-South cooperation (Kato 2012).

According to Suraya Wang binti Abdullah, who was director of the Economic Planning Unit of the Prime Minister's Office, Prime Minister Mahathir began to emphasise the perspective of South-South cooperation in the 1980s, which led CIAST to undertake third-country training in the manufacturing sector in the 1990s. Such a function of CIAST was already proposed in preliminary studies (JICA 1982a: 42) and implemented on a small scale since 1988. There are two dynamics behind the growing attention paid by Malaysia to South-South cooperation. She explained:

> The first is political. We espouse the principle that developing countries should move towards self-reliance. They must reduce their dependence on the countries of the North and forge strong friendships and solidarity among developing countries. The second is economic. We recognise the importance of pursuing a prosper-thy-neighbour policy rather than a beggar-thy-neighbour policy. Malaysia will benefit from a ripple effect of economic development in surrounding countries, and a win-win relationship can be established. The third-country training was designed through discussions between CIAST, JICA, and the Malaysian Ministry of Foreign Affairs. Malaysia welcomes the fact that Japanese values, culture and ethics are reflected in the training. I think Malaysia's values include a culture of tolerance, multiculturalism, and mutual understanding. We are pleased if other countries learn something from our values. [MYS 01]

Azmi bin Ali has often travelled abroad to design training courses since the 1990s. The training style can be learnt from any country. Regarding the content, however, we should take into account country-specific contexts.

> When we work with the Japanese, the training content should meet JIS (Japanese Industrial Standards). For example, the way of using a saw is different. In Japan, you pull the saw to cut a board, but in Europe, you push the saw. It's just the opposite. And now we pull the saw …. JICA approached us, and we went to Bangladesh as part of a CIAST mission to give technical advice. Then, I went to Kabul, Afghanistan, to train trainers and develop curricula and teaching materials. Malaysia is a Muslim country, so it is certainly easier for us to work in other Muslim countries. [MYS 06]

Norman bin Muhamad, who is in charge of international cooperation at the Ministry of Foreign Affairs of Malaysia, initially worked for Kawasaki Steel before joining the Ministry of Foreign Affairs. He argued that, because Malaysia benefited from development assistance, the country was responsible for contributing back to the international community. 'When it comes to technology transfer, there are cases where Japanese technology is too advanced to be transferred directly to developing countries. Malaysia may act as a bridge' [MYS 07]. Suimi bin Abd Majid of the Department of Skills Development at CIAST has visited Cambodia, Laos, and Vietnam to propose courses to develop manufacturing in the Indochina countries. He has high hopes for a two-way training project using CIAST as a hub to send lecturers to these countries and invite trainers from these countries [MYS 08]. There has been a remarkable increase in the mobility of industrial human resources in Southeast Asia. In the future, it will be necessary to harmonise vocational qualifications regionwide (Japan Institute for Labour Policy and Training 2005).

Technical cooperation has a life cycle. Institutions that have garnered good results at home spread their wings abroad, and technologies that have reached a saturation point in the original country begin their next life elsewhere. In the 1930s, the Japanese economist Akamatsu Kaname conceived the so-called flying geese model, which has been refined and critiqued as a theorem that explained the dynamics of regionwide economic development in post-war East Asia (Akamatsu 1962; Bernard and Ravenhill 1995; Kojima 2000; Lin 2012). Individual birds are similar, and one of them happens to fly ahead of the pack. The second line reaches the head point, followed by the third line. The flock of birds flies on, and eventually, all birds perch on a tree and have a rest. Until then, the transfer of development experience will continue to play a vital role in ensuring a smooth flight of the group.

3.3 Deliberation before Decision-Making: Eastern Seaboard Development Project (Thailand)

3.3.1 Anti-Japanese Sentiment and Industrialisation in Asia

Thailand was at the centre of the anti-Japanese movement in Southeast Asia. Hoshino Masako, who later founded the Japanese NGO Japan International Volunteer Center (JVC), went to Laos in 1965 as one of the first batch members of the JOCV and, after working as a Japanese language teacher and serving for the Japanese Embassy in Laos, moved to Bangkok, Thailand, in 1971 to work for Japan Airlines (JAL). When I interviewed Hoshino as part of my interviews with JICA Volunteers (Chap. 4, Sect. 4.3), she told me an interesting story about her time in Thailand.

At the time, the Indochina peninsula was in the midst of liberation wars and civil wars. An accidental attack on a Japanese commercial airliner had to be avoided by all means. As a JAL employee, Hoshino's job was to contact the Vietnamese air traffic control authorities from Thailand by telephone and use her French language skill to obtain permission for passenger aircraft to fly over Vietnamese territory. At the time, 'pollution export' from Japan was reported in Thailand. As Hoshino recalled, 'students at prestigious universities like Chulalongkorn and Thammasat who were concerned about environmental issues raised their voices' [VOL 10]. After her professional work with Vietnam ended, Hoshino took on the unusual task of transporting rice to poor villages in northeastern Thailand and distributing it as Japanese aid. It was a public relations activity by JAL, which was a semi-government company at the time, to appease the local anti-Japanese sentiment. They hired a European advertising agency with expertise to run such a campaign. Eventually, Hoshino distanced herself from the government and moved into the NGO sector when she volunteered to help with Cambodian refugees in Thailand.

In the 1970s and 1980s, actors of Japan's development cooperation sought better ways to help boost Southeast Asian economies and contain deep-seated anti-Japanese sentiment in the region. As discussed in Section 3.2, vocational training in Malaysia was one example of such responses. Meanwhile, in the southeast of Bangkok, a large-scale infrastructure project known as the Eastern Seaboard Development Plan was taking shape step by step (Ogino 1989). Combining yen loans and technical cooperation, the plan aimed to build deep-water ports as a base for export-oriented manufacturing industries. At the time, in addition to the so-called four major industrial zones (*Keihin, Chukyo, Hanshin* and *Kitakyushu*), industrial complexes, factories and warehouses were being built along Japan's east-west Pacific Belt—*Keiyo, Kanto* Inland, *Tokai* and *Setouchi*—where rustic fishing and farming villages were being transformed into the bases for modern manufacturing. The idea was to apply this experience to the development in Thailand.

The development of the eastern seaboard region is centred on two ports (Fig. 3.2). One is the Map Ta Phut port in Rayong province, about 190 km away from Bangkok. In 1973, natural gas was discovered offshore in the southern Gulf of Thailand by the US company Unocal, and in 1978 another natural gas field was discovered. A 425-km underwater pipeline was designed to transport the gas to a chemical factory complex to process chemical fertiliser, etc. It was decided to construct a deep-water port at Map Ta Phut, where large ships could dock, and to level the ground for an industrial estate around the port. The industrial complex was to be one of the largest in Asia as a base for capital-intensive industries.

The other is Laem Chabang port in Chonburi province, which is closer to Bangkok. To the south of Bangkok, a river-based port at Khlong Toei has long been in operation, but the shallow water level of the river makes it difficult for large vessels to access this urban port, and its river-side land is too narrow to accommodate industrial facilities. The plan was, therefore, to build a deep-water commercial port at Laem Chabang, not too far from Bangkok, some 130 km away. The intention was to create an industrial estate around the container wharf at Laem Chabang to produce labour-intensive light industrial goods and to expand the complex to promote the export industry at large. By employing workers from rural villages in northern Thailand, it was hoped that employment opportunities concentrated in Bangkok would be diffused to other regions, helping to reduce regional disparities.[17]

While Malaysia's vocational training was a micro project of technology transfer, Thailand's eastern seaboard development was a macro project, beginning with the construction of the so-called *hakomono* (literally, the box-style stuff, indicating hard infrastructure). The enormous industrial parks were expected to attract domestic and foreign firms, including Japanese firms, with advanced technological capabilities. Technology transfer would be endogenous; given a certain level of labour discipline, the next stage would be to nurture micro-skills through on-the-job training within factories and firms. In retrospect, the Eastern Seaboard Development Plan can be seen as a textbook success story of cooperation in infrastructure development. However, the project faced a serious crisis in its formative years, when no one could foresee what the project would look like a few months later. At one point, the project had to be frozen due to external intervention, as discussed in the next section.

[17] The eastern seaboard region now comprises three provinces, including the province of Chachoengsao to the north (close to the Cambodian border to the east). At the southern end of Chonburi province is Sattahip Port, which is used by the Thai navy. This was originally a military port used by the US military during the Vietnam War and did not have a commercial function.

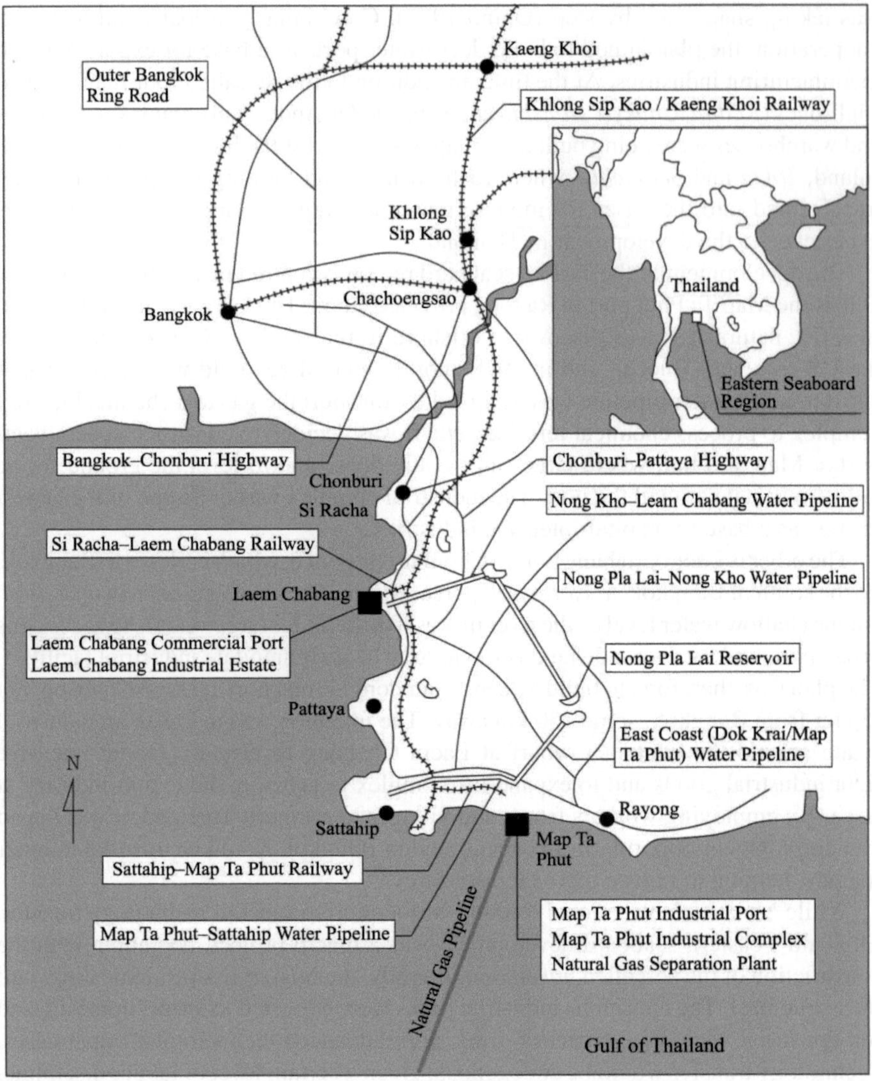

Fig. 3.2 Eastern Seaboard, Thailand. Source: Adapted from Yamada (2021: 145)

3.3.2 *Proponents and Opponents (1981–1985)*

The oil crisis of the 1970s was a major blow to non-oil-producing countries, including Thailand. The global recession led to a chronic balance of payments deficit as export prices of primary commodities (excluding energy sources) stagnated while import prices of manufactured products soared. At the time, the majority of Thailand's exports were agricultural food products, such as rice, natural rubber, and tin. There was an urgent need to upgrade the industrial structure and develop higher-value-added export industries. It also meant finding a way to consolidate Thailand's position as one of Asia's Newly Industrialising Economies (NIES).

Prime Minister Suzuki Zenko visited Thailand in January 1981, followed by a mission led by Okita Saburo in May. In exchange, Thai Prime Minister Prem Tinsulanonda visited Japan in October. On each occasion, the Japanese expressed their willingness to cooperate in the development of the eastern seaboard region, and by the end of the year, the Thai government formally announced its intention to embark on the development project for the region. The plan was included in the Fifth Five-Year Plan for 1982–1986, and various feasibility studies were conducted on the premise that substantial yen loans would be granted.[18] A natural gas pipeline was already completed in 1981, and a natural gas separation plant (to produce propane, LP gas, methane, ethane, gasoline, etc.) was constructed in Map Ta Phut in 1984, utilising yen loans. Originally, the eastern seaboard region was a relatively dry area with limited potential for rice cultivation. A lack of water for industrial use, drinking water, and field irrigation could hinder the overall development of the region. Therefore, from an early stage, emphasis was placed on providing a stable supply of water resources through a network of water pipes (JICA 1981c). For both Map Ta Phut and Laem Chabang ports, detailed studies were carried out on the development of infrastructure, including several industrial estates in the region (JICA 1982c; 1985c). The Eastern Seaboard Development Committee (ESDC), chaired by Prime Minister Prem, was established in the National Economic and Social Development Board (NESDB) as the government agency responsible for taking the plan forward. The first half of the 1980s saw the emergence of regional industrialisation plans, many of which seemed ready to take off.

In 1985, however, the project hit a major roadblock. As a result of a behind-the-scenes tug-of-war, in November of that year the Thai government announced a 'freeze' on the Eastern Seaboard Development Plan. This was principally due to the World Bank's opposition to the project. Shimomura Yasutami, then chief representative of the Overseas Economic Cooperation Fund (OECF) in Bangkok, witnessed, documented, and analysed this process at first hand.[19]

In the early 1980s, the World Bank and the International Monetary Fund (IMF) forced debtor countries in Asia, Africa and Latin America to undertake structural

[18] Before Laem Chabang was developed as a manufacturing base, an ASEAN-wide rock salt and soda ash project was planned. This was to transport rock salt by rail from northeastern Thailand, process it into soda ash (a raw material for glass and various other industrial inputs) at Laem Chabang, and export it to ASEAN countries (JICA 1981b). However, due to opposition from the neighbouring tourist resort of Pattaya, the proposed location of the plant was changed, and the project was eventually cancelled. A fertiliser plant using natural gas was also planned for Map Ta Phut, but the Thai government took no action about it.

[19] The following description in this section draws heavily on Shimomura (2017) (in Japanese). For English readers, Shimomura (2013) reconstructs the evolution of the project from the perspective of neo-institutionalist economics. Mieno (2013) reinterprets the project in terms of the regional development of industrial clusters. For an English summary of the main features of the Eastern Seaboard Development Plan, see: http://www.jsce.or.jp/e/archive/project/pj03.html.

adjustment programmes (SAPs). SAP loans were fast-track, non-project-based assistance to the developing countries that were struggling to repay their heavy debts, partly due to the high interest rates in the US at the time, and to restore their balance of payments deficits. The particular feature of this type of loan was that it encouraged, or rather coerced, a bold reform of the economic structure as a precondition for lending. Recipient countries were required to move away from *dirigiste* policies towards market-oriented policies, such as balancing public finances, rationalising public enterprises, privatisation, removing regulations and liberalising prices (see also the case of Tanzania in Chap. 2, Sect. 2.4). However, such conditionality tended to be a rigid, one-size-fits-all recipe that ignored the specific circumstances of each country. The SAP prescriptions did not consider the strategic promotion of long-term development projects or the dynamic creation of comparative advantages, as advocated by Japanese economists (Ishikawa 1990: Chap. 8; OECF 1992; Iida 1992; Ishikawa 1994; Goto 1996; Shimomura 2022: Chap. 8).

Faced with temporary deficits in the balance of payment, Thailand accepted SAP loans in 1982 and 1983, but by then the potential of the market economy had already been released in Thailand; the technocrats enjoyed autonomy in policy-making, the private sector was becoming more dynamic, and there were no restrictions on the activities of foreign (mainly Chinese) entrepreneurs. Therefore, the phase requiring a radical pro-market adjustment was supposed to be over in Thailand (Ishikawa 1990: 312). Nevertheless, the World Bank's prescription for Thailand during this period was as monotonous as those for other debtor nations; the priority was to curb borrowing and balance the fiscal and international accounts. The World Bank's message was: 'Don't take risks. There is little demand for industrial parks. Expanding the existing port in Bangkok, instead of building the Laem Chabang port, would suffice. Renovating the military port in Sattahip, instead of building the Map Ta Phut port, would suffice.' If a group of Washington-based experts removed the 'Hiding Hand' described in Chap. 1 (Sect. 1.3) and threatened local planners by saying, 'Are you really going to jump off a cliff?,' the planners would hold back and avoid taking serious risks.

The World Bank's representative in Bangkok, Quill Hermans, urged that the Thai Eastern Seaboard Development Plan be scrapped. Hermans was a South African-born economist. He held a senior position in the British Protectorate of Bechuanaland, became a citizen of the country when Botswana gained independence in 1965 and served as an adviser to Deputy President (later President) Quett Masire. In 1976, Hermans became the first governor of the Central Bank of Botswana before being seconded to the World Bank from 1977 to 1987 (Hudson 2018). As a diamond-rich, labour-scarce country, Botswana enjoyed abundant government revenues and achieved high growth with fiscal discipline. As *The East Asian Miracle* shows, the world's top leader in terms of GDP per capita growth between 1965 and 1985 was not an Asian country, but Botswana (World Bank 1993: 3). No matter how skilled an economist he was, it seems that he should not have applied the experience of a natural resource-rich African economy to a human resource-rich Asian economy. Thailand's comparative advantage at the time lay not in minerals but in (labour-intensive) industrial goods.

3.3.3 *Slow Decision-Making and Dramatic Growth (1986–1990s)*

At the end of 1985, the Thai government made a cabinet decision to 'maintain the framework' of the Eastern Seaboard Development Plan (in deference to the Japanese government) but to 'substantially delay' its implementation (in deference to the World Bank). At the time, supporters and critics within the Thai government were engaged in a heated behind-the-scenes debate. Proponents valued the impact of long-term development, while opponents were concerned about the short-term financial balance. At the same time, there was also a 'complex human drama in Thai leadership' (Shimomura 2017: 51). Prime Minister Prem came from the army, but according to Shimomura, politicians and the military were not much involved in the debate, while theoretical and professional discussions took place among educated technocrats in terms of economic calculation. It was also characteristic that the disagreements were not between organisations but between individuals within the organisation.

When Thailand was leaning towards a cautious approach, a major change came from an unexpected direction: the Plaza Accord of the autumn of 1985. Concerted intervention by the G5 countries led to a significant appreciation of the Japanese yen on the foreign exchange markets, making Japanese manufacturers uncompetitive in price and forcing them to relocate production bases overseas. Thailand's presence as a major destination of Japanese foreign direct investment (FDI) in Asia was bolstered by its political stability, the economic calibre of the ethnic Chinese, its solid infrastructure, and the fact that it had long sought export access to the Japanese market. While approved overall FDI in Thailand increased sixfold between 1986 and 1988, investment from Japan increased 12fold. In addition to labour-intensive industries, the expansion of large, high-tech factories producing electronics, electrical equipment, and transport machinery started to be discussed. SHARP Corporation moved to the suburbs of Bangkok, near the eastern seaboard region, and constructed a new factory. Thailand's industrial infrastructure was beginning to suffer shortages rather than excesses, as roads became congested, electricity was getting scarce, and container handling at ports could not keep up with the traffic. By the late 1980s, the headwinds against the Eastern Seaboard Development Plan had disappeared, and a strong tailwind began to blow (Shimomura 2017: Chap. 4).

Thus, the frozen Eastern Seaboard Development Plan was quickly thawed. In October 1986, it was decided to resume the project in Laem Chabang, and the commercial port became operational in 1991. An industrial park was created for 'non-polluting,' export-oriented, and labour-intensive industries, and all plots were sold by 1997. About 80% of the park was taken up by Japanese and Thai-Japanese joint ventures, including Mitsubishi Motors. Once the assembly plant was constructed, affiliated parts makers also moved in, creating robust industrial clusters. Map Ta Phut, meanwhile, was also making progress, with an industrial estate completed in 1990 and a large port in 1992. A number of petrochemical plants were also constructed. With Laem Chabang and Map Ta Phut as hubs, yen loans were also provided to build a network of railways and highways. From 1982 to 1993, the eastern seaboard absorbed 21.2% of the total yen loans to Thailand. The share of Eastern Seaboard in FDI Thailand accepted rose from 23% in 1991 to 75% in 1997, and 200 companies relocated from Greater Bangkok to the eastern seaboard region. The gross regional product per capita of the region was 2.6 times the national average and more than 80% of that of the Bangkok metropolitan area in 1995 (JBIC Project Development Department 2000; JICA and OECF 1999). All known Japanese automobile manufacturers have set up factories in the region, and the eastern seaboard has come to be dubbed the 'Detroit of the East'. Thailand's automobile production capacity exceeded one million vehicles per year in 2005 (Shimomura 2017: Chap. 5).

In retrospect, at the end of 1985, the Thai government adopted a deliberately ambiguous policy of keeping the Eastern Seaboard Development Plan floating and alive while postponing its implementation. It was a way of 'deciding when to launch the project without humiliating the Japanese government, and yet taking into account the World Bank's contention' (Yamada 2021: 146). As Shimomura indicated, the Thai attitude was 'not a mere postponement to gain time. There was a more positive intention, which was to make proponents and critics sit down and deepen their discussions,' and it aimed to 'sort out exactly which parts of the plan were feasible and which were not' (Shimomura 2017: 65–66).

Shimomura argued that Prime Minister Prem remained neutral and tried to make most of the collective wisdom of the technocrats to identify the problems. In the end, the Thai government decided to resume the overall plan to develop the eastern seaboard after assessing market trends. On the other hand, individual projects were implemented selectively by calculating their profitability, as seen in the cancellation of the Map Ta Phut fertiliser plant project, which had been supported by both the World Bank and Japan.

In the 1980s, mutual checks and balances seemed to work between the military, technocrats, political parties, and the business community in Thailand. If one's weaknesses were seized upon by the other, unfavourable information could be leaked to the mass media (Shimomura 2017: Chap. 6). The economist Amartya Sen argued for the instrumental value of democracy, taking examples of famines in South Asia and Africa. If a ruling party committed a grave mistake, such as failing to prevent a massive famine, the government would be severely criticised by the independent media, and the party would lose voter support and be defeated in the next election. As a consequence of ensuring media freedom, those in power are forced to pursue the right policies in order to survive (Sen 1999), and such a causality may have functioned in Thailand. The Thai government 'reviewed the content of the plan, the scale and timing of the investment, and made changes to the plan, including scaling down or postponing some where necessary, resulting in the scale and timing of the investment generally being within reasonable ranges' (JBIC Project Development Department 2000: 54).

So far, we have traced the dynamics of the eastern seaboard development based on a detailed study by Shimomura, who was part of the Japanese party himself. Thai policy-makers tried taming the development process autonomously while observing the directions the donors were taking. So how have these gigantic projects affected the ultimate beneficiaries, the grassroots people of Thailand? Towards the end of his project history, Shimomura shifted his focus from the bureaucrats to ordinary people and approached those living on the coast (Shimomura 2017: Chap. 7, Epilogue). In the following part of this section, I will attempt to continue Shimomura's work by presenting the voices of ordinary Thais.

3.3.4 Local Livelihoods and Environmental Concerns (1997)

Despite the COVID-19 pandemic, many Thai people, such as farmers, fishers, and workers, responded indirectly to my interviews.[20] It is generally accepted that the eastern seaboard development has multiplied employment opportunities, improved infrastructure, and raised people's incomes. When asking further questions, however, the remaining issues and hopes that the locals faced and harboured were revealed.

On the one hand, environmental activists from Rayong province, home to the Map Ta Phut heavy chemical plants, warned of environmental challenges. On the other hand, in Laem Chabang and the inland industrial estates, which are located in the broader eastern coastal region, pollution did not appear to be as much of a concern, even though air pollution from car congestion was a hot topic as in Bangkok. From the outset, the Laem Chabang Industrial Estate was designed to attract 'non-polluting' manufacturing industries (JICA and OECF 1999).

The focus of the pollution problem in the Eastern Seaboard has not been on manufacturing but on the petrochemical industry in Map Ta Phut. In June 1997, dozens of students and teachers at a secondary school were raced to hospital, and the school had to be relocated after a strange smell spread through the area. Several similar complaints led to a series of rulings by local and central administrative courts in 2009, which declared the area around the Map Ta Phut Industrial Estate a pollution control zone and issued injunctions to stop the launch of 76 new businesses. In May 2012, an explosion at a synthetic rubber factory killed 12 people, injured more than 100, and damaged many homes (Miyoshi 1999; Rackpanichamanee et al. 2016). Thailand's local government system is complex, and effective coordination of environmental policies across departments remains a challenge. Industrial estates are 'enclaves' that are not directly subject to environmental governance, and on-site inspections of factories are not easily conducted (Sato 2008; Funatsu 2013).

Ronnarong Thuamcharoen, who had worked at a petrochemical and steel factory in Map Ta Phut since the age of 22, had poor results in his medical check-up and was

[20] As the COVID-19 pandemic made my own field research impossible, the interviews in this section were conducted on my behalf by Uetsuji Hidenori who lives with his Thai family in Bangkok. After online discussions with me, Mr. Uetsuji travelled around the eastern seaboard region by car and motorbike from September to October 2021, conducting the interviews in Thai. Video footage of the interviews, photographs of the interviewees and their surroundings, and the map coordinates of the interview sites were provided so that I could 'walk' through the sites via Google Street View and imagine what was happening. It should be noted that the main interviewees were introduced by EARTH, a local environmental NGO, so the selection is not necessarily representative, but they are people who seriously engage in the future of their local communities and have their own opinions.

found to have chromosomal abnormalities at the age of 40. He took early retirement at the age of 42 after doctors told him they could not rule out chemical exposure as the cause of his illness. In the past, companies and governments were less concerned about workers' health. 'I used to work in a warehouse for raw materials such as plastics and iron. But they didn't give us safety equipment like dust masks, and I couldn't get medical check-ups as a benefit until I was 35' [THA 01]. Today, while his wife continues to work in the factory, he earns his living as a farmer, growing vegetables and fruits.

Chalermporn Klomkaew, from Rayong, used to work as a car mechanic in Kuwait but was forced to return home because of the Gulf War. Wanting to protect the natural environment of his homeland, he became involved in the environmental campaign. He saw plants dying and fish disappearing from coastal areas, particularly in Map Ta Phut. 'Near my home, for example, I feel that bees are disappearing and flowers are not blooming even when it rains' [THA 06]. Pinyo Srisutthi, who lives two kilometres from a petrochemical plant, said, 'There is a bad smell depending on the direction of the wind, and when it is quiet at night, you can hear the sound of the flares coming from the chimneys. The rainwater is undrinkable, and when it rains, it sometimes leaves stains on the plant leaves' [THA 02].

Pollution control involves latecomers' advantages. The technology for control devices such as filters and inspection equipment is advancing rapidly. We do not see the same pollution in the Thai eastern coastal areas in the 2020s as we witnessed in Japan in the 1970s—sludgy seas, foul odours in the rivers, and routine photochemical smog (see also Chap. 6, Sect. 6.3). Instead, the problem seems to be a lack of accurate information, which has led to growing mistrust among the population. Thuamcharoen insisted that workers and the local people have been relegated only to a secondary position in the process of economic development. 'This is clearly evidenced. Investors and their families would never want to live near Map Ta Phut' [THA 01]. Such perceptions may be a part of local reactions to the concentration of power in the hands of the people in Bangkok. For regional development to be sustainable, it is necessary to ensure that people can continue living in their hometowns and maintain links with traditional trading areas (Kitahara and Akagi eds. 1995).

With funding from the Toyota Foundation, a team from the Open Research Centre for Minamata Studies at Kumamoto Gakuen University once visited Map Ta Phut and tried to assess the actual state of environmental pollution with local activists. The method of sharing information about environmental and other risks and building mutual understanding among all parties involved is known as risk communication (Fischhoff 1995; Boholm 2011; Lundgren and McMakin 2018). It is a deliberative process involving all key stakeholders and differs from one-way, top-down public relations. However, there are few examples of risk communication in developing countries, and it was hoped that the Thai eastern seaboard area would serve as a model case (Nakachi 2009). Attempts were also made to support the establishment of a system to register pollutants emitted by factories and record their movements in Thailand (JICA 2016a). Shimomura noted that a lack of trust between the industry and the local people and NGOs in Map Ta Phut led to a 'long period of emotional tension' (Shimomura 2017: 117). In resolving local conflicts, it would be meaningful to repeat formal third-party evaluations such as Miyoshi (1999) and to share information regularly with the local community.

3.3.5 Broadening the Range of Choices

As Shimomura mentioned, the exclusion of Thai chicken, mangoes, and corn from the Japanese market was much discussed in Thai media in the 1970s (Shimomura 2020). In the twenty-first century, however, Thailand began to produce large numbers of Japanese-brand cars and export them from the Laem Chabang port to the rest of the world. The share of manufactured goods in Thai exports increased dramatically from 32.2% in 1980 to 81.5% in 1996 (JICA and OECF 1999). The establishment of a partnership between Japan and Thailand to capture the global market dynamics has successfully dissipated the deep-rooted anti-Japanese sentiment in Thailand (Shimomura 2020: Chap. 4).

The centre of gravity of growth industries in Thailand has shifted from agriculture and fisheries to labour-intensive and then knowledge-intensive sectors, and this process has been accompanied by a continuous migration of the labour force from rural to urban areas. Figure 3.3 shows the share of the rural population in several Southeast Asian countries and Japan. Thai society appears to be more resistant to urbanisation than Indonesia, positioned between Malaysia and Vietnam. While the dazzling attractiveness of metropolitan Bangkok is no different from that of Tokyo, Seoul, or Shanghai, about half of the Thai population resides in rural areas. In the 1980s, there was a debate among Thai policy-makers about becoming a Newly Agro-Industrialising Country (NAIC) rather than an upgraded member of the NIES. The idea was to achieve relatively slow income growth based not on high-tech manufacturing and heavy chemical industry but on agro-industry, i.e., agriculture, forestry, fisheries and other nature-based industries (Suehiro and Yasuda eds. 1987; Ichikawa et al. 1991). What characterises contemporary Thailand is the coexistence of the urban and the rural, and the assertiveness of each element. Expanding the range of choices and taking time to find a third way seems to be the Thai way of making decisions.

Many of the interviewees in the Eastern Seaboard region still have ties to farming and fishing. Pinyo Srisutthi, who lives in Map Ta Phut, worked in a factory after graduating from university, but at the age of 29 decided to take over his family's farming business. He thought that if he had left the land unattended, the soil would have become desolate, and he would not be able to restore the field back to its original state. He grew durian, mangosteen, rambutan, and natural rubber and employed four Cambodian workers.

> It was impossible for me to continue my life as a company employee, and after retirement, to take over farming back home. That was impractical because of physical weakness and lack of knowledge and experience. Considering these factors, I think it was a good decision to take over the farm when I was young. In addition, small agriculture is less affected by

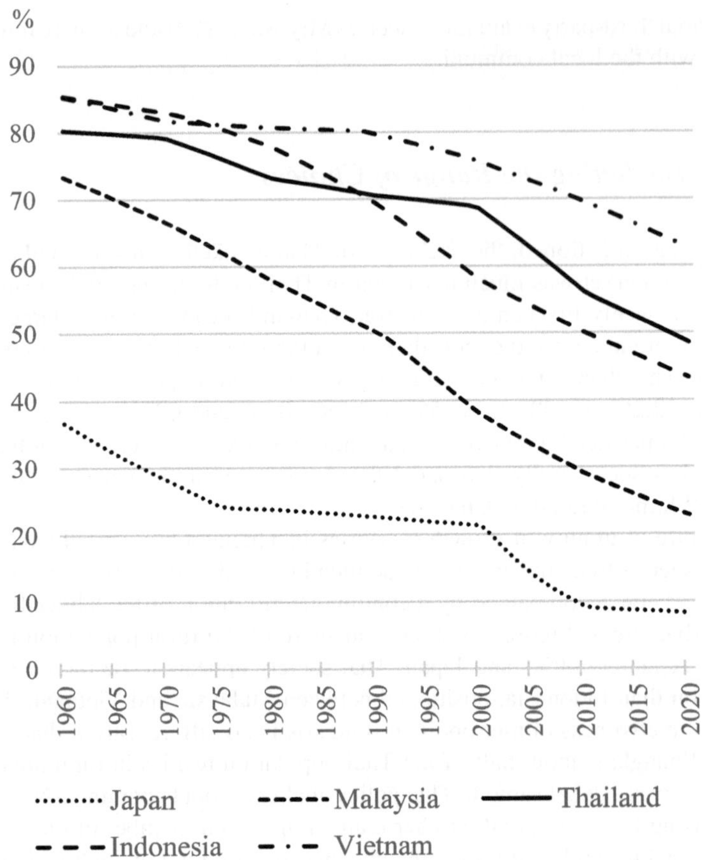

Fig. 3.3 Percentage of Rural Population in Several Asian Countries. Source: World Bank Data https://data.worldbank.org

> sudden changes, especially now that the COVID pandemic has stayed with us for so long. [THA 02]

Bancherd Ruangpon, a fisherman from Rayong, says his father is a Buddhist and his mother a Muslim, but 'I think any religion is fine because all teachings are important. Even Christianity is OK for me if the teaching is right.' At 67, he still goes fishing alone on a 7-metre boat. He continued:

> I think around 40-50% of fishermen of the same generation have given up. What do they do when they stop fishing? They become factory workers, or security guards, or work on construction sites. I'm proud of my job as a fisherman. I didn't want to be an employee or do a job I wasn't used to, so I continued fishing. I like going to sea, and I will go fishing as long as my body is fine. This is because being a fisherman is a job that I wanted, and to put it differently, I can only be a fisherman, nothing else. [THA 03]

A team of scholars at the Research Institute for Humanity and Nature (RIHN) has proposed the idea of 'area capability', which is to expand the range of livelihoods that people can choose, not as individuals but as a community. Local people are expected to steadily develop profitable livelihoods through trial and error while caring for the environment (Ishikawa and Watanabe eds. 2017). A good example is the fisheries in Rayong, Thailand. The approach is neither to promote a large-scale trawling method nor to advocate small-scale, household-based fishing. Japanese fishers and researchers are experimenting with a 'wait and see' fishery with set nets, modelled on the practice in Toyama, Japan, and are waiting to see how the fisher folk in Rayong will react: yes, no, or a third way (Arimoto et al. 2017).[21]

As factories were built, more and more people were employed and engaged in formal production work. Born into a poor farming family, Sawat Thamkonkar was adopted by a farmer in Pathumthani province and attended only four years of primary school. He moved to Laem Chabang, relying on his aunt-in-law, and worked as a day labourer in various jobs. He now works as a private transporter with his own small truck. He lives in a shack he built on the premises of the Laem Chabang Port Authority. 'It's illegal, maybe, but nobody chews me out.' His eldest son works for a subcontractor and lives nearby. 'My eldest daughter is married in Ayutthaya and works together with her husband in a big truck. When she comes nearby, she stops by.' He feels that when the industrial park was set up, more people from other provinces were hired than those who lived locally. 'When I hear stories from people who visited Japan, I wonder if I could also go and visit Japan. Uhuh…. That's a pipe dream!' [THA 07].

3.3.6 Working for Japanese Firms

Tawat Keethortet was born in the Pichit province of northern Thailand. After graduating from a local vocational school, he went to work for a Japanese-Thai joint company that manufactured automotive parts. Twenty years ago, he was transferred to the Laem Chabang branch factory, where he met his wife and has been working with her since then. His senior brother looks after the family's fields. 'I earn a decent salary with some benefits and overtime, and my wife also works for the same factory, so I think our income is sufficient. I'm happy with my job and the way they treat us. I have worked for this company for such a long time. This is because I am satisfied.' His wife's aunt in Buriram province takes care of their children so that he and his wife can concentrate on their work. When he retires, he plans to build an extra house on his land and live off the rental income. 'I have worked with many Japanese people, and some have been very open with me in private, even coming to my house for dinner. They have a lot of good ideas at work, and I greatly respect them [THA 08].

Samroeng Thaiwee, from Sukhothai province in northern Thailand, graduated from high school and worked for an automobile parts factory near Bangkok. He then joined a Japanese-Thai joint venture and was transferred to the Laem Chabang plant.

[21] JICA Hokuriku and Himi City collaborated on a three-year grassroots technical cooperation project from 2005 to train Thai fishers in set net fishing methods.

He also worked as a welder at a factory in Kawasaki City, Japan, from 1992 to 1994. 'I learnt a bit of Japanese during that time, and it was a good experience.'

> I am happy with my current salary because I also get benefits. My wife runs a small restaurant near the house, so combining the income from that, it's enough for us to get by, at least. I have worked for this company for 34 years, so I love this place. This company is like a family to me. But I will be retiring very soon. I want to continue working as a welder, but unfortunately, the company doesn't have an employment extension system, so I'm still wondering what I should do when I retire. I will probably help my wife in the restaurant. [THA 09]

Sitthisak Phiaia, a farmer from Nong Khai province bordering Laos, used to work as a welder in a factory near Bangkok, but when the factory moved, he returned home and helped with farming for a while. However, the income from the farm was unstable, so he asked his sister to take over the farm and came to the Eastern Seaboard region. He rode his motorbike around an industrial estate, found an advertisement for a job in a Japanese factory he had long dreamed of working for, and then applied. He failed but finally got the job on his third try. After his wife became pregnant with their second child and decided to concentrate on motherly duties, he worked overtime to make ends meet. He said:

> I only know Japanese people who work for the same company. As far as I know, in the past, managers and representatives of Japanese companies were sent to Thailand before they retired. I think they were from a generation with a lot of experience. I think they understood Thai people like us. But now, the managers are relatively young, around their 40s, and I don't think they know the local people very well. But we are the same Asians, so I think we have a lot in common. [THA 05]

Bunyuen Sukmai, who worked for a Japanese-owned foundry in an inland industrial estate, said that when he formed a trade union and became the leader, he was denied work and fired. The court did not find that he had been unfairly dismissed. But he obtained degrees in political science and law and now works as a lawyer specialising in labour disputes. 'I have worked with the Japanese for the past 20 years. The older generation respected the human rights of Thai workers, and I think they were reasonable people. My impression is that the younger people are preoccupied with results and profits and often demand too much of us.' In the early days of the development of the Eastern Seaboard region, incomes were higher and more stable in factories than in agriculture. However, 'recently, a lot of Chinese-owned companies have started investing in this area. I think their way of thinking is outdated, and there are some problems with labour rights' [THA 04].

It is likely that the Japanese who spent time in Thailand during the period of the anti-Japanese movement, especially those who assumed responsible positions, carefully controlled their behaviour, knowing that they were not always welcomed in Southeast Asian countries.

After the radical changes in the investment climate of the mid-1980s and the Asian economic crisis of the late 1990s, the Eastern Seaboard region appears to be at a third turning point in the 2020s. The focus of Thailand's growth industries is shifting from traditional manufacturing to next-generation vehicles, robotics and digital industries, as well as medical tourism, ecology and natural foods. With the prospect of regional development involving neighbouring countries such as Cambodia, Laos and Myanmar, as well as investment from Chinese companies, which now have a colossal presence replacing Japanese firms, the environment surrounding the Eastern Seaboard region—now often referred to as the Eastern Economic Corridor (EEC) as part of a broader development framework with Thailand being its hub—is undergoing radical change (Suehiro 2014; 2018). As we expect to enter the period of infrastructure renewal in Thailand, it is crucial to look back at the history of development cooperation in infrastructure building, which abounds in practical lessons.

3.4 Disseminating *Kaizen:* Advocacy for Industrial Development (Costa Rica)

3.4.1 War and Peace

Japan provided support to Asian countries in their quest for industrialisation in various ways, but there was some restraint or modesty. The anti-Japanese movements in Southeast Asia in the 1970s reminded the Japanese that Asian people did not forget the war. It was against this background that the Fukuda Doctrine of 1977 promised that Japan would never again be a military power and would establish a 'heart-to-heart' relationship with the nations of Southeast Asia. In places outside Asia, however, Japanese development cooperation unfolded in slightly different contexts. In countries geographically distant from Asia and not directly engaged in World War II, people have little negative personal memory. In the 1970s and 1980s, Japan was the only developed country that sustained substantial economic growth. In places outside Asia, the success of the Japanese economy, along with the global reputation of brand companies such as Toyota and Sony, was largely an object of curiosity.

Central America, the region discussed in this section, has a character of this kind. Located between the Atlantic and the Pacific Ocean, the countries of Central America endured devastating civil wars in the 1980s against the backdrop of the Cold War. In Nicaragua, the Sandinista revolution in 1979 brought in a left-leaning government, but pro-US right-wing guerrillas known as the Contras established military bases in neighbouring Honduras and Costa Rica in an attempt to overthrow the regime. In El Salvador, civil war between the state military apparatus and left-wing guerrilla groups escalated. Civil war also persisted in Guatemala, where the majority of the population were indigenous Maya. While socialist Cuba remained defiant, the countries of Central America could not afford to ignore the wishes of the powerful US, which did not hesitate to intervene militarily in its backyard.

In the 1980s, despite differences in regime and historical circumstances, there was strong momentum in Central America to achieve peace in the region through internal initiatives. The result was the Esquipulas II Accord signed at a meeting of the presidents of the five Central American countries in Guatemala in August 1987. Costa Rican President Óscar Arias, known for his strategic and principled pacifism, drafted this epoch-making, comprehensive agreement. Then, as early as the following September, Japanese Foreign Minister Kuranari Tadashi paid an official visit to Guatemala and delivered a speech in support of the peace process. In his memoirs, Kuranari looked back on this visit to Central America and argued that, citing the writings of French anthropologist Pierre Clastres (1974), native Americans in the rainforest resisted the emergence of centralised state power while maintaining social prosperity. When the West introduced statehood in the sixteenth century, the indigenous people were threatened with extinction, and the pre-Hispanic culture sank into the basement. Kuranari was born in pre-war Nagasaki City. The empathy with the defeated rather than the winners was shared by many Japanese of Kuranari's generation, who experienced World War II, irrespective of political creed (Kuranari 1988: 95–110).

Kuranari's personal enthusiasm was genuine, but there were also political factors behind the proactive Japanese attitude in supporting the peace process in Central America (Hosono 1990). The US unequivocally supported anti-communist forces in the region but could not take control of the entire region. It needed to involve supposedly neutral mediating forces in the peace negotiations without risking the balance tilting to the left. Therefore, involving actors such as the World Bank and Japan—whose attitudes towards the best way of development were fraught with tension, especially in the late 1980s, as we saw in Section 3.3—in the post-conflict economic reconstruction was considered effective. What, then, could Japan offer to Central America? This is where the agenda of industrial human resources development attracted attention. The economies of Central America were dependent on exports of primary commodities such as bananas, coffee, sugar, cotton and meat, and in the 1980s most countries suffered debt, budget deficits and serious inflation. Therefore, the region sought to promote exports of higher-value-added industrial products and get back on a growth trajectory, and human resources development was proposed for this purpose. For several countries in the region with higher levels of education, it was considered possible to apply the ASEAN way of human resources development. In the long term, it would have been expected that the region would become part of the Asia-Pacific economy.[22]

3.4.2 *Contribution to Human Resources Development in Central America (1987–1988)*

During his visit to Guatemala in 1987, Kuranari stated that once peace was achieved in Central America, Japan would contribute as much as possible to the reconstruction and development of the region. He expressed the idea that Japan would support

[22] In Japanese, Hosono (1995) presented a comprehensive research framework to understand Asia-Pacific Economic Cooperation (APEC) and regional cooperation in the Americas, including Central America. One of the first major overseas expansions of the Japanese spinning industry in the post-war period was the operation of Kureha Spinning in El Salvador in 1955 (Tanaka 1997: Chap. 7).

a development framework for the entire Central American region, rather than a specific country, so that peace would be consolidated and all Central American countries could unite by benefiting from the development initiative. In line with this proposal, the 'Seminar on Human Resources Development in Central America' was held in Tokyo in March 1988. A total of ten delegates (a director-general and an academic expert from each country) representing five countries—Costa Rica, El Salvador, Guatemala, Honduras and Nicaragua—were invited[23] to attend the seminar with their Japanese counterparts at the newly constructed JICA Ichigaya Building. Central America was the second regional unit, after Southeast Asia (Sect. 3.2), to receive Japanese assistance in human resources development through the framework of regional cooperation.

The seminar began with a commemorative address by Nagai Michio, Japan's former education minister and special adviser to the United Nations University in Tokyo. Nagai emphasised that Japan's modernisation was a process of democratising its social system, while preserving its traditional culture, by absorbing lessons from the West independently and selectively. Nagai argued, 'From this perspective, the Meiji Restoration should be added to the American, French, Russian, and Chinese revolutions, which are considered turning points in world history.' Drawing on his own experience in Mexico, he articulated his vision of a mutual understanding between Japan and Latin America that harbours 'a mixture of the civilisation of the Indigena that is to be revived, the Spanish civilisation that is to be preserved, and the Western civilisation that is to be oriented towards innovation.' (JICA 1988: 12). Nagai confidently declared that it was great to be a 'spiritual mestizo' and called for a version of modernisation that would retain non-Western cultural elements. Even though his historical perspective may have perplexed some participants, his provocative message seems to have given depth to the discussion.

The overarching theme of the seminar was economic development and human resources development. Economic development was necessary for peace to take root, and this required the expansion of manufacturing throughout the region, for which the development of industrial human resources was considered essential. Hosono Akio, associate professor at the University of Tsukuba, who gave the lead-off speech at the session for the director generals of the participant countries, noted that *hito zukuri* (human development) and 'human resources development' were two similar but different concepts. 'The term human resources development means that human beings are utilised as resources for development, similar to natural resources and capital. However, our talk about *hito-zukuri* is about the development of human persons with hearts and faces, those with individuality and autonomy. Therefore, it must be said that the word *hito-zukuri* does not at all mean that human beings are mere parts of production machines.' Hosono maintained that *hito-zukuri* required

[23] Central America includes Belize (English-speaking) and Panama, which hosts the US-controlled Panama Canal. These countries also participated in the later phase of the third-country training for the region.

'nurturing humans as comprehensive beings' (ibid. 32). His statement foreshadowed the human development paradigm advocated by the United Nations Development Programme (UNDP), which emphasised that human beings are not a means to economic development but an end in themselves. Human development is the process of expanding the range of people's choices so that they can live lives they value (UNDP 1990; Fukuda-Parr and Kumar 2009).

Hosono further stressed the importance of combining the best aspects of economic planning and market mechanisms. In Central America, intellectuals associated with the so-called Chicago School favoured laissez-faire market principles, while those influenced by socialist thinking in Cuba and the Soviet Union favoured a planned economy. Addressing representatives of nations torn apart by prolonged conflicts, Hosono argued that both ways of thinking were necessary and proposed the diffusion of micro-level practices such as OJT and the QC circle to raise productivity (ibid. 33–34). The idea that neither the right nor the left should deny the thinking of the other camp outright was necessary to make regional cooperation take off in Central America.

At the seminar, representatives from the five Central American countries presented their current situations and participated in honest discussions. While Japan provided bilateral assistance to individual countries, it was thought to be necessary to establish a solid base in a certain country from which technology could be transferred regionwide, using such schemes as the third country training. So which country was the most appropriate? The obvious choice was Costa Rica. In the wake of a civil war, Costa Rica abolished its army in 1948, enshrined this principle as a permanent decision in the constitution in 1949, and has played a key role as a mediator in conflicts throughout the region, appealing to the human rights norms the US prioritised, and at the same time declaring 'Perpetual, Active, and Unarmed Neutrality' in 1983 (Lipton and Barash 2019: 65). Costa Rica was by far the most stable society in Central America with a high level of education and a well-developed infrastructure. The country's status was enhanced by the fact that President Arias, who espoused a moderate social democratic creed, was awarded the Nobel Peace Prize in 1987 for his contribution to the peace process.

3.4.3 Costa Rica as a Regional Hub (1989–1992)

Following the seminar in Tokyo, a project formulation study was carried out between 1988 and 1989, after which the government of Costa Rica formally requested grants-in-aid and project-type technical cooperation. Just as the project to establish a regional centre for human resources development in Costa Rica was beginning to take off, something unexpected happened. Arias lost the election in February 1990, and Rafael Ángel Calderón Fournier of the centre-right Christian Social Unity Party was elected president. In any country, a new administration can leave the projects of the former government in limbo or even attempt to destroy them. So, I visited the home of Marvin Herrera Araya, who served as education minister in the post-Arias government, and asked him what happened to the project. He explained that the new government was working hard to ensure that the commitment of the Japanese side would not be lost despite the power shift [CRI 08].

Herrera explained that, when the government changed, the Japanese mission came to Costa Rica to see if the new administration wanted to continue receiving Japanese assistance. During the previous Arias administration, establishing a human resources development centre had been put on the agenda, but a decision had yet to be made on where it would be built. The Japanese mission apparently indicated that the aid might shift to Guatemala if the new Costa Rican government was no longer interested in the project. Against this backdrop, Herrera's first task was to find an appropriate construction site to show the commitment of the new government. He identified a space in Alajuela, in a suburb of the capital, San José, where the international airport is located. The site was owned by the Alajuela University College (CUNA: Colegio Universitario de Alajuela). The Ministry of Education began to take charge of this project not only because the proposed site happened to be an educational college but also because the Alajuela University College had a track record as a community college, providing two years of practical training for high school graduates, as well as hands-on training for technicians in companies and factories.[24] Although the technology transfer of the new centre was aimed at the business community rather than at students, the contents of what they were supposed to teach were similar. Moreover, from a practical point of view, the legal settings of tertiary education could easily be adapted to create the centre. Herrera recalled:

> Signatures were exchanged with the Japanese side in November 1990. And in January 1991, I went to Tokyo as a witness to ensure that the Japanese government's money was spent properly. This surprised me, because in Costa Rica, we don't go that far to check how public money is spent. I found that there were tenders and bids, and the budget was strictly managed. Everything was appropriate. [CRI 08]

Kajima Corporation began operations, and in March 1993 the construction of the building of the Centre for the Training of Trainers and Technical Personnel for the Industrial Development of Central America (CEFOF) was completed with grant funding. The latest equipment, including inspection machines, information equipment, and a library system, was brought in (JICA 1991c). Arlette Jiménez Silva, who has been working for CEFOF since then, confided that she was initially worried about being interviewed in a shabby place, but when she saw the brand-new building, she thought that this was where she had to work. CEFOF's equipment was state of the art, including an electronic blackboard, which was very rare in the 1990s and is still in use today [CRI 03].

[24] The fact that the tertiary institution gives formal qualifications to worker-students was expected to lower the barrier between the professional engineers and the machine operators (JICA 1990a: 9).

3.4.4 CEFOF'S Take-off (1992–1997)

CEFOF consisted of the department of quality and production control in food processing, textiles and clothing, and industry in general and the department for information processing. In the area of information technology, as early as in the 1990s Costa Rica was trying to provide personal computers in primary schools, and private computer literacy schools were mushrooming in major cities. CEFOF, therefore, aimed to train more advanced programming and systems engineers (JICA 1990a). In the first edition of UNDP's *Human Development Report,* Costa Rica was ranked high on the Human Development Index (HDI), better than South Korea and Singapore (UNDP 1990). Nevertheless, Costa Rica was identified as a recipient of Japan's assistance because of the expected spillover effects to other countries in the region.

CEFOF was launched in September 1992 in the middle of the construction of the building, and the project was to run for five years. According to the final evaluation report, 'In the first half of the project, the schedule tended to be delayed due to the dearth of local counterparts, differences in approach among [Japanese] experts and a lack of basic awareness of the industrial situation in Costa Rica among them.... but we recovered the loss in the second half, and the technology transfer went well' (JICA 1997a: 1). By the time of the final evaluation in 1997, 16 long-term experts had been dispatched from Japan, a total of 4546 people had participated in CEFOF seminars and courses, mainly from private companies, and many business enterprises had cooperated in the field training. Touring seminars were also held in various countries in the region. However, the retention rate of CEFOF staff was low. While 49 people worked for CEFOF initially, 18 left within five years. CEFOF had been under the jurisdiction of the Ministry of Education but was transferred to the Ministry of Science and Technology in 1994 (ibid.).

While the description in the final evaluation document was objective and prosaic, the interviews revealed the nuances of what happened. Enrique González Villalobos, a long-time staff member, said that the Costa Rican boss in the early years was 'someone who didn't even know what CEFOF was supposed to do', and the only thing the new staff were told was that 'if you join us, you can go to Japan.' As civil servants, they received ministry-level salaries, but as their skills improved, they naturally wanted to move for the private sector. Ironically, while sustaining *kaizen* in the workplace is critically important, the staff members did not sustain themselves and left one by one. Nor were the experts from Japan willing to create teamwork, secluding themselves in the 'three islands' of food, textiles and metals. As Villalobos witnessed, however, the government began to focus more on CEFOF, and the consultation with companies became more active in due course [CRI 02].

José Arce Brenes, who moved from CEFOF to the Ministry of Economy and Industry, recalled that CEFOF's work in the 1990s was truly pioneering. 'The idea of upending the hierarchical relationships between management and the factory floor was very unique' [CRI 01]. The fact is that most parts of the Japanese management models, without bothering to call it 'Japanese', are already embedded in Western management practices, such as Motorola's Six Sigma, the statistical quality management method in the US. Arce, however, drew attention to the aspect that *kaizen* had emerged from Japanese culture and brought 'creative destruction' to the Costa Rican work environment.

> Costa Rica and Japan have very different cultures. We've tried to follow, well, 90% of the Japanese method, while adapting the remaining 10% to fit the local context. In Latin America, there's a strong tradition of top-down decision-making. The gap between management and the shop floor is huge, and we felt it was important to bridge that divide. Top management in Latin America is quick to embrace *kaizen,* but only in theory. Honestly speaking, it is just a surface level. There's no real culture here that empowers factory workers to make decisions or take ownership of their tasks. So, what can we do about it? We have learnt that developing middle managers – the ones who directly oversee the shop floor – is the key. This way, we have tried to create more opportunities for self-determination in the workplace. [CRI 01]

This reminds us of the argument of Imai Masaaki, the early proponent of *kaizen.* Imai contrasted Japanese *kaizen* with Western innovation (Imai 1986; Imai 1997). Western companies emphasise innovation, which is result-oriented and requires rapid change, while workers are expected to maintain the system passively. If these two worlds stay unconnected, technological innovation will not trickle down, and the products that customers receive may not change in price and quality. This is where *kaizen* comes in, to bring about change in the middle ground between the two separate worlds. Rather than simply maintaining once-established standards, those who know the shop floor, be they workers, supervisors, or engineers, pool their wisdom, introduce new standards to the production sites, reduce waste, and start producing more and better goods at lower cost. Both the firm and the workers share in the fruits of better outcomes. As shown in Fig. 3.4, *kaizen* takes place in a space between management and workers, where workers make suggestions and management listens. In Costa Rican companies, 'workplace hierarchies are very tight, and the teamwork is lacking' [CRI 06]. It seems that Costa Rican companies have a more 'Western' orientation than European and US companies, so a conscious effort was needed to strengthen this very middle ground.

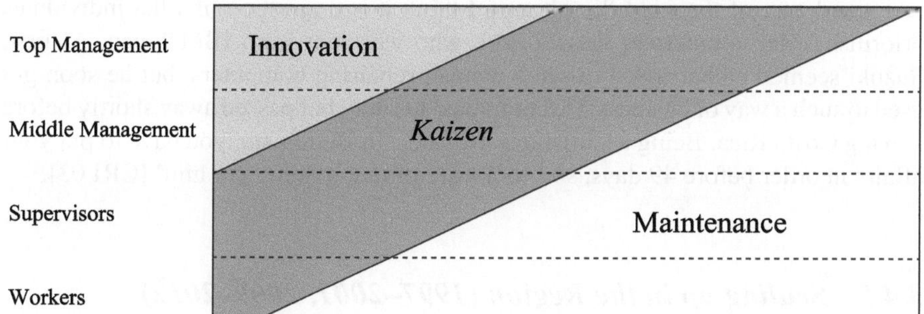

Fig. 3.4 Kaizen and Job Functions. Source: Imai (1986: 7)

According to Hazel Rojas García, director of CECAPRO-UTN (CEFOF's successor institution), the localisation of external practices is called 'tropicalisation' in Costa Rica. As part of *kaizen,* there is a system of spontaneous suggestions for improvements by employees. Initially, they were asked to write down their suggestions and put them in a box, but nobody was interested and dared to open the box and analyse them. So, in Costa Rica, they started asking people to speak out at meetings and make direct suggestions. Once workers began to give their ideas in those meetings, they competed with each other to express their opinions. It was also important not to complicate the methodology. No one will follow you when you instruct people to do too many things at once. *Kaizen* activities must be implemented step by step. It is important to teach them in a practical and flexible way [CRI 09].

As the Japanese and Costa Rican staff worked together to visit companies, teach *kaizen* methods, and invite workers to training sessions, relationships of trust between Costa Ricans and Japanese seem to have grown and matured. Luigi Longhi Córdoba said, 'We had 54 staff members from both countries working and eating together all the time, so we became a united team.' The Japanese experts wanted to get into the company's finances, which was very difficult in Costa Rica. 'So our policy was to start by teaching management techniques and then touch some of the finances as far as possible' [CRI 04]. Gregorio Arce Gómez learnt from Japanese experts practical ways of 'acting together, having conversations, and then providing suggestions'. The experts began by asking, 'Do you only want to hear good things, or do you want to know the truth?' However, 'I feel that the Japanese way of working is a bit too rigid compared to Latin American culture. For example, if there is a written notice on paper, the Japanese try to do what is written, even if it doesn't fit the reality' [CRI 06].

Arlette Jiménez, who was in charge of information processing, recalled that the first phase of the project was marked by a sense of pride held by both sides. She went to Japan for training in 1994. While she was impressed by the discipline and punctuality of the Japanese people, she also commented, 'I thought Japan was a technological superpower, but I was surprised to see an old lady sweeping the streets with a broom. I have the latest Samsung smartphone, but my Japanese friends still take good care of their old flip phones. I think it is a question of what individuals prioritise.' Her counterpart was Suzuki, who was sent from IBM Japan. At first, Suzuki seemed embarrassed to see a woman repairing computers, but he soon got used to such a way of business. He completed his duty but passed away shortly before leaving Costa Rica. Being a Christian, she said, 'In Buddhism, you have to put your affairs in order before 49 days, so I took care of many things for him' [CRI 03].

3.4.5 Scaling up in the Region (1997–2001, 2009–2012)

The first development cooperation project that engaged in *kaizen* was the human resources development cooperation project in Singapore in 1983 (JICA 1990b). Since the activities of CIAST in Malaysia (Sect. 3.2) were concerned with the transfer of production technology and did not prioritise the institutional and organisational aspects, the project in Costa Rica could be considered a direct successor to the one in Singapore, even though the term *kaizen* did not appear very often in the reports on CEFOF. *Kaizen* is a generic term for a set of methods that involve everyone in a factory, from the shop floor to the management, taking the suggestions of all employees seriously and working tirelessly to improve productivity and quality. There are various methods, including Total Quality Control (TQC), QC Circles, 5S (Sort, Straighten, Shine, Standardise, Sustain), PDCA (Plan, Do, Check, Act) cycle, Just in Time, etc.[25]

As we saw at the beginning of this section, the CEFOF project was designed to contribute to peace through economic development in Central America. Therefore, it included a dimension of regional cooperation from the outset (Fig. 3.5). As it started as project-type technical cooperation, bilateral cooperation between Japan and Costa Rica continued during the first five years (although CEFOF organised several on-site training events for other Central American countries during this period). This was followed by the CEFOF-based third-country training, combining lectures and factory visits, for two weeks each year from 1997 to 2001 (JICA 2000a). Then, from 2009 to 2012, a broader project was implemented in the Central American region to train facilitators for quality control in small and medium-sized enterprises (SMEs), primarily targeting officials of SME-related public institutions in the region, combining training in Costa Rica with on-the-job training in each country (JICA 2014). Ex-post empirical studies showed that workers' confidence was strengthened and working conditions improved in companies that participated in the *kaizen* projects. However, workers tended to take longer than management to accept the *kaizen* practices positively (Shimada and Sonobe 2018). In promoting regional cooperation, support was sometimes provided by the Inter-American Development Bank (IDB) to bridge gaps between different phases of JICA support. Taiwan also provided support through the Ministry of Economy, Industry, and Commerce of Costa Rica.

When communicating *kaizen* in other countries, the 5S slogan was often utilised as the most convenient and straightforward technique to get people involved. According to Enrique González, 'sort', 'straighten' and 'shine' are relatively easy to address, and the level of 'standardise' (original Japanese is *seiketsu* [cleanliness]) could also be gradually enhanced. 'However, we faced mixed reactions to "sustain" (original Japanese is *shitsuke* [discipline]). It is necessary to stay motivated, strengthen self-discipline, and improve mental attitudes to sustain the process. But I think this element is particularly challenging in Latin America.' [CRI 02] As Longhi indicated, the

[25] In a sense, *kaizen* is a Western method that was given a Japanese flavour and made into a simple motto; the marketing gimmick of the concept presented by Imai (1986) was brilliant. An interesting interpretation of the origins of *kaizen* in Japan is found in Shimada (2018; 2024). Shimada pointed out that there was a dual purpose of *kaizen:* to improve efficiency and to protect workers. The Japan Association of Corporate Executives (*Keizai Doyukai*), which brought together a group of relatively young entrepreneurs, played an essential role in introducing *kaizen.* There was also a political aim to keep the Japanese trade union movement in the Western camp, which was in line with a US strategy. There is a clear element of worker protection in *kaizen,* which is not recognised properly even by Japanese.

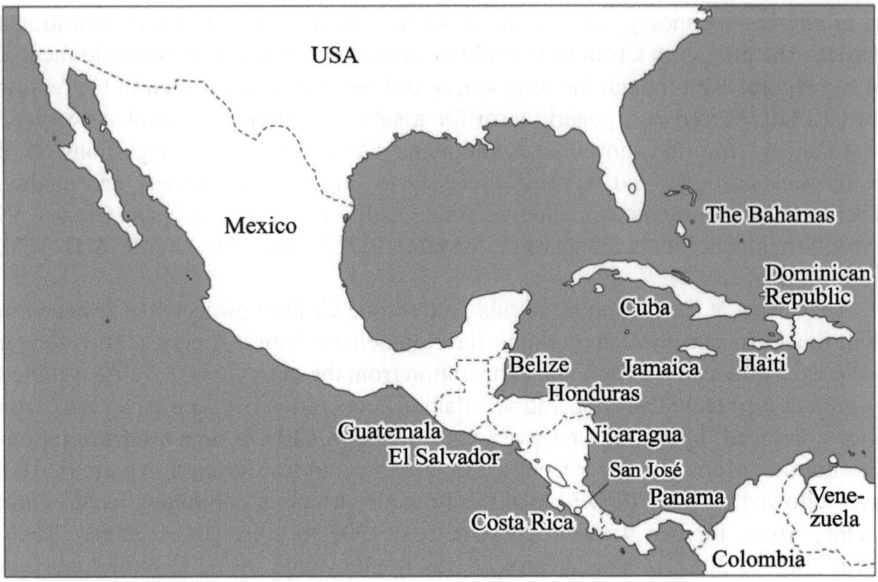

Fig. 3.5 Central America. Source: Author

reactions varied from country to country in the region. 'People in El Salvador try to accept and absorb everything. People in the Dominican Republic are less accepting and quick to ask questions.' On the last day of the field training, a gift to the organising staff from Dominican counterparts was accompanied by a card with the message: 'You were like tigers (you did a wonderful job)' [CRI 04].[26]

There was growing public opinion in Costa Rica that the country should focus on its own development first, rather than making sacrifices for neighbouring countries. Against such currents, CEFOF's long-standing staff members took responsibility for specific countries, visiting them sometimes with Japanese experts, and giving guidance on the 5S and other methods. In line with local efforts, the Japanese side developed a comprehensive aid strategy for the region: providing assistance to Guatemala for Chagas disease control, to El Salvador for police support and waste management, to Honduras for mathematics education, to Nicaragua for reproductive health, to Costa Rica for productivity improvement and support for judicial reform, to Panama for disaster management, and to the Dominican Republic for medical education. In this way, a division of labour for regionwide technology transfer took shape.[27] Each country developed its areas of expertise and learnt from the others

[26] The Dominican Republic occupies the eastern part of the island of Hispaniola, the second largest island in the Caribbean after the main island of Cuba, and borders Haiti. While there may have been a strategy to extend regional cooperation in Central America to the Caribbean, Dominica is also a country where Japanese migrants settled under difficult conditions. See also Chap. 6 (Sect. 6.2).

[27] In 2005, Prime Minister Koizumi Junichiro and delegates from the member states of the Central American Integration System (Sistema de la Integración Centroamericana: SICA) (Costa Rica, El

where they are lagging behind. The long-term goal, of course, was to eliminate the need for such division of labour through technology diffusion.

3.4.6 Organisational Restructuring (2001)

Marvin Herrera García, who was trained at UNITICA, a Japanese textile and chemical company, and took charge of the textile section of CEFOF, reflected on his past experience. 'The support from the Costa Rican government was not consistent. When the president and the ruling party changed, a symbolic project of the former administration could become a scapegoat'. Even so, he added, the fact that many staff members left CEFOF should not necessarily be seen in a negative light. 'Since what they learnt at CEFOF was so unique, they thought they could offer services based on it to business firms. Those people picked up what they learnt here and shared it with the outside world. It's cool' [CRI 07]. If the technology transfer was completed early and the employees went out as '*kaizen* evangelists', the low retention rate would actually mean that the project was successful.[28] Zianne Ramírez Arias, who started as secretary to the director of CEFOF and became a consultant, remarked, 'I worked with the Japanese experts from the 1990s until about 2005. It was a great time.' Eleven staff members were certified as management consultants by the Japan Productivity Center (JPC), and 'That gave us credibility in the market' [CRI 05].

Between 2001 and 2006, a series of productivity-enhancing projects were conducted throughout Costa Rica. CEFOF was involved in both national and regional projects. In 2009, however, it became part of the newly established National Technical University (UTN: Universidad Técnica Nacional) and changed its name to the Quality and Productivity Centre (CECAPRO: Centro de Calidad y Productividad). Many interviewees complained that the university did not understand the historical context and the unique value of CEFOF, as its staff members were transferred to

Salvador, Guatemala, Honduras, Nicaragua, and Panama) and the SICA associate member state (the Dominican Republic) agreed on the Tokyo Declaration. https://japan.kantei.go.jp/koizumispeech/2005/08/18press_e.html and https://www.mofa.go.jp/mofaj/area/latinamerica/j_latin05/pdfs/k_keikaku.pdf.

[28] According to a Japanese report on the first phase, 'the relationship between the leavers and CEFOF itself is good. An alumni association has been organised for mutual stimulation and collaboration through information exchange' (JICA 1997a: 19). Another, more detailed assessment was made at a later stage. 'This interim evaluation has confirmed the fact that competent counterparts shifted the jobs. However, it has become clear that they maintain their relationships with CEFOF as external consultants (based on the subcontractor method) even after they have left. Now, the question we should answer is how to evaluate the contribution of those consultants who carry out the work of CEFOF [outside CEFOF] from the viewpoint of self-help support. How to retain counterparts [in public agencies] is an old and new issue in technical cooperation, but it may be worth looking at this question from a slightly different perspective than before' (JICA 2003: 13). The case of Chilean salmon farming in Chap. 2 is another example in which counterparts left the home organisation and made a significant contribution to achieving the original objectives. The interviewees differed on which administrations in Costa Rica were particularly (un)favourable to CEFOF.

other organisations in the university, and its building began to be used by other departments. It is nonetheless true that the management has stabilised with institutional backing from a national university. CECAPRO continues to focus on extension activities that link the university to the business community, offering evening classes and consultancy services for firms.

At the end of my stay, I had the opportunity to visit several factories in Costa Rica. Ilex, a major detergent and food processing company, has a factory in Cartago on the outskirts of San José, where the 97-year-old owner agreed to start the *kaizen* campaign. Once it was launched, the *kaizen* practice received constant criticism from above, but it took root because the middle management got behind it. Even now, new employees are trained in the 6S (5S plus 'Seguridad: Security'). Although some workers resisted, questioning why they had to do things outside their formal duties, the 6S-based evaluation activities were eventually accepted, and both new and old employees were accustomed to doing the cleaning together [CRI 10; CRI 11; CRI 12].

Roma Prince, which has a factory in Alajuela, produces pasta for markets throughout Central America. The factory has been automated since the 1980s and now employs about 150 people. The company has been working with CEFOF since 2001 on *kaizen* for middle management and machine operators. Teams walk along the production line with digital cameras to identify problems, make dirty areas clean, and repair broken parts [CRI 13]. Senior workers look after junior workers and play football together, so that closer communication among workers ensures safety in the workplace [CRI 14]. One young worker, Andrés Jiménez Quiros, faced financial problems in his family, was forced to drop out of secondary school, and started working for Roma Prince. He has since worked his way through high school and is now studying production engineering at university. After working as an operator, he now measures the temperature of machines and the weight of products. He said he had loved machines since he was a child. 'I am proud of my company, and when a machine breaks down, it hurts me. I feel like the machine is myself' [CRI 15].

The new machinery and equipment installed at the Roma Prince factory showed that the pasta was processed on a fully automated line with almost no human intervention required until the final product was packaged. It is as if the whole factory was one machine. However, a limited number of skilled workers, i.e., the operators who know all about the machines and can react to sudden malfunctions, are needed to run the sophisticated systems (Nakaoka 1971: Chaps. 3 and 4). Until a widespread use of robots makes human labour totally redundant, artisan-type engineers will be needed to tame capricious machines and programmes. Young workers like Jiménez, who spoke of his genuine love of machines, will soon become excellent engineers. At the other end of the workforce, groups of auxiliary workers who transport raw materials and products, clean the factory, etc., are also necessary. It is not easy to introduce *kaizen* into this area of work, where little scientific skill is required. But there is also a middle ground. As Enrique González illustrated:

> There is a US company called Jockey, which manufactures and exports underwear. I went there with Mr Okamoto, and we found it was an intriguing case. I think there were about 800 female workers. One production manager was interested in *kaizen* and suggested to his

> boss that they should try it. We diagnosed the problem. We noticed that time was wasted everywhere. If there was a problem with a sewing machine, a technician would be called in, but there were only four qualified technicians, so work stopped until the person arrived. We thought it would be better if the sewing workers could do simple repairs on the spot. So we taught basic mechanics to the workers and told them to clean the machine with a brush to make it less prone to clogging. Yes, it was to 'Shine', an element of 5S. It is not nice for small fibres to get into sewing machines, so we suggested they clean it for five minutes during the changeover. Actually, it turned out to be a big incentive for the workers. Each of them had a quota of how many products one should make in a day, and when she reached it, she got a basic salary. If she had fewer problems with the machine, she could continue working, speed up the process, and finish more underwear than her quota. This means she got extra pay. In this way, *kaizen* was good for workers, too. The factory owner was an American, who visited the factory only once a month. In that factory, *kaizen* was suggested by middle management and spread to the shop floor. Proactive leaders were identified in the company to spread such a practice. It was a success story, but this factory located north of San José was shut down in 2013. This was because the cost of running a factory in Costa Rica, including labour costs, had risen too much and become unsustainable. Many women lost their jobs as the factories relocated to Asia. The same happened with Intel. The lesson is that macroeconomy is also very important. [CRI 02]

Even if the efficiency of the production lines is significantly improved through *kaizen,* factories may have to accept closure when they are unable to compete with their Asian rivals in price terms. Tireless efforts by the workforce can be wiped out in an instant by fluctuations in supply and demand in the global market. Any attempt to spread micro *kaizen* must be backed by long-term investment plans and strategies. Costa Rica accommodates cutting-edge US companies such as Intel in semiconductors and Baxter in medical equipment. The core workforce in these industries is not the kind of factory workers depicted in Charlie Chaplin's 1936 film *Modern Times.* Perhaps Costa Rica is entering a stage which requires the expansion of dynamic innovation in addition to the *kaizen* practice on the shop floor.

Chapter 4
Teaching Is Learning: Educational Cooperation

4.1 Education as a Means and an End

4.1.1 From Vocational Training to Primary Education

Development cooperation requires a 'marketing' effort. If we were to create a street advertisement to demonstrate that development aid is being effectively utilised, what kind of image would be most suitable? Whether we work for a government or an NGO, the answer may be similar: showing smiling children. Japanese readers may have read the classic popular novel *Twenty-Four Eyes* (Tsuboi 1957) or watched its film version. The story depicts the emotional bond between a teacher hailing from a city and children rooted in a remote fishing village. If we replace the scene of the Japanese elementary school with another elementary school in an African village, we can shoot a good picture.[1] The image of young JOCV teachers working at schools in Africa is not just a publicity stunt but a fact.

However, what I am describing in this book is a history. A primary school may be an effective symbol of educational cooperation in the twenty-first century, but the gravity of Japan's educational cooperation lay elsewhere in the twentieth century. For years, Japanese educational cooperation gave priority to human resources development, such as teaching young workers how to turn a lathe, grow vegetables, and treat patients in hospitals. Japanese educational cooperation from the 1950s to the 1980s concentrated on technical and vocational education and training (TVET) and higher education (Kayashima et al. 2022: 7–24). The world of *Twenty-Four Eyes* bore little resemblance to the typical practice of Japan's educational cooperation in the past century.

[1] Nishikata Norihiro, a JICA senior adviser on education, remembered that when he was in sixth-grade, the first time he could buy something with his own pocket money, he bought a paperback copy of *Twenty-Four Eyes* and read it with great pleasure. Nishikata became a teacher at a public elementary school in Niigata Prefecture, applied to join the JOCV, and then went to Honduras.

Y. Mine, *An Oral History of Development Cooperation*,
https://doi.org/10.1007/978-981-95-5479-9_4

This book has six chapters. Given that the majority of case studies in this book are about cooperation involving tertiary and secondary institutions, the educational sector could be overrepresented. However, this is not necessarily the case. In the last century, the assistance for TVET (Sects. 3.2 and 3.4) and university medical schools (Sects. 5.2 and 5.3) was not necessarily classified as educational cooperation. When JICA was established in 1974, the Ministry of Education[2] was 'pushed out of the power politics among the four powerful ministries – Foreign Affairs; Agriculture, Forestry and Fisheries; International Trade and Industry; and Finance' (Sato 2019: 48; Sugishita 2005: 78–81). Although the Ministry of Education had a strong presence in multilateral educational cooperation through the United Nations Educational, Scientific and Cultural Organization (UNESCO), the relationship between the Ministry of Education and JICA, which was responsible for bilateral cooperation, cooled down due to the relative detachment of the Ministry of Education from the ODA practice. When JICA wanted to dispatch university professors as experts, the Ministry of Education just approved it.

Until the 1980s, bilateral assistance for basic education was not only marginalised but also considered a sort of 'taboo'. The Ministry of Foreign Affairs assumed that aiding basic education (i.e., 'national' education) might impinge on the sovereignty of aid recipient countries and preferred to avoid possible political entanglements, especially given the anti-Japanese sentiments in East and Southeast Asia (Chap. 3). The Ministry of Education did not want to provide resources for the cooperation in primary education where the ministry is not involved in decision-making, either (Sato 2019: 41–49). There was also a positive aspect in concentrating on TVET and higher education. In the latter half of the twentieth century, Japan had a comparative advantage in the field of science and engineering. Even if Japanese experts were not good at English, as long as they engaged in hands-on experiments and practical training, their performance could be highly appreciated (Chap. 3). Returning to Francis Fukuyama's argument discussed in Chap. 1 (Sect 1.2.2) transferred technology in TVET and higher education is much more 'specific' than in primary education, and it is easier to measure the extent of progress in the former than in the latter.

In the era of TVET, there was modest support for basic education in the form of the provision of teaching materials. Nishikata Norihiro, a primary school teacher, worked as a JICA Volunteer in Honduras from 1987 to 1988. He travelled around local primary schools, driving a van loaded with teaching materials such as models of the human body and the globe. It was a kind of 'mobile classroom'. Nishikata and his colleagues also used a 16-mm film projector to show movies to local people, but he began to question whether this was genuinely an educational activity, and then he decided to work directly with primary school children on mathematics education (Nishikata 2017: 23–26).

[2] The official name is the Ministry of Education, Culture, Sports, Science and Technology, which is referred to simply as the Ministry of Education in the text hereafter.

4.1.2 Metamorphosis of the Project

It was only in the 1980s, with the growth of Japan's overall development cooperation, that 'Japanese-style educational cooperation' began to emerge. Concerning higher education, gigantic projects, such as the creation of whole new universities, started to be launched. In addition, the fields of assistance expanded from traditional ones like medicine to new ones such as agriculture and engineering. The exemplary projects include King Mongkut's University of Technology in Thailand and Jomo Kenyatta University of Agriculture and Technology (JKUAT) in Kenya, which is the subject of Sect. 4.2, the first case study of this chapter (Araki 2014; Kayashima 2022).

JKUAT was originally launched as a technical college with Japanese assistance in 1979 and accepted first-generation students in 1981. The college curriculum emphasised practical learning and aimed to train young people who were expected to play a key role in agricultural and industrial development in Kenya. It became a college attached to Kenyatta University in 1988 and was granted the status of a full-fledged national university in 1994. Today, JKUAT has established a reputation as one of East Africa's leading comprehensive universities with about 50,000 students.

However, things did not go always that smoothly. The largest crisis surfaced in 2000 when Japan withdrew its assistance from JKUAT, though the Kenyan side was unprepared for Japan's 'sudden' departure. Assistance may end anytime when the recipient country develops its capacity to manage the project on its own, as described in the transition from the state of Fig. 1.2 to that of Fig. 1.4; in the latter stage, the project is embedded within the internal cycle of the principal-agent relationship. But how can we safely judge whether the period of assistance has successfully concluded? For 20 years, Kenyans and Japanese had worked together more or less as equals in pursuit of a shared dream. Why, Kenyans asked, did the Japanese leave exactly when the project was about to take off? No, Japanese replied, we had already explained that we were going to leave, and we are not cutting ties but proposing to try something new based on the past collaboration. Whatever the case, something seems to have gone wrong between them, involving the question of mutual dependence, independence, and entanglements.

The year 1990 was the most significant turning point for Japanese educational cooperation at large.[3] Following the World Conference on 'Education for All' held in Jomtien, Thailand, the Japanese government shifted the focus from higher education and vocational training to basic education (including early childhood education, primary education, lower secondary education, and non-formal education). In 1992, JICA organised a study group on 'Development and Education', chaired by the economist Iida Tsuneo, which published a breakthrough position paper in 1994 (JICA 1994b). In addition to the new emphasis on basic education, the report also advocated the importance of education in science and mathematics, education for girls, education for vulnerable groups, reinforcement of educational administration, support for teacher training and capacity development, development of curriculum,

[3] Kuroda (2023) (in Japanese) is the only comprehensive study tracing the history of Japan's educational cooperation back from the period before World War II.

textbooks, and teaching materials, and improvement of school buildings and facilities. In the past, assistance in higher education was classified as technical cooperation involving university professors, but since the 1990s, as the stronger focus was brought to basic education, the endeavours involving universities 'began to be recognized as higher education cooperation in contrast to basic education cooperation' (Kayashima 2022: 211). Three main areas of educational cooperation were thus established: basic education, higher education, and TVET. However, as the appropriate balance between these areas should differ from one country to another, the 'Development and Education' report emphasised the special importance of 'assessing the current state of education in the partner country' (ibid.: 31).

Taking this new development into consideration, Sect. 4.3, the second case study of this chapter, examines cooperation in secondary education, one level below higher education (one step closer to basic education).[4] In Kenya, alongside JKUAT, Japan has been implementing a project called Strengthening Mathematics and Science in Secondary Education (SMASSE). Most science and mathematics education in Kenya is said to have been a one-way flow of knowledge; the teacher writes formulas with chalk on the blackboard, and students take notes and memorise them (education in Japan also used to be the same as I personally remember). However, science lessons disconnected from children's everyday life experience failed to capture their spontaneous interest. Teachers were therefore encouraged to design creative and imaginative lessons showing examples and using makeshift materials for active experiments so that students could share in the joy of *eureka!* Let us change the educational method from 'teacher-centred' to 'student-centred' so that both teachers and students can improve their practice in classrooms with confidence.

When SMASSE began in 1998, secondary education in Kenya seemed to be full of fresh spirit for such transformation. Careful preparations were made between Kenyan officers and Japanese experts, and it was agreed that new teaching methods would be disseminated through nationwide training of in-service teachers. Teachers gathered, learnt the new teaching methods, and returned to their classroom to put it into practice. SMASSE was transformed into an 'educational movement' that was eventually internalised in secondary education in Kenya. SMASSE was then exported to other African countries, particularly Zambia where it flourished in combination with an additional method of lesson study.

However, in the early stage of SMASSE, the Kenyan and Japanese stakeholders were not necessarily confident about its success. In this chapter, we pick up the issue of the provision of allowances. Teachers in the training programme complained that it was unfair that they did not receive compensation for attending the training on holidays, and some of them even tried to boycott the training. The counterargument was that the training was meant to benefit teachers as well as students. During the interviews, I found a complex logic at play on the part of those criticising the training and those trying to persuade them. In the end, the teachers embraced SMASSE because they accepted the training contents positively.

---

[4] Kenya followed the 8-4-4 school system from 1985 to 2017, with four-year secondary education before tertiary education.

4.1.3 Teaching and Learning

In the last section of this chapter, I will look at the activities of the JOCV in educational cooperation. JICA Volunteers were deployed to contribute to the projects in and around JKUAT and SMASSE. While working hard in their places of assignment, the JICA Volunteers also witnessed the dynamic evolution of the project from a half-amateur viewpoint.

By 2015, the 50th anniversary of the programme, the number of JICA Volunteers dispatched around the world had reached around 40,000. Maruyama (2022) argued that the history of the JOCV could be divided into three stages: the 'Rise' period (from 1965 to around 1980), the 'Doubling' period (from 1980 to the mid-1990s), and the 'Diversity' period (from the 1990s to the mid-2000s). In the early days, JOCV activities were focused predominantly on technology transfer. In the first half of the 1960s, most volunteers worked in the agriculture, forestry and fisheries sectors. However, during the period of doubling, the number of volunteers in the education and cultural exchange sectors increased. By 2000, these sectors had become a majority, accounting for over 40% of the total dispatch. In particular, the project of primary mathematics education in Honduras that began in 1991, the project of secondary mathematics and science education in the Philippines that started in 1994, and SMASSE in Kenya, a subject of this chapter, were considered flagship projects. JICA Volunteers, including in-service teachers, were sent in groups or teams to work with local teachers and give classes at local schools. In these interviews, we asked former Japanese volunteers who worked mainly in Kenya to revisit their experiences.

But why did I interview the Japanese? As explained in Chap. 1, even though the main actors in development projects are supposed to be the counterparts in the aid recipient countries, their narratives have rarely been presented. The Japanese narratives are often the 'strong' narratives that are effectively represented, while the local narratives are the 'weak' narratives that get less attention. In this book, I have reversed the roles and consciously kept the Japanese narrative low-profile as much as possible.

Nevertheless, I thought it was worth conducting the interviews with former JICA Volunteers, considering Fig. 1.5 in Chap. 1. Once the stage of 'teaching how to fish' is completed, the relationship between aiding and aided countries will transform into the one between equals, providing a room for mutual support and learning between peer nations and people ('Let's fish together'). Thus, horizontal international cooperation (the shaded area in Fig. 1.5) will develop between citizens (the principals) and between governments (the agents). Citizens who cross borders may not only influence people in other countries but also share their experiences with people in their home country after they return. Unlike the expectation of experts to 'teach' their counterparts, JICA Volunteers are expected both to teach and to learn in their places of activities. As the poet Tanigawa Shuntaro put it in praise of JICA Volunteers, 'When trying to help, you will be helped.' 'When trying to teach, you will be taught.' 'What cannot be seen can only be received. That is the most precious gift of all' (JICA 2016b: 34–35).

It is not just a question of attitude. The necessity of fostering mutual understanding and sharing the lessons in their home country is clearly stated as the objectives of the JOCV. The main goals of the JOCV are stated as follows: (1) to cooperate in economic and social development, as well as the reconstruction of developing countries, (2) to promote international goodwill and deepen mutual understanding, and (3) to develop international perspectives of volunteers and give back their experience to Japanese society. These objectives are plainly different from those of the usual development projects that mobilise professional experts to benefit developing countries.[5]

The content of this chapter starts with higher education, then proceeds to secondary education, and finally looks at horizontal cooperation in education. Education is a process of holistic human development through which individual persons become good citizens by learning and teaching (JICA 1994b: 1). Given that there is an educational element in all development projects, educational cooperation and development cooperation may intrinsically be the same. So to whom does education belong? If we adopt a student-centred rather than a teacher-centred approach, the answer will be that the process should be directed and ultimately owned by students. And when not only students but also teachers, volunteers, and local community members are all transformed into dynamic 'learners', the whole school is expected to be a space for everyone to co-create new knowledge and nurture new attitudes to life.

4.2 The Emergence of the House of Learning: Jomo Kenyatta University of Agriculture and Technology (Kenya)

4.2.1 Luring the President (1977–1981)

This book treats each development project as an independent entity. Many factors contribute to the birth of a project, but once it is launched, it grows on its own logic, affected by a combination of internal and external factors including assumptions and misunderstandings.

The big university was born small. Araki Mitsuya, who runs a Japanese periodical, *Kokusai Kaihatsu (International Development) Journal*, described the circumstances of the birth of the Jomo Kenyatta University of Agriculture and Technology (JKUAT) (Araki 2014). As he wrote, at the initial stage, what principally mattered was the political situation on the African continent. Before and after 1960, African countries were breaking with colonial rule and becoming independent one after another, but in southern African countries such as South Africa and Rhodesia (now Zimbabwe),

---

[5] These objectives are presented in various documents and websites including publicity materials. See the concise statement on JICA's official website: https://www.jica.go.jp/english/activities/schemes/volunteer/index.html.

white minority rule persisted. Japan imported natural resources from these countries and maintained trade relationships. If Japan's implication with these regimes was exposed and criticised by African nations, Japan could be diplomatically isolated, and its economic security could be in jeopardy.[6]

It was against this background that Japan tried to 'lure' the first president of Kenya, Jomo Kenyatta, as a diplomatic ally. It could be in parallel with Japan's assistance for rice production in the Kilimanjaro region in Tanzania (Chap. 2), an initiative strongly supported by Tanzania's President Julius Nyerere (Araki 2014: 32–42). In East Africa, Kenya, espousing the market economy principle, was a Western Ally, while Tanzania, advocating African socialism, was close to socialist China; it could be a rational decision for Japan, a resource-poor nation, to purchase insurance from both. In Kenya, it was decided to build an institution for human resources development, named after Kenyatta, which would align with his five-year plan. 'When it comes to diplomacy between heads of state, the formal "request-based" principle does not work. The so-called request was coordinated in advance at the administrative level' (ibid.: 48).

Thus, in 1977 and 1978, survey teams were sent from Japan to investigate the possibility of providing grant aid for establishing the JKUAT. In 1978 and 1980, additional survey teams were dispatched to examine the feasibility of technical cooperation. These teams were led by Uenosono Chikasa of the Faculty of Engineering at Kyoto University and Fukada Minoru of the Faculty of Agriculture at Okayama University. At the time, Kenya had only one comprehensive national university, the University of Nairobi. Therefore, a new school plan was elaborated based on the experience not of the exceptional institution but of the existing agricultural and technical colleges (JICA 1978a). The planned campus was about 200 ha in area and was located behind the town of Juja on the way from Nairobi to Mount Kenya (Fig. 4.1). The town is now sprawling, but in the 1970s there were only sisal fields; a clipping from a local newspaper reporting that the president donated the land was attached to a JICA project report (JICA 1978b). After 1979, with Japanese funding, a management building, classrooms, a laboratory building, a student dormitory and other facilities were constructed. For students to acquire practical skills in agriculture, it was also necessary to develop a university farm, which was gradually taking shape through irrigation and soil dressing.

Decades ago, Jomo Kenyatta was imprisoned for leading the struggle of the Kikuyu people against British colonial rule. He was around 70 years old when he was released in 1961, called 'Mzee' (elder), and revered as a national hero. He married a British woman and, after independence in 1963, veered to a pragmatic approach in diplomacy and economic policies and yet remained a strong-willed politician[7] (Kenyatta 1961). However, Kenyatta died in 1978, exactly when the construction of

[6] This consideration of political sentiments in African countries was also a strong background to the inauguration of the Tokyo International Conference on African Development (TICAD) process. See a series of articles written by a Japanese journalist, Shirato (2022) and Ampiah (2022).

[7] Kenyatta published an academic book entitled *Facing Mount Kenya* (Kenyatta 1961, originally published in 1938). He studied under the social anthropologist Bronislaw Malinowski while a student at the London School of Economics, and wrote this ethnography.

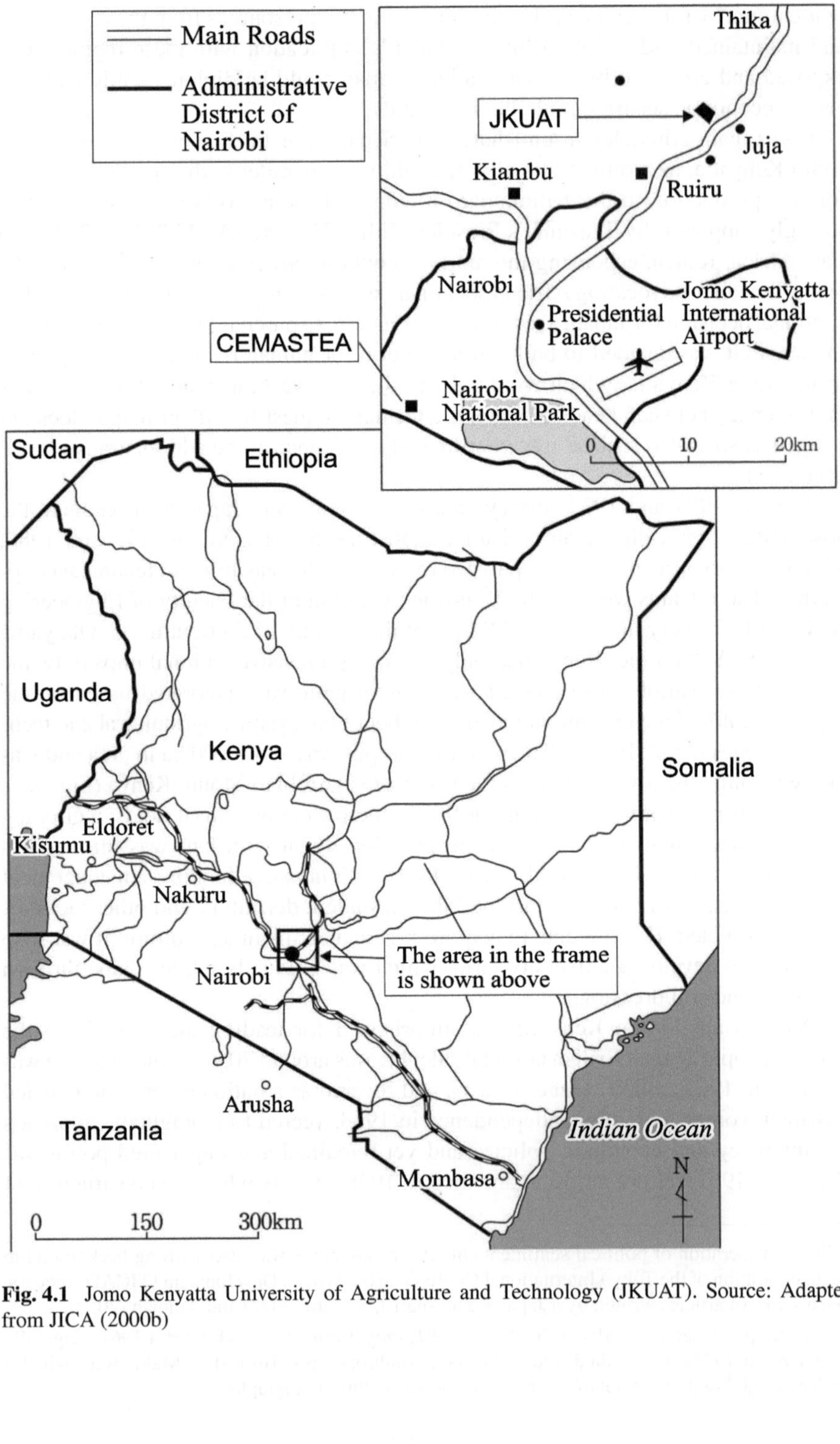

Fig. 4.1 Jomo Kenyatta University of Agriculture and Technology (JKUAT). Source: Adapted from JICA (2000b)

the school building was about to begin. Although Japan's attempt to 'lure' the president might not work, his successor, Daniel Arap Moi, happened to be a graduate of a teacher's college and was passionate about education. Under President Moi, the quest to establish a practice-oriented agricultural and technical university would gain momentum over the next 20 years. The college opened in 1981, with the faculty of agriculture covering horticulture, agricultural engineering, and food processing, and with the faculty of engineering comprising civil engineering and architecture, mechanical engineering, and electrical and electronic engineering. In the beginning, the college suffered a shortage of Kenyan lecturers; students enrolled at different times of the year; and the curriculum was still incomplete (JICA 1981d). During the first half of the 1980s, the college barely managed to fill its annual intake of 198 students (JICA 1991d: 46). It seemed that the opening of the campus was a rushed job.

4.2.2 Emphasis on Practical Learning (1981–1987)

The school's official name at the time of its establishment was Jomo Kenyatta College of Agriculture and Technology (JKCAT). It was a college, not a university. Johnson Muhara, a first-generation student, passionately recalled the early days of JKCAT.

> I was so excited because something new was about to begin. The facilities were amazing – state-of-the-art. Learning *karate* was a cool experience. Learning how to drive a tractor was also memorable. These were things I could never try in other universities. While I was there, I learnt so much from the Japanese way of doing things. It wasn't just about the skills; I also picked up their approach: for example, working thoroughly, staying focused, and being punctual. Mr Sugiyama was like a father to me, and my relationships with JICA Volunteers were great, too. They were a bit older than me, so it was like having big brothers around. Hanging out with friends after school was always a lot of fun. Oh, I even met my wife there! [KEN 10]

Muhara managed a company undertaking the production, collection, processing and export of macadamia nuts and was also a representative of the industry's association in Kenya.[8] He still maintained contact with his former fellow students [KEN 10]. The 'Mr Sugiyama' he mentioned is Sugiyama Takahiko, a legendary expert who provided support to JKCAT/JKUAT from 1980 to 1994. After helping to set up the university, Sugiyama played a key role in the SMASSE project, which will be discussed in Sect. 4.3.

In Kenya, all academic subjects, including science, are taught in English from the primary level, while all are taught in Japanese in Japan; it must have been challenging for JICA Volunteers to teach in English in front of English-speaking Kenyan students. Glaston Kenji, who had studied at Okayama University and ran the JKUAT laboratory,

[8] Muhara commented, 'It would be a good idea to include business-related courses in the curriculum because there are many JKUAT graduates who, like me, are active as entrepreneurs and can put their business skills to good use. Compared to countries like Japan, which are already developed, we have a lot of untapped business opportunities in Africa' [KEN 10].

said, 'Sure, there were some challenges with communicating in English, but I was surprised at how adaptable the Japanese were. The following year, the quality of teaching improved dramatically' [KEN 02]. The Chief Technologist-Laboratories Paul Nyota Karanja, said:

> Japanese and Kenyans have different teaching styles. The Japanese focus on teaching in a simple way that's easy to understand. When the JICA Volunteers stood in the class, their English was not always perfect and could be a bit difficult for students to follow, but the Japanese worked so hard that it never became a real issue. For us, practical experiments are more important than theory. I think it's all about showing the students how things work in the real world. [KEN 04]

The Japanese and Kenyan faculty at JKCAT tried to interact with the students in hands-on ways rather than just explaining concepts and theories. As we saw in Chap. 3, it was the comparative advantage of Japanese technology transfer. The project to create an entirely new university in Kenya was a 'test of the true worth of our nation's education and a model for African countries, which aim to develop autonomously, while building upon the educational system of colonial powers' (JICA 1991d: iv). In Kenya, like in Malaysia, a qualification-oriented norm was visible. People with higher degrees did not engage in practical work on the ground but made decisions that would affect all workers, while those without degrees conducted substantial jobs but were alienated from decision-making. This meant that there was a discrepancy between top-down decisions and bottom-up needs. Graduates of JKCAT were expected to acquire not only hands-on skills but also the capacity to think for themselves and make decisions congruent with practical needs in farms and workshops.

However, the bottom line was for the students to get their bachelor's degrees. 'Only about half of the first-generation students managed to pass the exam. The Japanese emphasised practical training, but the Kenyan academic system focused on theory. The practical aspect is the university's strong selling point. It is obvious. But the graduates could not even get started if they did not pass the examination. So, we decided to strike a balance by blending the Japanese and Kenyan approaches' [KEN 02].

By revising the curriculum, the pass rate improved dramatically by the late 1980s. However, as long as the teaching depended on foreign lecturers, the principal-agent relationship would not work. Thus, immediately after JKCAT opened, the Kenyan academic staff at the college were invited to Japan as government-sponsored students to take higher degrees so that they could teach more advanced classes (see also the parallel Zambian case in Sect. 5.3). The scheme was funded by the Japanese Ministry of Education (JICA's scholarships were not yet available at that time). With 1983 as a turning point, Japan's scholarship programmes for students from developing countries were expanding along with the rapid increase in the ODA budget (Sugimura and Kayashima 2022: 223). In the meantime, Japanese university professors took leave and went to Kenya to contribute to teaching. Nakagawa Hirotsugu at Kyoto University's Faculty of Engineering and Iwasa Junkichi at Okayama University's Faculty of Agriculture coordinated the domestic support committee.[9] The faculty from a total of 62 universities across Japan, including Kyoto and Okayama Universities, engaged in supporting the take-off of JKCAT (Araki 2014: 264). Vice-Chancellor Mabel Imbuga expressed her gratitude.

> JKUAT is gaining a higher profile not only in East Africa but also across the African continent. The most impressive thing is that almost all Kenyans who went to Japan to study have come back to Kenya and are now contributing to the university. This is different from what often happens with students who go to the US or the UK, where some choose not to return, which hampers Kenya's capacity development. [KEN 01]

Brain drain has been a nagging concern for the management of Kenyan universities. They welcomed the return of young scholars who acquired skills in Japan and then contributed to the development of their home university, though their willingness to return was partly because of the lack of a substantial African diaspora community in Japan.[10]

4.2.3 Becoming a Comprehensive National University (1988–1993)

Despite the efforts of all parties, it took years for JKCAT to become fully independent. In project reports in the 1980s, such evaluations were repeated as 'the teaching load of Japanese lecturers has decreased, but there is still a high level of dependence,' and 'the work attitude of the Kenyan teaching staff is not necessarily the best.' Some Japanese started to worry that they could not see a way out.

A featured article in the *Asahi Shimbun* newspaper (8 April 1989 morning edition) entitled '10 Billion Yen Invested, But the University Still Unable to Stand on Its Own' honestly reported the concerns of the Japanese stakeholders. As written in the article, the 'handover' of the project from Japan to Kenya was supposed to be completed by 1985, but due to a shortage of teaching staff, the support for the college was extended to 1990. Despite the substantial amount of budget consumed, 'there is no prospect of the college becoming self-sufficient. The consensus among those involved is that if aid was withdrawn now, the quality of teaching would decline quickly.' The article concludes, "The shortage of lecturers is due to a lack of bachelors in science and

[9] In particular, Nakagawa Hirotsugu served as the head of the support committee for JKUAT for 20 years, visited Kenya numerous times, and played a significant role in helping JKUAT get off the ground. A mimeograph written by Nakagawa records the detail of his interactions with his Kenyan counterparts, and Araki (2014) made an extensive use of this document (in Japanese). I would like to express my deep gratitude to Prof. Nakagawa for sharing his observations with me prior to my visit to the JKUAT.

[10] The survey conducted by the Japan Student Services Organisation (JASSO) showed that, in 2004 (2022), 22.9% (44.3%) of international students found employment in Japan after graduation, 45.9% (19.9%) continued their education in Japan, and 12.6% (7.3%) found employment in their home country. In recent years, the number of African students seeking employment in Japan has increased dramatically. https://www.studyinjapan.go.jp/ja/statistics/career-and-degrees/.

poor working conditions. But this is a problem common to all developing countries. It could have been predicted before the college was set up. Who is responsible for the decision to grant no less than 10 billion yen without foresight?'

The question was whether they would continue assisting the take-off of the full-scale JKUAT as a national 'university' with a resolve to invest further funds or be content with keeping the position of JKCAT as a medium-sized 'college' that would emphasise hands-on learning. As we saw in Chap. 3, in the 1980s, Japanese development cooperation started to place a renewed emphasis on *hito-zukuri* (human resources development) in Southeast Asia and beyond. If the primary objective of the assistance was vocational training (or capacity development for government officials), the core institution does not have to be a comprehensive university. Concerning JKCAT, the original focus was on training a large number of field engineers and extension workers, and it seems that some of the Japanese planners of the project did not want the college to be promoted to a comprehensive university. On the other hand, Araki noted that some officers involved at the level of the Japanese Ministry of Education were insisting that the college must become a university. This could possibly be due to some involvement of politicians, or perhaps due to a bureaucratic turf war: it is the Ministry of Labour, rather than the Ministry of Education, that has jurisdiction over vocational training schools (Araki 2014: 118). In Kenya's technical colleges, the salaries of the teaching staff were around half those of university faculty, and the government, rather than the college management, held the power to make decisions on the personnel. The survey team concluded that, in terms of incentives, it would be impossible to attract motivated staff unless the college was upgraded to a full-fledged university (JICA 1987a: 11).

Opinions varied on the Kenyan side as well. As noted by Araki, the initial response from the Kenyan government officials was simply like this: 'We don't need a university' (Araki 2014: 117). Apparently, the existing universities did not want their rivals to grow, and there could also be a turf war between the ministries like that in Japan. If the college transformed into a university, the ministry in charge of the college would be transferred from the Ministry of Vocational Training to the Ministry of Education. Ratemo Michieka, who later became vice-chancellor of JKUAT, said, 'There were political moves to slow down the process, as they felt the college was growing too quickly' [KEN 11].[11]

Nevertheless, opinions gradually converged. Vice-Chancellor Imbuga explained:

> The students' parents objected, complaining that they would have to pay higher tuition fees to learn things that were of no practical use. Some of the lecturers were afraid that if the college became a university, their degrees would be too low, and they might lose their jobs. However, no other institutions in the country taught practical agriculture and practical engineering like ours. It's very unique. So, we have decided. If we have to become a university, we should become an excellent university, not just a university. [KEN 01]

[11] Michieka said he was criticised for being conservative, as he believed that JKUAT should not expand into the social studies but concentrate on its original fields such as agriculture, engineering, and natural sciences. 'Whether it was a good decision to make the institution a comprehensive university will be judged by future generations' [KEN 11].

In September 1988, Jomo Kenyatta University College of Agriculture and Technology (JKUCAT) was established temporarily as a branch of Kenyatta University. George S. Eshiwani was appointed its principal. The new university college could now recruit the teaching staff and raise the standard of its educational and research activities on its own initiative (JICA 1989b). In 1992, when Eshiwani became vice-chancellor of Kenyatta University, Michieka followed in his footsteps and was promoted to principal of JKUCAT. In 1994, the Kenyan Parliament enacted a law establishing JKUAT as the fifth full-fledged national university, and Michieka became its vice-chancellor.

In the 1990s, JKUAT began to engage in income-generating activities to supplement and diversify its financial resources. Activities to process and sell agricultural products harvested on the university farm are still in place. The university farm 'sells all its products. We supply the university canteen, so students eat food grown on the farm every day' [KEN 09]. In the 1990s, Japanese documents made little mention of the importance of commercial activities at universities; instead, it was considered critically important that the Kenyan faculty members should set their own research topics and carry out advanced research now that the institution had transitioned from a college to a university (JICA 1994c). Until the 1990s, the prevailing view in the Japanese educational sector was that a national university should be a sacred temple of academic knowledge where the teaching staff do not have to worry about financial management. In this respect, it seems that Kenya was more advanced than Japan. It was not until 2003 that Japan's national universities were transformed into corporations to strengthen their financial self-reliance.

4.2.4 Gaining a Foothold (1994–2000)

Let me write a little more about Michieka, who became the first vice-chancellor of JKUAT when it was formally upgraded to a full-fledged university in 1994. In the early 1990s, the attempt by Kenyan universities to raise tuition fees provoked student rebellion. At the time, Michieka as principal of JKUCAT was in charge of student affairs. As described in his autobiography, Michieka opened the door of his office to visiting students and faculty, treated students as his equals, and always tried to listen to their opinions. He dealt with noise, fights, theft, eating and running, police intervention, entanglements of love, and ethnic strife. He even received midnight phone calls to deal with students' youthful indiscretions. He queued with students in the canteen to get his food and visited college dorm rooms to talk to them. Michieka was proud that he had never expelled students except those with poor grades. Thanks to his honest conversations with student leaders, the college developed a reputation for its relative peace that enabled classes to take place regularly according to the academic calendar, contributing to steady student recruitment (Michieka 2012: Chaps. 6–7).

In July 2018, I met Michieka in a hotel restaurant for an interview. When I arrived three minutes late, the big gentleman was already seated, his back straight, and he said, smiling mischievously, 'If you're Japanese, you have to arrive a little early for an appointment' [KEN 11]. Actually, while reading his autobiography, I found this passage: 'If you have an appointment with any Japanese here in Kenya, you must ensure that you arrive for the function a few minutes earlier…. If by any error you get to an appointment late, your negotiation power starts to decline immediately and you are construed as a person who is not serious. If they arrived at a meeting late, which occasionally happened, because of traffic jams in Nairobi, then I knew I was on top of the bargaining power! It actually worked and many times to my favour' (Michieka 2012: 89). So, he arrived at the restaurant a few minutes earlier and waited for me.

Under the leadership of Michieka, JKUAT grew significantly. 'The town of Juja also expanded a lot. Since the campus dorms couldn't accommodate all the students who needed them, many apartments mushroomed, and new shops opened up around the town. Things developed so quickly that basic services like water, sewage, and electricity couldn't keep up. New primary schools were constructed, land prices skyrocketed, and the cost of building materials followed. It was also a challenge to make sure students living near the university were protected from physical attacks' [KEN 11].

At the time when JKUAT was taking off as a full-fledged university, Vice-Chancellor Michieka often discussed the university's next direction with Nakagawa of Kyoto University. Michieka said, 'Professor Nakagawa is a great son of Japan.' On the other hand, some young Japanese staff 'were too immature to deal with the senior staff and failed'. There was even a case where a Japanese short-tempered expert unfairly scolded a Kenyan, a big fight broke out, and Michieka had to step in. Michieka's role was to intervene and restore harmony when relations became strained, whether between Kenyans or between Kenyans and Japanese.

Before the end of the Japanese assistance, in the late 1990s, some forms of third-country training began to be conducted in all departments of JKUAT, except architecture. In addition, domestic training for women leaders in the Kenyan countryside was implemented on the university farm to improve their farming techniques (JICA 1999a). Naomi Nduhiu, a technical officer at the farm, explained the rationale for focusing on women.

> Many men take part in the training. But in rural areas, women do almost everything. They handle all the housework, take care of children, and also do most of the farm work, including caring for the livestock. But when they sell cash crops, the money usually goes into the account of their husbands. Sometimes wives make a little money by selling chickens, eggs, or milk, but that's rare. We wanted to improve women's status by helping them get more cash income. It's important to redistribute money more fairly within the household. [KEN 09]

Nduhiu then emphasised the value of exchange.

> When we worked together on the farm, we spoke Swahili instead of English. Japanese people learnt Swahili words one by one, so we could feel we were really working together. It was also an excellent experience for me to go to Kagawa Prefecture for a short training course and learn about things like growing tomatoes in greenhouses. I was able to see and make sure for myself where the Japanese people in Kenya came from. [KEN 09]

Anticipating the day when Japanese support would terminate, a group of Japanese volunteers led by Nakagawa of Kyoto University set up the Babaroa Scholarship in 1996 to support talented and financially challenged students at JKUAT. The name was taken from the French-style cold dessert, *bavarois*, Nakagawa savoured at a restaurant near Nairobi station. The French word bavarois is transcribed as *babaroa* in Japanese. It has no meaning but may sound like an African word.

4.2.5 End of Assistance (2000)

Then came a major turning point. Japan decided to terminate its assistance for the main body of the JKUAT. Those involved in the Japanese ODA know that if assistance continues for no less than 20 years, the project will not continue as before, whether its outcomes are considered successful or not. The US or France may continue to assist certain projects to protect liberalism or cultural prestige, but not Japan. The tone of the *Asahi Shimbun* article quoted above also reflected the grassroots conservatism of Japanese taxpayers, who loathe the idea of their money being used lavishly for the benefit of foreign countries, with possible patronage and clientelism.

In 2000, JICA's final evaluation report of JKUAT proudly asserted, 'Japan's support over the past 20 years has steadily borne fruit, and it is clear that the project's goal of producing graduates with sufficient knowledge and skills in agriculture and engineering has been mostly achieved.' Despite some problems regarding research and administration, the JKUAT project contributed to the goal of producing practice-minded professionals in higher education in Kenya, and 'it can be judged that the foundations for the university to operate independently have largely been established.' Since the original objectives had been met, the project could be concluded as a success (JICA 2000b: 7). In terms of future involvement, it was suggested that JKUAT should be positioned as a hub institution for *hito-zukuri* (human resources development) in the broader African region to address specific problems Africa faced. This new orientation of continent-wide scaling-up was considered a natural option as most academic departments of JKUAT had already been involved in third-country training.

However, the university management regarded the withdrawal of Japan as a bolt from the blue. When I conducted the interviews, almost 20 years had passed since the end of assistance, but the disappointment at Japan's 'sudden' departure was remembered by many as a major crisis JKUAT encountered. Vice-Chancellor Imbuga, who had been dean of the Faculty of Science at the time, explained the coping strategies:

> When Japan decided to withdraw in 2000, we were not prepared. We were stunned. We tried to generate income by setting up business and management courses that did not require physical facilities. We also started to recruit self-supporting students who would pay their own fees. In this way, we tried to raise the budget for equipment and supplies in the engineering department. [KEN 01]

Bernard W. Ikua, principal of the College of Engineering and Technology of JKUAT, argued, 'Japan's withdrawal was a major turning point. Just as the university was about to expand, its financial support was substantially reduced. It was a big challenge, but perhaps we'd been too dependent on Japan' [KEN 06]. Kenji, who studied in Japan, was more critical. 'The Japanese give and then leave. The Japanese should have involved the Kenyans from the beginning. They simply come, do things, and then leave the place. Such practice doesn't leave anything behind nor motivate the locals to protect what is there' [KEN 02]. As Japanese and Kenyans went to lecture rooms and laboratories every day to look after the students, they came to feel that they had built a unique place for learning together as peers. It may be difficult to determine whether the withdrawal was too early or too late, but the fact is that there remained a lingering sentiment that Japan quit too early.

Then came China. Given the Japanese investment in JKUAT, China's support for JKUAT appeared to be modest, though a botanical garden was being constructed next to the farm with support from China. Peter K. Kihato, head of the workshop of the engineering department, commented, 'The impact of Japan's withdrawal was huge, so the Chinese picked up where the Japanese left off. Japan and China share a similar development philosophy, so Kenyans cannot tell the difference between them' [KEN 07]. Mwikamba Kaibui, who had been in charge of the university farm for many years, contrasted the differences between the West and the East rather than between Japan and China. 'Japan and China came after the period of structural adjustment, and I think it was good for Kenyans to see that there are ways of doing things that are different from the Western ways' [KEN 08]. He continued:

> I think the Japanese respect Kenyan ownership. In the beginning, we relied on Japanese assistance, but as time went on, the dependence diminished. In the college days, the lecturers were all Japanese. But slowly and gradually, the Japanese trained Kenyan lecturers and assisted them to be promoted to senior positions. In this sense, the Japanese withdrawal was not sudden. If you had observed this process carefully, it would have been predictable. [KEN 08]

The idea of self-help may have reached the people and got internalised in their hearts and minds. Nduhiu, a technical officer at the farm, said the purpose of the Japanese assistance had been achieved. She told me confidently:

> At first, there was an attitude like 'The Japanese are still here, so we can leave it and let them decide.' People take care of things that they feel are their own. After the Japanese left, I think we are able to maintain the farm as our own. [KEN 09]

When I visited, Chinese workers were paving the gravel road under the trees, which were planted in the early days of JKCAT. The workers noticed us and looked curiously at us, fellow East Asians who were indistinguishable from Chinese by appearance. Arnold Onyango, a lecturer in the Department of Food Science and Technology who studied at Okayama University, said, 'I think we will collaborate with China in the field of biotechnology. I met my Chinese wife, a foreign student like me, in Japan. Japanese people are gentle, and Chinese people are more direct in what they say' [KEN 03]. Daniel Ndaka Sila, a young researcher, wanted to study in Japan but eventually studied at the Katholieke Universiteit Leuven in Belgium. 'I feel there is a stronger sense of hierarchy in Japanese society than in Europe. Europeans are more outspoken. Japanese avoid saying "no" and try to handle the situation carefully' [KEN 05].

4.2.6 The Roads Crossing Again (2000–)

JKUAT continues to grow and flourish. According to the official history, which covers the 20 years from 1994 to 2014, the number of graduates, which was 498 in 1996, increased to 1460 in 2004, 4447 in 2011 and 6109 in 2014 (JKUAT 2014: 19). The pace of expansion, especially after Japan's withdrawal, was remarkable, and the number of students reached 40,895 in 2016 (JKUAT 2018: 13).[12] The academic fields taught at the university have enlarged beyond the original agriculture and engineering to science, information, architecture, human resources development, and health care, and the status of some of the departments in agriculture and engineering seem to be comparable to those of the prestigious University of Nairobi (JICA 2000b: 34). Dean of Engineering Ikua explained the trick. 'I think JKUAT keeps a practical diploma culture even after it transformed to a full-fledged university. It takes pride in its excellent hands-on training' [KEN 06]. The hands-on traditions of the college were carried on to the educational practice of JKUAT, which is still alive. However, there have also been substantial changes. Technologists at the university laboratories have a lot of contact with the students. As narrated by Karanja, today the disposition of students looks the same all over the world. He noted:

> I feel students used to have more leeway. They used to spend more time doing research and reading more books. Nowadays, students use smartphones and PCs as part of their everyday lives. The Internet is essential for exploring research literature, but I don't think it's a good idea to depend on it too much. [KEN 04]

Even after the Japanese assistance terminated in 2000, Karanja continued to maintain the old experimental equipment. However, if spare parts ran out, there was little he could do. When the faculty succeeded in obtaining competitive research funding, the latest research equipment would be acquired.

As the first woman vice-chancellor of JKUAT, Imbuga was seeking to set up opportunities for direct conversations with girl students to make them study with confidence [KEN 01]. Women have a substantial presence on campus in all departments; I witnessed an exercise class on the groundwork for building construction, where half of the students wearing blue coveralls were women, who were busily laying bricks. In the Gender Gap Index released by the World Economic Forum, Japan has long since been overtaken by Kenya (Kenya was 75th and Japan 118th in

[12] Several faculty members expressed concern that if student enrolment increases without parallel expansion of lecturers and facilities, the quality of education will deteriorate. Students who overflow the classrooms already have no choice but to watch the experiments from outside the classrooms [KEN 02] [KEN 03].

2024).[13] When it comes to gender equality, Japan has little advantage over African countries.

After the Japanese support for JKUAT ended, a new building of the African Institute for Capacity Development (AICAD) began to take shape by the main entrance of the campus, and the construction work was completed in 2003. AICAD is a centre for human resources development operated by the governments of three East African countries—Kenya, Tanzania, and Uganda—and carries out extensive training activities involving JKUAT faculty members. In addition, to serve as the East African base for the Pan-African University established by the African Union, a graduate school specialising in science and technology innovation was established at JKUAT and began operations in 2012. JKUAT is gaining a reputation not only in Kenya but also on the continent. However, the staff of JKUAT were not happy that AICAD, built in a prime location on the campus, was institutionally independent of JKUAT. They pointed out that they were not even allowed to enter the building freely.

When the college was inaugurated in 1981, the Japanese complained about the lack of enthusiasm on the part of Kenya. In hindsight, since the project was initiated unilaterally from the Japanese side, it is not surprising that Kenyans were not very keen on it. Nevertheless, as practical cooperation progressed on the ground, the Japanese experts and their Kenyan counterparts forged strong bonds through their daily educational activities. After Japan pulled the plug in 2000, both sides sought to redefine their modality of cooperation. For Japan, all in all, the project of assisting the birth of JKUAT remains a prototype for Japan's subsequent collaboration in higher education cooperation in Africa and elsewhere.

4.3 Science Is Interesting! Strengthening of Mathematics and Science in Secondary Education (Kenya)

4.3.1 Narrow Escape (1996–1998)

Thus far, I have tried to relate to the experiences and feelings of the local counterparts rather than those of the Japanese. Yet, sometimes, veteran local counterparts still speak fondly of certain Japanese, such as Shiraishi Yoshikazu and Nagasawa Aliaky in Chile and Kasahara Shohei in Malaysia. In the SMASSE project, Sugiyama Takahiko is such a figure. Since 1969, Sugiyama worked in Tanzania as a JICA Volunteer to teach science and mathematics, and after working as an expert at the Faculty of Agriculture, the University of Dar es Salaam (today's Sokoine University of Agriculture), he served as an expert at JKUAT from 1980 to 1994 (the Japanese team leader from 1985). After JKUAT became a full-fledged university, Sugiyama began to be involved in SMASSE. Then, in 1996, the Ethiopian Airlines flight on which

[13] https://www.weforum.org/publications/global-gender-gap-report-2024/. Namibia ranked 8th, South Africa 18th, and Mozambique 27th.

Sugiyama was travelling was hijacked shortly after take-off at the Addis Ababa Airport and crashed into the Indian Ocean. While 123 out of the 175 passengers and crew on board were killed, Sugiyama survived with fractured bones. After this incident, Sugiyama seems to have decided to devote his heart and soul to educational development in Africa (JICA 2009a: 35).

By the time Sugiyama recovered and took up his post, the direction of the SMASSE project was under careful discussion. A project formation survey was conducted in the mid-1990s, and it was recognised that human resources development was an urgent issue in Kenya. Given the success of JKUAT, it was intended to expand the assistance to science education down to the lower level of education, i.e., secondary education. The research team dispatched to the area in 1996 explored the possibility of strengthening secondary mathematics education. It proposed in-service teacher training using the cascade method, with which JICA had already experimented in the Philippines (JICA 1997b).

In the typical cascade model, the training is first organised at the national level, and those who have attended the national training sessions go back to the regions they hailed from and train local teachers, who then take what they have learnt back to their schools and put it into practice. As a form of training, in-service training (INSET) is often organised to improve the skills of teachers by having them participate in training while they continue serving their schools. In this way, it was hoped that the training outcomes would become immediately visible nationwide. Teacher training is a type of assistance that is to 'teach people how to fish' (teach teachers how to teach) as described in Chap. 1 (Sect. 1.2). In SMASSE, the Japanese taught the Kenyans how to manage classes, and then the Kenyan teachers taught their colleagues. Once the training content was accepted, even after the Japanese disappeared, the learning cycle would continue to revolve in Kenya.

Samuel Kibe, who chaired Kenya's national association of secondary school principals and played a critical role in establishing SMASSE in Kenya, indicated that parallel attempts were already made by donors other than Japan. In the early 1990s, UNESCO, the World Bank, the Association for the Development of Education in Africa (ADEA), the Commonwealth, the Department for International Development (DFID) and the German Agency for Technical Cooperation (GTZ) paid keen attention to in-service teacher training, joined by Israeli educationists. Given that the DFID was working on primary teacher training, it was decided that SMASSE would concentrate on secondary teacher training to avoid duplication. The fact that there were far fewer secondary schools than elementary schools was also considered [KEN 12].

While Kibe was bringing together Kenya's secondary school principals, Sugiyama recruited his chief counterpart, Bernard Njuguna. Originally a chemistry teacher, Njuguna became the leader of the Kenyan SMASSE team and was later described by Sugiyama as an 'evangelist of SMASSE'. Njuguna recalled, 'I was greatly influenced by Sugiyama-san's professional ethics. We met almost every day for eight years and discussed the project over a beer in the evening' [KEN 13]. In old Japan, critical business decisions were often made during evening drinking sessions rather than daytime meetings. As described by Njuguna, this kind of cosy relationship could also be established between Japanese experts and their counterparts.

4.3.2 Launch of the Education Campaign (1998–1999)

In 1998, Phase I of the SMASSE project was launched in Kenya. Based at the Kenya Science Teachers College (KSTC) established with Swedish assistance, the cascade of teacher training was to be carried out in nine pilot districts and, if successful, expanded to districts nationwide. The training content was considered critically important. SMASSE was expected to have a considerable impact because the teaching methods introduced in the training were seen as a revolutionary departure from the old ones deployed in Kenya. Kenya's science and mathematics education was teacher-centred (like pre-war Japanese education). The teacher wrote formulae on the blackboard as they appeared in the textbook, and students copied and memorised them. The students were not expected to ask 'why'. Experimental equipment was either not available at school or otherwise covered in dust. Knowledge was seen as something that was transferred unilaterally from teacher to student.

The SMASSE team then introduced the distinctive slogan, ASEI-PDSI, which had no meaning in Swahili or Japanese. ASEI stands for A (activity), S (student), E (experiment), and I (improvisation): teachers were encouraged to introduce an *active* element into the classroom (A), prioritise the interest of *students* rather than teachers (S), incorporate *experiments* into lesson plans (E), and *improvise* practical lessons using makeshift materials (I). PDSI signifies the sequence from P (plan) to D (do), S (see), and I (improve), which is a variant of the PDCA (plan-do-check-act) cycle in the *kaizen* practice. Teachers were encouraged to carry out what they planned in advance and evaluate the results, use them to improve the lesson, and then revise the plan for the next academic term.

Muyanga B. Mutua, a trainer who studied in Wuhan, China, on a UNESCO scholarship, said:

> With the PDSI cycle in mind, secondary school teachers began to plan, implement, evaluate, and improve. This was a feedback system of trial and error. The 'ASEI' in the slogan ASEI-PDSI was initially mistaken for Japanese, but I think that is not necessarily a mistake because the slogan was a kind of Japanese *kaizen* in education. People's minds are complex. Teachers' reactions were not always positive, but there is no doubt that their teaching skills improved. Classrooms became more lively, and scores improved, so overall, there was no opposition to this campaign. [KEN 17]

Takemura Shigekazu, an educationist who retired from Hiroshima University and participated in SMASSE as an academic advisor, was respected by the local Kenyan teachers as a *mzee*, senior professor. The figure of Takemura jumping up on a chair and gesturing flamboyantly to demonstrate his lesson style made a strong impression on the trainees. Don't cram too much into the students. Teach them only the essential things. Mutua said he was particularly impressed by how Takemura cut out diagrams from a thick teaching manual with scissors, pasted them on paper, and made photocopies. This was precisely 'cut and paste'.

Takemura published a Japanese book, *Kyoiku Kakumei (Education Revolution)*, which encapsulates his attachment to the SMASSE project. The first chapter traces the history of Western science education, beginning with Greek natural philosophy; the second chapter introduces the trends in science education in the twentieth century; and the third chapter looks at the student-oriented education movement in Africa. The book abounds in concrete examples that could be used in the classroom, and Takemura states that 'the new ASEI/PDSI movement is driven by the needs and demands of African people and bears the character of a mass campaign carried out by Africans themselves for educational innovation.' He likened SMASSE to the 'black churches in African Christianity' (Takemura 2008: 252). SMASSE prevailed not only because its project design was reasonable but also because it ignited teachers' passion.

But why was Japanese involvement accepted? Kibe, who worked as a technical coordinator at JICA's Nairobi office after his retirement, explained:

> In light of the history of colonialism, I think Japan's position was relatively neutral. The philosophy of *Harambee* and Japan's philosophy of self-help are essentially the same, aren't they? We have not just accepted the policies advocated by Western countries. Together with Japanese, we tried to transform them, show results, and increase the efficiency of development aid. [KEN 12]

Harambee (meaning 'let's all pull together and work together') was proposed by President Jomo Kenyatta as a slogan for Kenya's bottom-up development (Ng'ethe 1983; Ngau 1987; Hill 1991). Instead of rejecting Western ideas outright, Africans adapt them to their local knowledge system and proactively reinterpret them. Kibe thought that Japan, as a non-Western country, could be a good partner for such an endeavour.

4.3.3 The Allowance Issue (1999–2000)

Initially, there was strong resistance to SMASSE from teachers because, although they availed themselves of holidays to attend the training, they did not receive any compensation. Typically, in donor-funded projects (including NGO activities), participants are paid an allowance in addition to necessary expenses pertaining to travel and accommodation. This training was conducted by JICA, and the teachers were working on holidays, but they were not paid anything, which caused dissatisfaction among the participating teachers.

The fact is that Sugiyama and Njuguna consulted closely and decided beforehand not to pay anything. Njuguna said, 'It was not Sugiyama-san, but me, as a Kenyan, who handled the situation on the front line. Our logic was that the teachers would benefit from the training, so it was unreasonable for us to pay something for their attendance. Actually, there was another reason, or true reason, for our decision. If the project is rolled out nationwide, the number of participants will dramatically increase. This means that, if we pay allowances to participants, the training will soon become bankrupt' [KEN 13]. The project must be financially self-sustaining. Each secondary school collected school fees from parents, some portion of which was set aside to improve the quality of teaching and learning. Then, it was decided that this pool of money would be used to cover the necessary training costs. Therefore, the implementation of the SMASSE training would not affect the budget of the Ministry of Education. Even if Japan withdrew, the system would continue to evolve as long as the content was considered good for everyone and the Ministry of Education did not deliberately abolish it. It was a smart calculation.

When the training began, however, there were teachers who were not convinced of this arrangement. In August 1999, those who had been appointed as national trainers attended the training at the KSTC, but they expressed strong dissatisfaction about the lack of compensation and even went on strike. As the second training approached in 2000, the organisers were worried, 'What if no one shows up?' In fact, the teachers returned to the training. 'Eventually, even more teachers attended than in the first year, and thus the foundation of the system was established' (JICA 2009a: 40–41, 100).

Teachers' dissatisfaction was not unfounded. Firstly, there was a sense of pride among teachers for having college/university degrees and being fully qualified; they believed there was no need for additional training. This was particularly the case for teachers in so-called 'elite' secondary schools. Second, many teachers supplement their meagre salaries by spending their holidays working in their agrarian gardens or tutoring students. Naturally, they felt it was unfair that only science teachers were forced to attend the training while humanities teachers continued with their second jobs. Thirdly, having to stay in student dormitories during the training was something that teachers resisted even more fiercely than the issue of the daily allowances. Teachers found it humiliating to have to sleep in the beds of students. Fourth, although it was mentioned little in the JICA report, the teachers' trade union opposed the training.

Teachers' dissatisfaction and resistance persisted for a while, but after the training started to be implemented nationwide in 2003, the complaints became less frequent. The authorities made participation compulsory. The Ministry of Education took a tough stance, and from the second phase onwards, a certain amount of penalty was to be deducted from the salaries of teachers who did not attend the training. In addition, the school principals strongly encouraged teachers to attend the training.[14] On the other hand, incentives were provided. Concerning accommodation, it was accepted to commute from home or to stay in nearby B&Bs. The teachers' union was invited to participate in decision-making, so that organised resistance also disappeared. Above

[14] The fact that Kibe, who was the leading figure of the secondary school principals in Kenya, promoted SMASSE from the outset was a very significant factor. Jennifer Katumbi Mwiltea, a secondary school principal, said that, in recent years, training for school principals has also been introduced to make schools more aware of the importance of teacher training [KEN 25].

all, the teachers found the content of the training attractive and useful [KEN 16; KEN 17; KEN 18; KEN 19; KEN 21; KEN 24] (JICA 2007: 26–36).

SMASSE is generally known for its innovative teaching methods, which include hands-on experiments and outdoor activities. However, the training sessions in Kenya did not start with those elements. The training was initially organised in four cycles, each lasting two weeks. Njuguna explained:

> The content of the first cycle was the same for all teachers. This was to change teachers' psychological attitudes. Originally, many of them wanted to be doctors or engineers but gave up their dreams because their academic performance fell short of it, a little bit. So, they eventually ended up becoming teachers. They didn't choose their career, they became teachers because they had no other choice. The first cycle was designed to give these teachers confidence in their profession. [KEN 13]

In the second and the third cycles, the teachers were divided into groups by subject (physics, chemistry, biology, mathematics, etc.), and the focus was on explaining how to teach the units that they found most difficult to teach. They were taught methods that could be used immediately in the classroom. Only in the final fourth cycle did the teachers learn the tricks to change their lessons qualitatively. When teachers can stand confidently in front of their students and answer their questions, their lives as teachers will never be the same. No teacher wants to be disliked by their students.

4.3.4 Changes in Teaching (2000–)

As the training proceeded, the quality of teaching in the classrooms changed. As Makoba Edmond Kizito, one of the trainers, remarked, the content of what teachers learnt at college or university was much more advanced and complicated than what they had to teach at secondary school. In colleges, they did not receive practical training adapted to the teaching in secondary schools. Hence, when they stood in front of students, they had no choice but to teach the way they had been taught in secondary school themselves. However, 'when we teach strategically in the classroom, the students show great interest, and the classroom comes alive.' In biology, native plants, local materials, such as ashes to preserve food, were used to make the lessons attractive. 'We did it together with Japanese experts, so I think they enjoyed it, too' [KEN 18].

Takemura of Hiroshima University reflected on his experience in Kenya:

> I always told the experts who would come after me not to bring anything from Japan. I told them that I would take them to rural areas so that they could see the situation there for themselves and go from house to house looking for teaching materials and making things by hand. If we bring something sophisticated from Japan, people will reject it.... In Japan, we say we should learn by looking at the back of the person we respect, but this does not work over there.... Once, a teacher requested me to observe her class, so I went to see it. But the teacher told me, 'I couldn't do it as I had intended. I want to have another class with a slightly different style, so I want you to come and see it again.' When I went to see that class, it was completely different. The class was successful, so the children applauded. The

> teacher shouted, 'I did it!' and ran over to me with her arms stretched. She was in tears and seemed so happy. (JICA 2009a: 72–73)

Samuel Thuku Chege, who taught physical chemistry at Tala Girls High School, said teachers should use a variety of examples in their lessons rather than just asking students to memorise a formula. He gave the examples he learnt in training.

> When I teach about pressure in physics, I give an example like this. There is a person who wears gym shoes and another who wears high heels. If they step on your foot, which one will give you more pain? The smaller the area of contact, the greater the pressure. The students will understand it immediately. I also explain why big lorries have so many wheels. As you know, this is to increase the contact area so that the road lasts longer with fewer repairs. When I teach this way, the students never forget. [KEN 29]

Robert Atsiaya Mukanzi, a science and mathematics teacher at Kiambu High School, concurred.

> At a teacher training session I was leading, a mathematics teacher in his fifties raised his hand and said he couldn't figure out how to teach triangulation. So, I took the teachers outside and explained how to explain it to students, using a guidebook for professional surveyors in the field. They became confident. This is a good example of activity-based teaching. [KEN 21]

Kenneth Benson Muya, a young mathematics teacher at Loreto Kiambu Girls High School, remembered that his teaching style had changed after participating in SMASSE. 'Teachers used to teach students from the top down, but now teachers help students learn. I think our students started to learn on their own, even when the teacher is not in front of them' [KEN 22].

Student-oriented science and mathematics education is spreading from secondary schools to elementary schools. We spoke to several teachers at an institution where elementary school teachers were trained. 'SMASE [a general form of SMASSE that includes primary education][15] is more about attitude than about the content of lessons. In a nutshell, I think it is about strengthening critical thinking.' 'Elementary school pupils are not shy. They raise their hands and ask questions, so you have to improvise more than in secondary schools' [KEN 26]. They tried to 'arrange the fruits around them as miniature planets to teach the solar system' [KEN 27] and 'make pupils craft their own scales using tree branches' [KEN 28].

> I think back to my own school days. My goodness, I remember that we were forced to learn multiplication by heart, and when we failed, the teacher used to beat us. Corporal punishment is now prohibited, of course, but it was different in my day. [KEN 28]

So said Stephan Kasyoka, aged 55. I am of a similar age, and I remember that the Japanese schools were similar. As SMASSE entered Phase 2, the Centre for Mathematics, Science and Technology Education in Africa (CEMASTEA) was established as a national teacher training institution to replace the KSTC, and it began to operate in 2005. Nchabira Lydia Muriithi, deputy director of CEMASTEA, was teaching

[15] When SMASSE (Strengthening of Mathematics and Science in Secondary Education) spread to primary education, it became known as SMASE (Strengthening Mathematics and Science Education) by dropping the word 'Secondary'.

biology at a secondary school when the SMASSE project started. In those days, teachers had to carry out experiments using the equipment as described in the textbooks, or otherwise they would just give up practicing it. She said it was wonderful to realise that 'if you improvise, you can do the same experiments in the natural environment,' since it was out of the question to prepare all the necessary equipment with the school's limited budget [KEN 16].

4.3.5 Consolidation and Expansion (2003–)

The original style of the cascade was a three-tier waterfall: those trained at the Nairobi centre give training at the district level, and those trained at the district level then train teachers at the sub-district (cluster) level. David Mwangi Kareri, a chemistry teacher who was a trainer at the district level, recalled, 'I instructed the trainers, who were scattered in different places, not to add anything, not to subtract anything, when they conducted training locally. In this way, the same teaching method was supposed to spread throughout the country' [KEN 20]. However, the three-tier system turned out to be too complicated, and in 2001, the structure was changed to a two-tier system consisting of Nairobi and local districts (which were reorganised into counties in 2013). The improvement of the training facilities in the districts/counties made it practical for local teachers to be trained directly at the county level. The training format was thus simplified, and in 2003, with the launch of Phase 2, the training started to be delivered nationwide.

The SMASSE system was to tap into the pool of tuition fees borne by parents, so it did not place a financial burden on the Ministry of Education but was self-sustaining as long as the training content was good. However, as the size of the pool depends on the number of students, small schools in remote areas tend to suffer a shortage of funds to send all teachers for training. Therefore, the government decided to provide subsidies to schools that lacked funds. In addition, teachers' participation in training was made compulsory by law, making in-service teacher training fully integrated into the Kenyan educational system [KEN 16].

Chege, the physics and chemistry teacher, said, 'I think Kenya is now taking ownership of SMASSE. The people giving the training are not foreigners but Kenyan teachers like us' [KEN 29]. The trainer, Kizito, said:

> Parents trust the school. The classroom atmosphere has changed. Now parents know that, when children move around the classroom in the middle of class hours, they are not playing. When SMASSE became popular, some humanities teachers started to complain that they had no chance to receive such training. I think the SMASSE method should also be extended to the humanities class, because ICT is now used widely in every subject. [KEN 18]

As the cascade training system for in-service teachers had already been implemented in the Philippines, the stakeholders in Kenya and the Philippines could exchange their experiences. The SMASSE was scaled up to cover areas outside Kenya, and Strengthening of Mathematics and Science Education in Western, Eastern, Central and Southern Africa (SMASE-WECSA) was founded in 2003 (Ishihara 2012). From 2009 to 2013, Phase 3 of the project provided in-service teacher training in all member countries: the project began with 11 members: Ghana, Kenya, Lesotho, Malawi, Mozambique, Rwanda, Swaziland (Eswatini), Tanzania, Uganda, Zambia and Zimbabwe, and gradually expanded to involve 27 countries by 2011.[16] The practice in Zambia is a case in point. Instead of the cascade model, school-based lesson study (*jugyo kenkyu*) is being developed in Zambia. Lesson study, in which a carefully prepared research lesson is observed by a team of colleagues and the content is expected to improve continuously through peer discussions, is a kind of participatory teacher training/empowering system that has gradually developed in Japan since the Meiji period (JICA 2005: 271–283). Lesson study was introduced and adapted to Zambia's unique contexts (Baba and Nakai 2009), and Kenya and Zambia are good rivals in science and mathematics education and are the two driving forces of the SMASE movement in Africa. Like 'tropicalisation' of *kaizen* in Costa Rica (Sect. 3.4), this process is considered a good example of translative adaptation (Ohno 2024).[17]

The education sector is faced with the tough question of whether to increase the amount of teaching or to selectively refine the teaching content. Practical, hands-on teaching requires time, and therefore, teachers need special skills to complete all the compulsory teaching units within the school year [KEN 18; KEN 22; KEN 24]. Mathematics teacher Muya said:

> More girls are taking science and mathematics courses than before. Their academic performance is also much improving. Talking about SMASSE teaching, the most challenging task is time management. If there is a lot to teach in the curriculum, we have to stop the practical lessons even when the students start enjoying creative experiments. Then, we have to go back to the textbook. It's a pity. [KEN 22]

When I visited a high school in Kambu, I met a lively girl student who confidently expressed her wish. 'I want to be an engineer. I want to build roads in villages' [KEN 23].

In Japan, in response to criticism of the tight cramming system, the Ministry of Education introduced the *yutori kyoiku* (relaxed education) policy with more simplified teaching curricula in 2002. Although some sharply criticised that the policy caused a decline in academic performances, no evidence-based research proves that this really happened in Japan. Turning to Kenya, the empirical evidence remains insufficient to demonstrate that the introduction of SMASSE has significantly improved the academic performances of Kenyan secondary students (Irungu and Mercy 2013; Kiige, and Atina. 2016; Dennis et al. 2017; Wanjala et al. 2020). Yet, the bottom line is that teachers have become more confident in their everyday teaching and that more children are interested in science and mathematics. One of the

---

[16] See the pamphlet commemorating the 10th anniversary of SMASE-WECSA: https://www.jica.go.jp/Resource/english/our_work/thematic_issues/education/pdf/smase.pdf.

[17] See Murata and Lee (2021) and the titles from WALS-Routledge Lesson Study Series: https://www.routledge.com/WALS-Routledge-Lesson-Study-Series/book-series/WLSS?srsltid=AfmBOorRZKv91oVVoyEEWnxy6fxdDHyki31ZkxZ4r1v0p4kUq7Y3T_3I.

effects of SMASSE was that it laid the ground for information and communication technology (ICT) education in Kenya. Stephen Njoroge, Director of CEMASTEA, remarked that teacher training in Kenya started to be integrated with ICT education, and a reward system for teachers who deliver excellent lessons was also in place [KEN 15].

Simon Kariuki, a young national staff at the JICA Kenya office, told me, 'Our generation can achieve a lot without working very hard, toiling and sweating. Perhaps, we lack a sense of duty, activeness, and dedication. But I think we, young people, also need to learn from the old people's values and incorporate something into our lifestyle' [KEN 14]. For the younger generation, for whom ICT gadgets are part of everyday life, there may come a moment when SMASSE-style hands-on learning is appreciated anew.

4.4 Sustained Passion: The Experience of Japan Overseas Cooperation Volunteers (Kenya)

4.4.1 Everyone Was a Novice

Experts working in developing countries are sometimes referred to as *kuroko* (黒子: stagehands) in Japanese. In the performing arts, *kuroko* wear black clothes and hide their faces to erase their identities, so that they can move around the stage and help the actors perform effectively. In a puppet show, however, the *kuroko* can be a manipulator controlling soulless marionettes. In development cooperation, experts are expected to act like the former rather than the latter, and the bottom line is that they are supposed to have valuable skills and experience. What if they happen to fall on the stage or tangle the strings? How would a nurse feel when giving a real patient an injection for the first time?

The former Japan Overseas Cooperation Volunteers (I use the terms JOCV and JICA Volunteers interchangeably) I interviewed are now university professors, consultants, or NGO activists. This time, I asked them not about their current jobs but about their motivations, failures, and achievements when they were young volunteers. In his acclaimed classic *Pedagogy of the Oppressed* (1968), the Brazilian educator Paulo Freire called for the 'problem-posing' model of education, which overturns the conventional 'banking' model in which teachers fill children as empty vessels (like piggy banks) with textbook knowledge. In the problem-posing model, learners become teachers, and teachers become learners, initiating a process of making all people critical, 'conscientised' thinkers and contributing to the co-creation of knowledge (Freire 1970). In this section, I will discuss the institution called the JOCV, which is expected to function as a catalyst for problem-posing (social) education.

As for the origins of the JOCV, in addition to the normative influence of the US Peace Corps, the ambitions and strategies of several key stakeholders such as Japanese youth organisations, the Liberal Democratic Party (LDP), and the Ministry of Foreign Affairs played certain roles as discussed in Okabe (2024). However, the actual motivations of individual volunteers were extremely diverse. When I asked about their honest motives for application, the interviewees gave a variety of answers, such as 'I wanted to see wild animals,' 'I longed for the nature of Africa,' 'I wanted to do science experiments in front of children,' 'I was impressed by NHK's special TV programmes,' 'I rebelled against the closed atmosphere of the countryside,' 'My postgraduate research wasn't going well,' 'I was tired of the busyness of my daily life as a school teacher,' 'I just received an application form,' 'I remembered seeing an advertisement on the train,' 'I wanted to wander around as a backpacker and help poor children,' and so on. Some interviewees were ashamed about the banality of their reasons and ideas.

Whatever their motivations, they shared something in common. For them, their time living in a community in the partner country was a life-changing experience and an undiluted joy. We will look at some more examples of citizens engaged in international cooperation and mutual learning in Chap. 6. In this section, I will focus on the stories of former JICA Volunteers, particularly science and mathematics teachers in secondary schools. Their narratives will also shed light on the JKUAT and the SMASSE projects discussed in Sects. 4.2 and 4.3 from the other side of the cooperation.

4.4.2 The Transformation of Individuals

Soma Takashi, executive director of the consulting company PADECO, was an ordinary JICA Volunteer in his 20 s [VOL 08]. From 1990, he taught mathematics at a junior high school in northern Ghana. He recalled, 'I was struggling to survive. I felt so lonely that I once ran away from the school to visit another Japanese volunteer working 120 km away.' As there were no mobile phones at that time, the only way of communicating was by sending and receiving postal letters. Soma said that the turning point for him was when he was infected with malaria. After that, he changed his attitude and started eating at his colleague's home every night, living the same life as the locals. Then, 'Everything started to go well.' He became a popular teacher who gave classes seven hours a day without slacking off. He was thrown out to the field as an individual, felt a searing sense of loneliness, and eventually became a full member of the local community.[18]

Some of the volunteers experienced embarrassing moments. Baba Takuya, who now works for Hiroshima University, recalled, 'I was lucky to have survived as a teacher' [VOL 05]. While he volunteered in the Philippines from 1984, 'The students started to complain and stormed the principal's office, demanding, "That teacher doesn't speak English. You should bring in someone else!" It was a terrible shock

[18] In May 2021, four former JICA Volunteers who now work as consultants for PADECO held a roundtable discussion via Zoom [VOL 08]. This section quotes some of the statements given by the participants.

to me.' Uchiyama Hazuki, who worked as a science and mathematics teacher in Lukulu in western Zambia from 1993, had a similar experience [VOL 04]. Many volunteers must have faced such a reaction from their students. In the case of Baba and Uchiyama, after having gone through problems in adaptation at their schools, they began to feel completely at home in the community and found their life enjoyable. Uchiyama remarked, 'What I realised when I taught in Zambia was that all children are the same. They fussed when I didn't prepare for the lesson or forced them to follow my instructions. But they were delighted when we had science experiments. It was even more fun when the students came to visit my accommodation. We became friends.' A volunteer, who started working as a science and mathematics teacher in Kenya in 1993, said that when she walked into a classroom, she felt that Kenyan and Japanese schools were the same [VOL 03]. 'Some students didn't like the lessons but liked the activities. It was great fun to go on trips with students and make video clips together.'

What about the contents of the learning? Naganuma Keiichi, who was sent to Zambia as a science and mathematics teacher in 1996, taught in the second-best school in the area, only to find that many students could not do even the four arithmetic operations [VOL 02]. The results of short tests were devastating, and he confessed, 'I thought it was really bad. I prayed, "Please, please get better marks." The fact that they weren't getting good marks meant that they didn't understand what I was teaching, so I realised that their low marks were low marks for me. If the students don't change, it's because I'm teaching poorly, so I felt sorry.' He started to teach more carefully, and the marks improved. At the same time, Naganuma identified a reason for the problems he encountered. He indicated that Zambia's examinations were 'designed to weed out students who won't become elites', which destroyed the motivations of the majority of students. Naganuma also worked on science experiments that excited students, and this became a small success story for him. 'I realised that the local teachers didn't want to fail. If they kept failing, the students would look down on them, and if that kept happening, teachers would hate the job. I thought the teacher training wasn't going well.' Naganuma eventually became an expert with SMASSE in Kenya. For him, the insights he obtained from his time as a JICA Volunteer in Zambia laid the foundation for his subsequent career.

4.4.3 Pros and Cons of Teamwork

A JICA Volunteer must have strong personal capacity, especially the capacity to empathise. In some cases, JICA Volunteers are dispatched not as individuals but as a team or a group of individuals to work together in coordination. Let us look at some examples related to the JKUAT and SMASSE.

When Koaze Hiroshi was a graduate student at Obihiro University of Agriculture and Veterinary Medicine, he heard that his academic supervisor, who had connections with Okayama University, was looking for a young person to help set up the JKUAT. He immediately raised his hand [VOL 01]. 'I thought it would be wonderful if I could help establish a new university in Africa.' In 1981, he began to engage in this task. At the time, the JKUAT campus was just a collection of whitish buildings on a dry, empty plain. Koaze and his colleagues were the first to enter the new buildings and test the equipment before the Kenyan staff arrived.

At the time, Koaze was still a young man in his late twenties, just graduated from a university, and in that respect, no different from the average JICA Volunteer. But his duty in Kenya was clearly defined from the outset. He was required to team up with an expert and teach at the new college. Koaze's senior partner was Sugiyama, the expert who would eventually become the driving force behind SMASSE. At the end of Araki (2014), all names of the experts and JICA Volunteers involved in the early years of the JKUAT were listed. Between March 1981 and July 1990, 53 volunteers and 58 long-term experts provided support, meaning that teamwork between young volunteers and senior experts was roughly one-to-one. Koaze said, 'Mr Sugiyama told me that dictation alone wouldn't be enough. We should also make everything printed on paper. In those days, there was no computer, no photocopy, so we used typewriters and mimeographs to prepare teaching materials.' As in Japan, they worked late into the night on weekdays. However, on weekends, 'We went to Nairobi with the experts, began drinking in the daytime, and discussed everything.'

Most experts were former JICA Volunteers, so their relationship was good. For Koaze, Sugiyama and other experts were like older brothers, and the Kenyan students like younger ones. One of the first-generation students, Muhara (Sect. 4.2.2), was an outstanding student. The person who taught him *karate* was an agricultural engineering volunteer, Tokita Kunihiro. In the opening days of the college, everything was handmade. 'The students maintained the sports grounds themselves and built basketball and volleyball courts and the athletics tracks. I have wonderful memories of inviting the graduating students to my house to have a big celebration party.' However, the fact that only five out of ten students in the first generation passed the national examination shocked everyone. Koaze continued, 'Japanese technical education places a great weight on the graduation work. The exam comes after all this work. But in the JKUAT, there wasn't enough time to prepare for the exam. So we got past exam papers and analysed them, and from the second generation we incorporated exam preparation into the curriculum. We worked really hard because the university's reputation could be ruined if we failed to raise the pass rate.' The Kenyans and the Japanese worked as one team. The Kenyans could not believe it when the Japanese announced they were pulling out, as discussed in Sect. 4.2.5.

Next, let us turn to the stories of JICA Volunteers in the field of science and mathematics in secondary education. Having taught science in the Solomon Islands, Nakai Kazuyoshi was sent to the Philippines to oversee a team of volunteers as a senior member [VOL 06]. In-service teacher training in science and mathematics started to be provided in the Philippines in 1994, using the same cascade approach as the one that would be adopted in Kenya a few years later. Teacher trainers in the Philippines were not always good at experiments, so JICA Volunteers stepped in and taught them how to do it as necessary.

> Individual volunteers had their own ideas. I assumed the volunteers understood the team's goals and objectives, but some preferred to teach in their own ways. I gave them guidance and explained that working as a team would benefit them in the long run. Working as a team is a valuable skill when they return to Japan. The volunteers were assigned in three regions and met and worked in groups a few times each month. They travelled by car to schools far from the local science education centre, where they demonstrated experiments and introduced inquiry-based learning, similar to what's done in Japan. Educators in the Philippines welcomed them, and it worked well because they involved children in both the preparations and the activities. [VOL 06]

Team dispatch is formally arranged based on agreements with partner countries. Group dispatch is similar, but its conditions of activities are less strict. Later, the lessons of science and mathematics education were transferred from the Philippines to Kenya. Uchiyama Hazuki, responsible for coordinating the SMASSE group dispatch in Kenya, was sent to Makueni District as a senior JICA Volunteer in August 2000 [VOL 04]. Uchiyama initially worked as a primary school teacher and later as a junior high school teacher in Nagano Prefecture. In Kenya, she and her counterparts, the teacher training supervisors, visited schools nationwide to converse with school principals and observe how subjects were taught. 'Volunteers would assemble once a month in Machakos to have discussions. I explained to less experienced volunteers about the progress of SMASSE so far, emphasising that education is a team effort. I encouraged them not to struggle alone but to broaden their horizons and collaborate with their colleagues. I also told them about the overall achievements at the district level. The volunteers worked very hard, so I respected them all.'

On the other hand, Jibutsu Kenichi, who was dispatched to a different district from Uchiyama's, confessed that he did not like the group system.

> I tried to do things my way, but I kept getting told to do this and that as part of the group, which frustrated me. Everyone in the group was complaining to each other about it. Since I didn't have any teaching experience, the expectation put on me was overwhelming. The experts kept telling me how to teach, but their advice didn't work for me. I was caught up in preparing for the next day's lessons and it was all I could manage. When I returned to Japan and started teaching at a junior high school, I finally felt comfortable with my teaching style. [VOL 18]

First of all, JICA Volunteers should face the students in classrooms. At the same time, volunteers also need to connect with their colleagues to improve their activities at the school. Volunteers from Japan and local teachers are required to work in groups, at least. It is always challenging to find a good balance between individual responsibility and group collaboration.

4.4.4 *The Plight of Local Teachers*

So how did JICA Volunteers see the conditions surrounding local teachers? A volunteer who stayed in western Kenya found that many Kenyan teachers were giving up their jobs. 'Life in rural villages is inconvenient and boring. There is no adequate accommodation. The pay is far from good. The schools don't have enough budget to pay the teachers properly, so they have to supplement their meagre salaries by working in their gardens.' The high turnover of local teachers meant that JICA Volunteers who taught 'for free' were considered a great asset to both the schools and the local communities. When she arrived in the village, the village chief was waiting for her at the bus stop, which was served only once a day. The kindness seemed to be a mixture of the chief's integrity and the villagers' gratitude for her voluntary work [VOL 03].

In the previous section, I discussed the question of allowances in SMASSE. It could be unreasonable to ask teachers working in poor villages who engaged in side jobs to make ends meet to attend training on holidays without compensation. Uchiyama, who was a senior JICA Volunteer during the second phase of SMASSE, remembered that Kenya's Ministry of Education took a tough stance regarding the allowance issue. 'I think the teachers feared they would be in trouble if they were absent from the training. The Ministry of Education was serious about the training.'

On the other hand, the training itself seemed to be an enjoyable experience for the participating teachers.

> The teachers bonded with each other, and in the evenings they'd often hang out and watch movies together. It felt just like being back in college days. Since the training was interactive, no one got bored, and even the younger teachers felt comfortable discussing things as equals with senior teachers. The staff at the designated schools worked hard to serve excellent meals. At first, there was a bit of hesitation about sleeping in the student dorms, but we provided brand-new mattresses for them. Everyone seemed to have a great time, and one participant even said she wanted to name her future child 'Smasse'. [VOL 04]

Nishikata, who used to engage in mathematics education in a primary school in Honduras, said that neither local teachers nor JICA Volunteers would change their attitudes by being told abstract ideals. They must have a clear motivation. He offered some tips to young volunteers:

> Some people are too ambitious and spin around. They say, 'I want to do this, I want to do that,' but I ask them if it is OK just to think of 'what I want'. If you assume what you know is the best way of education, or you want to teach them the Japanese method, which you believe is the best, the local people won't take you seriously. First of all, you have to share your values with them. Then you should reflect on whether that is really what you can do. And you must be able to show them how they will benefit from what you do. [VOL 07]

If you begin by blaming your counterparts, you won't be able to collaborate with them effectively. You must trust them. Nishikata said it was important to understand the gaps in perceptions between volunteers and local teachers. What is the goal? What are the problems? How can we solve them? Nishikata advised the young volunteers to try to achieve things step by step and have a sense of accomplishment.[19]

[19] https://www.jica.go.jp/activities/issues/education/useful/advice/advice_01.html (in Japanese).

4.4.5 Learning from the Field Experience

It is indispensable for a JICA Volunteer to nurture historical imagination. In discussing mathematics education in Kenya, Baba of Hiroshima University endorsed the concept of ethnomathematics, proposed by the Brazilian pedagogist Ubiratan D'Ambrosio (Baba 2003). D'Ambrosio argued that mathematics had a cultural aspect. Different cultures have different ways of counting, measuring, and calculating. Even though 'Western' mathematics has been historically sophisticated and has universal applicability, mathematics education will become richer and more acceptable to local children by teaching them other ways of mathematical thinking, referring to their historical and cultural contexts (D'Ambrosio 1985, 2006). It is true not only of mathematics but also of the Western system of art and music, for example, the equal temperament. Japanese folk songs evolved with the perfect fourth as a basis of musical scale.[20]

Kenyans think in similar ways. Muyanga Mutua studied in Wuhan, China, with a UNESCO scholarship and is well-versed in Asian culture. He then became a trainer at CEMASTEA. He explained his idea.

> Even if it's broken, Kenyans always try to speak English. I think there is a mindset that English is a superior language. I think this is a result of mental colonialism. Some people say that physics transcends languages, but we have the problem of which language we should choose as the language of instruction. Linguistic differences may bring confusion to children. For example, in English, we say one-third, a fraction, but in Japanese, I know you are saying 'san bun no ichi' (three divided by one). The order of the numbers is different. For small children, who are learning fractions, such a difference can be quite confusing. [KEN 17]

Given the colonial legacy, Samuel Chege, who taught chemistry and physics at a girls' high school, remarked that Kenyans had no choice but to continue using English because the country would fall apart if they did not use a third-party language.

> It may be a legacy of British colonial rule that science, mathematics, and other subjects are taught in English in Kenya, but I was taught that way myself, so I have no problem using English. There are over 40 ethnic groups in Kenya, and it is difficult to communicate with each other without using English. It is common in schools to have students from several ethnic groups, which makes it practically impossible to choose one ethnic language. There is a nationwide personnel transfer system for secondary school teachers in Kenya. I think this system contributes to the national cohesion of Kenya. [KEN 29]

While interacting with students in the classroom and local community members outside the classroom, JICA Volunteers encounter unexpected, sometimes embarrassing facts and stories. In an essay reflecting on his experience as a volunteer in the Philippines, Baba of Hiroshima University noted that a relative of the owner of his

[20] See Bangura (2012) for 'African mathematics'. There are two ways to tailor a kimono: one is to convert the measure based on *Shakkanho* (the Japanese measurement units) into the metric system and then tailor; the other is to directly tailor the kimono using *Shakkaho* and then measure the size of the product using the metric system. With the first method, one can only make something that is 'roughly similar' to a kimono (Nakane 1967: 12–13). This intriguing description of 'residuality' is somehow omitted in the English edition of Nakane's classic work on Japanese society.

boarding house was killed by Japanese soldiers during World War II, and the owner was initially reluctant to accept a Japanese person like Baba into her home (Baba 2007: 59). Baba told me another story:

> There was an anti-Japanese atmosphere in the Philippines in the 1980s. A senior volunteer was even stoned. I once visited a refugee camp in Bataan where the death march had taken place. I was travelling in a jeepney. I had already learnt a little Tagalog, so I overheard a conversation among Filipinos in the same car, and one of them said that he was the child of a rape by a Japanese soldier during the war. I don't think they knew I was Japanese. I was at a loss, and I just shrank away. I encountered many similar incidents. [VOL 05]

When Baba worked as an expert in Kenya, he heard a volunteer criticising British colonialism. He thought that was too naive because the Japanese committed evils in Asia, as the British did in Africa. Baba thought the remark by the Japanese volunteer was irresponsible, as the person spoke casually as if his people were innocent. On the other hand, in Britain, Baba met a British who called President Jomo Kenyatta a 'terrorist', referring to the Mau Mau rebellion in Kenya. He said, 'If your position was different, you would express a completely different opinion. We should look at things from different angles.'

Sekine Reiko, who specialised in early childhood education, used to work in a kindergarten, a special education class, and a nursery close to a railway station in Japan [VOL 08]. However, after turning 30, she felt something was missing, so she applied for the JOCV. In Syria, where she was posted, she worked on early childhood education and participated in a wider training programme involving Egypt, Jordan and other countries. She will never forget how her colleague in Aleppo, Syria, who was the same age as her, welcomed her like a family member.

> Once, she asked me what my family looked like. Then she drew a form of trapezium. The parents are located at the top and the children are at the bottom. And she said that was what her family looked like. She meant that a husband and a wife were equal. After I came back from Syria, I lost my father. When she heard about it from a new team member, she phoned me in Japan to express her condolences. [VOL 08]

Syria, once a heartland of educational cooperation in the Middle East, was torn apart by the civil war that began in 2011, and Aleppo, where Sekine spent her years as a JICA Volunteer, was ruined. The Syrian accomplishment of human development was lost in a moment.

4.4.6 After Returning to Japan

Many former JICA Volunteers faced 'reverse culture shock', maladjustment when rejoining Japanese society. Yoshioka Itsuo, who spent years in Ethiopia, was unable to find work after he returned to Japan, could not readapt to society, suffered hallucinations in hearing Amharic at midnight, and started to have serious stomach problems (Yoshioka 1998: 183–189). A former volunteer concurred, 'Nowadays, there is an option to enrol in graduate schools. At that time, few former JICA Volunteers could find jobs in international cooperation. It depended on their area of expertise, but many JOCV returnees just became 'weird persons' and could not find work' [VOL 03].

JICA Volunteers who have developed a strong attachment to the developing world may eventually become experts, consultants or researchers in specific fields. However, Sekine, who works for PADECO, remarked, 'There were fewer people around me who wanted to become professionals. I think there were more who wanted to work for NGOs.' Baba, who returned to Japan from the Philippines in 1986, engaged in NGO activities on the issues of deforestation in Malaysia at a time when Japanese ODA was harshly criticised. 'At that time, people thought joining the JOCV was hypocritical' [VOL 05].

In civil society, the person who had the most significant impact on the image of JICA Volunteers was probably Hoshino Masako, who became a Japanese language teacher in Laos as a member of the first batch of JICA Volunteers dispatched as early as 1965. Turned 89 years old, Hoshino recalled that the moment of Japan's defeat in the war had a lasting impact on her career.

> During the war, I looked after army horses, I was trained with bamboo spears, and I sincerely tried my best, believing we would win the war. I was a dedicated military girl, and that's why I became so angry. I thought, 'What does it mean to endure the unendurable?' The fact that the war was wrong meant we didn't know the truth. I thought we shouldn't be confined to the small islands of Japan and that we had to look at Japan from the outside to discover the objective truth. [VOL 10]

Before the war, Hoshino's father lived in Hawaii as an emigrant but returned to Japan because of sickness. When Hoshino, then a young child, saw poor children on the street and blurted out 'Those guys are poor', her father admonished her, saying, 'You shouldn't speak like that. We were the same. We were all poor.' After graduating from university, Hoshino worked as a full-time housewife for 10 years and then got divorced. While reading a newspaper at the National Diet Library, she came across an advertisement to recruit the first batch of the JOCV and applied immediately.

In Laos, many of the students in Hoshino's language classes were ethnic Chinese, who apparently wanted to use their multiple language skills for their business, as visitors from Japan were expected to increase. In Thailand, in the late 1970s, she became a coordinator for Japanese housewives helping Cambodian refugees and served as an interpreter for Ogata Sadako, who visited the Thai-Cambodian border region. In 1980, Hoshino and others founded the Japan International Volunteer Center (JVC). While working with the UK-based NGO, Oxfam, they were invited to join Oxfam and establish its Japanese branch, but they declined in favour of independence. In the meantime, Hoshino ensured that all discussions in JVC's overseas offices should be conducted in English. 'The decision was not necessarily welcomed, but I thought we had to do it that way to make the organisation effective.' Hoshino returned to Japan in 1982 and committed herself to JVC's activities from the headquarters in Japan, but she was always prepared to 'bury my bones in Laos [make Laos my final home]', and said that if there was a parallel world, she could easily see herself living there [VOL 10].[21]

As a pioneer of her generation, Hoshino lived a life of continuous trial and error, but the younger generation appears more strategic. Miyazaki Atsumasa, who worked as a science and mathematics teacher in Malawi and was involved in a SMASSE follow-up project, applied for a graduate school in the UK while working as a JICA Volunteer and moved to London as soon as his term was up. While writing his Master's thesis, he accessed the job search website for international cooperation, PARTNER,[22] and applied for a post offered by an NGO, the Association for Aid and Relief, Japan (AAR Japan). Miyazaki said he wanted to work for an influential NGO because he 'wanted to feel a sense of touch' which he enjoyed in his JICA Volunteer days. Miyazaki was dispatched to Uganda as an AAR staff member, but the spread of COVID-19 forced him back to Japan after less than six months. He said, 'I am frustrated about working remotely like this. The local staff continue working hard. The decision to have Japanese people leave the site and give instructions from Japan must be the right choice, but it's frustrating' [VOL 09].

Most of the educational volunteers I interviewed were science and mathematics teachers, though Hoshino was a Japanese language teacher. The last person I met online, Ogawa Akiko, consistently pursued a 'dual career in international cooperation and making things'. She thought it was necessary to acquire specific skills to become a JICA Volunteer, so after graduating from university she trained for four years as a furniture maker in Hida Takayama and Nagano. She loved crafts (as opposed to the fine arts), 'things that are rooted and used in everyday life'. She passed the JOCV examination in the field of art and was assigned to a national vocational school in Honduras, Central America, where 'I actually taught maths – things like how to use a ruler, how to draw a line, and how to count numbers with a unit. I taught them how to look at things through art.' Through her experience as a JICA Volunteer, she strengthened her capacity to 'imagine what is happening' in places other than Japan. After returning to Japan, Ogawa worked as a furniture maker for another four years before joining Shapla Neer, an NGO founded in 1972 that promoted fair trade in handicrafts made in Bangladesh and Nepal, among other activities. She now wanted to broaden the scope of her work in Japan, for example, by having students sell Shapla Neer's commodities on consignment at school festivals. 'I think there's value in things that can only be made by humans, things that remind you that there are people living on the other side of the globe, things that AI can never replace' [VOL 11].

If the JOCV's mission is only to contribute to development cooperation, it may be more effective to recruit volunteers with more specific expertise, carefully examine the nature of their skills, mobilise them as junior experts, and dispatch them in teams with definite assignments. However, such a reform may undermine the very basis of the JOCV. Even when their activities do not bear fruit, many JICA Volunteer

[21] Hoshino struggled with illness at the time of the interview. She passed away in Tokyo in 2022 at the age of 90.

[22] The website (in Japanese) is managed by JICA: https://partner.jica.go.jp/.

alumni say that being thrown out as a bare individual was the 'real appeal of the JOCV.' A former science and mathematics teacher in Kenya said, 'If the goal is to be effective, I think it would be better to provide the country with the equal sum of money as needed to hire a JICA Volunteer and use it to employ capable local teachers. Nevertheless, the value of the JOCV is priceless, because this has enabled local people and JICA Volunteers to learn from each other. After experiencing hardships in unfamiliar places, former volunteers can intuitively understand how to help foreigners in Japan after returning home' [VOL 03]. As Hoshino hoped as a child, those who experienced the JOCV could observe Japan objectively from outside perspectives.

Although the presentation of narratives of former Japanese volunteers in this section could be a deviation from the emphasis on the narratives of counterparts in Japan's partner countries, it is still crucial to consider the future of international cooperation beyond the principal-agent framework by highlighting the mutual learning involving citizens across nations. The theme of broadening the horizons of cooperation by promoting citizen participation will be discussed again under the theme of human security in Chap. 6. Before doing so, let me return to the appraisal of activities in which specificity plays a critical role: cooperation in the medical sector.

Chapter 5
The Right to Health: Public Health Cooperation

5.1 Science, Institutions, and Outreach

5.1.1 The Living System in Question

Tolstoy's *Anna Karenina* begins with the famous passage: 'Happy families are all alike; each unhappy family is unhappy in its own way.' Consider the example given by Amartya Sen in *Development as Freedom* (Sen 1999: 54–56). Annapurna can hire only one out of three poor people who want to work for her. First, Dinu is the poorest in terms of income. Second, Bishanno recently lost his job and is the most depressed. Third, Rogini has a chronic illness and is debilitated, and the money she could earn from the work would enable her to afford treatment in hospital. Which of the three, then, should Annapurna hire? Should we look at income (money), subjective well-being (utilities) or the range of critical options available to individuals (capabilities)? Each aspect is important. However, Sen wrote that while there were a lot of discussions and research about incomes and utilities, not much attention had been paid to human capabilities and the quality of life.

The role of health in human development is analogous to that of education, which we examined in Chap. 4. Children who attend school, learn to read, write, and do maths, and become creative and socially disciplined will be transformed into valuable human resources and contribute to economic growth. However, beyond its instrumental value for economic development, education also has intrinsic value; going to school broadens people's life choices and enhances their well-being so that they can live lives they value. The same is true of health. Workers who are physically and mentally healthy and take no sick leave contribute to economic development as valuable human resources. But being healthy also involves broadening one's life experiences. Raising life expectancy from 40 to 80 years would, at least potentially, double life's opportunities and enjoyment. Living a longer and healthier life is good for everyone, not just for society.

Y. Mine, *An Oral History of Development Cooperation*,
https://doi.org/10.1007/978-981-95-5479-9_5

To ensure healthy lives for all, hospitals should provide appropriate medical services, vaccines should be widely distributed, nutrition should improve, and the health insurance system should work. However, whether a person gets sick or not is largely a matter of chance and physical traits. The COVID-19 pandemic is a good example. We are all human beings; if a rich and a poor person share the same room, both are equally susceptible to infection. In 2020, the spread of COVID-19 in Western countries was dramatic. Rich people with underlying diseases were more likely to develop critical symptoms than healthy poor people.

At the same time, the fact remains that poor people are particularly vulnerable to serious diseases. In both the United States and Western Europe, the number of victims of COVID-19 was particularly high among people of non-European descent, probably because of their exposure to the virus through unsafe key-worker jobs and the insufficient coverage of health insurance. As Ulrich Beck pointed out in *Risk Society*, air pollution crosses national borders and harms the health of rich and poor alike, but it is the latter who live in dangerous low-lying areas and are swept away by climate change-induced floods. 'There is a systematic "attraction" between extreme poverty and extreme risk' (Beck 1992: 41). The United Nations warned in March 2020 that the socio-economic impact of COVID-19 would be more significant in developing countries (UNSG 2020), though the ex-post research on the exact magnitude and consequences is still ongoing.

Diseases are not just about humans and human society. In fact, domestic and wild animals also play a key role in the emergence and spread of major infectious diseases. After the World Health Organization (WHO) declared the eradication of smallpox in 1980, people assumed that humanity had finally overcome major deadly infectious diseases. However, as historian William McNeill described in *Plagues and Peoples*, the balance between human hosts and disease organisms has been thrown into an 'unusually dramatic and drastic disturbance' (McNeill 1998: 10), and the process is intensifying. When living creatures, whether human or livestock, live in close proximity to each other in large numbers, it becomes a favourable feeding ground for parasites, where an explosive infection is likely to occur, as discussed in the case study of salmon farming in Chile (Chap. 2, Sect. 2.3). 'Most and probably all of the distinctive infectious diseases of civilization transferred to human populations from animal herds' (ibid.: 69). The modalities in which humans interact with other living things are in question, and the traditional boundaries between human medicine, veterinary science, and biology are being blurred.

5.1.2 Cooperation in Advanced Medicine

Given the importance of medicine for human society and planetary health, I present three projects in this chapter in the context of the history of Japan's medical cooperation. Can we identify changes in the trend of development cooperation in the health sector that parallel those in other sectors discussed in other parts of this book?

Development cooperation in health poses challenges that are qualitatively different from those in education, even though these two sectors are often grouped under the single umbrella of human development. Medicine requires highly specialised training. Education to obtain national medical qualifications takes longer than that for teachers. Becoming a teacher in primary and secondary schools also requires skills and qualifications, but for schoolteachers, improving teaching skills in the classroom is far more important than learning in teachers' college.

Let us revisit the principal-agent framework (Chap. 1, Sect. 1.2). Medicine is a field in which 'specificity' weighs greatly. The manuals for examination, diagnosis, surgery, medication, and follow-up are in place and constantly updated, and all medical professionals are required to follow the procedures. While special knowledge and expertise are required to address emergencies and treat rare diseases, medical malpractice that occurred due to the negligence of standard procedures is prosecuted. At the same time, the scope of medical practice is not as broad as that of education. Many children spend far more time with their teachers than medical professionals. Children go to school every day, but they go to hospital only when it is necessary.

Given the importance of specific skills in the medical field, Japan attempted to send doctors and nurses to developing countries from the early period of medical collaboration. Japan's official development cooperation in the health sector is said to have begun in 1958 with the dispatch of medical experts to Ethiopia.[1] 'Initially, the main focus was on sending mobile teams to carry out medical activities locally and providing necessary equipment such as special vehicles. Although the project was highly appreciated by the residents of the areas where the medical treatment was provided, the activities were not sustainable in the aid recipient countries, and the project had to end with only temporary results. This was because there was no human resources development through technology transfer to the personnel in the recipient country' (JICA 1984b: 80). In 1966, after such evaluation, the Medical Cooperation Office was set up in the Overseas Operations Department of JICA, and relatively large-scale project-type technical cooperation, combining the dispatch of experts, the acceptance of trainees, and the provision of equipment, was promoted. In 1970, the Medical Cooperation Department was established in JICA, and from 1974 to 1983, 71 projects were implemented in the health sector (in addition to five projects in population and family planning). If charismatic doctors had been dispatched to a place empty-handed, they could not have made a difference. By combining the technology transfer with the provision of equipment, it was hoped that medical cooperation would have a significant impact (ibid.: 78–80).

A good example is the Noguchi Memorial Institute for Medical Research (NMIMR) in Ghana, which I take up as the first case study of this chapter. This project, named after the Japanese bacteriologist Noguchi Hideyo, received an unprecedented amount of funding from the Japanese government. Support for the University of Ghana in the area of medical cooperation began in 1968. It was the third oldest of the 12 major medical cooperation projects in Africa, after the Nakuru Hospital in Kenya

[1] Before the war, a group of Japanese Christians privately provided medical aid to Ethiopia, according to research by Professor Takahashi Motoki of Kyoto University.

(cooperation started in 1966) and the Imperial Central Laboratory in Ethiopia (cooperation started in 1967). In the above period, the number of experts dispatched from Japan to the project in Ghana was 69, the second largest of all project-type technical cooperation (after the 79 experts sent to Bolivia for research on digestive diseases). Even more outstanding is the provision of equipment, which totalled 875.86 million yen. It was the largest project-type technical cooperation at the time (plus buildings constructed with grant aid), surpassing the project with the budget of 593.12 million yen for vaccine production in Brazil (ibid.: 78–79).

Ghana in West Africa is home to a wide range of tropical diseases, and the need for medical cooperation has been substantial. In addition to the strong local needs, there were also circumstances in which a lot of resources had to be transferred from Japan to Ghana in medical cooperation. In the first half of Sect. 5.2, I will describe the historical background of the NMIMR in some detail. In the second half, I present interview narratives of those Ghanaians who were familiar with the situations after the NMIMR was established, in which the ownership of the project was in question.

The project-type technical cooperation for the NMIMR ended in 1985.[2] In the same year, the project to establish the School of Veterinary Medicine at the University of Zambia (UNZA) was launched (Sect. 5.3). Support for veterinary science at UNZA could be classified under either agriculture (animal husbandry) in Chap. 2 or education (higher education cooperation) in Chap. 4. In this book, the cooperation in Zambia is presented as the second case study of the medical cooperation of this chapter, given the close causal relationships between infectious diseases of humans and those of big and small animals, as evidenced by the emergence of various types of zoonoses. From a biological point of view, medicine and veterinary science can be regarded as fundamentally the same as the science of living creatures including humans.

Looking at the support for the NMIMR and UNZA, we can see an interesting pattern of project evolution. Initially, Fukushima Medical University became the mainstay of support for the NMIMR, which was called the 'Fukushima Medical University Model.' In the case of the School of Veterinary Medicine at UNZA, the entire Japanese veterinary community was involved, with the School of Veterinary Medicine, Hokkaido University, taking the lead. In contrast to the Fukushima model, which was discontinued at the height of cooperation, Hokkaido University stayed committed to providing support to and collaborating with UNZA even after JICA's full-scale assistance ended.

---

[2] The NMIMR project (Phase I and II) was implemented for over ten years from 1986. In preparation for the second phase, there were requests for new projects from Ghana, including research on malaria, but the Japanese research team considered that, 'if possible, we would like the research topics to be universal ones that would be beneficial and interesting to Japanese researchers as well' (JICA 1990c: 7). As will be discussed later, the Ghanaian side was not satisfied with the Japanese response.

5.1.3 Catalyst for Institutional Development

The two projects described above have played a significant role in establishing advanced medical and veterinary science in Africa. The NMIMR has focused on research, while the School of Veterinary Medicine at UNZA prioritised education, and both eventually became proudly autonomous organisations in their own right.

While these are examples of the transfer of highly specific technologies, the third case study in this chapter concerns building a nationwide system to deliver basic healthcare to every citizen. While population policies existed in all countries, they tended to be top-down campaigns, often accompanied by coercive measures. However, the family planning initiatives that emerged out of the 1994 International Conference on Population and Development (Cairo Conference) spread around the world as democratic joint ventures of governments and civil society, promoting women's empowerment. In the project in Jordan, as will be discussed in Sect. 5.4, village health workers have been visiting households in rural villages since 1997, advising local women on a range of issues from contraception and maternal and child health to domestic violence.

In order to occasion people's behavioural change, individual citizens need to be convinced that the new modality of life will benefit them as well as larger society. The importance of linking scientific knowledge with people's everyday practice was appreciated all over the world in the vortex of the COVID-19 pandemic. In the context of development cooperation, it also highlights the necessity to integrate behavioural economics into evidence-based development studies.[3]

The three projects presented in this chapter all reached maturity, but it is also necessary to note that each went through a period of unexpected crisis. Medical cooperation in Ghana was temporarily suspended due to the oil crisis, and when the construction of the building was completed, the Ghanaian government was overthrown in a military coup, with other serious events including a famine constantly buffeting the project. The School of Veterinary Medicine at UNZA was threatened by a crisis of organisational sustainability from the beginning. Without the spirit of independence of Zambians and the persistent support from Hokkaido University and other institutions, the project could have been derailed and delayed. The project in Jordan grew steadily, but the project in its neighbour, Syria, which would become an integral part of regionwide reproductive health cooperation, was destroyed by the civil war that began in 2011. This brings home to us the fact that peace is the cornerstone of human development.

---

[3] See the works of Esther Duflo, Abhijit Banerjee and Michael Kremer, the winners of the 2019 Nobel Prize in Economics, such as Banerjee and Duflo (2011).

5.2 The Legacies: Noguchi Memorial Institute for Medical Research (Ghana)

5.2.1 *The Life of a Prodigy*

In Ghana, the name 'Noguchi' refers to the Noguchi Memorial Institute for Medical Research (NMIMR), one of Africa's leading medical research institutes. In order to understand why the institute, named after the Japanese bacteriologist Noguchi Hideyo, was established in Ghana, let me briefly recount Noguchi's life.

Noguchi Hideyo was born in 1876 in a village on the shore of Lake Inawashiro in Fukushima Prefecture. When he was one and a half years old, he fell on the hearth and suffered severe burns to his left hand. With the support of his mother, Noguchi studied medicine and worked at the laboratory of Kitasato Shibasaburo, a distinguished medical doctor and bacteriologist, in Tokyo. In 1900, Noguchi moved to the US and carried out research on the spirochete of syphilis at the Rockefeller Institute for Medical Research, for which he was nominated several times for the Nobel Prize in Medicine. In 1918, he was sent to Ecuador to study yellow fever, which was feared to be one of the deadliest tropical infectious diseases, but the mechanism of the disease was not exactly known.[4] In 1927, Noguchi travelled to Accra in the British Gold Coast Colony (today's Ghana) in West Africa to investigate its pathology. However, he contracted yellow fever himself and died in Accra at the age of 51.

Dozens of books on Noguchi, mostly biographies, have been published in Japanese over the past century, and new ones continue to appear. Japanese children learn about Noguchi 'much as American children learn the story of George Washington and the cherry tree' (Plesset 1980: 10). In 2008, the Japanese government established the Hideyo Noguchi Africa Prize to honour people who have made outstanding achievements in the fields of infectious disease control and public health in Africa, and the awardees have been announced on the occasion of the Tokyo International Conference on African Development (TICAD).[5] In real life, Noguchi was no saint and used the money he borrowed from his friends to go on a spending spree. Noguchi adopted the American value of innovative competition; his achievements were recognised globally, except in Japan, during his lifetime.

Noguchi's greatest misfortune was that he could not verify his most important hypothesis. The causative agent of yellow fever is not a bacterium, which Noguchi was frantically looking for, but a virus. Noguchi and his assistants raised several hundred monkeys for experiments in Accra, dissected them all night, and searched for a pestilent pathogen of yellow fever with optical microscopes. An electron microscope would have been needed to find the virus, but this was not available in his time.

---

[4] Since there was a geopolitical need for the US to eradicate yellow fever to defend the Panama Canal, the Rockefeller Institute for Medical Research prioritised funding for this project. As for Noguchi's life in the US, see Eckstein (1931).

[5] See the Cabinet Office website: https://www.cao.go.jp/noguchisho/english/index.html.

Noguchi was somehow convinced that he had acquired immunity to yellow fever, and his last words were, 'I don't understand….' The mystery remained unsolved.

In the early days of Japan's international cooperation, Noguchi was a role model for many experts and JICA Volunteers. Many must have read paperback biographies of Noguchi to overcome their loneliness and be encouraged to vie with Western aid workers. Noguchi was not only a powerful 'natural man' but also 'considered working with his hands to be his forte' (Koizumi 1939: 178–179). 'There are two kinds of researchers: those who work with their heads and those who work with both their heads and their hands. People like Ehrlich get others to do the work they have thought up. That way, they can do good work, but I can't trust anything outside my own hands.' This is a quote from Noguchi during his time at the Rockefeller Institute. Noguchi would not let his assistant wash test tubes at the time of critical experiments. 'He would wash them himself, check them himself, and use them himself' (Okumura 1933: 416–417).

Ghana was the frontrunner of the African independence movement, and some Japanese policy-makers wanted to carry on Noguchi's legacy and contribute to Ghana's nation-building. Immediately after Ghana achieved independence in 1957, Japan established diplomatic relations and appointed Okuma Nobuyuki (the grandson of the Meiji statesman Okuma Shigenobu) as the first Japanese ambassador to Ghana. Near the laboratory used by Noguchi, a Japanese garden was laid out, and a statue of Noguchi was erected. When a commemoration of the 42nd anniversary of Noguchi's death was held at this site in 1970, one participant, Minami Kazumori, a bacteriologist at Fukushima Medical University, had the opportunity to hear from a Ghanaian who had worked as Noguchi's assistant. He said Noguchi was physically small but when he began to talk, he 'suddenly appeared like a giant'. Noguchi had a good memory, and all the experimental data was 'stored in his head'. He worked mostly at night, so the boiler man kept the coal burning at night (Minami 2004).

5.2.2 The Land of the Black Star

In order to recount the story of the NMIMR in Ghana, it is necessary to describe not only the Japanese but also the Ghanaian context. The northern part of today's Ghana had thrived since ancient times as part of the Islamic trade routes. In the mid-fifteenth century, the Portuguese arrived on the southern coast and began to build castles and fortresses, such as today's World Heritage Elmina for the slave trade. Meanwhile, in the interior, the Asante kingdom with Kumasi as its capital rose to power and, by the early nineteenth century, controlled a vast area. The British, however, attacked the Asante kingdom in alliance with the Fanti kingdom in the south, and by 1902 controlled the entire area of present-day Ghana as the British Gold Coast. The capital of the colony was established in Accra.

During the colonial period, commercial cocoa farming spread in the southern part of the Gold Coast, and British-style education was diffused in urban areas. In 1927, the same year Noguchi arrived in Accra, the Achimota School was founded to educate the local elite equipped with a combination of the 'European' intellect and the African mind. At that time, Nigeria was the pivotal British tropical colony in West Africa, and its capital, Lagos, and the capital of the Gold Coast, Accra, were in a state of rivalry. The Rockefeller Institute, to which Noguchi was affiliated, had a base institution in Lagos, where key researchers were critical of Noguchi's work, so he avoided Lagos and opted to conduct research in Accra.

The man who led the Gold Coast colony to independence was Kwame Nkrumah. Born into a village family in the western coastal region in 1909, Nkrumah entered the newly established Achimota School the same year that Noguchi arrived in Accra and became a teacher at a Catholic school after graduation. In 1935, like Noguchi did in the past, Nkrumah went to the US with high aspirations and studied at Lincoln University, where he had to work hard to make a living. In 1945, Nkrumah went to London, became a charismatic pan-Africanist leader, and returned to the Gold Coast in 1947. He then headed the independence movement, and when legislative assembly elections were held in 1951, he stood as a candidate from prison and was elected, and in 1952 he assumed the position of prime minister. In 1957, the Gold Coast became the first British colony in sub-Saharan Africa to achieve independence as the Republic of Ghana. The national flag of Ghana has a black star in the centre to represent the spirit of independence.[6]

As the national leader, however, Nkrumah suppressed his political opponents, tried to redistribute resources without due regard to financial sustainability, and imposed taxes on cocoa exports to achieve quick industrialisation. However, the construction of the gigantic Akosombo Dam failed to serve effectively as a catalyst for growth,[7] and in the Cold War context, Nkrumah's socialist rhetoric gradually drove him to the position of an enemy of the US. In February 1966, while Nkrumah was out of the country, a *coup d'état* took place, and Nkrumah was deposed. From then until 1981, Ghana experienced a series of coups and regime changes, and its economy stagnated. Nkrumah's economic policies relied on state intervention and his government pursued top-down industrialisation at the expense of rural areas. These policies failed but, in retrospect, aligned with the mainstream thinking of development economics at the time, such as import substitution industrialisation and the 'big push' (Killick 1978; Frimpong-Ansha 1991). In a way, Nkrumah was like Noguchi. Both did their best under the constraints of the times, became suspicious of others, and were criticised by thinkers of later generations.

Although the political forces that rallied behind Nkrumah's socialist principles disappeared, few people deny his massive contribution to guiding the Ghanaian nation to independence from Britain. In terms of a national legacy, the historical position of Nkrumah in Ghana may resemble that of Mao Zedong in China and Sukarno in

[6] There are countless studies on the process leading to Ghana's independence. Apter (2008) vividly captured the dynamics of political turnaround. Cooper (1996) situated Ghana's experience of decolonisation in the context of the transition in both Anglophone and Francophone Africa.

[7] Murphy (2006) examined Nkrumah's economic policies, cocoa exports, and dam projects, and wrote that all these were linked to the advisory activities of the World Bank and the United Nations Development Programme (UNDP) in Ghana.

Indonesia. In Japan in the 1960s, the achievement of Nkrumah's Ghana was viewed favourably by both progressive and conservatives.[8]

5.2.3 Carrying on Noguchi's Legacy (1968–1978)

A development project often moves forward because of the firm will of a single individual. In Accra, where Noguchi died, Honda Kenji, a Japanese medical scientist, played a key role in establishing a distinguished centre for radically upgrading the standard of medical research in Africa. Unlike the diminutive Noguchi, Honda was a giant weighing 100 kg. Born in Miyagi Prefecture, Honda studied at Tohoku Imperial University, and after working as an assistant professor at Tohoku University, he became a professor at Fukushima Medical University in 1959.

In 1968, after consultation with the Ministry of Foreign Affairs, the faculty decided that Fukushima Medical University would begin medical cooperation with its counterpart in Ghana. The way in which a specific university takes responsibility for a particular development project was to be called the 'Fukushima Medical University Model'. As mentioned in the foreword contributed by Hogen Shinsaku, then president of JICA, to Honda (1983), the success of the NMIMR project was attributable to the university's full participation, 'which helped to avoid the academic factionalism and rivalry in the area of medicine that have often hindered medical cooperation' (Honda 1983: vii). Honda was initially not particularly enthusiastic about working in Ghana but was gradually drawn into the project.

The counterpart of Fukushima Medical University was the Ghana Medical School, which was established in 1964 and transformed into the University of Ghana Medical School in 1969. Its home institution was the National Hospital at Korle Bu, southwest of Accra, where Noguchi concentrated on his research in his last years (Fig. 5.1). In 1968, an agreement was reached between the governments of Ghana and Japan on medical cooperation, focusing on basic rather than clinical research. The plan was to develop virology utilising sophisticated equipment in the implicit hope of realising Noguchi's lost dream. Expensive equipment, such as the electron microscope manufactured by Hitachi, was provided to Ghana as part of the medical-technical cooperation project. Many local and international guests dropped by to look on the machine situated in Korle Bu.

Microbiologist Julius Mingle, who returned to Ghana in 1973 after studying in Canada, witnessed the collaboration between Japan and Ghana. His laboratory is still located in the corner of the building where the first electron microscope was installed. The place is also very close to the laboratory where Noguchi carried out his experiments.

> It all started in this building in 1968. This [where we were standing] is exactly the place where the electron microscope was installed. When we entered, we had to put on slippers to

[8] The selected works of Kwame Nkrumah (five volumes) were published in Japanese by the Japanese publisher Rironsha in 1971.

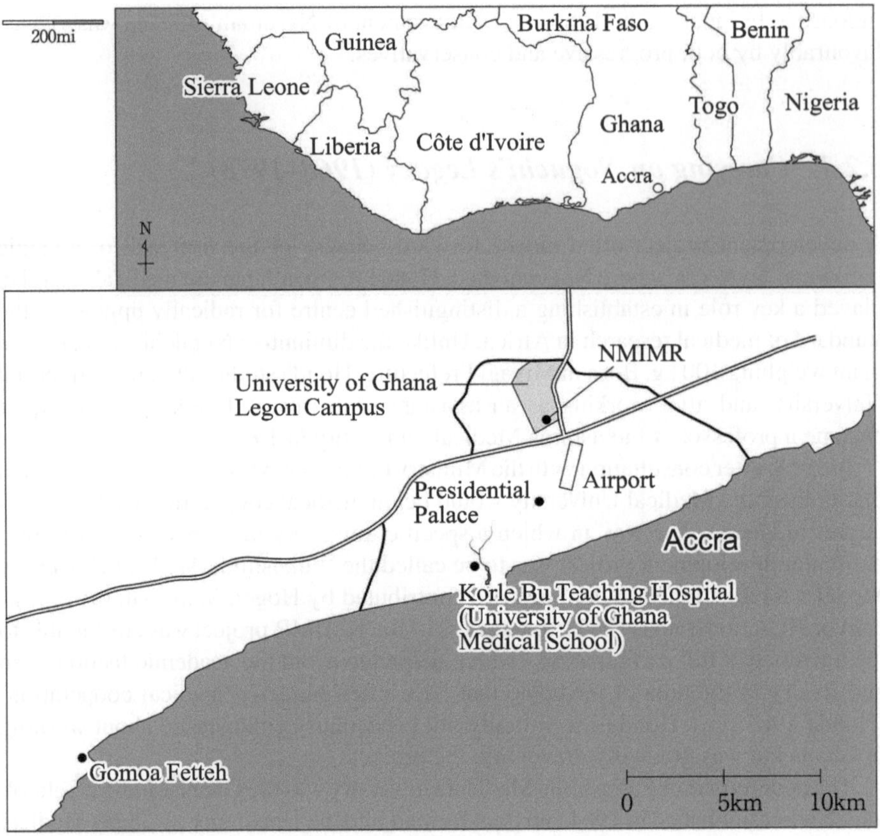

Fig. 5.1 University of Ghana and the project location. Source: Author

> avoid bringing sand into the building. The Hitachi refrigerator next to you is a 1976 model, which we still use today. Speaking about Dr Honda, well, he was a true giant. He had a big heart. He was a man who laughed a lot. [GHA 08]

In the 1970s, researchers from various departments at the University of Ghana began to use the electron microscope, which proved to be useful for diagnosing viral diseases in the laboratory. In 1972, the research team led by Honda also met with the head of state, Acheampong, who seized state power in a *coup d'état* that year. It was decided that future cooperation would include a clinical element such as nutrition and ophthalmic infectious diseases, and the idea of establishing a new research institute was tossed around. Honda recalled that when he had visited the Japanese Ministry of Foreign Affairs, he had been told, albeit jokingly, that a budget of 10 billion yen (about $30 million) should be drawn up (Honda 1983: 272).

However, when the oil crisis broke out in October 1973, the economies of developed and non-oil developing countries, including Japan, went into deep recession, and the tide turned against such big projects. Japanese experts were no longer sent to Ghana, and the Japanese ambassador to Ghana openly stated that the plan of constructing a new research institute would not be materialised. There was a widespread feeling that the medical cooperation that had begun in 1968 had come to an abrupt end.

Honda hit back furiously. 'If the project was cancelled, I would resign from my professor position to take responsibility. I would go to Ghana with my family, atone for my sins, and devote the rest of my life to the people of Ghana' (Honda 1983: 188). From 1974 to 1975, Honda repeatedly visited JICA, the Ministry of Foreign Affairs, and the Ministry of Finance, making desperate pleas. The Ghanaian government also suggested that the Japanese government should establish the institute in 1976, the centenary of Noguchi's birth. Mike Fransisco Ribeiro, who administered the University of Ghana Medical School and the NMIMR from 1970 to 1989, looks back at those days.

> I think the Ghanaians were also in panic. The head of the Ghanaian side was Dr Kwarkpong. He was very worried because he was working on a big ophthalmology project with Fukushima Medical University. I remember. It was Dr Kwarkpong who suggested that we should name the institute after Noguchi. [GHA 02]

The Ghanaians pressed the Japanese side, asking if Japan really meant to cancel the project when it would bear the name of Noguchi, the 'best child' of Japan.[9] Honda also met with Minister of Finance Fukuda Takeo (later prime minister), through Kobari Rekiji, the president of Fukushima Transportation, the local magnate, and before long it was decided that the new research institute would be constructed with a budget of 2 billion yen. As originally planned, the site was identified in Legon, where the main campus of the University of Ghana was located. Legon is a hill north of Accra, north-west of the international airport. Once the research institute was established near the main entrance to the campus, the plan was to move the Medical School, then housed at the Korle Bu Hospital under the Ministry of Health, to Legon Hills and create a medical school village. The design was finalised in 1976, and the ground-breaking ceremony in that year was attended by the governor of Fukushima Prefecture, Matsudaira Isao, who planted a commemorative flame tree. Andrew Anthony Adjei, who currently works in the President's Office at the University of Ghana, recalled that he was thrilled to see the NMIMR building gradually taking shape. 'The construction was very quick, and we found the building so beautiful. Everything was brand new, and it turned out a wonderful place. The researchers chatted and laughed in the pagoda' [GHA 05]. Ribeiro said, 'I remember we were excited because the building was designed in Japan. It looked completely different from other buildings on the campus' [GHA 02]. The third phase of the project in pathophysiology and immunology began in 1976. Expectations grew in both Ghana and Japan that their medical cooperation would soon enter a new phase.

---

9 A report in 1973 stated that stakeholders in both countries were keen to establish the 'Noguchi Hideyo Memorial Institute of Medical Research' by 1976, the centenary of Noguchi's birth (OTCA 1973b: 10). Another report in 1976 presented the building design and referred to the institute simply as the 'Basic Medical Research Institute.' However, this report also obliquely stated that the Japanese side 'refrained' from naming it the 'Noguchi Memorial Institute', while calling it the 'Noguchi Institute' was 'the real wish' of the Ghanaian side (JICA 1976b: 14).

5.2.4 *The Coup (1979–1980)*

However, around the time that construction of the NMIMR was in full swing, an incident occurred at Fukushima Medical University, which Honda described as an evil whirlwind. Along with news about political and economic instability in Ghana, 'malicious rumours' were circulated in Fukushima that a committee headed by Honda was involved in fraudulent accounting. According to Honda, this was intended to remove the university's president and neutralise Honda.[10] Adhering to the Fukushima Medical University Model, in which the whole university engaged in a development project, became practically impossible, and it was decided to set up a national committee consisting of medical scientists from different universities, which would take over the task of steering the project on the Japanese side. In July 1978, in addition to the faculty of Fukushima Medical University, medical scientists from Iwate Medical University and Kagoshima University were invited to attend the first meeting of the domestic support committee (Honda 1983: 260–262).

In Ghana, despite military confrontations, economic crises, and persistent shortages of supplies, construction of the building on Legon Hills continued and was completed in March 1979. However, in May and June of the same year, a series of coups were staged by radical soldiers led by Air Force Flt. Lt. Jerry Rawlings. The head of the military, Fred Akuffo, who was supposed to be the guest of honour at the opening ceremony of the NMIMR, and President Acheampong, who had long been the formal head of the medical cooperation project on the Ghanaian side, were arrested and executed. In September, state power was transferred from the military to a civilian government. The new president, Hilla Limann, gave a congratulatory speech at the opening ceremony of the Noguchi Institute in November. However, given the volatile political situation, Rawlings staged another coup in December 1981, dismissing Limann and reinstating military rule. The Ghanaian people, who had been critical of the governments that had followed Nkrumah's, generally supported the revolution initiated by Rawlings.

The situation was highly precarious, but as the building had just been completed with grant aid, Japan had no option to withdraw. Following the discussions at the domestic support committee, diarrhoea and malnutrition were chosen as the themes for the fourth project, and a mixed team of experts from Fukushima Medical University and other universities was dispatched from Japan. At the time of President Limann, the security situation deteriorated. In August 1980, a group of armed robbers broke into the private house of the project leader, Minami Kazumori, and some of the experts began to express their fears openly. To appease their anxiety, Minami invited them to his house and organised a party, drinking the beer the robbers had left behind (Honda 1983: 303–306). Similar incidents occurred from time to time. Once, armed bandits broke into the NMIMR at night and robbed the Japanese of their

[10] Concerning the engagement of Japanese universities in international cooperation, the Ministry of Education advised that the process driven by individual researchers' initiatives should be transformed into more institutional collaboration (Kayashima 2022: 213). The attempt of Fukushima Medical University appears to have been aborted at a critical stage.

money and goods [GHA 10]. And, 'A Japanese researcher went to collect mosquitoes for research, but because the place was in the military premise, he was targeted, and the military came to the NMIMR and captured him' [GHA 03]. Despite these risks, however, there was no discussion of withdrawing the Japanese experts from Ghana. For Honda, born in 1918, this level of turmoil was probably nothing compared to his memories of the Pacific War.[11] On the Ghanaian side, people did not agree that public security was so bad around 1980 [GHA 08] [GHA 10]. Ghanaians said that the food shortage caused by the 1983 famine was much more serious.

In the meantime, research continued. After the whirlwind in Fukushima and the great storm in Accra, the NMIMR's activities gained momentum in 1981. Ribeiro, the chief administrator at the time, said, 'Ghanaian society was in a difficult situation. We didn't have enough food. But, unlike the surrounding areas of Accra, the NMIMR was getting by, as all the research equipment and materials were imported from Japan. The only expenses the Ghanaians had to pay were electricity and water bills' [GHA 02]. As recalled by Isabella Akyinbah Quakyi, who joined the NMIMR in 1980, 'When people had to finish work at 3 p.m. and go out to look for food, we were able to continue experiments right up to the last minute. We couldn't do the same at the medical school in Korle Bu. The wonderful architecture and the wonderful resources gave us hope' [GHA 07].

However, when people are confined in a small space in a tense situation, their emotions may become introverted and interpersonal conflict can arise. The story of Honda was that the Ghanaian director and administrator hid the keys so that the Japanese researchers could not get the things out of the warehouse (Honda 1983: 311), but the Ghanaians said the situation was the opposite. The parasitologist Maxwell Alexandar Appawu told me, 'There were times when the Japanese researchers did not give us the key, and we could not get in' [GHA 03]. Perhaps, there was a scramble for the key. Ribeiro indicated that there was a 'tyrannical type of Japanese who nagged the Ghanaians' and made them feel 'treated like tools', with emotions on both sides getting entangled [GHA 02]. Adjei summarised: 'When the NMIMR was established in 1979, there were three problems. Firstly, the Japanese side wanted to investigate topics which they thought were important. But the Ghanaian side was not very interested in those topics. Secondly, JICA brought in excellent machines, but they did not teach the Ghanaians how to use them, and they brought in experts from Japan. The third point concerned management. Before important matters were communicated to the Ghanaian side, JICA and the Japanese experts and advisers would discuss them among themselves and make decisions' [GHA 05]. The NMIMR stands out as a successful example of medical cooperation, but it seems that there was not necessarily a beautiful honeymoon.

So what was the cause of the conflict? Some said it was due to cultural differences. George Armah, a microscopist with a PhD from Osaka University, remarked,

[11] Honda (1983) expressed great concern for the families of the experts. Until the 1980s, however, the typical women who were mentioned in project documents were housewives selflessly supporting their husbands, and I rarely encountered the names of female experts on either the Japanese or the Ghanaian side.

'When it comes to communication, Japanese people don't say yes or no clearly, but Ghanaians are very direct, and when they say 'Yes', they mean it. If attitudes are not open, problems become more complicated, and it takes time for both sides to soften their stance' [GHA 04]. Appawu said, 'It would have been better if we had involved the Ghanaians sufficiently in advance and proceeded on the basis of consensus. From time to time, we had problems because of a lack of communication. But, we solved them by sitting down and having an open conversation. And there was no problem regarding the content of the research' [GHA 03].

There was also an institutional bottleneck at the University of Ghana. One of the problems unique to the NMIMR was that the medical school remained at the Korle Bu National Hospital, which meant that the NMIMR in the Legon campus was physically separated from the medical school. Many Ghanaian researchers had a dual role, teaching at the Korle Bu medical school and doing research at the NMIMR in Legon. Korle Bu and Legon are about 18 km apart, cutting through the centre of Accra, so it was not easy to travel back and forth especially due to the heavy traffic. Meanwhile, the Japanese researchers could concentrate on their research at the NMIMR. 'The Ghanaian researchers were working at two places. So I think it was inevitable that our productivity was affected' [GHA 02].

More seriously, the political and economic turmoil caused a large number of Ghanaian researchers to leave the country. According to Honda, the dean of the Faculty of Medicine at the University of Ghana complained that a third of the teaching staff had left in 1982 (Honda 1983: 40). Armah remembered, 'Some went to the WHO, but others went to universities in Nigeria and Bantustans in South Africa. I think there were also people who went to Zimbabwe and Zambia. Skilled nurses emigrated to the UK to look for work' [GHA 04].

5.2.5 *Towards Self-Reliance (1990s)*

However, the Ghanaians with first-hand knowledge of the past agreed that the serious problems had disappeared by the mid-1980s. Ribeiro said, 'Japan had already invested a lot, and Ghana had benefited from it, so everyone wanted the situation to normalise' [GHA 02]. By the end of the 1980s, 'I think the NMIMR was able to take off. As the NMIMR became better known, people who had left Ghana began to return. Instead of a brain drain, we now have a brain circulation' [GHA 04]. Importantly, Ghana's political economy stabilised. Rawlings, who respected Nkrumah, also learnt from the failure of Nkrumah's adventurous economic and foreign policies. Realising that support from the Eastern bloc was limited, Rawlings changed the direction of foreign policy and re-established relations with the West. In 1983, Ghana accepted the structural adjustment programme (SAP) promoted by the World Bank and the

IMF (see also Chap. 3, Sect. 3.3). Ghana's economy recovered, and Rawlings introduced a multi-party system in 1992. He was voted in the same year as president and retired in 2001.[12]

It seems that the NMIMR adopted two strategies to realise sustained growth of the institute. The first was the recruitment strategy. Ribeiro said, 'The best researchers were leaving the country. So, we decided to identify young talented students, train them carefully, give them degrees, and retain them in Ghana' [GHA 02]. Ghana has a system of national service for university graduates; they are obliged to work in the public sector in a place other than their home region, and only after engaging in such activities do they become full members of society. This is a legacy of the Nkrumah's administration, which sought to promote national unity by overcoming ethnic conflict and bridging the gap between the elite and the people (Langer 2013). Appawu, the parasitologist, also said that his first involvement with the NMIMR was through national service after graduating from university. 'I was delighted to be able to do my research here with the best facilities. I completed my PhD thanks to this opportunity' [GHA 03].[13]

The second was the diversification of donors. Ghanaian researchers wanted to work on eradicating malaria, the most serious infectious disease in West Africa, but the Japanese side did not attach much importance to this issue [GHA 03] [GHA 04]. Alexander Nyarko, a clinical pathologist with a PhD from University of the Sciences, Philadelphia, who served as director of the NMIMR from 2006 to 2012, explained the request-based principle, one of the hallmarks of Japan's development assistance.

> I don't think it was because Japan was not interested in malaria. It was not the case either that they didn't have the technology to deal with malaria. The Japanese side often asked the Ghanaian side for ideas. I think the process was that the Ghanaian side made a list of what they were interested in, and the Japanese side looked for Japanese researchers who were interested in working with Ghana, and then the Japanese side made their choice. I think that's why malaria research was not included. This is my understanding. [GHA 13]

Still, the NMIMR had high expectations for collaboration in malaria research, and the natural solution to this mismatch was to secure funding from a donor other than Japan. Consequently, the NMIMR's partners began diversifying in the 1990s. Armah said, 'I think, because of our relationship with Japan, in a sense, the NMIMR refused to grow on its own' [GHA 04]. At the same time, the experience of collaboration with Japan made it easier for Ghanaians to build relationships with other donors. Adjei said, 'It was very nice that the Japanese experts taught us not only how to do research, but also how to interpret the results of experiments, and how to write good proposals to attract research funding' [GHA 05].

---

[12] After retiring from the university and ending his direct involvement with the NMIMR, Honda travelled around the world as the head of the Japan Medical Team for Disaster Relief (JMTDR). Honda was especially active in mobilising resources for the sufferers of the 1984 Ethiopian famine (Honda 1988). The JMTDR transformed into the Japan Disaster Relief (JDR) with JICA serving as its liaison agency since 1987.

[13] Director Anang said that, in the late 2010, the NMIMR accepted around 50 Ghanaian youth annually.

The funding for the research on malaria was provided by the US National Institutes of Health (NIH). 'Yes, the project was funded by the US, but that didn't mean we worked with American researchers' [GHA 13]. It was a commissioned research project in which the NIH provided financial resources, the NMIMR conducted the research, and the NIH evaluated it and made the audit. When it came to Japan's collaboration, JICA provided resources, and the Ghanaians and the Japanese worked together. They quarrelled sometimes but shared the research outcomes. 'I think a kind of symbiotic relationship was established when the needs of the Ghanaians and the Japanese converged. In the end, everyone gained benefits. The resources sent from Japan, such as equipment, could be used by different research departments' [GHA 13].

Kwame Gabriel Attorkwe, who was responsible for the NMIMR's accounting from 1982 to 2009, has seen the process from an administrator's point of view. Compiling the accounting reports was a demanding task when research grants came in from the WHO, NIH, etc. When the NIH funded the research on malaria control in the 1990s, he was invited to the US for training to learn how to use specific accounting software. 'From the researcher's point of view, JICA's budget may not be easy to implement, but from the administrator's point of view, I didn't have to touch it, so it was very easy' [GHA 10].

When I talked to Ghanaians, I sometimes found that they were very good at telling parables. Microbiologist Armah compared the Japanese-Ghanaian collaboration to a parent–child relationship: 'When a child grows up, he tries to work with their parents as an equal. Think of a child born into a bakery and growing up working in the shop with his parents. The child will eventually become independent and may work with other people. That's OK. It's important not to break up the family bond' [GHA 04]. The NMIMR has become independent, and Japan is now just one of the partner countries. Yet, it is important to renew the ties, remembering the first encounter.

The people of Korle Bu may have felt a little desolate and lonely as the NMIMR left the National Hospital in Korle Bu for the Legon campus. Korle Bu is where Noguchi worked with his microscopes. It is also close to congested, poverty-stricken, yet vibrant inner-city areas such as Jamestown. Mingle, who knows the era of the electron microscope in the 1970s, said, 'You shouldn't neglect your children until they grow up. Parents' interest may shift to the new baby, but they shouldn't ignore the first child. Next to this building, you can find the Dr Noguchi Memorial Laboratory and the Japanese Garden. Many students have heard of Noguchi, but they don't really know who he was. I always talk about Noguchi in my classes' [GHA08].

5.2.6 *Expanding into Effective Outreach*

During the 1980s and 1990s, the NMIMR trained new generations of researchers and diversified its partners. In addition, clinical activities were remarkably strengthened. The laboratory of Richard Berko Biritwun, a public health scientist mentioned several times in Honda (1983), was still working at the Medical School in Korle Bu. He said that conducting research in Korle Bu was more convenient than in Legon because the former was closer to the research field. With Biritwun, we visited the fishing village of Gomoa Fetteh, about 30 km west of the Korle Bu Hospital, going through the heavy weekend traffic. This village was chosen in 1982 as a field for the NMIMR's Epidemiology Unit to collect clinical evidence. As the village was densely populated and somewhat isolated from the surrounding area, the NMIMR team was able to carry out a thorough health survey of the residents to construct panel data. The 1983 famine provided a natural experiment to observe the effects of poor nutrition on the human body. The NMIMR not only conducted research on malaria and parasites but also provided treatment, so the researchers were very well received by the villagers [GHA 06].

The village of Gomoa Fetteh sits on a hill overlooking the sea. Anette Annan, the 83-year-old wife of the chief, said, 'I remember well when Dr Honda and his wife were here. We talked about how we would give Dr Honda a proper burial in Gomoa Fetteh when he died' [GHA 15]. The former clinic staff who gathered at the chief's house said, 'The Japanese staff also participated in door-to-door visits and made efforts to understand the Fanti language spoken by the villagers' and 'there was a Japanese woman who was called by a local name.' The memory of the 1983 famine was still vivid. The NMIMR staff gave flour, cooking oil, rice, and yellow maize to the people who came to the clinic, and they were so grateful [GHA 16] [GHA 17].

In the 1990s, NMIMR also undertook activities to promote parasite control in schools throughout Ghana. The momentum was given by the Hashimoto Initiative announced by Japanese Prime Minister Hashimoto Ryutaro at the G8 Summit in Denver, US, in 1997 [GHA 01]. Along with Mahidol University in Thailand and the Kenya Medical Research Institute (KEMRI), the NMIMR became one of the global hubs of this initiative. Michael David Wilson, a parasitologist trained at the University of London and the Netherlands Agricultural University, kept pieces of picture story shows they made for school children. 'I think we should consider developing longer-term programmes rather than jumping on a project that will disappear after five years' [GHA14].

It was the Ghanaian women who stressed the importance of fieldwork and communication with people. The chief's wife, Anette Annan, said that a shared value of the people of Gomoa Fetteh was that the adults 'treat boys and girls as equals' [GHA 15]. Margaret Armar-Klemesu, a nutritionist at the NMIMR, said, 'Nutrition is all about the fieldwork. If you want to know about nutrition, you must go to the community and find out what people are eating. Once you have identified the problem in the laboratory, you have to intervene and collect evidence in the field' [GHA 09]. Isabella Akyinbah Quakyi, who founded the School of Public Health at the University of Ghana, stressed the importance of fostering a spirit of research in young people rather than just forcing them to memorise and pass exams. She remarked:

> In Ghanaian culture, we relate different things to each other through stories. Colonialism never respected local culture. Colonialism never tried to appreciate it. Our languages were branded as inappropriate, and during that time, the meaning of life, the philosophy of life, was lost. In medicine, we discover the scientific causality of disease, but you should remember

that the practice of keeping everything clean and not catching a disease is qualitatively different from understanding what the disease really is. [GHA 07]

Quakyi left Ghana in 1983 to conduct research on malaria at the NIH and elsewhere in the US and returned to the NMIMR in 2001. She mentioned that as an African woman, she had some uncomfortable social experiences overseas. She also expressed her gratitude to her parents for investing in her education, which reminded me of Noguchi who was always grateful to his mother in his village days. As she described, it was not easy for a woman to climb the ladder, but there were many roles for women. One could be a mother, an educator, a professional—one can be anything. Housewives should also be respected, but she said that they should not stand in the way of other women doing other things [GHA 07].

The clinical work overlaps with the remit of the Ministry of Health, but the outreach is indispensable for any applied science. As Armah explained, 'The NMIMR is under the Ministry of Education, but people outside the university assume that the institute is an agency of the Ministry of Health. Whenever there is news about an infectious disease, people ask, "Where is Noguchi?"' In fact, the activities of the NMIMR seem to be highly regarded by the Public Health Bureau of the Ministry of Health. When there is an outbreak of an infectious disease, experts from the Ministry of Health collect samples and bring them to the NMIMR for examination. They then work together to monitor and control the spread of the disease. With Japanese scholarships, young NMIMR researchers typically study in Japan for their PhDs, while the staff of the Ministry of Health study for their Masters [GHA 11]. When a health crisis occurs, 'everyone wants to hear what the NMIMR has to say. The NMIMR and the WHO are special. They give advice based on solid evidence, which is very helpful to policy-makers' [GHA 12].

The NMIMR has come to fulfil three important missions. Director Abraham Kwabena Anang explained, 'The first mission is, of course, research. The second is capacity building, which includes training graduate students and young researchers to nurture the next generation of scientists. It also includes community capacity development involving local schools. The third is specific diagnosis and surveillance of serious emerging diseases. In the past, it was difficult to diagnose HIV/AIDS locally, so we had to send samples abroad. Now we can do it here at the NMIMR' [GHA 01].

In 2008, Tokyo Medical and Dental University set up a joint research centre at the NMIMR, and in 2018 the construction of the Advanced Infectious Diseases Research Centre at the NMIMR was completed with Japanese grant aid. Its modern grey architecture is reminiscent of the science buildings at Japanese national universities. On the site next to the NMIMR, a new medical training hospital has opened, and the medical village in Legon finally seems to be taking shape. The critical role played by the NMIMR in addressing health emergencies such as Ebola and COVID-19 has been appreciated: for example, at the peak of the COVID-19 pandemic, the NMIMR performed 67% of the PCR tests in Ghana. The Institute has a strong presence in West Africa as a centre for third-country training in the field of health and medicine, and it is hoped that cooperation with Japanese companies and hospitals, as well as with JICA, will be further enhanced. Under the leadership of its first woman director, Dorothy Yeboah-Manu, the NMIMR strengthened the clinical, applied research activities on top of its already strong basic research capability.[14]

Looking back on the 40-year history of the NMIMR, we are reminded of the importance of teamwork and the power of strong, dedicated leadership.[15] Even at difficult times, the Japanese side did not compromise and continued to send the best equipment, build the best buildings, and try to send the best researchers to Ghana. The impact of this sustained effort was considerable, though Japan should not take for granted the appreciation of the Ghanaian side, as efforts have always been mutual and interactive. The Ghanaian institute stood up on its own, with the Japanese assistance, drawing on its own potential.

5.3 Nurturing Local Veterinarians: School of Veterinary Medicine, University of Zambia (Zambia)

5.3.1 Local Context (1983–1986)

Following Ghana's independence in 1957, the wind of change blew across the continent, and dozens of African nations became independent of the colonial powers. However, the surge of autonomy was blocked in Southern Africa (Fig. 5.2). In South Africa and Rhodesia (now Zimbabwe), former British colonies, and Mozambique and Angola, former Portuguese colonies, the white settlers and their descendants monopolised political and economic power and denied the black majority even the right to vote (Fig. 1.3). Nevertheless, the Portuguese colonies gained independence in the 1970s, followed by Zimbabwe in 1980. In the same year, the independent nations in the Southern African region formed the Southern African Development Coordination Conference (SADCC) and began to promote regional cooperation for self-reliance to isolate the apartheid rule in South Africa. The founding conference

[14] See the conversations of William K. Ampofo, Ishikawa Koichi, Dorothy Yeboah-Manu, and Ozawa Maki. 'Sharing Tales of Japan-Ghana Trust and Cooperation,' *JICA Magazine*, April 2024 Issue, https://jicamagazine.jica.go.jp/en/article/?id=202404_4f. On the occasion of the Great East Japan Earthquake in 2011, to demonstrate Ghanaians' goodwill and solidarity, the NMIMR led by Director Alexander Nyarko donated tons of chocolates to the citizens of Fukushima. 'Noguchi Institute Donates to Fukushima Earthquake Victims,' *Ghanaweb*, 21 April 2011, https://www.ghanaweb.com/GhanaHomePage/NewsArchive/Noguchi-Institute-donates-to-Fukushima-earthquake-victims-207246.

[15] The director of the NMIMR, F. K. Nkrumah, was the son of President Nkrumah. He contributed a column to *The 25-Year History of JICA*, describing the NMIMR as 'a monumental symbol of friendship and cooperation in health and medical research between Ghana and Japan' (JICA 1999b: 165).

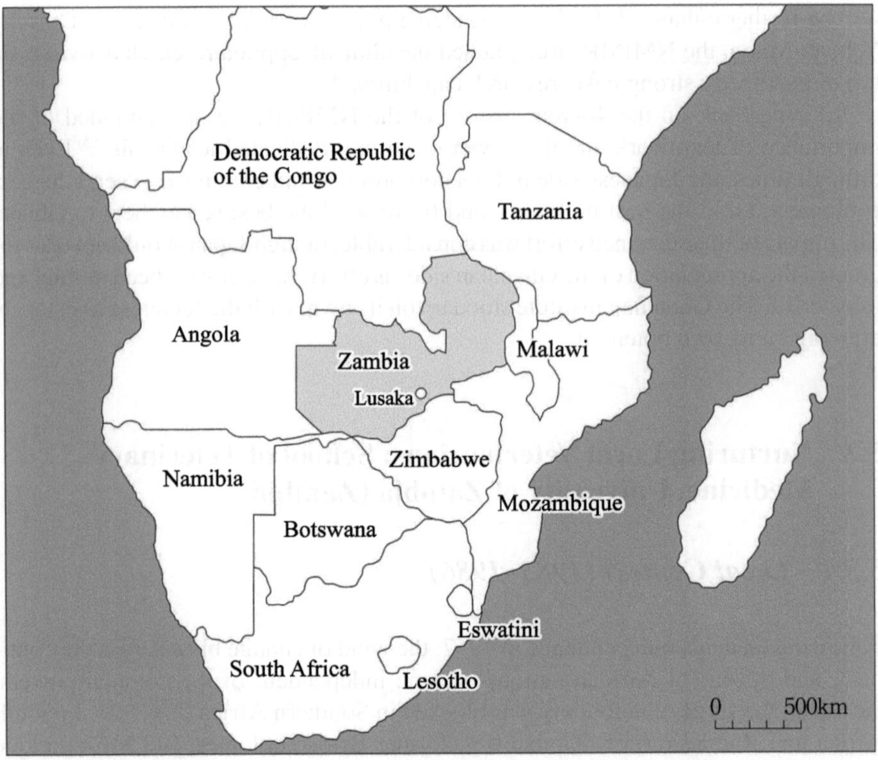

Fig. 5.2 Southern Africa and Zambia. Source: Author

was held in Lusaka, Zambia. Zimbabwe, which had just achieved liberation, also joined the SADCC.[16]

As the white minority rule in Africa clearly went against the historical trend of self-determination of nations, the United Nations and even the former colonial powers criticised apartheid rule in South Africa and supported the development efforts of the countries that joined the SADCC. It was in this context that FAO proposed the establishment of a regional hub to train veterinarians in Zambia in 1981. However, after discussions within the SADCC, it was decided that a regional centre for veterinary medicine should be located in newly independent Zimbabwe, a decision endorsed by the European donors. Mutale Mike Musonda, who became the first Zambian dean of the School of Veterinary Medicine in 1996, explained the historical background.

> In colonial times, Zambia, Zimbabwe and Malawi formed the British protectorate of Rhodesia in a federal framework. When all three countries achieved independence, Zambia

[16] As for the rationale of the SADCC/SADC, see Hanlon (1986). Southern Africa has a rich regional history of ecology, peopling, and political dynamics. See Mlambo and Parsons (2019) and Alexander et al. (2020).

> didn't want to see new development projects concentrated in Zimbabwe. I don't think President Kaunda was happy about Zimbabwe becoming the regional base for veterinary medicine. To be honest. I have the impression that the reason the EU supported Zimbabwe was because of the presence of British farmers, who stayed in Zimbabwe after independence. [ZAM 09]

At the time, Zambian President Kenneth Kaunda was a popular African socialist, and the country was politically stable. In addition, copper, Zambia's main export, was globally sought as an essential input for the electric industries. In 1982, the Zambian government requested Japan to support the establishment of a veterinary school at UNZA. In 1983, then Crown Prince Akihito and Princess Michiko visited Zambia, Tanzania, and Kenya, and the project in Zambia quickly kicked in. The question of competition with Zimbabwe was resolved by classifying the proposed veterinary school in Zambia as a 'national school' within Zambia rather than a regional hub. At the time, it was estimated that Zambia would need 500 veterinarians to look after 2.15 million livestock, while in 1982, there were only 70 veterinarians, of whom only eight were Zambian (JICA 1983: 15). The demand for veterinary professionals in Zambia, a country with a strong commercial livestock industry, was very high, like in Zimbabwe.

Thus began the project of the School of Veterinary Medicine at UNZA. The construction of the school building started in 1984 and was completed in 1986. The design of a two-storey building with a beautiful courtyard in the centre was similar to that of the NMIMR. Kennedy Choongo, who enrolled as a second-generation student in 1983, recalled, 'I attended classes at the nearby Faculty of Mining while watching the construction work progress. I remember we were very excited to see the modern building was coming up, and the best equipment was installed' [ZAM 05].

However, although the school building had been built anew, there was a paucity of qualified Zambian veterinarians who could teach in the classrooms. This was a rather unusual case of Japanese development cooperation; there must already be local counterparts in the partner country to which technology will be transferred from Japan. In the University of Ghana, the Japanese experts had been working with medical scientists at the School of Medicine for a decade before the building of the NMIMR was constructed. In Zambia, it was necessary to recruit future counterparts from the student population.

By referring to the principal-agent framework discussed in Chap. 1 (Sect. 1.2), we can easily understand the nature of the problem Zambians faced. There were not enough agents (Zambian professional veterinarians) to serve the interests of the principals (Zambian citizens, including livestock farmers). The British colonial authorities had brought in veterinarians from Europe and British colonies. After independence, Zambia wanted to break away from the situation like Fig. 1.3 by fostering A-β, but non-Zambian experts employed by the Zambian government continued to provide services. Therefore, the policy of Zambianisation (or 'indigenisation') was introduced to accelerate the process of transition from Fig. 1.3 to Fig. 1.2 and then to Fig. 1.4. An attempt was made to encourage young Zambians to obtain professional degrees so that Zambians could teach Zambians how to treat animals and keep them healthy.

The process required a long-term commitment. After negotiations, the School of Veterinary Medicine at Hokkaido University took the lead in supporting its counterpart in Zambia. Kanagawa Hiroshi and Hashimoto Nobuo, both famous veterinary scientists of Hokkaido University, participated in designing the school building and started to be involved in the domestic support committee in 1985 (JICA, IDCJ, and IDJ 2013: 70–71).[17] Compared to medicine in general, the world of veterinary medicine was small and brimmed with a sense of unity. Japanese veterinary schools and universities, veterinarians, and local municipalities started to gather together to support the new school at UNZA.

5.3.2 *Education First (1987–1996)*

However, the process of trait-making (Hirschman 1967: 135–139) was by no means easy. In hindsight, the process appeared to have been a brilliant success story, but in fact, the project at UNZA faced difficulties in its early years. Mikami Takeshi, an expert dispatched from Hokkaido University, pointed out in his 'personal opinion' document (hereafter the Mikami Report) in 1987, two years after the commencement of the project, that the future prospects of the project were unfortunately bleak.[18] Now that almost 40 years have passed since this JICA document was internally circulated, let me quote a passage. After acknowledging that the Zambian students 'attended the classes very seriously, accepting the language handicap of the Japanese lecturers,' Mikami wrote:

> After graduation, the first-generation students of the Sapporo Agricultural College [in Hokkaido] under the tutelage of Dr. Clark,[19] played active roles in various fields. I told the [Zambian] students that they should be aware of their role and responsibility as the very first graduates of the veterinary school and that they should have a spirit of sacrifice for their alma mater, using examples such as how the Sapporo graduates contributed to their school

---

[17] The story of the popular Japanese comic series, Sasaki Michiko's *Doctors of Animals* (動物のお医者さん), is set at the School of Veterinary Medicine at Hokkaido University. Kanagawa and Hashimoto were the models for the strange vet profs at 'H University'. The first person to head the Japanese domestic support committee was Ogata Manabu, who later became president of Azabu University.

[18] The gist of the Mikami Report, which emphasised the role of education, seems to have been influenced by the ideas of Hashimoto Eiji, who was then coordinating the project and later became JICA's Executive Director. Mikami said that he received 'a lot of criticism' about the Mikami Report, but in the end, the project moved in the direction of the recommendations presented in the report. Zambia achieved independence in 1964, the year of the Tokyo Olympics. The team from 'Northern Rhodesia' marched in the opening ceremony, but the closing ceremony happened to coincide with the country's independence day, thus the same team of athletes paraded the Japan National Stadium on the final day as the Zambian national delegates with Zambian flags proudly draped around their necks, cheered heartily by the Japanese audience. Hashimoto remembered, 'When I told this story to Zambians, they were all very happy' (JICA 2009b: 63, 75–76, 94).

[19] William Smith Clark was a US agricultural educationist. He was invited by the Japanese government to establish the Sapporo Agricultural College (SAC) in 1876, which was later transformed into Hokkaido University. His motto 'Boys Be Ambitious' is known to all Japanese people.

> as educators, and how the high level of education in Japan today was achieved thanks to the efforts of Japanese youth in the Meiji era, who studied in Western countries and then returned to their home country to devote themselves to teaching the next generations. I wonder if this kind of preaching would have been appreciated by Zambians with individualistic minds. (Mikami 1987: 1)

In retrospect, it is clear that Mikami's concerns were groundless, as his 'preaching' was well received by young Zambians. When the project began, the veterinary community in Zambia was dominated by foreigners, including Japanese. Due to President Kaunda's African socialist principles, many lecturers were recruited from non-aligned countries. In the mid-1980s, of the 23 faculty in the veterinary school, six were long-term JICA experts, and the others were one British, two Ghanaians, two Tanzanians, one Nigerian, one Ugandan, one Sudanese, two Indian, one Sri Lankan, one Czechoslovakian, and four Zambians who had only their Master's degrees. The other two senior technologists were Irish, and the separate administrative dean and his subordinate senior technologists were British (ibid.: 4, 32).

However, the transition from this state to full Zambianisation appeared to be slow. While some research-oriented Japanese experts complained that '[teaching] was a heavy burden and there was little professional benefit for us' (UNZA Support Committee 1998: 5), the Mikami Report honestly noted that the Japanese staff were isolated and looked down upon by both Zambians and foreigners because of their poor English skills (according to the Mikami Report, this was not a unique problem in Zambia but one of the 'biggest concerns' in Japan's development cooperation at that time). However, this question was being addressed, and there was a more serious bottleneck; it was difficult to recruit and retain new expatriate lecturers, whether Japanese or not, because the salary, accommodation, and other benefits UNZA could offer were not good enough. In addition, it seems that some of the foreign staff members were resistant to the strategy of increasing the number of Zambian lecturers (Mikami 1987: 23). It was feared that if things continued as they were, only the school buildings built by Japan would remain, and the teaching staff would disappear except for a small number of settled expatriates.

The Mikami Report emphasised that the short-term goal of the project should not be research but education targeting young Zambians. Priority must be given to establishing educational systems, such as curriculum development, providing educational equipment, and training qualified Zambian lecturers. To achieve this end, it was necessary to encourage Master's students to pursue PhDs and to show a pathway for undergraduates to obtain Master's and PhD degrees. Various scholarships should be used to invite Zambian students to Japan, and Japanese scholars with a passion for education should be dispatched to Zambia as a bridging measure until the students achieve their degrees and return to Zambia. The report also suggested that an education-oriented Japanese dean should be appointed; this 'interim' dean should be heavily involved in the management of the faculty and then transfer the power to a Zambian successor as soon as possible. The Mikami Report concluded that a decision on possible withdrawal would have to be made by 1990, if the parties could not agree on such a direction.

Eventually, the withdrawal option was not chosen, and the second phase of the project began in 1992. However, the Zambian researchers who had been studying abroad had not yet returned, and the project was in jeopardy. Although a graduate school had been established, no Zambian students moved to the postgraduate level because they could not secure scholarships. Enthusiasm on the Japanese side also appeared to be waning; the position of Japanese team leader had been vacant for a year and a half. In 1994, however, Norway began to offer scholarships, which enabled more Zambians to pursue Master's degrees. In the second half of the 1990s, Zambian students who had studied abroad in the UK for their Master's and in Japan for their PhD began to come back to Zambia one by one (ibid.: 7–9). It was like the adult fish that grew up in the ocean returning home.

5.3.3 Consummation of Zambianisation (1997)

The strategy to focus on education turned out to be effective.[20] From 1985 to 1997, 36 long-term experts, 61 short-term experts and 16 JICA Volunteers were sent from Japan to fill the gap left by the absence of Zambian staff. The transition was smooth. By the time the project ended in 1997, all department heads and dean of the School of Veterinary Medicine had been replaced by Zambian scholars, and the number of Zambian faculty members had reached 21 (ibid.: 20, 23). At the time, HIV/AIDS was raging across southern Africa, and young, promising researchers were falling victim, but those who had completed their PhDs abroad started to teach at UNZA. By 2020, almost all faculty members at the school had been replaced by Zambians.

Zambianisation took about 15 years to complete. I asked several Zambian faculty members with degrees from Japanese universities how they interpreted Zambianisation and assessed their experience of working with the Japanese. Kennedy Choongo, a toxicologist, said, 'Honestly speaking, the Japanese experts were not very good at English, but the handouts were excellent. I was also inspired by their hard work. Compared to other countries, I think studying in Japan is different because the relationship with the supervisors is much closer. Thanks to this, we could start new joint research' [ZAM 05]. Surveys have confirmed that researchers who studied abroad in Japan tend to continue collaborative research with their Japanese academic supervisors (Kayashima 2019; Kayashima et al. 2024).

Henry Chimana, who taught at the Department of Biomedical Sciences, said that Zambianisation was not about people's faces but their attitudes. 'I think Zambianisation is about maturing. It means learning from the people who came to Zambia to help us, so that we can take responsibility for ourselves. It means learning from

[20] In the late 1980s, Japan's assistance to higher education from the perspective of *hito-zukuri* (human resources development) was not yet mainstreamed as part of educational cooperation (Kayashima 2022). The project of Jomo Kenyatta University of Agriculture and Technology (JKUAT) discussed in Chap. 4 (Sect. 4.2) and that of the University of Zambia discussed in this chapter were the pioneering examples. Support for the NMIMR in Ghana was considered part of medical rather than educational cooperation (ibid.: 227).

what the Japanese do. They clean up after their experiments, even the desks and chairs' [ZAM 04]. Victor Zulu, who obtained his PhD from Rakuno Gakuen University, said, 'In Japan, professors and students have casual conversations with those who clean up the laboratory. In Zambia, today, people who have become rich often look down on other people' [ZAM 10]. Edgar Simulundu, a virologist who enjoyed skiing in Hokkaido, said, 'African universities send samples to foreign universities, where scholars examine them. But with Hokkaido University, we can conduct real collaborative research based in Zambia' [ZAM 03].

Girja Shanker Pandey, born in Uttar Pradesh, India, moved to Zambia in 1980 and taught at the veterinary school at UNZA from 1983. He obtained his PhD from Azabu University in Japan in 1988. He is an ethnic Indian veterinarian who observed Zambianisation from the inside, with empathy for Zambians and Zambian animals. For Pandey, Zambianisation meant radically increasing the number of veterinarians working in rural Zambia to meet a variety of needs in those areas.

> I think Zambianisation was meant to address the shortage of Zambian veterinarians, especially in rural areas. Japan understood this problem very well. It was a time-consuming process because nobody could just go and grab a PhD. Zambia is moving towards decentralisation, so the number of districts is increasing. We need more professionals. We still face a serious shortage of animal doctors at the village level, so the needs are huge on the ground. [ZAM 07]

Pandey's perception resonated with the discussions in the domestic support committee. The narrowly defined Zambianisation, i.e., replacing the foreign faculty with Zambians, had been achieved. The next step was to Zambianise the content of the educational activities. 'The Western textbooks used in Zambia contain more descriptions of diseases that have been well researched in the West than those about African diseases, and the research areas tend to lean towards those which interest Western researchers rather than those which would meet Zambian needs. To achieve "Zambianisation of practice", it is necessary to train veterinarians with the qualities required by the local communities and to carry out research and extension activities, which respond to the needs of the local communities. All these should be made in the spirit of a "national university"' (Mikami 1987: 23).

As we saw in the case study of the Jomo Kenyatta University of Agriculture and Technology (JKUAT) in this chapter (Sect. 5.2), Japan is willing to provide training opportunities not only for faculty members but also for technologists and assistants. Wilmot Benkele, who became a technologist, was trained at the Hyogo International Cultural Exchange Centre and the Hyogo Prefectural Himeji Livestock Health Centre from 1984 to 1985 and studied at the Obihiro University of Agriculture and Veterinary Medicine from 1988 to 1989. He said, 'The work of a technologist is like an interpreter. When students have questions, they first come to me. If I can answer them, I do, and if not, I advise them to ask a particular professor. It's like growing a tree. It takes time for students to become independent' [ZAM 06]. After retiring from UNZA, Benkele taught Japanese to ordinary Zambians in town.

Amoni Mwelwa, a young technologist who attended a two-month short-term training programme at Hokkaido University, shared his understanding of Japanese society. 'Zambians often talk to fellow people they don't know. I found it interesting that Japanese people respected their own personal space and ignored each other even on the bus. Yes, Japanese people are hardworking. But I thought their organisation was like a pyramid, and there was a rule like everyone should follow a senior person who gives instructions' [ZAM 02].

Mutale Mike Musonda, who was one of the few Zambian faculty members when the veterinary school was established, returned to UNZA after completing his PhD at Azabu University and was appointed the first dean of the School of Veterinary Medicine in 1996. Musonda said, 'Dr Lee was the first dean, and Dr Lovelace was married to a Zambian. I think they both understood the necessity of Zambianisation' [ZAM 09]. In practice, the Zambianisation of staff appointments was a variant of affirmative action based on the principle of redressing historical injustice.[21] However, Musonda maintained that the promotions were based on merit.

> You should know. We did not put people in important positions who lacked the ability. When I became dean, I was voted for in an election, which was strictly based on the university regulations. My colleagues judged me as a qualified person, and the decision was based on an objective assessment of my academic achievements. We always follow the same procedure. [ZAM 09]

5.3.4 Beyond Collaboration in Veterinary Medicine (2000s)

Zambianisation was ultimately successful not only through Japanese cooperation but also by mobilising support from other donors. Kenny L. Samui, who succeeded Musonda as dean of the School of Veterinary Medicine in 1998, had studied for six years at an agricultural university near Kyiv on a scholarship from the Soviet Union. He then went to the US and obtained his degree, thinking it would also be nice to study in the West. Samui remarked, 'Veterinary medicine is an applied science based on evidence. So it has nothing to do with ideology' [ZAM 11]. Regarding collaboration with Japan, Samui mentioned that there was some division between the faculty who worked with the Japanese and those who did not. He also commented that he felt JICA's regulations were sometimes stubbornly inflexible, for example, when it came to registering equipment.

While the highlight of medical cooperation with Ghana around 1970 was the provision of the electron microscope, the fact is that around the same time, two electron microscopes were installed at UNZA. These were not grants from Japan but from the Soviet Union. Eventually, the machines became obsolete, and in 1985 the US bought one of them, and the Soviets disposed of the other (Sato 1993: 174–175).

In UNZA, the School of Veterinary Medicine had a high research productivity alongside the School of Medicine. Except for several South African institutions,

---

[21] In the post-independence period in Zambia, it was thought that the nationalisation of the copper mines was a precondition for resource sovereignty, decolonisation, and equitable redistribution. While some argued that inequality between Zambians widened as Zambian elite classes began to grow after independence (Daniel 1979), others criticised nationalisation for distorting the market forces and hampering structural adjustment (Gulhati 1989).

UNZA's veterinary school became the finest research hub of veterinary science in sub-Saharan Africa. Dr Katendi Changula, a young clinical veterinarian, obtained her PhD from UNZA instead of a foreign university. She noted that in academia, men and women, Zambians and non-Zambians, are judged solely on the quality of their research output. Zambianisation, where locals take the lead, is already complete in the School of Veterinary Medicine. However, she said, 'If Zambians are isolated from the outside world, they won't be able to produce cutting-edge research results. Academic challenges are universal, so nationality, gender, and other factors are irrelevant.' Changula continued to say that she did not feel discriminated against because of her gender, but in her view this was probably because 'the university space is relatively isolated from the rest of Zambian society' [ZAM 08].

While some graduates pursue their careers as professional researchers, others work in the extension service. The number of Zambian veterinarians (most of whom are UNZA graduates) reached 284 in 2007, and 200 of them were scattered around the country as veterinary officers for the Ministry of Agriculture (JICA 2009b: 18–19). Danstan Mwiinga, who graduated in 2013, was a veterinarian for the Zambian livestock company Zambeef. 'Working from four o'clock in the morning is really hard, but it's a great learning experience. I was the first Zambian vet of Zambeef, but after me, six vets have been employed by the company.' He commented on his alma mater:

> To be honest, I think the practical aspect of the curriculum is weak. The animals we deal with at the school are mostly small ones, and students graduate without enough practical experience, so they don't have much confidence in what they can do in the field. Graduates sometimes find work in companies which have nothing to do with veterinary medicine, such as marketing. Otherwise, if they have good academic talent, they may become researchers in human medicine, using their experience in basic science. Anyway, many villages still have no veterinarian. I think the demand for animal doctors is still very high in local villages throughout Zambia. [ZAM 12]

There has also been an international dimension to the development of the school. Its official name is the Samora Machel School of Veterinary Medicine, the University of Zambia. Samora Machel was a freedom fighter in the independence movement of Mozambique, became its first president in 1975, and died in a plane crash in 1986, a reminiscence of the mysterious death of Dag Hammarskjöld, the UN secretary-general, in Zambia on the way to the Congo. Despite the assumption of becoming Zambia's national school, the school was named after the hero of the independence movement of a neighbouring nation in a spirit of regional solidarity. In 1999, third-country training began for veterinarians from the member countries of the Southern African Development Community (SADC), which had evolved from the SADCC. Zimbabwe, which had embarked on radical land reform, could not serve as a regional base for such training, at least for the time being. In the meantime, students from Namibia and other countries in the region began to study at the School of Veterinary Medicine in UNZA. Samui emphasised the importance of third-country training. 'As animal diseases spread throughout the region, we should work with other countries in the region. Thanks to the third-country training, we have produced a good textbook and laid the foundation for the expansion of international students' [ZAM 11].

Kasuka Muwauluka, former president of UNZA, stated:

> Zambianisation and internationalisation reinforce each other. Zambianisation should go hand in hand with internationalisation. If we favour only Zambians, the university will die. It is wonderful that the veterinary school is now vigorously tackling issues that transcend national borders, such as the spread of infectious diseases. We should address cross-border threats, which affect all of us in the region. [ZAM 13]

In 2007, the Hokkaido University Center for Zoonosis Control in Zambia (HUCZCZ) was established at UNZA and has been conducting advanced research on viral and bacterial infectious diseases. One of the joint research projects between Hokkaido University and UNZA was 'Visualization of Impact of Chronic/Latent Chemical Hazard and Geo-Ecological Remediation (Solve the lead (Pb) contamination problem through a multi-disciplinary approach!)', a project of the Science and Technology Research Partnership for Sustainable Development (SATREPS) administered by JICA and Japan Science and Technology Agency (JST). This evidence-based study investigated possible pollution due to lead (Pb) mining in Zambia. John Yabe, a pathologist involved in the project, had the opportunity to visit Minamata (Chap. 6, Sect. 6.3) while studying at Hokkaido University. He said:

> Back in 2010, I went to Kumamoto for a toxicology conference. One of the most unforgettable experiences was visiting Minamata with other students. We were completely shocked. I didn't know that such serious pollution and disease existed in Japan. Local people didn't understand why the patients were getting sick, and sadly, they were even isolated from their community because people wrongly thought the disease was contagious. That visit opened my eyes. I realised how important scientific knowledge is. [ZAM 01]

Hokkaido University opened the Lusaka office in 2012 as its fourth overseas base after Beijing, Seoul and Helsinki, and its staff were trusted by researchers and students visiting Zambia from various Japanese universities. The Lusaka Office also served to expand opportunities for African students to study abroad in Japan, not only for Zambians but also for all students in sub-Saharan Africa, based on the scholarships provided by the Ministry of Education. The relationship between Hokkaido University and UNZA, which began with support for the School of Veterinary Medicine, has evolved into an equal research partnership and comprehensive student exchange linking Africa and Japan. Although appropriate 'exit strategies' have often been discussed among donors, we have another option: not to leave but to stay and collaborate for mutual benefit. The 'Hokkaido University Model', which emphasizes education as well as research, has been a good example of sustained educational cooperation based on the trust forged between two universities, though it remains to be seen how the model will evolve in the next stage.

5.4 Empowerment in Action: Women's Rights and Family Planning (Jordan)

5.4.1 Population, Family, and Women (1994–1996)

Medical cooperation in Ghana was launched in the late 1960s, and activities expanded from basic research to clinical studies and outreach, while maintaining and developing research capacity. The project at the School of Veterinary Medicine, University of Zambia, started in the 1980s and has expanded from education to applied research and outreach. The final example in this chapter is a family planning project in Jordan, which focused on full-scale outreach: the dissemination of knowledge and institution building encompassing remote areas.

While population issues were much politicised across the North and the South in the last century, there has been a growing consensus about the need to rethink top-down policies and instead promote bottom-up approaches in recent years. The importance of ensuring reproductive health and rights for every individual, especially women, rather than imposing macro-level coercive population policies, has been accepted in both industrialising and industrialised countries. There has also been a growing recognition that the most rational way to prevent the so-called population explosion is not to forcibly reduce the number of children, but to spread the fruits of economic development and raise the social status of women. In any country, as urbanisation progresses, as women begin to work outside the home, as children's education becomes a higher priority in household finances, and as contraceptive methods become more widespread, the birth rate steadily declines as a result of people's own choices (Mine 2022: Chap. 2). Japan has a long history of supporting reproductive health in developing countries, most notably through disseminating the Maternal and Child Health Handbook in Southeast Asian and other countries (JICA 2012).

Globally, the turning point in mainstreaming reproductive health was the International Conference on Population and Development held in Cairo, Egypt, in 1994, after which the basis of population policy-making shifted from a state-centred to a people-centred, more comprehensive approach. National governments and multilateral agencies elaborated measures to improve the health of pregnant women and infants, promote contraceptive methods, provide information to young people, combat infectious diseases, and empower women, taking cultural contexts into account (JICA 2004b). The Cairo Conference also provided momentum for abolishing laws based on eugenic ideology in all countries, including Japan. The following year, in 1995, the Fourth World Conference on Women was held in Beijing, and it became a norm for policy-makers to incorporate the enhancement of women's status and self-determination into policy designs.

Against this background, in 1994, based on the outcomes of the Cairo Conference, the Jordanian Hashemite Fund for Human Development (JOHUD) expressed interest in promoting reproductive health, and the Higher Population Council (HPC) of Jordan requested Japan to assist. Princess Basma bint Talal, the king's sister, was particularly enthusiastic about this initiative. For JICA, it was the first attempt in the Islamic world to design a project that combined family planning with women's empowerment. Sato Tokiko, an expert in reproductive health who had worked in Kenya, was assigned to Jordan and played a central role in coordinating the project. According to Sato, in this project, women's empowerment 'means that, rather than the husband unilaterally deciding how many children they should have, the wife confidently participates in decision-making, and that she has the power to implement family planning in agreement with her husband' (Sato 2012: 10). JOHUD, an organisation with considerable influence and legitimacy in Jordan, is not a government organisation but an NGO run by the royal family; from a technical point of view, it was not easy for JICA, a government agency, to work with a non-governmental organisation as an official counterpart. Therefore, a tripartite partnership was established on the Jordanian side, involving JOHUD, HPC and the Ministry of Health.

The project was initially intended to cover the southern part of Jordan, a vast, sparsely populated nomadic area where healthcare services were lagging behind. The location for the first project in the south was carefully selected (Fig. 5.3). Nuha Hanna Muhreiz, who worked for JOHUD, said, 'We thought of Ma'an, but it was a challenging area as the locals tended to be insular and did not accept outsiders easily. So we gave up and decided on Karak, where diverse groups live together. We chose a region where the birth rate was relatively high and people were relatively poor' [JOR 02]. The aim was to experiment in a small area and gradually scale up. The first phase, from 1997 to 2000, began in the South Ghor region in the south of Karak Governorate, with a population of around 30,000. The second phase was from 2000 to 2003, intended to extend the project to the whole of Karak. In the third phase, from 2006 to 2011, the scope of the project was expanded to cover the entire southern region of the country (Karak, Tafileh, Ma'an and Aqaba Governorates). The main activities were: first, improving the facilities and the skills of the staff of the village health centres that served as base institutions; second, making home visits by health workers from the centres; and third, raising community awareness. In addition, small income-generating activities were organised for local women (Komasawa 2005; Sato 2012).

5.4.2 Health Workers Visiting Villages (1997–2003)

The most significant impact of these activities was probably made through the mobilisation of home visits by health workers.[22] As Sato explained, 'Unmarried women, who were not satisfied with just helping with household chores after graduating from high school, and married women, who were not satisfied with their current situation

---

[22] Although we refer to them as health workers generally, their official title, status, and system changed over time. In the first phase, they were called Community Development Promoters (both men and women), and in the second phase, the workers were renamed as Community Support Teams (women only). When I visited Jordan, they were called Health Educators. As the system changed, new recruits were sought, so the same people were not always employed.

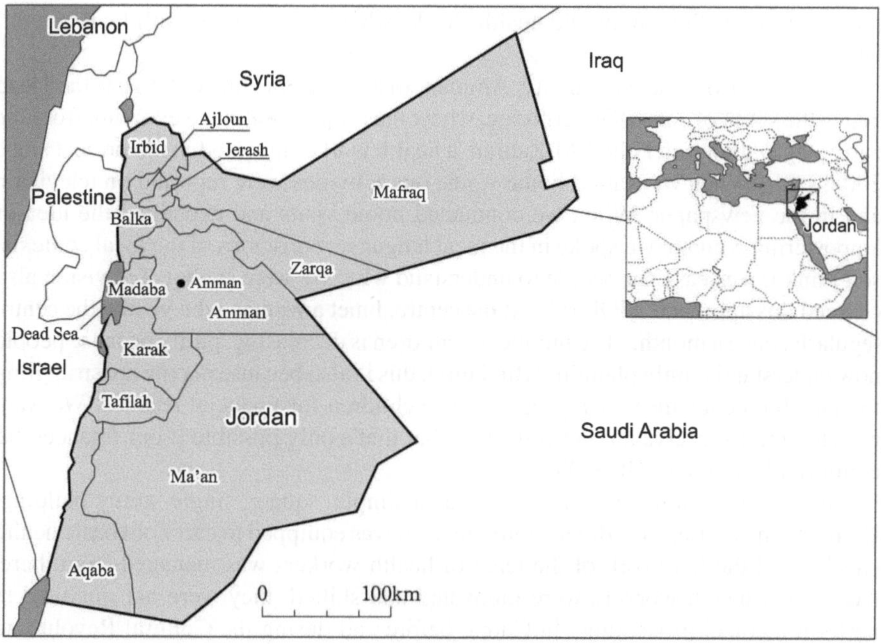

Fig. 5.3 Administrative map of Jordan. Source: Adapted from Sato (2021: 2–3)

after their marriage, participated in the selection test for health workers in search of inner change and life regeneration – I think those women were already being brave deep inside' (Sato 2012: 20). Based in the village health centres, they visited homes to provide advice on a wide range of issues facing women, including family planning. They became skilled community workers. Khawla Kawwa, the former head of the family planning division of the Ministry of Health, explained:

> The health workers spoke to women in every home about important topics like breastfeeding, how to take care of children, and hygiene. The husbands were also listening! Southern Jordan is about half the size of the whole country. It was not common for an international project to engage in this kind of work in such a big rural area. I think it was a very special project, even compared to the big USAID ones run in the same area. [JOR 01]

Kittie Tawfig Jamil Hijazeen, who has been working as a health worker in a village health centre on the outskirts of Karak city in Karak governorate since 2008, engaged in tasks such as breast cancer screening and blood pressure measurement, as well as family planning education. She did not just speak to married women. 'I also deal with various family issues, such as the problems old people face, domestic violence, and difficulties in raising children. Antenatal and postnatal care are also needed.' She discussed family planning as well, but that was only part of her work. 'We travel on foot, so it's hard when the houses are far apart. We are also scared of stray dogs' [JOR 05]. A woman who happened to be visiting the centre at the time of the interview told me cheerfully. 'I come here regularly. I don't want to get pregnant again. Kittie does a great job. She kindly did health checks when my mother wasn't feeling well' [JOR 06].

I travelled from the capital city, Amman, to a village health centre near the Dead Sea in the south of Karak Governorate, where the project continued evolving from the early stages. Fawzieh Fahed Al-Zahran, a health worker involved in the project since 2008, said, 'When we started home visits, our activities were reported on television and in the newspaper. When we conducted home visits and explained the idea of empowering women, we spoke in the local language, conscious of the local contexts, so I think it was easy for people to understand what we were saying. Television also covered this approach' [JOR 08]. At the centre, I met a woman who visited the centre regularly, once a month. 'The number of children is decreasing, partly because people now understand family planning. But I think this is also because people are struggling to make both ends meet. They cannot have children for financial reasons. We want our children to receive a good education, but that's only possible if our finances are comfortable at home' [JOR 09].

The village health centre I visited was a simple, square, single-storey building, similar to the houses of ordinary Jordanians. It was equipped to carry out basic health checks, and the fieldwork of the team of health workers was managed from there. Even if the health workers were motivated and skilled, they were not qualified to perform medical procedures. In China, before and during the Cultural Revolution, such people worked as 'barefoot doctors' and examined patients (Horn 1969). In any country today, however, the national health system will be disrupted if health workers start doing the same work as doctors and nurses. Once, the head of a local government in Jordan tried to have health workers give vaccinations, but the Ministry of Health intervened and stopped it [JOR 01].

Nevertheless, the health workers were not isolated; they continued to work effectively within the communities. Various awareness-raising events were organised, involving influential people in the villages. Abdulmonim Malkawi (the only male interviewee in Jordan), who had been working for the HPC since 1998, said, 'In the first phase, we brought religious leaders to the villages and asked them to give talks about our activities. Like it or not, men are the decision-makers in the family. If men say no, the project will fail. So we showed that family planning, such as spacing births, did not conflict with Islamic teachings' [JOR 03].[23] As the project area expanded, JICA provided four-wheel-drive vehicles, which could be used to travel between the villages. The workers walked around for the daily activities in the villages.

Women's empowerment and family planning are closely linked. Involving women in income-generating activities is expected not only to contribute to poverty reduction but also to increase women's influence over men and reduce unwanted pregnancies. JOHUD had always stressed the importance of income generation, and in this project JICA provided goats and bees as 'equipment' to give a stimulus to microcredit activities. The use of living creatures as equipment was almost unprecedented except

[23] Voices of villagers who participated in workshops in Karak (attended mostly by women but also men and children) were vividly captured and reported in Hagiwara and Malkawi (2003).

for laboratory animals. In the first phase, both women and men were recognised as beneficiaries, but in the second phase, only women were eligible, and the target area was expanded. Sahryeh Rawashdeh, a housewife living on the outskirts of Karak, had eight children. She used the loan in the second phase to buy five goats and increased her herd to 30, selling some milk to make yoghurt. 'Every time my children became school age, I sold some of the goats to pay for their school fees. It was an excellent investment. My children were very enthusiastic about taking care of the goats. I think they developed a sense of responsibility by helping with their mother's project. Even my husband, who is in the army during the week, goes to the market to buy food for the goats, and he even cleans the house, which is not very common in this society' [JOR 07]. It seems that her business activities had a significant impact on both her children and her husband.

The overall objective of the project was to reduce the total fertility rate (the average number of children a woman has in her lifetime). The UN demographic statistics shows that the fertility rate in Jordan was around 8.00 in the 1960s, but around the time the project started, it declined to 5.06 (1995–2000), and continued falling to 2.77 (2015–20). In the same period (2015–20), the fertility rate of Saudi Arabia, Jordan's eastern neighbour, was 2.34, and that of Israel, its western neighbour, was 3.04.[24] Contraceptive methods such as intrauterine devices (IUDs), pills, condoms, sterile operation, and breastfeeding became well-known to Jordanian women, and simple ones were made available at village health centres. Given the means, partners' consent, and motivation, the fertility rate will decline. Dr Hiam Hamie, who was born in Lebanon and studied medicine in the Soviet Union, emphasised the importance of the economic factor: 'It's not so easy to change people's behaviour. You can't force it from the top down. It's impossible to just go into people's homes and make them change what they believe in. Yet, the birth rate is falling. I think the main reason is economic. The shape of the family will not change without material necessities' [JOR 04].

Manal Fares Al-Ghazawi, who joined the project in its third phase, praised the changes that had taken place in the community as a result of the health workers' home visits. But she also noted that the status of women in Jordan as a whole had not changed so much. It was true that women had been empowered to some extent; Jordanian women were educated well, even better than men. However, there had been little change in economic statistics, such as the labour force participation rate [JOR 10]. Not only women but also men and society need to change. It is impossible to bring about a radical change in the behaviour of the entire population of a country in a project period of three or five years. However, the support provided at the right time can be the catalyst for changing the social tide. International cooperation may work as a midwife, standing by and empowering people.

---

[24] See the UN statistics: https://population.un.org/wpp/. The birth rate in Israel has been higher than in neighbouring countries. Although the project on reproductive health was intended to expand the range of life chances available to women based on the outcomes of the UN conferences in Cairo and Beijing, it was sometimes subject to misplaced but understandable criticism for trying to reduce the 'birth rate of Arabs' (Sato 2012).

5.4.3 *Progress in Institutionalisation (2000s)*

Setting up the institution of a self-sustaining health worker system by the Ministry of Health was probably the most outstanding achievement of the project. As discussed in the case study of SMASSE in Chapter 4 (Sect. 4.3), development projects sometimes face the question of allowances. In the second phase of the project in Jordan, which covered the whole of Karak Governorate, JICA paid allowances of 40 Jordanian dinars (about $56) per month to health workers who made 20 to 40 home visits (Komasawa 2005: 40). The third phase covered a large area in southern Jordan, and with the completion of this phase, JICA's financial support was terminated. The Jordanian government then extended the project to the north on its own initiative. Home visits became a public system, and health workers were employed by the Ministry of Health, which paid them regular salaries. The system was thus internalised.

When I asked local counterparts in other countries what they thought of the Japanese experts, their reactions were not always positive. In Jordan, however, it seemed that Japanese experts enjoyed an excellent reputation among their local colleagues. 'I think what makes JICA different from other donors is that JICA people are sensitive to local culture. They try to decide things from the bottom up and make plans with local people' [JOR 02]. 'The USAID officers may have been jealous because I often talked about JICA. JICA values what is happening on the ground. We address the needs of local people, who are our sisters, cousins, daughters and husbands' [JOR 01].

As mentioned several times in this book, development cooperation, especially technology transfer projects, may have unintended positive social impacts. HPC's Malkawi told me that he would never forget the experience of visiting a primary school in Japan in 1999.

> The principal was cleaning the floor together with the school children! I still like to tell this story to people around me. In this country, a school principal would probably wave a stick around and chase the children, shouting, 'Clean up, now!' But if the children saw the principal actually doing such work himself, they would probably say, 'Please take a break, sir. We'll do it. [JOR 03]

The fact is that not all Japanese elementary school principals join in cleaning, but some would. The principal's job is to manage the school, and the school's most important goal is supposed to improve the children's academic performances. The humble attitude of teachers is praiseworthy, but it may not be an essential quality for them. What is intriguing in Jordanian contexts is that such behaviour of the Japanese school management was perceived with a sense of surprise as something that could galvanise social change, at least potentially, as was the case with *kaizen* in Costa Rica.

Concerning the Noguchi Institute in Ghana and the veterinary project in Zambia, the core of transferred technology was highly specific, advanced technology. In contrast, the women's empowerment project in Jordan required a general change in social norms and values. In Jordan, it was hoped that the value system would change gradually and steadily. In order to achieve such a goal, it was necessary to understand the context of the society in which the project was embedded.[25]

In Jordan, local stakeholders joined the initial baseline survey, and there was a high level of participation and a sense of project ownership from the outset. The Project Design Matrix (PDM) is a figure popularised in the 1990s, which is to logically configure a set of objectives, conditions, inputs, and expected outputs of a project. At the end of the first phase, Jordanians participated in meetings with JICA and contributed to drafting the PDM for the second phase [JOR 02] [JOR 03] (Komasawa 2005: 38). I do not think it very common that PDMs are drawn up in such a bottom-up approach with the participation of local stakeholders. Al-Ghazawi, an HPC staff member, talked about several points for improvement in the future. 'I believe the project could have focused more on young people. It's really important to teach the basics to people who have not got married yet. And, I think we should provide education to both women and men' [JOR 10].

The Jordanian lessons were disseminated to neighbouring countries. In June 2008, an international workshop on reproductive health was held in Aqaba, a port city in southern Jordan, attended by representatives from Palestine, Syria, Sudan, Afghanistan and India in an attempt to share the Jordanian experience (Sato et al. 2008). In October the same year, a study tour was organised in Aleppo, Syria, in which Jordanian nurses and midwives participated, and the honest exchange of ideas strengthened the ties between the country representatives. However, in March 2011, a civil war broke out in Syria, and the country's health system totally collapsed. Large numbers of Syrian refugees fled their homeland and poured into northern Jordan. As Muhreiz, a former JOHUD staff member, described, 'Syrian refugees and poor Jordanians are competing for resources. Jordanians think that Syrians get more benefits because they have more children than Jordanians. The refugees must be empowered. I don't think it's good for refugees to remain dependent on handouts' [JOR 02].

'This project is like my baby,' said Khawla Kawwa, who took charge of the project at the Ministry of Health. She was originally from Palestine. The majority of Jordanians, especially urban citizens, are of Palestinian origin, and people of various refugee backgrounds and their children now play an essential role in Jordanian society. When Khawla incidentally remarked, 'I think we should write a book documenting this project by ourselves' [JOR 01], I realised that this oral history would only be a makeshift attempt by an outsider. As Khawla hoped, the time will come when the counterparts write a history with their full ownership.

5.4.4 Seeking Environmental Security

Given its sound success, the family planning project in Jordan could have been replicated in a much broader region of the Middle East, just as the SMASSE project

[25] Along with prevention and comprehensiveness, the context-specific approach is regarded as one of the pillars of human security practices. See JICA ORI (2022, 2024).

that began in Kenya spread across the African continent. However, the unexpected outbreak of civil war in Syria has made it difficult to scale up the project. This was a painful reminder that political stability is a prerequisite for sustainable human development.

Jordan is not endowed with rich natural resources such as oil, and its outlet to the sea (the port of Aqaba at the southern tip) is extremely narrow. A country where power is concentrated in the royal family, Jordan was originally an artificial state designed to be a part of the British Empire. In light of geopolitics, Jordan has hosted refugees from neighbouring countries one after the other—Palestinians, Lebanese, Iraqis, and recently a large number of Syrians. Had the political circumstances been slightly different, the presence of refugees would have become a factor of serious conflict, but the political landscape of Jordan as a 'politely run authoritarian state' (Robins 2019) has been surprisingly stable by recent Middle Eastern standards.

The development of this project can be primarily attributed to the consistent support of the Hashemite royal family, the skills of the expert Sato, and the teamwork of her open-minded and donor-experienced Jordanian counterparts. Before coming to Jordan, Sato worked in Kenya and was completely new to the Middle East. The Japanese audience should not overestimate the 'pro-Japanese' general sentiment and attitudes, if any, of partner countries. Jordan's heavy dependence on humanitarian and development aid from the US[26] must have contributed to the favourable attitude of Jordanian policy-makers to Japan as an alternative donor.

Sato moved to Japan after the completion of the project but has since returned to Jordan several times to conduct research on Syrian refugees in the northern province of Mafraq. Jordan was originally an administrative unit of Greater Syria until the establishment of the Kingdom of Jordan, and ethnically speaking there is little difference between the people of southern Syria and the people of northern Jordan. Life in refugee camps places a heavy burden on both mothers and children, and there is a great need for ensuring reproductive health and family support. The prolonged refugee crisis, compounded by the spread of COVID-19, has put a strain on the lives of people in northern Jordan, both the locals and the refugees. There appears to have been an increase in domestic violence and divorce (Sato 2021).

The research in Jordan for this oral history was carried out in January 2020, just before COVID-19 began to spread worldwide. In the years that followed, as I was unable to take international flights, I spent my days organising my research notes from various fields I had visited. A particularly memorable scene for me in Jordan was the landscape I observed while travelling to visit the project in the Karak Governorate. We drove down to the Dead Sea, which is located 430 m below sea level and is situated southwest of Amman. On the way, I passed Mount Nebo, where Moses is said to have died. On the other side of the Dead Sea is the West Bank of the River Jordan, now encroached upon by Israeli settlements. The surface area of the Dead

[26] According to OECD statistics, just before the outbreak of COVID-19, the largest donor to Jordan in 2018–19 was the US with assistance of $1.126 billion, followed by Germany with $459 million, and Japan ranked seventh with $102 million. https://www.oecd.org/countries/jordan/aid-at-a-glance.htm.

Sea has been gradually decreasing for various reasons, including the development of irrigated agriculture around the River Jordan, the increased consumption of water for daily life due to population growth, and the reduction in rainfall caused by climate change. At the time of my visit, the surface area of the Dead Sea had shrunk to about 600 square km, around 60% of its size in the mid-twentieth century.

The course of the Israeli-Palestinian and Syrian conflicts and wars will configure the future state of women's rights and family planning in Jordan and the wider region. When the water shortage caused by population growth and agrarian and industrial development is seriously felt throughout the region, an environmental crisis could transform into a political crisis. Development projects take on various meanings in the context of unpredictable political development and creeping environmental degradation.

Chapter 6
Towards Human Security

6.1 Networking Beyond Nation-Building Support

6.1.1 Drifters in Development Cooperation

Thus far, we have made a series of journeys to visit development projects. While each project bears a unique character, their classification into agriculture, fisheries, manufacturing, education, and health, and the distinction between technology transfer and infrastructure building through yen loans and grants could be considered safe and orthodox. In this final chapter, I want to discuss different types of efforts. I shed light on projects that readers already acquainted with development cooperation practices may consider somewhat outside the mainstream.

The primary objective of Japan's development cooperation in the second half of the twentieth century was to support nation-building. Japan assisted in strengthening the functioning cycle of principal-agent relationships in developing countries. As discussed in Chap. 1, although it is rarely remembered today, the motto of Japan's development cooperation in the 1980s was 'Human Development, National Development, and Heart-to-Heart Communications'. It was considered important not to catch fish directly for the local people but to teach them how to fish. Efforts were made to train human resources in farms, factories, schools, clinics, research centres, ministries, municipalities, etc., tapping into local people's quest for self-help. The construction of hard infrastructure was accompanied by efforts to develop local human resources to maintain it. The hope was that this would enable the aid recipient country to develop its own functioning institutions, thereby accumulating national wealth and improving the well-being of the people in newly-born nations.

However, in the historical process of nation-building support, horizontal cooperation and mutual learning between nations and peoples also gradually emerged. This is partly because of the success of nation-building efforts (due to which nations become substantially equal), and partly because of the nature of global challenges—climate change, natural disasters, pandemics, war, economic crises, etc.—that affect people

Y. Mine, *An Oral History of Development Cooperation*,
https://doi.org/10.1007/978-981-95-5479-9_6

across national boundaries. Thus, in addition to cooperation between sovereign nations, a greater effort of solidarity is required between people (UNDP 2022) as illustrated in Fig. 1.5 in Chap. 1. At this stage, people's interaction, as well as inter-governmental collaboration, matter.

Solidarity between people is consolidated by people's face-to-face communication. People cross borders, encounter each other, and learn from each other's experience. From earliest times to the present day, homo sapiens has been a special kind of animal that is constantly on the move (Miller 2023). On the other hand, since modern nation-states are premised on national territories and boundaries, support for nation-building tends to be a closed, self-contained practice. 'Endogenous development', proposed by Japanese sociologist Tsurumi Kazuko as a framework for development against top-down state-centric modernisation, is to promote participatory practices in ecological communities smaller than a nation-state (Omi 2024). Inspired by the thoughts of John Dewey and the Chinese sociologist Fei Xiaotong, Tsurumi advocated endogenous development, resonating with the concept of 'alternative development' proposed by the Dag Hammarskjöld Foundation in 1975, which presaged today's sustainable development.

In her reflections, Tsurumi also developed a theorem to avoid the isolation pertaining to self-contained national and communal development. It was a focus on 'drifters' (漂泊者, which can also be translated as 'vagabonds', 'wanderers' or 'itinerants'), who take action across 'regional communities' (地域, which can also be 'regions', 'areas' or simply 'communities'). In a regional community, there are leaders among 'settlers' (定住者, who are also called 'residents'), who tend to be 'trusted and respected by the locals and more cautious in their thoughts and actions'. However, these settlers constantly interact with 'drifters who tend to be more radical in thought and action'.[1] The drifters connect rural areas with cities, communities with other communities, and nations with other nations. As described by Tsurumi, a regional community where people live together and discover each other are

> places where settlers live their lives based on soil and water. It is also a place where settlers and drifters interact. Settlers become temporary drifters when they leave their settlements to move elsewhere, but they eventually return to their original places. For settlers, drifters are transmitters of foreign information, values, ideas, etc. By drifting temporarily, the settlers also encounter different cultures, which they transmit back to other settlers. A regional community can be redefined as a place with the potential to create new common bonds through the interactions between settlers, drifters and temporary drifters. (Tsurumi 1996: 26)

Tsurumi assumed a constant exchange of roles between the settlers and the drifters. When a sufferer of Minamata disease visits an indigenous community in Canada, she or he becomes a temporary drifter. When a Native Canadian visits Minamata, the indigenous person also becomes a temporary drifter. When their travels intersect, mutual learning of experiences occurs (Tsurumi 1996: 189). Broadly speaking, it

[1] Tsurumi described Kawamoto Teruo, a radical leader of an association of Minamata disease sufferers, as a drifter who embodied a *suiten* (focal point) where various forces and networks intersect (Tsurumi 1996: 163–169) (in Japanese). Kawamoto's father was a Chisso employee originally from Amakusa, and Kawamoto had roamed around various places and occupations while he was young.

may even be possible to position technology transfer in development cooperation as the institutional mobilisation of temporary drifters who possess specific skills.

6.1.2 People Move, Water Flows

The first case study of this chapter focuses on human migration and drifters' life experiences. At a symposium organised by the Ministry of Foreign Affairs to commemorate the 70th anniversary of Japanese emigration to Brazil, Ishikawa Tomonori, known for his work on Okinawa, gave an overview of the history of Japanese emigration (Ishikawa 1979). Recruitment-based emigration in modern Japan began in 1868 (the first year of the Meiji era), with Hawaii and Guam as the main destinations. Subsequently, emigration from various parts of Japan to the United States (mainly Hawaii and the West Coast) and Canada accelerated, but from the 1920s onwards, the target countries shifted to Brazil and other Latin American countries. After World War II, a new wave of Japanese migration occurred; they have been resettled chiefly in the Amazon region of Brazil since 1952. A breakdown of Asian migration worldwide in the 1970s shows that Chinese migrants numbered no less than 20 million, Indian migrants nearly 5 million, and Japanese ranked third at 1.6 million (the largest population was the ethnic-Japanese Brazilians at 760,000). In 1940, the three main prefectures of origin for Japanese emigrants were Hiroshima (72,484), Kumamoto (65,378) and Okinawa (57,283). For the *issei* (the first generation) migrants, the psychological bonds to their hometowns, i.e., the villages where they were born and grew up, may have been stronger than the general attachment to their home country, Japan.[2]

The reader may wonder why migration is discussed in the final part of a history of Japan's development cooperation. One important reason is that assisting Japanese emigration was part of the original mission of JICA. In 1963, the Federation of Associations for Japanese Emigration (FAJE) and the Japan Emigration Promotion Co., Ltd (JEPC), which were both responsible for overseas migration, merged to form the Japan Emigration Service (JEMIS). A policy document described the activities of JEMIS, which had offices in all prefectures, as 'a pillar of human exchange with more lasting "depth" and "weight" at the mass level, than just the short-term tutelage and cooperation or the exchange of a handful of intellectuals' (Japan Emigration Service 1973: 4, 8–9).

---

[2] According to the brochure *The Nikkei, Connecting Japan and Latin America* (2018) published by the Japanese Ministry of Foreign Affairs, the number of *Nikkei* worldwide reached more than 3.6 million, of which 2.13 million lived in Latin America, with around 1.9 million being Brazilian *Nikkei*. https://www.mofa.go.jp/mofaj/press/pr/pub/pamph/japan_latinamerica.html. Spanish and Portuguese versions are also available on this website. It is difficult to know the exact number of *Nikkei* across generations, as Japan does not recognise dual citizenship. I express my sincere gratitude to Yurisawa Masaru, himself a young *Nikkei* networker, who guided me in Brazil, especially in Belém.

In 1974, JEMIS and OTCA merged to form the Japan International Cooperation Agency (JICA). After the merger, the emigration support services were downsized, but the human resources and know-how of JEMIS were transferred to JICA and utilised to recruit JICA Volunteers and to dispatch experts with valuable local knowledge. While development projects by Western donors tend to be run as a centralised project by the national governments, Japan's cooperation is more decentralised. JICA has 15 domestic offices rooted in local communities from Hokkaido to Okinawa. Were something akin to the dismantling of USAID attempted in Japan, strong opposition would arise from local governments.

Even now, JICA is carrying out projects to support ethnic Japanese citizens in Latin America, including the elderly of Japanese descent.[3] This chapter describes the 'Japanese Language School Students Training' project, which began in 1987. The *Nikkei* (ethnic-Japanese) youth, selected from Japanese language schools throughout Latin America, learnt about the history of Japanese migration, stayed with Japanese families, attended Japanese public schools, made Japanese friends, and experienced Japanese culture. The project was renamed the 'Education Programme for *Nikkei* Next Generation' in 2012. I interviewed Brazilian *Nikkei* citizens who participated in the training for junior high school students.

Cooperation between Brazil and Japan went further beyond the support for *Nikkei*. In 1992, the United Nations Conference on Environment and Development (Rio Summit) was convened in Rio de Janeiro, Brazil. That year, a young Brazilian chemical scientist, Olaf Malm, arrived in Minamata, Kumamoto Prefecture, Japan. Concerned that the Amazon basin was being rapidly contaminated by mercury from gold mines, Malm, a chemical scientist at the Federal University of Rio de Janeiro, brought samples, including frozen fish, to Japan; apparently, there were not very strict rules about luggage on international flights in those days. The samples were then tested at the National Institute for Minamata Disease (NIMD) located on a hill overlooking the Shiranui Sea in the suburb of Minamata City. They were found to contain unusually high levels of mercury [BRA 16].[4]

Section 6.3, the second case study of this chapter, explores the cooperation between Minamata and Brazil in preventing mercury pollution. The Kagoshima-born independent-minded, experienced chemical scientist Akagi Hirokatsu played a unique role as a key figure in this cooperation. Akagi began his career as a researcher at the National Institute of Public Health at the Ministry of Health. After conducting research in Canada, he moved to the NIMD in Minamata under the Ministry of the Environment, where he developed a precise technique for measuring mercury, known as the 'Akagi method'. After his retirement, Akagi established a private laboratory in

[3] The history of JICA's support for emigrants is explained in JICA (1984b: Chap. 6) and JICA (1999b: Chap. 1, Sect. 4; Chap. 2, Sect. 4; Chap. 4). The total number of Japanese emigrants handled by JICA and its predecessor agencies amounted to 73,035 (of which 53,657 are in Brazil) as of 2017. https://www.jica.go.jp/regions/america/support.html.

[4] The NIMD was established in 1978, one year before the establishment of the Noguchi Institute in Ghana, as a research institute of the Environment Agency (Ministry of the Environment since 2001). http://nimd.env.go.jp/english/about/history/.

Minamata and continued collaborative research and training activities with scholars from Brazil and other parts of the world.[5]

Minamata disease and the gold mines in the Amazon basin in Brazil became known worldwide through the art of photography. The American photographer Eugene Smith and his wife, Aileen Mioko Smith, lived in Minamata and exposed the reality of this human tragedy to the world (Smith and Smith 1975). By contrast, the Brazilian photographer Sebastião Salgado shot lively pictures of the gold miners—exposed to mercury—in the Amazon known as *garimpeiros* (Salgado 1999; Salgado et Francq 2013). While the situations in Minamata and in the Amazon were being publicised through the activities of renowned artists, civil society activists and municipal officers in Minamata strived to repair social divisions and regenerate the community. As described in this section, lessons from these locally-led initiatives, along with the dangers of mercury poisoning, have been shared worldwide through JICA training.

6.1.3 Peace at Sea, Peace on Land

From the Korean peninsula to Jeju Island, Tsushima, the Goto Islands, Nagasaki, Amakusa, Koshikishima, and the Nansei Islands including Okinawa, to Taiwan, islands large and small line west of Kyushu. The Shiranui Sea, which washes Minamata, is a quiet inland sea in part of this maritime area. Section 6.4—the final case study of this chapter—opens the view from Minamata to the southwest, taking the reader on a journey towards Okinawa and further into southeast Asia.

Threats to the survival, livelihood and dignity of humanity surround us. The most immediate threats are wars involving civilians—post-World War II history is not one of peace but of violent wars, including civil wars, and the wars in Ukraine and Gaza in the 2020s have only added another page to this history. In war and war-like situations, the nation-state, which is supposed to protect human security, can turn into a source of threats to people's survival. In considering the experience of Japan, the horrific ground battle in Okinawa in the final stages of the Pacific War should be remembered. The Battle of Okinawa lasted from March 1945, when US troops landed, until the Japanese were disarmed in early September. One of the factors that contributed to the prolonged fighting was the Japanese military's manoeuvring operation in Okinawa, known as 'bloodshed for endurance', intended to delay an imminent large-scale battle on the Japanese mainland. As US forces quickly occupied the northern and central parts of Okinawa's main island, the southern part became the scene of the fiercest fighting. Japanese forces retreated to Mabuni (where the Okinawa Prefectural Peace Memorial Museum is now located), while up to 100,000 Okinawans wandered the battlefields where the so-called 'Iron Storm' raged. Official records show that the

[5] The manual of the Akagi method can be found at: http://nimd.env.go.jp/kenkyu/docs/march_mercury_analysis_manual(e).pdf. One of Akagi's colleagues at the NIMD in the 1980s was Tamaki Hidehiko, who was originally from Okinawa. After joining WHO to work on the Global AIDS Strategy, Tamaki moved to Hokkaido and was instrumental in establishing Hokkaido University Nitobe College. https://nitobe-college.academic.hokudai.ac.jp/en.

death toll in the Battle of Okinawa comprises 94,000 Okinawan civilians, 28,228 local servicemen and military personnel, 65,908 Japanese soldiers from the mainland, and 12,520 on the part of the US military. Okinawan civilian casualties are comparable to the military casualties.[6]

The Okinawa Prefectural Peace Memorial Museum is a prefectural institution that collects evidence of people's wartime experiences and passes on the facts and lessons of the ground war to future generations. Since the end of the war, Okinawa, being under the yoke of the US military bases, has become a dynamic home for drifters. Not only has Okinawa sent many of its youth out into the world, but it has also welcomed those who have returned, and its stunningly beautiful sea and cultural heritage continue to attract outsiders. Since its opening in 2000, the museum has welcomed around 400,000 visitors every year, many from outside the prefecture and abroad.

Once its reputation was established, the museum was expected to spread its wings to the outside world. After some discussion, the Tuol Sleng Genocide Museum in Phnom Penh, Cambodia, was selected as a partner institution. The building of Tuol Sleng (a hill of poisonous trees) was originally used as a high school (lycée) but was converted into an interrogation facility targeting citizens suspected of being spies or counter-revolutionary activists during the Pol Pot regime from 1976 to 1979, when systematic abduction, torture, and murder took place. The number of detainees, ranging from former regime collaborators to innocent civilians (mostly the latter), reached nearly 20,000, and almost no one made it out alive. Even today, Cambodians continue to struggle with coming to terms with the history of mass killings perpetrated by fellow Cambodians. On the other hand, there are memories of the historical glory of the Khmer Kingdom in Cambodia. Museum staff from Tuol Sleng spent time in Okinawa, interacting with the public and receiving training in storage, display and outreach, which they adapted to improve the museum in Cambodia.[7] Section 6.4, the third case study, traces such grassroots exchanges and technology transfers between peace museums in Okinawa and Cambodia, followed by a story of collaboration in the field of water supply.

This chapter deals with issues such as migration, mercury pollution and memories of killings. In the JICA training, the methods used to address these issues were plainly practical, drawing on the accumulated knowledge of multicultural education, scientific mercury measurement, and museology. Furthermore, the projects discussed in this chapter were all carried out in participatory ways involving a wide range of non-state actors, including ordinary citizens—junior high school students, teachers, laboratory scientists, local government officers, and NGO members. From within the framework of supporting 'nation-building,' the practice of promoting 'heart-to-heart' communication between citizens across borders gradually took shape. No

[6] Figures are from the 'Peace Study' website of the Okinawa Prefectural Peace Memorial Museum. http://peace-museum.okinawa.jp/heiwagakusyu/index.html (Japanese). A general introduction to the museum is available at: http://peace-museum.okinawa.jp/english/index.html.

[7] In July 2025, the Cambodian memorial sites for peace and reflection including the Tuol Sleng Genocide Museum were formally inscribed on the UNESCO World Heritage List.

country can flourish without ensuring peace, well-being, and security for every individual in society. The growing recognition of this fact is a momentous shift in the history of development cooperation, from support for nation-building to shared human security.[8]

6.2 Youths Connected and Energised: Fostering the Next Generation of *Nikkei* People (Brazil)

6.2.1 Taking Part in the New World

The earth is round. One country diametrically opposite Japan is Argentina, which adjoins Brazil. If we intend to travel from Japan by airplane, we should be prepared for a journey of more than 24 h to get to São Paulo. However, we can choose the route relatively freely. The standard one is across the Pacific to the US and then heading south, but there are also alternative routes via Europe or the Middle East. In the mid-1990s, on my way back from a research trip to Cape Town, South Africa, I was on a Malaysia Airlines flight. A young man sitting next to me asked me if I was Japanese. He happened to be a *Nikkei* Brazilian who worked in a factory in Mie Prefecture. He took a flight in Buenos Aires, crossed the Atlantic, landed in Cape Town, and crossed the Indian Ocean to Kuala Lumpur, before changing the flight to Japan. He told me that it was the cheapest flight connecting his hometown with his workplace. The route from Argentina to Malaysia is no longer in operation, but it was probably the longest scheduled flight using the same aircraft in the southern hemisphere.

There were two established travelling routes for Japanese emigrants: the eastbound (from the Japanese perspective) Pacific route from Japan to Central and South America and the westbound Indian-Atlantic Ocean route similar to the one of the Malaysia Airlines mentioned above. Based on his own experience of travelling to Brazil via the westbound route on the vessel *La Plata*, Ishikawa Tatsuzo published the novel *Sobo* (meaning 'grassroots people') in 1935. The work, which won the first Akutagawa Prize, depicted the lives of the emigrants on their journey by having the characters speak local dialects and describing the stressful life and entertaining events on board. The migrants boarded the ship in Kobe and, after a 45-day voyage through Hong Kong, Saigon, Singapore, the Straits of Malacca and South Africa, disembarked at the port of Santos in Brazil and were then dispersed by train to farms in the state of São Paulo. Although life there was equally poor, it was different from Japan where people were 'tormented by taxes and social obligations' (Ishikawa 1951: 194, 241).

[8] Key literature on human security includes Thomas (2000), Kaldor (2007), Tadjbakhsh and Chenoy (2009), Martin and Owen (2014), and UNDP (2022) among others. The JICA Ogata Research Institute publishes a report on human security every two years (JICA ORI 2022).

The *Nikkei* people, who had worked hard to establish themselves in Brazilian society, were torn apart after World War II between the 'victorious' group, the majority who believed that Japan had won, and the 'defeated' group, the minority who believed that Japan had lost. In 1946 and 1947, there were even fatal victims due to terrorism by the extreme right-wing *Shindo Renmei* (League of the Moral of the Emperor's Subjects) against influential figures of the 'defeated' group. The unrest spread to non-*Nikkei* Brazilians, and the Brazilian National Congress debated a constitutional amendment that would ban the acceptance of Japanese immigrants. The vote was close, with 99 in favour and 99 against, and the chairperson's casting vote narrowly turned down the proposal. This 'victorious versus defeated' conflict was a massive crisis in the history of the Japanese-Brazilian community, but the fact of Japan's defeat was gradually accepted in the whole of *Nikkei* community, and the conflict subsided by the mid-1950s.[9]

The year 1978 marked the 70th anniversary of the history of Japanese emigration to Brazil. Following the disembarkation of 791 people from the *Kasato Maru* at the port of Santos in 1908, the Japanese-Brazilian community spread throughout Brazil, and with the emergence of the second and third generations, *Nikkei* citizens were gradually integrated into Brazilian society (Fig. 6.1). In June 1978, the *Mainichi Shimbun* newspaper organised a symposium in São Paulo to commemorate the 70th anniversary of Japanese migration to Brazil. In December of the same year, another symposium with the same purpose was held by the Ministry of Foreign Affairs and JICA in Tokyo. The keynote speeches at these two symposiums were delivered by Umesao Tadao, the founding director of the National Museum of Ethnology (Umesao 1978, 1979). Umesao spoke passionately about the historical significance of Japanese migration to Brazil in the context of human civilisation beyond the perspective of individual migrants. The Americas were a 'new continent' for both Europe and Japan, 'the property of all humanity' (Umesao 1978: 13), and the Japanese were participating in the new venture of human history to unleash the potential that lay latent in the land—this, Umesao argued, was the civilisational essence of Japanese migration to Central and South America.[10] Umesao proposed the slogan 'We take part in the New World (われら新世界に参加す)'. The banner with this slogan was still hanging at the entrance to the Historical Museum of Japanese Immigration in Brazil in São Paulo when I visited the city 40 years after the symposiums.

Umesao understood that Brazil was in the process of transforming itself into a unified nation. It was therefore important to note that the *Nikkei* were no longer

---

[9] As for the conflict between the 'victorious' and the 'defeated' groups, see a balanced account given by Ota (1995) in Japanese.

[10] Umesao noted that 'to put it bluntly, the destinations of Japanese emigration all belonged to the New World. There was a brief period of emigration to the Asian continent in the form of the mobilisation of settlers in Manchuria, but this ended in a miserable failure' (Umesao 1979: 20). If we take the worldview of Umesao's ecological history of civilizations presented in 1967 to its logical extreme, it could be that North and South America was a joint frontier colony of the West and Japan, which was collectively referred to as Zone 1 (Umesao 2003: 96). In his world history, Umesao did not really touch on the question of indigenous peoples in the Americas and the transatlantic slave trade.

Fig. 6.1 Brazil and the Amazon river basin. Source: Author

Japanese but Brazilian citizens. 'The view of the *Nikkei* colony as an extension of Japanese society will certainly lose its power' (ibid. 17). Umesao said that the *Nikkei* were more like relatives than family members; they were like 'uncles' who hailed from the same clan and settled in different villages. While proud of the common ancestry, Umesao remarked that he was inclined to tell them, 'Please continue to contribute to the village in which you live' (ibid. 18). The *Nikkei* people share qualities such as hard work, passion for education, and collectivist ethos. They tended to anchor themselves in the 'middle class' of the country in which they settled (Umesao 1979: 27). The *Nikkei* community would continue to contribute to Brazilian society while retaining Japanese culture and inheriting the Japanese value system. And today's young Japanese would still have to 'leave their country and work abroad as foreigners' (ibid. p. 30). Umesao said that many countries besides Brazil were waiting for a new civilisation to emerge.

Nikkei immigrants in Central and South America faced constant hardship, being overworked on farms, left to fend for themselves in desolate, stony wastelands, suffering from malaria, and being targeted by anti-Japanese campaigns. The situation of the immigrants sent to the Dominican Republic in Central America was appalling and could only be described as being 'deserted' (Konno and Takahashi, 1993). However, to see all *Nikkei* as pitiful victims is to underestimate the strength of the people who survived against all odds. The idea that the Japanese who crossed the oceans struggled at the forefront of human history was nothing but a grand historical vision characteristic of Umesao. However, it was also a forceful message of life encouragement that gave confidence to the *Nikkei* individuals and communities in Latin America.

6.2.2 Nikkei *Youth*

Supporting overseas migration through various measures, including publicity campaigns and matching, was part of JICA's official mission in its earlier days. However, when the post-war labour surplus came to an end, overseas migration ceased to be a policy objective. The number of emigrants handled by JICA's predecessor organisation peaked at 8,386 in 1960, but then fell to 1,526 in 1963, when the Japan Overseas Migration Association was established, and to 534 in 1974, when JICA was formed through a merger, and the project formally terminated with only 31 people in 1993. Although this marked the end of the era of systematic emigration, JICA continued to provide support to the *Nikkei* communities that grew in Latin America. The hope that 'the existing *Nikkei* communities will serve as stronger bonds with our country' remained constant, but the purpose of support for the *Nikkei* people has shifted from 'settlement and stability of life' of migrants to 'welfare of the elderly and human resources development'. There were initiatives such as training by inviting *Nikkei* youth to Japan, activities of JICA Volunteers (in the fields of Japanese language teaching, elderly care, sports, etc.), collaboration with the private sector, and public relations.[11]

The rest of this section discusses the Junior High School Student Invitation Programme, a part of the *Nikkei* Community Next Generation Training, which targets young students of Japanese descent in Central and South America. The original name of the scheme at the time of its launch in 1987 was the Japanese Language School Student Training. This was for students who were equivalent to junior high school students in Japan, studying in Japanese language schools run by *Nikkei* organisations, and recognised as having excellent grades, good conduct, and sufficient potential to

[11] Information is taken from the JICA website: https://www.jica.go.jp/regions/america/support.html https://www.jica.go.jp/regions/america/ku57pq0000207h3n-att/pamphlet_201903.pdf (both are in Japanese) The Overseas Migration Museum was established at JICA Yokohama in 2002 and has become a centre for outreach and research on migration. https://www.jica.go.jp/english/domestic/jomm/outline/index.html https://www.jica.go.jp/Resource/english/publications/reports/annual/2020/c8h0vm0000fc7q2b-att/2020_27.pdf.

contribute to the development of the *Nikkei* community in the future.[12] The training lasted approximately one month and included a combination of activities such as learning about the history of Japanese emigration, visiting facilities, experiencing life in Japanese junior high schools, homestays, and group trips to places such as Hakone, Tokyo Disneyland, and temples and shrines in Kyoto. The training ran twice a year, with the first group of students coming from North and Central America (mainly Canada and Mexico) and the second from South America (mainly Brazil). The second group stayed in Japan in January or February, so if they were lucky they could see a snowy landscape that they would not see in Brazil. The trainees used to stay with their relatives in the past, but more recently they stayed with volunteer citizens for a few days before travelling to Kansai.

In São Paulo and Belém, I interviewed participants in the training who belonged to different generations of *Nikkei,* all of whom spoke to me in perfect Japanese. Jerson Hideaki Onishi, a 45-year-old banker and second-generation immigrant from Wakayama Prefecture, participated in the first youth training in 1987 when he was 14 years old. It was his first trip abroad.

> Attending Negishi Junior High School was a great experience. I thought Japan was a rich country, but some aspects of the real Japan were different from my original image. I remember the school had many enjoyable club activities, music, and physical exercise. Subjects like natural science were difficult. When I played football, I could join the group very quickly. I stayed with my relatives in Tokyo. After I returned to Brazil, I kept in touch, for a while, with the Japanese students I had met at junior high school in Japan and other *Nikkei* students who participated in the training. Terada-kun, who was from São Paulo, enrolled in the University of São Paulo, the same university as me. I still meet him. I think there were six trainees from Brazil, and one each from Argentina, Paraguay, Peru and Bolivia. [BRA 02]

Only those students who made it to the finals of the essay, interview and speech competitions were selected to participate, representing their Japanese language schools. It must have been a great honour for them, as well as for their families, to be chosen and join the training.

6.2.3 The Linguistic Situation of Nikkei

The social role and position of Japanese language schools in Brazil changed over time. In the past, most first-generation immigrants wanted to return to Japan after making their fortune in Brazil. Therefore, they tried hard to remember the Japanese language and customs and raise their children as Japanese nationals so that they could adapt to Japanese society when they returned. However, it took longer than expected to save the money, and given the physical distance between Brazil and Japan, it

[12] An overview of the training is available on this website: https://www.jica.go.jp/regions/america/middle_school.html (Japanese) Reports on recent training are available on the JICA website. Activities during the COVID-19 pandemic were conducted online. https://www.jica.go.jp/Resource/english/publications/reports/annual/2007/pdf/110.pdf, https://www.jica.go.jp/Resource/english/publications/reports/annual/2018/c8h0vm0000dxws0g-att/2018_27.pdf.

was not easy to visit home. Before and during World War II, Japanese, German and Italian immigrants were subjected to militaristic, ethno-centric education, which contradicted the goal of national integration promoted by the Brazilian government. While Japanese-language schools were shut down and Japanese-language newspapers were suspended, the first-generation *Nikkei* people strived to preserve the Japanese language. As I wanted to hear the story of the first generation, I was introduced to Mizuno Masayuki, who had moved to Brazil from Nagoya in 1933 at the age of nine. I met him in the foyer of his apartment. As a child, Mizuno worked like a slave on a coffee plantation during the day and studied Japanese at night. A man in the neighbourhood had brought 24 lecture notes from Waseda Middle School, so he borrowed each one and spent every day secretly copying the notes into his notebooks. After the war, he went to São Paulo, but he couldn't find a proper job because he had no academic qualifications. However, his self-taught Japanese was excellent, so he was hired as a proofreader by the Japanese-language newspaper *Jornal Paulista* [BRA 10].

Onishi, a second-generation *Nikkei,* attended a Japanese school from kindergarten and spoke only Japanese at home. He said that when he heard Portuguese outside the home, he wondered what the strange language was. For him, learning Portuguese was more of a self-study process, and it was something of a struggle.

> For most *Nikkei,* Japanese is a third language, coming after Portuguese and English. I think it's nice to encourage young people to learn a third language. It is the responsibility of parents to give their children a good foundation. After that, the parents should leave the choice to the individual children. Brazil is a Western country, basically, but staying in touch with an Asian country is an advantage for young people. [BRA 02]

Maria Julia Tobase, a university student studying law, is third-generation. Her grandfather came from Kumamoto in the 1920s, and her grandmother from Hiroshima. They had difficulty communicating with the local people, so they wanted their children to be fluent in Portuguese. Consequently, Tobase's parents could only speak Portuguese, so they hoped their daughter would learn Japanese. Tobase participated in the training in 2013, when she was in the third year of junior high school. When she was shortlisted, her father, who was in the hospital, was jubilant at the news all the more because he did not understand Japanese [BRA 01]. Rumi Koroku Hisataka, a fourth-generation student who was about to major in natural science, was in her third year of junior high school at the time of the interview and told me that she had just attended the training that year. In addition to Portuguese, she speaks English and Japanese. She said that more and more young non-*Nikkei* people around her were interested in Japan because of animation and other cultural factors [BRA 03].

Some children resist their parents' advice, while others follow it. The situation varies from family to family and from individual to individual, but the fact that Portuguese has become the first language of the younger generation is undeniable. Daniel Akira Hashimoto, a third-generation university student, said, 'My parents understand Japanese, but they speak it very little. They mix it with Portuguese. *Nikkei* people call this language *Colonia*' [BRA 04]. Yoshio Leandro Maruoka, whom I met in Belém, Pará, said, 'When I look around my third generation, I see they are losing their identity as being *Nikkei.* For the third generation, it's nice to please their grandparents by speaking Japanese, but the fourth and fifth generations don't have to do that, and they are losing interest' [BRA 11]. The young people selected as trainees are fluent in Japanese, but they know they are in the minority in their generation.

A language that is spoken within a family and passed down to next generations is called a 'heritage language'. If children are exposed to everyday conversation in this language at home, they only need to learn how to read and write it formally. However, if the language is no longer spoken at home, one cannot but learn it as a 'foreign language'. While JICA has supported the teaching of Japanese as a heritage language for *Nikkei* families, the Japan Foundation, the cultural wing of the Ministry of Foreign Affairs, has popularised Japanese as a foreign language for Brazilians at large. There has also been policy discussion about better coordinating these two efforts (Ehara 2007). Given the reality of the linguistic situation of young Brazilians, it would be better to put a renewed focus on nurturing Japanese conversational skills and the values of multicultural coexistence rather than on memorising Japanese characters and instilling traditional ethics (Shibahara 2016).

6.2.4 *Visiting the Home Country of Parents*

So what came to the mind of the *Nikkei* youth who participated in the training, when they saw Japanese society through their own eyes? In the library of JICA Yokohama, I found bound essays written by young students. The oldest is a collection of essays from the second training in 1988. Cecilia Sayaka Nishida (then 14 years old) from Mogi das Cruzes wrote one entitled 'My Country', which ends as follows:

> People say Japan is the richest country in the world, but when I came here, I thought that was not the case. Brazil may be a country full of debt, but I feel that everyone there has a richer life. During the carnival, they may spend the money they have earned over the year in just three days, and they like travelling on their days off. They have a lot of fun doing so. In the eyes of a Japanese, you might think, 'What idiots, these people?' But this is our Brazil. We try to enjoy the best of life.... The strictness of Japan may be all right for the people who live here. It's a bit tough for me sometimes, but I think this way of life expresses what Japan is all about. This training has made me realise how Japanese I am. I am proud of that, but I am also very proud of being Brazilian. Even though Brazil is such a country, I also realised that I cannot leave it and exchange it with another foreign country.

Even though it is full of problems, Brazil is still my home country, wrote a Brazilian junior high school student vividly in the Japanese language. While Nishida was upset to see sausages dipped in the Japanese *oden* soup, she wrote that the first thing she wanted to do when she returned to Brazil was to 'taste my mother's home cooking' (JICA Overseas Migration Center 1989).

In the interviews, many students mentioned how they perceived Japanese students of the same age. 'I thought Japanese and Brazilian junior high school students were very different. In Brazil, even junior high students go out with their boyfriends or girlfriends, but that doesn't happen in Japan. People say Japanese people are cold to others, but I found many of them wanted to be friendly and make friends with us' [BRA 03]. 'I felt Japanese junior high school students were childish and we had a sort of gap' [BRA 05]. Abuno Shizuo, a young farmer who worked hard growing flowers, also felt that the Japanese students were immature, but he calmly observed that 'I thought they were growing up little by little while enjoying their time at school in a naive way' [BRA06]. In Brazil, people have to start thinking about how they are going to make a living as soon as they enter high school. In the collection of essays, the strictness of school rules, the hierarchical relationship between *sempai* (seniors) and *kohai* (juniors), and the noise the students made in class were honestly noted, but many of the trainees wrote that they were eventually able to make friends.

It is widely known in Brazil that the *Nikkei* who go to Japan to work are treated frigidly in the country of their roots. Hashimoto said:

> Some Brazilians think the Japanese are cold-hearted. In Brazil, you look people in the eye. But some think the Japanese are focused only on what they have to do, and they don't look at other people's faces. Well, they may be nice people, but they can't be real friends, and the image is that they don't like foreigners. This is what Brazilians tend to think, but I found that's not true of all Japanese. [BRA 04]

Daniel Sadayoshi Otsuki, who had participated in the training in 1991 as a delegate from a Japanese language school in Belém, ran a chicken hatchery. His parents moved from Fukushima to Brazil after the war. His uncle, a dairy farmer, was affected by the nuclear accident and could no longer sell his milk product. He talked about an advantage of Japanese schools that was often mentioned by counterparts. 'In Japanese schools, the students clean up the classrooms. At the Japanese language school in Belém, students do the same. But in Brazil, normally, the students make it dirty and someone else sweeps it up' [BRA 13]. Many young interviewees said that it was an enlightening experience to learn about the history of the *Nikkei*, as it allowed them to understand the origins of their communities from a different perspective.

6.2.5 Living as Brazilians

The Next Generation Training in Japan was a journey of self-discovery for the *Nikkei* youth. Onishi, a participant in the inaugural year of training, said he wanted to make the most of the advantages of Japan and Brazil. His parents told him to respect senior people, but he said, 'In Brazil, you must be assertive to survive. You can't cope well if you're reserved' [BRA 02]. After participating in the training in 2006, Takamura attended another training for coordinators of Japanese cultural activities, representing a youth association, in 2008. While discussing the current situation with other young leaders, he noticed that the number of people who identified with *Nikkei* was declining everywhere. He suspected that this weakening of *Nikkei* activities might have been caused by the stubbornness of some people who 'don't want to change, don't want to make a difference'.

> Brazilians are from all over the world. If everyone started claiming their own roots, Brazil would fall apart and disappear, so it's better to think of ourselves as Brazilians. Of course, we should not forget that our ancestors came from Japan. But if we stick together too much and think we are superior to others, we won't be able to accept other Brazilians. [BRA 05]

Tobase, who was studying international relations, said she did not want Brazil and Japan to fight but to mix.

> In Brazil, many people get along and socialise, but some do not. White people sometimes think black and Asian people are dirty, or even they should go back to their countries. There are also stereotypes about Japanese people. For example, the Japanese are quiet and lacking courage. This can be a disadvantage when it comes to finding a job. Many people, including *Nikkei* in the US, wonder who they are. In Brazil, people who are not *Nikkei* look at me as Japanese. In Japan, they treat me as a Brazilian. I am both Brazilian and *Nikkei.* I think I am a *Nikkei* Brazilian, and otherwise I can't be myself. [BRA 01]

Hashimoto, who also studied international relations, recalled that he was not really a Brazilian until he visited Japan. The training made him realise that he was not simply Japanese. 'Instead of comparing Japan and Brazil, I began to think I am a mixture of the two, and that is who I am' [BRA 04]. Abuno, who grows flowers, said, 'I feel Brazilians are not very patriotic.'

> I feel that Japanese people appreciate and cherish Japan. They don't throw rubbish on the ground. 'This is my country, so I want to make it better.' They share that kind of thinking, don't they? In Brazil, your house is your own, but it's nobody's business outside the house. You don't care. Brazil is a good country, so I think we should take better care of our own country. [BRA 06]

In interviews in Belém, at the mouth of the Amazon River, I encountered slightly different reactions. Otsuki, a second-generation *Nikkei* from Fukushima, had moved to the big city, São Paulo, hoping to reconnect with friends he had made during his training. He started working for Siemens, using the IT skills he had acquired at university. He did well with the German company, but when Siemens was taken over by Nokia, he left the company and returned to Belém to look after his old parents. He said that *Nikkei,* including himself, were forgetting the Japanese language, but 'even if we don't speak Japanese, I think *Nikkei* people trust each other' [BRA 13]. On the other hand, also in Belém, I had the opportunity to interview a young third-generation *Nikkei* who did not speak Japanese at all. Through an interpreter, Jonathas Hisamitsu told me that he did not even know where his grandparents were born in Japan. When he travelled to Japan with his family in 2016, he was taken aback. 'I saw a person with a child, but the bus didn't wait for them. It just kept going! No one can imagine that happening in Brazil' [BRA 14]. Hisamitsu eventually decided to join the Brazilian Navy. 'You forget a language you don't use. I don't speak Japanese. My heart is in Brazil, and I think Brazil is my home. Brazilians have warm hearts. My love for Brazil is very strong' [BRA 14].

Hiromi Hayashi, a third-generation *Nikkei* who taught at the Japanese language school in Belém, attended a junior high school in Sakuragicho, Yokohama, as a temporary student in 2004. She was worried when she heard that some trainees had been involved in a scrap with Japanese students in another school. In the interview,

Hayashi said that at the school in Belém where she taught, the number of non-*Nikkei* students was increasing, and as a positive side-effect, some *Nikkei* began to think positively about Japan and the Japanese language. Karaoke is also popular among ordinary Brazilians. According to Hayashi, while young people with both *Nikkei* parents were inclined to stay away from such places, in the case of mixed marriages, the non-Nikkei side of the parents was often willing to take up the microphone in karaoke bars. There were many *Nikkei* who travelled to Japan from Belém, but they could be divided into two types: those who had stable jobs in Brazil and wanted to go to Japan for fun, and those who were dissatisfied with their life in Brazil and wanted to earn money [BRA 12].

People's identity is expressed by attaching a possessive adjective to a group or a place to which one belongs, as in 'right or wrong, my country,' or 'the wronger the myer.' (Hirschman 1970: 104). We may feel that we are obliged not to abandon our hometown where we grew up. Even after we turn our backs on the place, we continue to be apprehensive about what has become of it. Brazil has become home to the majority of the *Nikkei* people. The training appears to have become a journey for them to rediscover Japan and redefine their relationship with both countries.

6.2.6 The Youth Networks

The young *Nikkei* interviewees spoke passionately about their identities, while choosing their words carefully. As Umesao noted, they were not so much Japanese as Brazilian. Many of them tried to contribute to the nation-building of Brazil by incorporating elements that were considered part of the Japanese way of life—such as punctuality and hard work—into their life attitudes.

However, while I was listening to their talk about their sense of belonging, I realised that there was a positive side effect of the youth training that I had not anticipated. The *Nikkei* participants were selected from countries in the Americas, mainly Latin America. The largest group of Brazilian participants was made up of delegates from different states of Brazil. With such a variety of backgrounds, the participants were curious about each other's experiences and tried to find out what they had in common and what made them different [BRA 04]. Apparently, most participants had smartphones and kept in touch even after the training.

> During break times, I made friends with Latin American *Nikkei* people. I learnt about the history of migration to each country and the differences in culture. I already knew that there were many Japanese immigrants in Brazil, but I didn't know anything about those in other countries. We spoke in a mixture of Portuguese, Spanish, Japanese, and English, like the *Colonia* language. We set up a group on WhatsApp and still exchange various news. [BRA 01]

Rumi Koroku Hisataka, a junior high school student, said, 'I get so many messages that I don't have time to read them all' [BRA 03]. Willian Kengo Tsukahara Ochi said, 'Social networking looked exciting at first, but now I don't use it very much. I think it's more important to go and see people in person. It's better to meet people by yourself. I went to Bolivia and Paraguay and met people who had participated in the training. There was also a friend who came to Brazil from Argentina.' Tsukahara Ochi's dream was 'to start my own business. I want to start a company with my friends from all over Latin America' [BRA 07].

The horizontal bonds among the *Nikkei* people that transcend national borders have been discovered and strengthened through training. Similar examples are also observable in their parental generation. Eduardo Masao Tsukahara, director of NGK Spark Plugs, a major Japanese company in Brazil, once applied for JICA's Advanced Training Course for *Nikkei* people and studied electrical engineering at Tokai University. He received training at the expense of Fukushima Prefecture, his father's birthplace, and even worked climbing electricity poles. 'Participating in JICA's advanced training course was the beginning of everything. I made friends and people-to-people connections for work. We know where others are' [BRA 08]. His wife, Isabel Satoko Ochi Ito, was born in Paraguay, qualified as a dentist in Argentina, and studied at the Kochi Dental Association and Nihon University School of Dentistry as part of the Advanced Training Course. She also kept in touch with those who attended the training. 'When the children get together for a *Nikkei* youth camp, the parents of the participants often know each other. I think the effect of the training may become visible as a network of work one or two decades after the children have finished the training' [BRA 09].

This book has discussed several examples of South-South cooperation through third-country training (Sects. 3.2, 3.4, 4.2, and 5.3). When bilateral cooperation matures to a certain extent, a counterpart organisation in the partner country becomes the basis for further regional cooperation, in which the pivotal country invites trainees from other countries and carries out technology transfer in a networked style. Japan provides financial and logistical support when needed, but in theory it can only observe what happens because the counterparts in the 'third' country (neither the donor nor the ultimate beneficiary) have already acquired the necessary skills. The *Nikkei* youth training was somewhat different in that a horizontal network transcending national borders was formed through the voluntary initiative of individuals rather than an institutional arrangement such as third-country training. There was no base country, no expert guidance, and no clearly stated objectives for the networking. Nevertheless, young people began to connect voluntarily. This was a critical side effect of the project that could have a lasting impact in the future.[13]

[13] The ABE Initiative (African Business Education Initiative for Youth), launched in 2014, is a more recent project. The project aims 'to develop human resources for industry in Africa and to train navigators to support the business of Japanese firms in Africa' by inviting young people from African countries to Japan and providing them with opportunities to obtain Master's degrees and to undertake internships at Japanese companies.

6.2.7 Two-Way Support

To conclude this section, I would like to present the story of Mizuno Masayuki, a first-generation *Nikkei* pioneer [BRA 10]. Immediately after becoming a proofreader for the newspaper *Jornal Paulista* (Sect. 6.2.3), Mizuno was caught up in the 'victorious versus defeated' confrontation. During the war, the teaching of the Japanese language and the publication of Japanese newspapers were banned, even though few people in the *Nikkei* community could read Portuguese. With no information coming in, some people began to believe what they wanted to believe, and the majority of them became part of the 'victorious' group, convinced that Japan had won the war. *Jornal Paulista* was affiliated with the 'defeated' group, those who accepted that Japan had been defeated. Mizuno was given a pistol to protect him from possible violent attacks and hid it in his desk drawer for a while.

The influential members of the 'defeated' group organised the Japan War Refugee Relief Association in collaboration with the Japanese American community in the US to take part in LARA activities. LARA is an acronym for Licensed Agencies for Relief in Asia, an organisation that operated from 1946 to 1952 and was known for transporting relief supplies such as skimmed milk powder, flour, and daily necessities to post-war Japan, with US Christian organisations and Japanese Americans playing a central role.[14] The chairperson of the relief association in Brazil, Sugayama Washizo, was a merchant from Fukushima Prefecture who had collected money from *Nikkei* customers like a commercial bank, but according to Mizuno, Sugayama was criticised by the 'victorious' group for 'behaving as if he was the representative of the *Nikkei* community though he was only a defeated one.' His business came to a standstill as many customers withdrew their deposits.

> LARA thought that it would be better if individuals made donations rather than organisations taking up charity work. Think about it – people wanted to send five kilos of sugar and clothes to relatives, and they could send it through LARA's distribution channels. They could do it as an anonymous donation, but LARA also allowed individuals to send goods to individuals using this network. This way of contribution became very popular. Then something unexpected happened. People received thank-you letters from their relatives in Japan, which said, 'Thank you. Japan lost the war.' Even those who were part of the 'victorious' group believed what was written in the letters from their relatives and began to accept the truth. [BRA 10]

Mizuno moved to the newspaper *Diário Nippak*, and while sending sugar to his relatives in Nagoya, he continued to report on the assistance *Nikkei* Brazilians provided to Japan through LARA. It is assumed that Japan's development cooperation is something that Japan gives and developing countries receive. However, as seen in the aftermath of the Great East Japan Earthquake in 2011, when many countries, both developed and developing, offered assistance to the disaster-affected area, the bonds can function as two-way traffic. It is worth remembering that Japanese people living in the ruins of war were supported by *Nikkei* people on the other side of the

[14] LARA's food distribution is also the origin of the school lunch system in Japan. For more information on the history and activities of LARA, see Tatara (1999) and the Church World Service (CWS) website. https://cwsglobal.org/our-work/asia/japan/.

world, and this also helped to dispel misunderstandings and heal wounds within the *Nikkei* community.

Eventually, Mizuno thought that there was little future in the Japanese-language press, and he began working at the Japanese Chamber of Commerce and Industry of Brazil in São Paulo. He then spent almost a year in Japan, editing the *Brazilian Economic Yearbook* (Japanese Chamber of Commerce and Industry of Brazil 1957) to attract direct investment from Japanese companies. Mizuno, then 32, travelled to Japan by the Pacific route via the US, but the route was cut off between San Francisco and Los Angeles, and he was forced to travel by train. He had problems communicating because Portuguese was not spoken in the US, but then he met a Japanese-American passenger on the train who took him to an orchard on the outskirts of the city. When they parted, he was given a tin of raisins. He was told that urban expansion in São Paulo was more vigorous than in Los Angeles, and he was inspired to try his hand at running an orchard when he returned to São Paulo. This is how Mizuno made his fortune. The unexpected horizontal encounters between *Nikkei* people led to a chain of business innovations—from the times of the 'victorious versus defeated' confrontation to the era of training the next generation; there is continuity across *Nikkei* generations in the quest to sail forward.

6.3 Engineers Protecting People and Nature (Minamata and Brazil)

6.3.1 Minamata's History and Social Layers

The Japanese word *kogai* (公害: public bad) has been in use since the Meiji period as an antonym of *koeki* (公益: public good). The former referred to what economists call negative externalities. During the period of rapid economic growth in post-war Japan, however, the word *kogai* began to take on a more urgent and emotional meaning. As the bodies of people were exposed to the hazards of industrial activities and damaged irreversibly, it became clear that the very basis of human existence was being threatened by the process of modernisation, which the Japanese seemed to have accepted unequivocally. In the 1960s and 1970s, citizens became deeply concerned about the severity of pollution, and the tragedy of Minamata disease attracted keen attention as a symbol of the destruction of human beings and living creatures. Minamata disease, Niigata Minamata disease, Itai-itai disease, and Yokkaichi asthma were known as the four major *kogai* diseases in Japan. The company that caused the Minamata disease, Chisso, was a general chemical manufacturer, and its Minamata plant was at the forefront of the growth of Japanese manufacturing. The mercury contained in large quantities in the factory's effluent was a catalyst for producing acetaldehyde, a chemical utilised to make things like vinyl chloride. Chisso was originally known as a manufacturer of chemical fertilisers, but was also gaining fame for its production of liquid crystals and electronic components.

In Minamata, the power centre lay in the Chisso factory and the town, surrounded by fishing villages on the coastal periphery. There lay a deep-seated social structure in which the powerful townsmen (settlers) looked down on poor fishers (drifters), who had migrated mostly from the Amakusa Islands, on the other side of the Shiranui Sea (Fig. 6.2). Minamata disease was caused by the consumption of contaminated fish and the absorption of methylmercury into the human body. This is why the disease first appeared in large numbers among fishing families. In the community of Minamata, it was maintained that if the sufferers 'made a fuss', Chisso would go bankrupt (and the fish could no longer be sold either). The patients were forced not to raise their voices.[15]

The multi-layered structure of the society of the Shiranui Sea also had an international dimension. Before World War II, those who were associated with Chisso travelled to the northern part of the Korean peninsula to work on the construction and operation of massive hydroelectric power plants and fertiliser factories—the leader of these projects was Kubota Yutaka, from the Aso region of Kumamoto Prefecture, who was also the driving force behind the development of the Brantas River basin as mentioned in Chap. 2 (Sect. 2.2.2) The extensive oral history compiled by Okamoto Tatsuaki and others revealed that the people from Minamata who went to Korea enjoyed life in 'another world' in the settlements in Korea, but after the war they became refugees and barely managed to return home (Okamoto and Matsuzaki 1990). Before the war, independently, the fisher folk of Amakusa sailed north to fish in the seawaters from Jeju Island to Dalian (Okamoto 1978). In contrast, women originally from Amakusa, Shimabara and Nagasaki were sold to Korea, Manchuria, Taiwan and the Pacific in a system that would be called human trafficking today. In her masterpiece, *Karayuki-san*, Morisaki Kazue used the ironic term 'inter-people diplomacy' to revive the experiences and dreams of these women, destitute and resilient, and to contrast them with the bombastic 'Asianism' expressed in contemporary men's grand speeches (Morisaki 1976).[16]

Based on their unique life history, patients who could talk about Minamata disease were appointed as official 'storytellers' at the Minamata Disease Municipal Museum, sharing their lived experiences with not only visiting schoolchildren but also JICA trainees from overseas. I visited Meisui-en, a sanatorium for Minamata disease patients, to hear the story of 91-year-old Ueno Eiko. She said that there used to be a lot of fish around the Hyakken outfall, from which contaminated water was discharged into the sea, and that the area started to smell like rotten apples. At her

---

[15] In 2007, I had an opportunity to visit the home of Sugimoto Eiko, a well-known storyteller in Minamata. She told me that the fishers of Minamata and Amakusa divided the time they spent fishing in the Shiranui Sea so that no one party would monopolise the marine resources. If one of them broke the agreement, they would chase each other across the water. She told us about the dynamic interplay, laughing heartily and gesturing as if she were explaining a sumo wrestling match.

[16] Just as Umesao (1979) dismissed Japanese emigration to Asian colonies as a 'miserable failure', Yano Toru concluded that the Japanese experience of the engagement in the 'South' was a 'futile century' (Yano 1975: 205). These may be undeniable facts, although the question is more one of right or wrong than of success or failure.

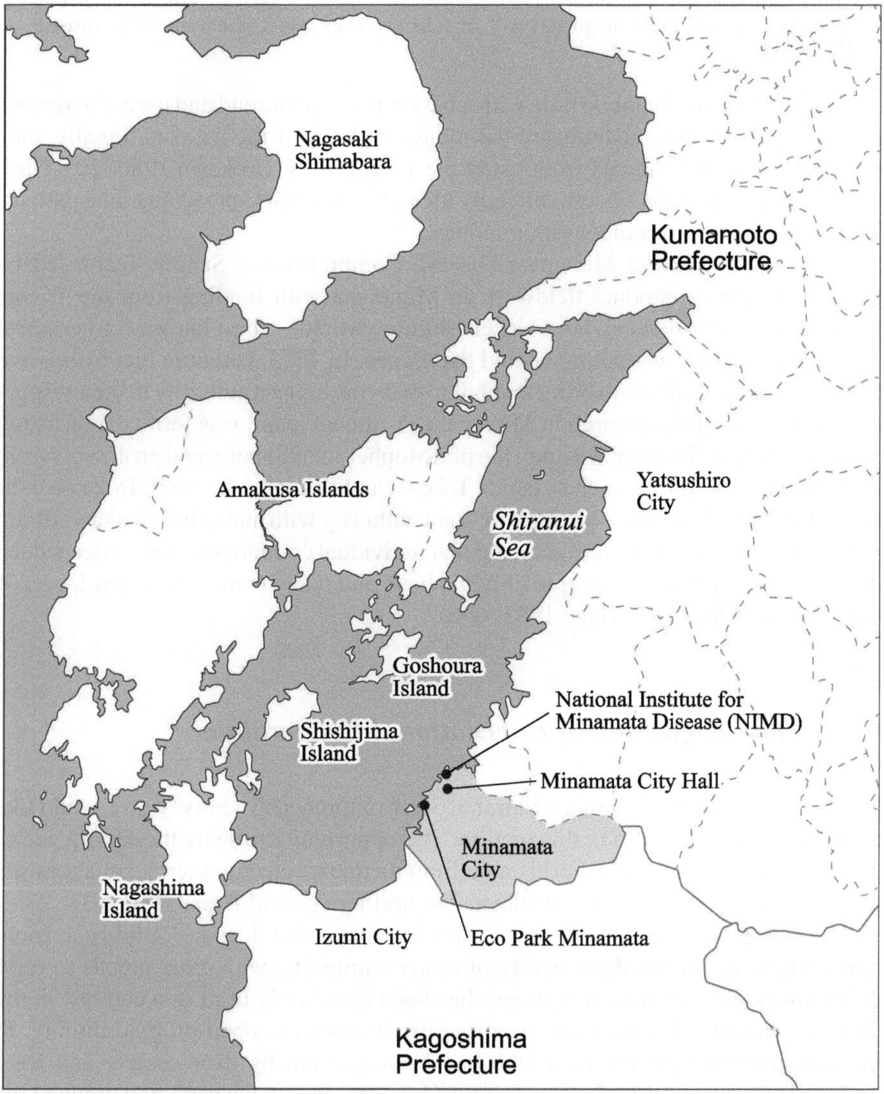

Fig. 6.2 Shiranui sea and Minamata. Source: Author

husband's family home, 'I was told, "You are contaminating us. Go away!" My daughter Ryoko was not accepted as a member of the family.'

> My father used to take care of a lot of fishermen. He looked after them as if they were his family, even though they were not, and shared his fish with them. But then he got sick, he could no longer move, and he lost his voice. It was so hard for him not to be able to work. He couldn't do anything. He was healthy when he was young, but after he suffered Minamata disease, he just lay there and said, 'Aah....Aah....' I don't need my property. Everyone bullied us. The house we lived in was abandoned and collapsed. When I went shopping at Sakamoto's

store, they wouldn't take my money with their hands. They said it would spread the disease. [MMT 04]

'They obtruded a bamboo pole with a basket hung on the end and used it to receive the money. They even disinfected the money in front of the patients. Finally, they even prevented the patients from using the village well' (Irokawa 1980: 20). Once the patient certification system officially kicked in, rumours spread that fake patients were applying to get compensation money.

In this situation, the Minamata Disease Comprehensive Survey Team, led by Irokawa, began to conduct fieldwork in Minamata with funding from the Toyota Foundation. The Amakusa-born writer Ishimure Michiko, best known for her novel *Kukai Jodo* (1969), was acting behind the scenes. In 1975, Ishimure met Irokawa in Minamata and asked him to bring in scholars with the highest authority in their respective fields to conduct research in Minamata. A 'dream team' was formed, consisting of the sociologist Tsurumi Kazuko, the philosopher Ichii Saburo, and professors from the University of Tokyo, such as Ishida Takeshi and Kikuchi Masanori. Irokawa indicated that it was Ishimure's strategy to 'fight authority with authority' (Irokawa 2020: 309–313). However, Ishimure also said that individual commoners 'have a deep, deep desire to speak directly to people of noble birth and make their stories heard, even if only once in a lifetime' (Haga 1983: 646).

6.3.2 The Beginning of International Cooperation

Much has been written about the Shiranui Sea Comprehensive Survey, so I would like to discuss something else in this section. The opportunity to share the experience of Minamata with the outside world came from an unexpected quarter: a collaboration to address the pollution in the Amazon, the northern part of Brazil (Fig. 6.1).

Mercury (chemical symbol Hg) is the only metal that does not solidify at room temperature, and it has the property of easily combining with other metals to form compounds. For this reason, mercury has been commonly used as a catalyst in the chemical industry, but its most extensive use has been in open-pit gold mining. In the Amazon basin, rough men who had been cast out by their society and were looking for a quick fortune, known as *garimpeiros,* dug up the earth and dredged the mud with mercury to extract the gold. When an amalgam of gold and mercury was burned, the mercury evaporated, leaving the pure gold behind. In this way, mercury-laced vapours constantly drifted around the gold mines that sprang up in the Amazon basin.[17]

[17] Zuleica Castilhos of CETEM said, 'Many women engage in small-scale mining. Some own the land, some own their machines, but few people pay attention to them' [BRA 17]. David Cleary, a British anthropologist who assisted Olaf Malm and his team in their fieldwork, predicted that even if the use of mercury in gold mining was restricted, it would continue to be used underground (Cleary 1990: 228).

Although inorganic mercury was already toxic at this stage, it eventually fell to the ground, entered rivers, and underwent chemical reactions in the natural environment to form methylmercury. It was absorbed by small fish and concentrated in larger fish, and at the top of the food chain, it destroyed the central nervous system of humans, causing the symptoms of Minamata disease. Indigenous people living on fish from the Amazon basin were thought to be most at risk. Brazil has a long history of gold mining. Marcelo de Oliveira Lima, who ran the mercury laboratory at the Evandro Chagas Institute, said, 'I may look white, but I have black blood. My family was poor when I was a child. Brazilians are extremely diverse and mixed. Historically, the use of gold in the Inca Empire goes back more than 1,000 years, while the use of mercury to extract gold began only half a century ago. It has always been processed by hand' [BRA 22].

In 1992, the year of the Rio Summit, at an international conference on tropical medicine held in Belém, at the mouth of the Amazon River, Olaf Malm from the Federal University of Rio de Janeiro met Harada Masazumi from Kumamoto University as well as a group of Kyoto-based lawyers involved in the Minamata disease lawsuit. It had been reported that people living in the Amazon basin were suffering from symptoms similar to those of Minamata disease. Malm was invited to Japan and visited Minamata, Toyama, Niigata, Hiroshima, and Nagasaki. Malm recalled that the director of the NIMD told him, 'These lawyers are communists. Don't associate with them.' He paid no attention to the warning and associated with everyone.

Malm returned to Brazil and visited Japan again, this time with a big quantity of samples, including fish and human hair. 'Some said it was not right to bring the data to Japan, a foreign country, but I thought solving the people's problem should be the priority' [BRA 16]. When Akagi Hirokatsu of the NIMD tested the sample with his equipment, it was found to be heavily contaminated with mercury. When Akagi showed it to the officers at the Environment Agency, 'They were terribly shocked. Within the Environment Agency, there were divergent views on whether to focus on local matters or on global issues. But it was just after the Rio Summit, and the data from Brazil was so serious that they decided to proceed with the research and then work with JICA' [MMT 02].

In Brazil, too, there was a tailwind in favour of large-scale research in the Amazon. According to Jean Remy Davée Guimarães of the Federal University of Rio de Janeiro, the photographs of the Amazon by Sebastião Salgado and the BBC's special programmes had galvanised public opinion. He said:

> Scientists from São Paulo suggested that they should go to the Amazon to investigate mercury contamination and gold mining. They attempted to cross the border into Bolivia, visited the Tapajós river basin, and brought back samples to gauge the seriousness of the situation surrounding the miners, known as *garimpeiros*. It was thought that the problem of mercury contamination needed to be controlled in order to guarantee the sustainability of agriculture in areas where slash-and-burn agriculture was practised. [BRA 15]

Against such a backdrop, the Brazilian Federal Congress allocated a budget for a large-scale research project in the Amazon, and the Mineral Technology Research Centre (CETEM: Centro de Tecnologia Mineral) of the Ministry of Science and

Technology was to coordinate the research [BRA 17]. There were a multitude of Brazilian counterpart institutes that were about to analyse possible mercury contamination: CETEM, the Federal University of Rio de Janeiro, the National Department of Mineral Production (DNPM) of the Ministry of Mines and Energy, the Institute of Tropical Medicine of the Federal University of Pará, and the Evandro Chagas Institute. Gradually, the research base converged on the city of Belém, where the Evandro Chagas Institute had been engaged in clinical research in the Amazon (Maura de Jesus et al. 2016). Other things being equal, an institution closer to the Amazon would likely have more knowledge and experiences about what was happening at the sites of pollution. As Malm said, 'In Japan, scientists at Kumamoto University know more about Minamata disease than those in Tokyo' [BRA 16]. The Evandro Chagas Institute was a world-class centre for tropical medicine and, as such, could be a powerful partner for Japanese institutions.[18]

Akagi of the NIMD oversaw projects for the Environment Agency, JICA, and WHO in various locations worldwide. Countries involved in these projects include Brazil, Kyrgyzstan, Cambodia, Bangladesh, Indonesia, Nicaragua, China, Kazakhstan, Vietnam, Indonesia, Mongolia, and French Guiana. Projects implemented by the NIMD with JICA in Brazil include the 'Mercury Pollution Analysis Project' (1994–2000), the 'Project to Strengthen the Health Monitoring System for Methylmercury Pollution in the Tapajós River Basin' (2007–2010), and the 'Project to Strengthen Health Monitoring for Mercury Pollution in the State of Acre' (2011–2014); the last one was a participatory grassroots technical cooperation project (community proposal type).[19] Through these projects, technology transfer progressed with the establishment of mercury laboratories at major research institutions in Brazil, combined with the training of young Brazilian researchers in Minamata.

6.3.3 The Akagi Method and the Evandro Chagas Institute

The mercury analysis technique, known as the Akagi method, consists of two parts: the measurement of total mercury using atomic absorption spectrometry and the measurement of methylmercury using gas chromatography. As methylmercury is the causative agent of Minamata disease, the latter is particularly important for risk

[18] Carlos Chagas, a contemporary of Noguchi Hideyo, is known as the discoverer of an insect-borne infectious disease now called Chagas Disease that ravaged Central and South America. There is a detailed project history of Chagas disease control in Central America involving JICA Volunteers (Hashimoto 2013). Evandro Chagas, Carlos's son, was renowned for his research on tropical diseases such as yellow fever, but died in 1940. The institute that bears his name was originally founded in 1936 as a research centre for infectious diseases in the Amazon basin.

[19] 'The Grassroots Technical Cooperation Project is a joint project in which JICA entrusts to the proposing organisation the implementation of international cooperation activities based on the knowledge and experience accumulated through the past activities of Japanese NGOs/CSOs, local governments, universities, private companies and other organisations willing to engage in international cooperation.' https://www.jica.go.jp/partner/kusanone/what/index.html (in Japanese).

assessment. The Akagi method, which can accurately measure even trace amounts of methylmercury, has been accepted by scientists around the world, but its dissemination was obstructed in Japan. At the NIMD, the unique national centre for the research of Minamata disease, the research equipment was once taken into a separate room and locked away to silence Akagi (MMT 02). However, when it was decided that joint research with Brazil would move forward in the wake of the Rio Summit, international cooperation was positioned as a pillar of NIMD's activities. Akagi, who at one point had considered resigning, was appointed to be the director of NIMD's Department of International Affairs.

Elizabeth C. de O. Santos, who set up the mercury analysis laboratory at the Evandro Chagas Institute, said, 'The legacy we have received from Dr. Akagi is his rigour, accuracy, and commitment to getting the right data.' I asked her why Akagi visited the Amazon so often. 'Dr. Akagi was a scientist, but the problems the Amazon faces are staggering and very complex. I think that's why he was fascinated by the Amazon, wanted to know more, and visited the Amazon again and again' [BRA 19]. She continued:

> We carried out tests on local people in the Amazon, sampling their hair, blood, faeces, and urine, and they were grateful for the health checks, which were beneficial not only in dealing with mercury poisoning but also in addressing diseases like malaria. What surprised me was that, even when the mercury levels were very high, they did not reveal obvious symptoms.... Mr Edilson examined the soil samples and showed that mercury levels were higher in certain parts of the Amazon than in other places, but he was killed by robbers. [BRA 19]

Many scholars voiced the name of Edilson. He collected all the material needed for his thesis, but his life was cut short. Terezinha Maria Cid de Souza, who was in charge of the DNPM's mercury laboratory in Belém, explained that foreign researchers used to take samples to their home countries for analysis. Once the Akagi method was accepted by local researchers, Brazilians were able to analyse mercury within Brazil. She continued:

> I tried rice planting in Minamata. I met the patients, too. Dr Akagi and Dr Miyamoto came here for training. I like learning, so I worked at weekends. Dr Akagi told me to translate the manual for the mercury examination into Portuguese. The Akagi method is very complicated. I tried to explain it more clearly and adjust the equipment, so that people could use it more easily. In the laboratory, I communicated carefully with Dr Akagi and others in English, but there were some matters we couldn't understand until we actually touched the machine and analysed the sample. [BRA 20]

Patrícia Correia de Araújo of CETEM did not have a chance to receive training in Japan, but she improved her skills under the guidance of Akagi, who visited Rio de Janeiro. She filmed the five-day training to explain the method to the next-generation researchers [BRA 18]. Kleber Freitas Faial of the Evandro Chagas Institute used the Akagi method to analyse hair, urine, blood, fish, soil, sediment, dust, and water collected in the Amazon. He said he was committed to this work because of a sense of accomplishment as he accumulated accurate data.

> I went to the Amazon with Dr Akagi. Sampling may look easy, but there are detailed procedures to follow when dissecting fish and collecting soil. In case of hair, we have it thoroughly

> washed, cut a small amount from the nape and examine it at 1 centimetre intervals. We then cut it into minuscule pieces and dissolve it in acid. The results of various tests are reported to the research participants. In June this year, we took samples from 120 gold miners and examined them. We have their addresses and contact details, so we are now going to give them back the results. [BRA 26]

Mercury released into the environment is difficult to recover. 'What I'm particularly worried about is whether symptoms will emerge among children and pregnant women. We are examining umbilical cords to see if there are any effects on the foetus' [BRA 21]. The transfer of mercury measurement technology from Japan to Brazil was successful. This was not only due to the large research capacity on the Brazilian side, but also to the empathy developed between the Brazilian researchers and the citizens of Minamata as described below.

6.3.4 The Expansion of Minamata Training

In 1991, the United Nations University in Tokyo took the lead in organising the Minamata International Conference on Industry, the Environment and Human Health (Rasool 1992). Another conference was held in 1992, the year of the Rio Summit, and Minamata gradually opened up directly to the outside world. The United Nations Environment Programme (UNEP) prepared an international agreement to reduce the risks of mercury pollution, and in 2013 the draft text of a treaty was agreed on by delegates of the UN member states in Geneva, Switzerland. In October of the same year, more than 1,000 representatives from governments, international organisations, and NGOs met in Kumamoto and Minamata to unanimously adopt the Minamata Convention on Mercury. Inorganic mercury is widely used in fluorescent lamps, thermometers, and batteries, but when it undergoes a chemical change in nature and becomes methylmercury, its toxicity increases dramatically. Therefore, it is essential to prevent the release of mercury into the environment and to collect patiently any that has escaped.

Young Brazilian researchers not only received training to learn experimental techniques in Brazil but also visited Minamata as JICA trainees. While the training at the NIMD was technical in nature, the Minamata City Government started to offer training in environmental restoration and capacity development for the creation of eco-cities in 2001. Brazilian scientists were involved in participatory field activities with trainees from other countries (JICA Kyushu 2014). As the Tapajós River Basin Project from 2007 and the Acre State Project from 2011 incorporated community outreach activities from the outset, Brazilian researchers showed great interest in the activities in Minamata.

De Oliveira Lima, who was in charge of the mercury laboratory at the Evandro Chagas Institute, said, 'I went to Minamata three times. The first time, I learnt about the Akagi method, but the second and third times I visited different places to learn about environmental issues. We also went to a recycling plant. The homestay was an unforgettable experience' [BRA 22]. In Brazil, as discussed in Sect. 6.2, while young *Nikkei* people tend to turn their backs on Japanese culture, other Brazilians were sometimes more curious about Japan. For João Paulo Góes Pereira, a young researcher at the Evandro Chagas Institute, the stay in Minamata was an interesting intercultural experience.

> I was impressed by the waste recycling in Minamata City. I learnt about specific analysis methods and also about the efforts of environmentally conscious citizens. My interest in Japanese culture is partly due to watching anime on TV. At school, I learnt that Japan had lost the war but recovered and prospered economically. I think they have the power to recover from pollution and from the tsunami. [BRA 24]

Jean Remy Davée Guimarães of the Federal University of Rio de Janeiro visited Minamata many times since 1992. He said he had a memorable experience at the 2013 Conference on Mercury at Minamata/Kumamoto, where the Minamata Convention on Mercury was adopted. He said:

> The conference was huge, but there were not many hotels in Minamata. So participants stayed with local families. I was accepted by a fisherman's home, and all family members wanted to speak English to me. The bicycles parked in the town were not locked, but no one ever tried to steal them. I remember a lot of local people attending the conference. [BRA 15].

Davée's host family were Ikeda Toshio and Ikeda Mitsuko, who worked for the rehabilitation of young patients with Minamata disease. Toshio said, 'When I was a primary school child, there was a Chisso hospital next to the school building, and I saw with my own eyes how cats suffering mercury intoxication were crazily spinning around within a cage in the laboratory. That scene is still burnt in my mind' [MMT 09]. Mitsuko attended an English conversation class for Minamata citizens set up by the Minamata City Government and continued to study English conversation afterwards. Mitsuko had a big smile and continued, 'Mr. Davée kindly made a Brazilian-style seafood hot pot for us, and we all ate it together. He was very popular among Minamata citizens and rode his bicycle everywhere. I remember one time he came home late at night and tried to go up the stairs quietly, step by step, so that he wouldn't disturb us. But I was awakened and noticed him!' [MMT 10].

Matsumoto Naomi, who hosted the JICA trainees, said her involvement in the volunteer work began when she met Akagi at an after-school childcare club. 'My third son, who is now a high school teacher, went to Niger as a JICA Volunteer and worked in youth activities. I visited Niger to see him. My son was dedicated to the activities, so I thought I should work hard, too' [MMT 07]. Her friend Tashiro Hisako was born in Tokyo. 'I think how you see Minamata depends on how you entered this area and who showed you around.' When a group of four good friends from Minamata went to Belém in 2009, scholars of the Evandro Chagas Institute and Cid de Souza of DNPM, who had visited Minamata several times, accompanied them and showed them around [MMT 08]. Group pictures shot together with several Brazilians I interviewed were displayed in the living room of Matsumoto's home.

Most of the JICA trainees who stayed with Matsumoto were from Asian or African countries. She recalled:

> I remember a trainee from South Africa was saying something like this. 'You can never forget the memories of oppression, but you can still forgive the perpetrator of the crimes.' This is not something that people who did not suffer the Minamata disease could say to a patient. Yet I was touched by this statement. I thought it was extraordinary that someone who had direct experience of apartheid was talking about forgiveness. [MMT 08]

The Soshisha, which attracted young people from all over Japan to support patients with Minamata disease and to campaign against Chisso and the government, was once considered a haunt of extremists, although it has recently been involved in training in cooperation with JICA Kyushu. In an interview in the 136th issue of Soshisha's newsletter, *Gonzui*, Akagi expressed his expectations for this 'stable and robust' association, stating that he hoped it would become a strong and capable international NGO, engaging in training programmes that would disseminate mercury measurement methods based on the 'principle of prevention'. In the same issue of *Gonzui*, Endo Kunio, a director of Soshisha, wrote, 'For me, the national government is not so pleasant,' but if it could lead to a new vision of society, 'I would like to work with JICA, the Ministry of the Environment, Kumamoto Prefecture, and Minamata City, and even with JNC [Chisso].'

I asked Endo, Nagano Michi and Koizumi Hatsue, who coordinated the training, to share their experiences. Initially, Soshisha was only responsible for a certain part of the training, but in 2013, they were approached by the Kumamoto Prefectural Government, and from 2014 they took on the responsibility of running the training for three years. 'Basically, the people of Minamata like outsiders and welcome their visits.'[20] Endo said:

> The anti-pollution movement came to a standstill, and we started working with the government. I think there was a mutual need. The people in the government didn't know what was happening on the ground. The national government, the prefecture, and patients are in different positions and are critical of each other. So I think the network of Soshisha has been useful in bringing everyone together. [MMT 01]

The training was designed so that participants could share problems in their own countries and learn from each other. 'Conversations among the trainers were just as valuable as listening to the lectures given by experts.' The homestay programme in Minamata was very popular, and 'there were even people who wrote only about the homestay experience in their feedback sheet, so we had to stop accepting them for a while.' The host families came to the ceremony on the final day to congratulate them. The trainees were mostly government officers responsible for implementing the Minamata Convention, but the situation varied from country to country. 'When the storytellers talked about discrimination, some people said they couldn't understand why they were suffering, while others cried out of sympathy' [MMT 01].

The Hot House, a care facility where patients with Minamata disease live together, was constructed with the support of the Ministry of the Environment. Groups of overseas guests, including those from Brazil, visited the facility about ten times a

[20] Nagano, who was born in Minamata, commented, 'We don't necessarily have an atmosphere of discussing everything freely within Minamata. It may not have changed much from the past' [MMT 01].

year. The patients told me that the dialect of Minamata was sometimes not properly interpreted, leading to misunderstandings, and that the trainees, representing their countries, listened carefully to the patients. When the experience of the Hot House was presented at the international conference for the Minamata Convention in 2013, participants from Africa hugged each of the patients and said, 'You are fighters' [MMT 05].

6.3.5 Towards Moyai Naoshi *(Mooring Again)*

A *moyai,* or a mooring rope, is used to tie two ships together, and the term *moyai naoshi* (もやい直し) refers to the act of mooring separate ships together again. The Minamata people's endeavour to overcome the social divisions in the community was born from within Minamata and given momentum by international events such as the Rio Summit in 1992 and the Minamata Convention Conference in 2013. As the effort of an NGO, Soshisha, was described in the previous section, I present the innovative activities on the part of the Minamata City Government in this section.

Yoshii Masazumi was elected to the Minamata City Council in 1975, became chairperson of the Council in 1983, and served as mayor of Minamata from 1994 to 2002. Soon after becoming mayor, he expressed an unequivocal apology to the victims of Minamata disease.[21] Yoshii also attended two international conferences in Brazil on mercury contamination and took the opportunity to visit his *Nikkei* relatives. Minamata signed a sister city agreement with the port city of Devonport in Tasmania, Australia, and Yoshii led a group of councillors to Australia. A women's group visited Germany. The official visits by delegates from Minamata to environmentally advanced municipalities abroad completely changed the mindset of the 'hardline' council members who had believed that industrial development should take precedence over the environment. Yoshii had worked in farming and forestry in the mountains but regularly ate the fish caught in the Shiranui Sea that local traders came to sell. The drastic measures that Yoshii took seemed as if the mountain people had stepped in to put an end to the assault by the town people on the sea people. In forestry, it takes 50 years from planting a tree to harvesting it. 'If you plant a tree when you are 20 years old, you will harvest it when you are 70.' Yoshii, who described Japan's forestry policy as a complete disaster, stressed that developing a policy vision with a time horizon of at least half a century was indispensable.

I listened to him in the tatami room of his old farmhouse located in a mountain valley.

> Nothing will change unless citizens decide to do something about it. I don't think individual attitudes change easily. Real change will occur when the next generation becomes

---

[21] Yoshii was a politician of the ruling Liberal Democratic Party (LDP), but he enjoyed a wide range of friendships with representatives of the citizens of Minamata, regardless of political affiliation, sharing the common goal of regenerating the community of Minamata. For his own retrospective account, see Yoshii (2017). He passed away in 2024 at the age of 92.

> the majority. In the past, Minamata was made up of people born in the Taisho era, who were emotionally attached to Chisso. For them, the priority was how to rebuild Chisso. Those people were also working at the centre of the municipal government. But in the 1990s, the gravity of the city shifted to people born in the Showa era. This generation had grown up with the knowledge of the pollution, and they had not received any special benefits from Chisso. For these people, international conferences and research missions were part of everyday life. In the past, Minamata was a high-income city thanks to Chisso, but we began to think about the future of humanity, not just about Minamata. Minamata began to open to the outside world. [MMT 03]

While working as a municipal officer aiding Mayor Yoshii, Yoshihmoto Tetsuro developed the experiences of the village community in the inland, mountainous part of Minamata into a universal method of community regeneration knowledge, or locality studies (地元学). Instead of asking what was missing, Yoshimoto proposed looking for what was already there. Fieldwork activities such as walking around a village and drawing a map of local resources by asking questions of local elders were incorporated into the training. Local villagers also benefited from these activities by rediscovering the local potential with the young Japanese and foreign ‘drifters’ (Yoshimoto 1995, 2008).

The local government policies and citizens’ campaigns played essential roles, but those who really matter are those who suffer. I had the chance to listen to the story of Ogata Masami, a furniture craftsman who came to Soshisha’s tatami meeting place for the interview. Ogata was exposed to extremely high levels of mercury during his childhood, but the authorities refused to recognise him as a Minamata disease patient. When the screening documents used by Kumamoto Prefecture were scrutinised, grave breaches of confidence were found, such as using his school grades without his consent, which had nothing to do with the disease. After an administrative appeal, the decision by the local government was overturned, and he was officially recognised as a Minamata disease patient.

However, Ogata recalled, ‘Somehow, I was far from happy. I was at a loss. I didn’t know how to react to the news.’ Ogata said that he initially tried to run away from the disease, then fought against it, and finally reached the stage where he could squarely face his fate.

> I believe it is critical to face the facts and live an honest life. If you want to play a game with the government, you can’t win. You’ll destroy yourself. Acting out of anger against Chisso and the prefectural government will never solve the problem. I’ve been trying to get rid of my anger to find a solution, not to take revenge. You can’t pretend things did not happen. But you can change your life. [MMT 06]

Ogata said that people have their own yardsticks and that we should honestly communicate how we think, how we measure things, to other people. ‘If you hide your feelings, people will poke around and discriminate against you more seriously. We should not hide anything about what happened in Minamata.… I called the governor of Kumamoto, Ms. Shiotani Yoshiko, my “mother”. When I’m suffering, my mother is also suffering. The governor was the mother of all the people of Kumamoto

Prefecture.' Ogata was also vocal about his feelings in front of the trainees who visited Minamata.[22]

Factories built on the ground do not move by themselves. Many of the hydroelectric power stations built in northern Korea under Japanese colonial rule are still in operation, and in particular, the massive Sup'ung Dam Hydroelectric Power Station remains at the centre as North Korea's national emblem. Infrastructure is tied to the land and promotes industry. Ships, on the other hand, can go anywhere on the water. Ogata Masami's uncle, Ogata Masato, took the helm of a wooden fishing boat called the *Nichigetsumaru* in the summer of 1996 and sailed from Minamata to Tokyo via the Seto Inland Sea and the Pacific Ocean. 'This route is the way to push back the poison. In other words, all bad things come from Tokyo' (Ogata 2020: 134).

6.3.6 Science and Truth

The mercury pollution in Minamata and the Amazon may seem like a thing of the past, but this is not necessarily true. Minamata Bay was reclaimed, and all the contaminated matter was buried in a section of the sea on which the spacious Eco Park Minamata was constructed. However, like the sarcophagus of the Chernobyl Nuclear Power Plant, the partitions in the sea will eventually reach the end of their useful life. Turning to the Amazon, De Oliveira Lima, head of the mercury laboratory at the Evandro Chagas Institute, was concerned about the rising levels of mercury in the Amazon basin.

> The number of gold mines has increased. In addition, mercury is now brought in from neighbouring countries such as Bolivia, which is upstream of Acre, rather than from Brazil. There are places in Colombia where the levels of mercury in the air are the worst. Mining is also expanding in the state of Roraima, bordering Venezuela. As long as gold mining continues, the problem will not be solved. Mercury levels are particularly high among miners, refiners and indigenous people. The high levels among the indigenous people are probably caused by the fact that they eat a lot of fish. I think we should monitor the situation. We don't know who will develop symptoms of Minamata disease in the future. [BRA 22]

The Amazon basin covers an area of no less than 6.3 million square km. Given that many of the gold mines are illegal and their locations are unknown, it is not easy to get an accurate picture of mercury pollution in such a vast area. Mercury does not have a half-life period like radioactive materials. Antonio Marcos Mota Miranda of the Evandro Chagas Institute proposed mapping the whole area and then conducting intensive surveys in the most contaminated areas [BRA 25]. Iracina Maura de Jesus also studied environmental education and recycling in Minamata with trainees from Tanzania, Indonesia and other countries. In Brazil, she had been

---

[22] JICA's magazine, *MUNDI*, January 2014 issue, https://www.jica.go.jp/publication/mundi/1401/ku57pq00001l9zvp-att/10.pdf (Japanese). Ogata (2016) contains the full text of his lecture on the occasion of the visit of the emperor and empress of Japan to the Minamata Disease Museum (October 2013). In preparing the lecture, Ogata was encouraged and inspired by Ishimure Michiko.

working on a surveillance project in the state of Acre, but faced some difficulties because the state government was not necessarily supportive of the surveys. She said:

> We found that pollution in Acre, where there are no nearby gold mines, was just as serious as in the Tapajós river basin. This is probably due to the gold mines in the neighbouring country, which are located upstream. As part of our environmental education, we produced teaching materials, visited schools, and carried out awareness-raising activities with local people. In 2014, citizens of Minamata attended a symposium together with researchers. We combined all these activities and embarked on an important project, third-country training. We brought together people from Bolivia, Peru, Ecuador, Suriname, Guatemala, Colombia, and Venezuela in a pan-Amazonian framework. [BRA 23]

Góes Pereira adapted the materials he received during the training in Minamata to create leaflets for Brazilian schoolchildren and citizens. 'I put pictures of fish on the wall and explained that although big fish are delicious, we should eat small fish as much as possible. I also added playful elements so that people who can't read and write could understand the danger of mercury' [BRA 24]. It is difficult to assess the success and failure of efforts to prevent a tragedy. Although prevention is far more effective and cheaper than reactive responses, its benefits are often underestimated. A Brazilian variant of Minamata disease may have been barely prevented by widespread publicity about mercury pollution and awareness campaigns in indigenous villages and among gold miners in the Amazon.[23]

Around the time when the COVID-19 pandemic became rampant in Japan in April 2020, Akagi spoke about the rigour, necessity, and fascination of scientific training. In an interview conducted by Gaia Minamata, a company that grows oranges in the area, he said:

> If you haven't mastered the technique, you will be at a loss when people get stuck. What will you do when your partners get stuck? This is where we start talking about technology transfer. For example, anyone can sew, but some critical stitches require specific skills. If you can show a solution, saying, 'This is how you can fix it,' it will open up a whole new world for everyone. No matter what kind of work you do, you should always be mindful of this moment. It's not just about getting rough numbers. It must be accurate, reproducible, and precise. When it comes to mercury contamination, this is the kind of analysis we need to practice.[24]

The Brazilian research community appreciated Akagi's ceaseless quest for scientific verification. In other chapters of this book, we have seen many experts like Akagi involved in development projects across the Global South. However, while he

[23] Many researchers in Brazil pointed to the puzzling fact that very few people in the Amazon show symptoms of Minamata disease, even when extremely high levels of mercury were confirmed in their hair. One hypothesis was that this was because many people ate nuts that contain selenium [BRA 16] [BRA 21] [BRA 25]. Akagi also said, 'We can't do human experiments, so we should be patient. But theoretically, it is possible that the diet is effective' [MMT 02].

[24] Gaia Minamata's interview series, Episode 6: 'In Quest of Science of Truth'. https://gaiaminamata.net/taimen-series-6 (Japanese). Akagi was undergoing treatment for his illness at the time of my interviews and passed away in August 2020. Regarding the contribution of science to human security in the post-Fukushima era, Maruyama Masato of the Human Security Program at the University of Tokyo highlighted the role of nuclear power regulation based on scientific knowledge (Maruyama 2015) (in English).

generously shared his laboratory techniques with his global counterparts, Akagi also wanted to put down roots in the local community of Minamata. Akagi, who 'drifted' to Minamata from Makurazaki in Kagoshima Prefecture, told me that he felt obliged to bring something valuable to Minamata. Akagi said that this was because he had 'received so many blessings from the people of Minamata'.

6.4 Passing on the Memories of War and Peace (Okinawa and Cambodia)

6.4.1 Recording the Experience of the Battle of Okinawa

Ishimure Michiko, the author and the key figure of a project called the Shiranui Sea Comprehensive Academic Surveys, which was launched in 1976, contributed an imaginative essay entitled 'Milky Currents' (see Preface of this book) to the final project report, *Revelations of Minamata*. During the research, Ishimure once travelled to Yonaguni Island in Okinawa, leaving the Tokyo-based research members stranded in Minamata. She wrote that this journey to Okinawa was a 'prayer ritual' necessary for her to face the spiritual world of the Shiranui Sea again. The sea fig (kin to the banyan trees), which propagated northwards from the southern sea, grew in clusters on the shores of Shiranui with its roots twisted and its branches extended towards the source of the currents. It 'appears to assert that life was created from the sunlight and the sea.' One can see 'the shine of the Mediterranean Sea, filled with the scent of figs, olives, and grapes, before the time of the Psalms of the Old Testament, if one follows the currents in the direction from which emerged the land and people', which rest in 'the periphery of this country' where Ishimure's imagination was born. Otherwise, we see 'the colour of young oak leaves' when this country had no name yet. In this way, Ishimure's illusionary vision follows the women of the Amakusa Islands who have dispersed to the 'Arafura Sea' in the south. In the real world, she visited an old woman who had converted to Islam in a nursing home in Kuala Lumpur. Conducting a dialogue in the Amakusa dialect, Ishimure delved into the folds of confused memories of the lonely old woman, who murmured, 'Dream, dream.... Everything is a dream.... Japan, the rotten dragged bowels....' (Ishimure 1983).

Takara Kurayoshi, a renowned historian of the Ryukyu Kingdom, begins his book *The Age of the Ryukyus* by describing his experience of strolling around the streets of Melaka, a place he had longed to visit. He wrote that in this strait city at the crossroads of Eastern and Western history, he could find no trace of the historical glory of the intersection of human civilisations; there were few visible reminders of the Islamic Sultanate of Malacca or the Portuguese Sea Empire. The lack of historical evidence disappointed Takara because he knew that there had been trade and cultural exchanges between the Ryukyu Kingdom and its counterpart kingdoms of Southeast Asia, including the Kingdoms of Siam and Malacca, which thrived during the fifteenth and sixteenth centuries (Takara 1998; 2012) (Fig. 6.3). Unless sorted, stored, and disclosed, historical facts will fade from people's memories, if not be lost altogether.

In this light, the Okinawa Prefectural Peace Memorial Museum is a miraculous place: the graceful and expansive building, newly constructed in 2000, is situated on

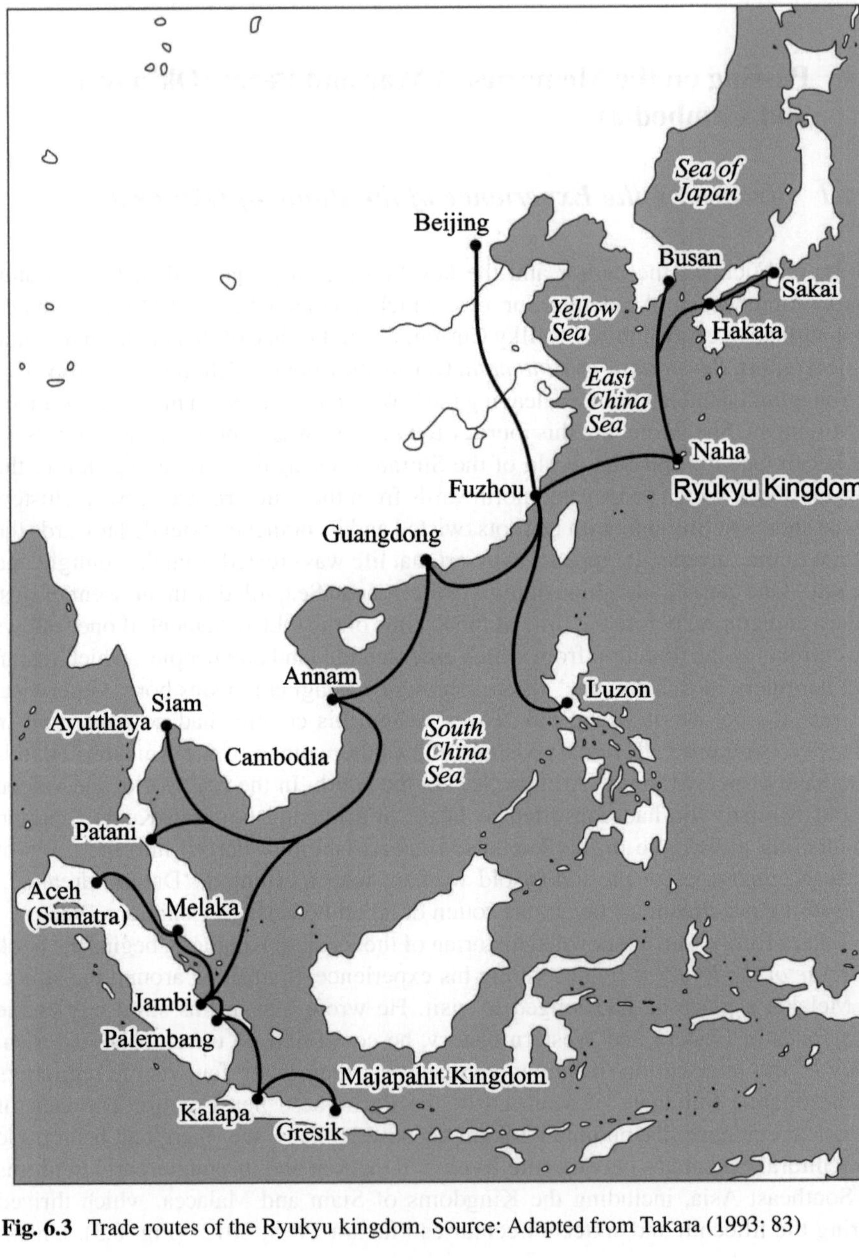

Fig. 6.3 Trade routes of the Ryukyu kingdom. Source: Adapted from Takara (1993: 83)

a hill overlooking the Pacific Ocean. As mentioned at the beginning of this chapter, southern Okinawa was the field of a ferocious ground battle, and Mabuni Hill in Itoman City, where the museum is now located, was the site of the last deadly battle. It is said that after being cornered, Japanese soldiers saw US warships gathering off the coast and then threw themselves off the cliff in despair. However, several hundred years ago, the same hill was never a corner of desperation from which one could see no escape. The Ryukyu Kingdom once flourished as a hub for transit trade between China, Japan, Korea and Southeast Asia, and merchant ships from various ports sailed the same sea busily and peacefully without brandishing weapons. In the vast garden area in front of the museum building, layers of numerous stone monuments have been erected, inscribed with the names of all known victims, both Okinawan citizens and soldiers from mainland Japan and the US military.

The main feature of the Peace Memorial Museum is an expanding collection of people's testimonies. The museum was originally established in 1975, the year of the Okinawa International Ocean Exposition. As a large number of specialists were recruited and dispatched to the Expo, the museum could not be adequately prepared but opened only as a makeshift, rather shabby 'military museum', displaying helmets, medals and Hinomaru flags, which faced mounting criticism. Especially because the museum lacked the presentation of Okinawan citizens' experiences, it was decided fairly quickly to start over from the planning stage, and a consensus emerged that the new museum should be based on people's memories and testimonies as the primary source of exhibition material (Sonohara 2016). The current displays of the museum are diverse, but it is the testimonies of Okinawans in the second half of the exhibition that leave a particularly strong impression on visitors. In a large, quiet, dimly lit room, a series of notes float in the light, allowing visitors to face the witnesses squarely and individually by reading the transcribed texts. When I visited the place, a young, uniformed officer of the Japanese Self-Defence Force was reading one of the testimonies utterly still, as if absorbed in the spiritual world of a particular war survivor.

A curator of the museum, Hirata Mamoru, has been dealing with the testimonies of the Battle of Okinawa.

> For about 20 years, since the new museum building was constructed, we have been collecting video testimonies. About 1,000 footages have been collected, but people's narratives are inevitably subjective. They have to be checked and monitored to ensure that they are compatible with historical facts. For example, there were some people who wrongly remembered the places of evacuation or gave place names that were simply impossible. We try not to include these parts in the archives that are open to the public. [OKW 05]

As discussed in Chap. 1 (Sect. 1.1.4), no one can blame a witness for his or her misremembering the facts. No matter how objective one tries to be, the details of memory are always subject to some degree of distortion or partial loss. Therefore, writing oral history, like other forms of history, requires careful verification of facts and context. Oshiro Toroku, an adviser to the Okinawa Peace Memorial Museum Fellowship, a group of storytellers, said, 'Whether we can pass on the experience to future generations depends on whether or not the government prioritise it. There is already a lot of material in the museum's storage area' [OKW 06]. Director of the Peace Memorial Museum Hokama Hirotomo had participated in preliminary research on the Tuol Sleng Genocide Museum in Cambodia in 2009, as a member of the Okinawa Prefectural Government. He said that the museum would have to collect testimonies about the immediate post-war period, when 'many people died of starvation due to serious food shortages in the devastated areas' [OKW 04].

Sonohara Ken, who was the chief curator of the museum, was the pivotal figure in opening the museum activities to the outside world through cooperation with Cambodia.

> I enrolled in the University of the Ryukyus in 1977 and went on to study English literature at the Faculty of Law and Letters. Then I visited Tokyo. When I mentioned I was from Okinawa, I was told, 'You speak good Japanese!' That shocked me. I thought it was a waste of time to learn English, and I changed my major to sociology and anthropology. I wanted to study Okinawa more deeply and look into my own community. After this turnaround, the so-called Okinawa boom began, when the TV drama *Wind of the Ryukyu Islands*[25] was broadcast. [OKW 01]

Takara Kurayoshi begins his *Ryukyu Kingdom* (Takara 1993) by noting that Okinawan historians often receive 'fanatical requests', such as asking how to help the goddess who is about to descend from the moon to the US military base. A historian may act as a holy medium. In academia, the life of the Okinawan people was regenerated by Iha Fuyu, known as the researcher of a collection of poems and songs, *Omoro Soshi,* and as the father of Okinawan studies (Iha 2000; Kano 2018). Iha was also known for his energetic efforts to popularise his academic findings through activities such as public lectures. The Okinawa Peace Museum functions as a hub for the historical study of contemporary Okinawa and the empowerment of people as history-makers. It is necessary to remember that in Okinawa today, the dialogue between the present and the past is progressing not only through the work of intellectual giants but through the collective efforts of numerous individuals who are willing to be part of the living archives.

6.4.2 Genocide in Cambodia

Let us now turn to the cooperation between the Peace Memorial Museum in Okinawa and the Genocide Museum in Cambodia. The Khmer Empire and the Ryukyu Kingdom were contemporaries in Asian history. In the twelfth century, the power of the Khmer Empire was at its zenith in Cambodia, where the stone-built Hindu edifice complex of Angkor was being constructed. Around this time, Okinawa entered the *Gusuku* period, and stone fortresses were being constructed on hilltops in various parts of the archipelago. The Khmer and the Ryukyus were hewing and stacking stones simultaneously in their respective places. The Ming Dynasty of China, founded in the fourteenth century, established a regionwide tribute trade system to contain

[25] The drama was produced and aired by NHK, Japan Broadcasting Corporation, in 1993. https://mubi.com/en/jp/films/wind-of-the-ryukyu-islands.

private piracy. Under this system, the Ryukyu Kingdom began to actively send out ships that connected the nodes of the trade networks (Takara 1998; Hamashita 2008; 2011). By this time, the Khmer Empire had lost its earlier momentum and been pushed back by the Kingdom of Siam, but present-day Cambodia, the interior of the Indochina Peninsula, must have continued trading with the Ryukyus (Fig. 6.3). The Ryukyu Kingdom was conquered by the Shimazu clan in 1609, and its autonomy was substantially weakened. The Ryukyus were incorporated into Japan in 1879 and became Okinawa Prefecture, while Cambodia became a French protectorate in 1863. The French government educated a handful of urban elites in the French language but was reluctant to change the lives of the rural masses. The contrast between the past glory of the Khmer Empire and the poverty in front of them would have stimulated the national consciousness of the Khmer elite.

After a brief occupation by Japan in 1945, Cambodia achieved independence from France in 1953. The historical sequence was analogous to those of Indonesia and Malaysia described in Chaps. 2 and 3. As the Cold War intensified, however, Cambodia was continuously buffeted by the multifaceted wars in Indochina. In April 1975, as North Vietnam's victory became palpable, the pro-US Cambodian government led by Lon Nol collapsed, and militias under the command of Pol Pot (whose real name was Saloth Sar) entered the capital city, Phnom Penh.[26] In the same year, the International Ocean Exposition was held in Okinawa to commemorate its return to Japan. US troops were withdrawing from Vietnam, and there were widespread expectations of a significant shift towards peace in the Asian regional political order.

In Cambodia, however, having perceived that the new regime was under siege, Pol Pot and his followers went berserk. Citizens of Phnom Penh were evicted to the countryside and forcibly mobilised for collective labour. Money, private property, commercial markets, schools, and cultural activities were suppressed, and those with professional skills and knowledge were fiercely persecuted. Wearing glasses is known to have been a reason for killing as a sign of belonging to the intellectual class. It is estimated that about one in five Cambodians lost their lives due to malnutrition, disease, forced labour, and executions under the Pol Pot regime, a rate similar to that of the Okinawans who died in the Battle of Okinawa. After seizing power, Pol Pot and his forces became suspicious of 'microbes' infiltrating their organisation and accelerated their efforts to identify and eliminate enemies and traitors (Chandler 1992: 136–137).

In 1971, several years before the change of the regime, a French scholar of Buddhism, François Bizot, was kidnapped by Pol Pot's militias while conducting fieldwork and detained in a rural camp, where, despite the constant threat of execution, he developed a strange friendship with the head of the camp, Duch (Kang Kek Iew), a former mathematics teacher and a revolutionary activist. Bizot was eventually released, and Duch continued to carry out his duties, interrogating and nonchalantly executing prisoners. After 1975, Duch was promoted to chairman of

[26] Concerning the personality of Pol Pot, see Kiernan (1985), Chandler (1992), and Short (2004). Even after reading these excellent biographies, the true nature of the man remains something of a shroud.

a secret interrogation facility codenamed S-21, where he meticulously read through voluminous 'confession' statements while overseeing the torture and execution of 'anti-revolutionary elements', including not only former government officials but also his own subordinates. As mentioned in Sect. 6.1.3, in this facility, formerly a high school, nearly 20,000 people were imprisoned, tortured, and killed over a three-year period. When Vietnam invaded Cambodia in 1979, Duch and the cadres fled without disposing of evidence such as torture equipment, documents, photographs, and even some corpses. Vietnam preserved the S-21 facility (later widely known as Tuol Sleng) and opened it to the public as a genocide museum, being aware that it would remind international society of the Bergen-Belsen concentration camp in Germany (Short 2004: 446–447). The fugitive Duch later converted to Christianity, hid his identity, and worked for a refugee relief organisation in the Thai border region, where he was discovered, arrested, and brought before the international tribunal in 1999.[27]

In her famous essay on the 'banality of evil', Hannah Arendt observed the trial of Adolf Eichmann, who was responsible for the mass transport of Jews to Auschwitz, and found that he was not the monster as expected to be but an ordinary petty citizen who lacked empathy for others, could only think in stereotypical ways, and obediently followed the laws and regulations of Germany at the time (Arendt 1963). He was integrated into the system, processed paper, and set the killing machine in motion. In Cambodia, Duch, a former mathematics teacher, was placed in the same position. However, Bizot perceived Duch as an extraordinarily intelligent and attractive person, which posed a riddle about the genocidal institution in Cambodia.

This book began with a case study of the development of the Brantas River basin in Indonesia, where the project was interrupted by the political upheaval in 1965, when the military and its allies mercilessly killed suspected communists. A decade later, self-proclaimed communists massacred innocent people in Cambodia. Despite the opposite political ideologies, the two historical events share the bare fact that countless people were killed without understanding why they had to be killed at all. It would be even more absurd if future generations did not remember the slaughter and stopped thinking about why these genocidal acts had occurred.

6.4.3 Beginning of Collaboration

Preparations for international cooperation at the Okinawa Prefectural Peace Memorial Museum began in 2008. Hirata, one of the curators, said, 'At the beginning, we wanted to collaborate with an institute in the areas occupied by the Japanese military during the war' [OKW 05]. Sonohara also said, 'We were keen to work in Saipan. The place was a fierce battlefield before the Battle of Okinawa' [OKW 01]. However, JICA is a bilateral development cooperation agency that can only work in

[27] See Bizot (2000) for more on Duch and Chandler (1999) for a detailed account of S-21. After being given a life sentence, Duch died in Phnom Penh in 2020.

an aid recipient country. Hence, the partner could not be Saipan, which is part of the US, which is a developed country. Cambodia and East Timor were shortlisted, and the final choice was Cambodia, where conditions were more stable and conductive to civic cooperation. Another context was Japan's deep involvement in the UN-led peace process in Cambodia.[28]

In May 2009, a research team led by Okawa Yoshiko, director of the Peace Memorial Museum, visited Cambodia and found practical problems with the operation of the Tuol Sleng Museum. In addition to physical deficiencies such as the breakdown of air conditioning and the deterioration of materials due to the high humidity, 'the guides lived off the fees paid by visitors, so the information attached to the objects was made unfriendly. If the labels were written carefully and extensively, the guides would no longer be needed and would lose their jobs' [OKW 01]. While lax management may seem typical of developing countries, we can see rational reasons for persistent poor quality. In the first place, the Cambodians may not have wanted to show the outside world what had happened at Tuol Sleng. Not only could they not be proud of the mass killing of Cambodians by Cambodians, but also the fact remained that the Vietnamese immediately publicized their discoveries of Tuol Sleng. 'Some people may have worked unwillingly for the Pol Pot regime, and perhaps it was not desirable to expose the past of these people too much' [OKW 01]. If such was the case, the philosophy of the museum should be reconsidered so that the place of violent folly would be transformed into a place of prayer for universal peace.

In any case, at that time, Cambodia lacked the human resources to run a museum. Here, let us revisit the argument presented in Chapter 1. Although Cambodia's governance structure corresponded to Fig. 1.3 in the colonial period, it was about to develop towards Fig. 1.4 in the post-independence phase. However, the Pol Pot regime completely destroyed A-β, which had already been weakened by regional wars and a civil war. The newly independent state needed to train professionals, such as teachers, medical doctors, engineers, and agricultural extension workers, regardless of political ideology, to act as people's agents. For a while, the government could be assisted by foreigners or those who had studied abroad, but in the long run it would be necessary to nurture local professionals who would graduate from local schools and be willing to work for the local community. However, the Pol Pot regime considered these professionals to be counter-revolutionary and tried to physically exterminate them. The pool of human resources literally dried up, as even senior party members who were in a position to give instructions to the people were purged one by one. According to *State of the World's Children 2024* by the United Nations Children's Fund (UNICEF), Cambodia's secondary education completion rate was only 27%, lower than Laos (31%) and East Timor (52%) (UNICEF 2024: Statistical Compendium). It is not easy to grow teachers from the zero point. In the

[28] In 1992–1993, Japan deployed the Self-Defence Forces, civilian police, and election observers to contribute to the Cambodian PKOs. Akashi Yasushi, who worked for peace in Cambodia as the United Nations Special Representative of the Secretary-General in Cambodia, wrote an insider's account of this period (Akashi 2017). In 1993, two Japanese, UN Volunteer Nakata Atsuhito and Lt. Takada Haruyuki, were killed on duty. For the contexts of Japan's cultural diplomacy in Cambodia, see Peycam (2020: 257–263).

cooperation with the Peace Museum, it was attempted to train the staff who were already working there to become professional curators with specialist knowledge. This seems to have been an appropriate and realistic approach.

Why should this cooperation take place in Okinawa and not elsewhere? The JICA Okinawa International Centre, which served as a bridge between the Peace Memorial Museum in Okinawa and the Genocide Museum in Cambodia, was established in 1985. As mentioned in Chap. 3 (Sect. 3.1.2), Japanese Prime Minister Suzuki Zenko proposed the ASEAN Human Resources Development Project during his visit to Southeast Asia in 1981 and established centres in five ASEAN countries; the development of the centre in Malaysia was discussed in Chap. 3 (Sect. 3.2). The Okinawa International Centre was set up as part of this initiative in Okinawa Prefecture, 'which is geographically close to ASEAN countries and shares many similarities in climate and culture'. Furthermore, 'in recent years, the internationalization of local cities has been progressing nationwide, and it was hoped that the Centre would play a complementary role to the various international exchange programmes promoted by Okinawa Prefecture and contribute to the internationalization of the Prefecture' (JICA 1995b: 1). Museum cooperation between Okinawa and Cambodia expanded the scope of collaboration between Japan and ASEAN countries, from manufacturing to peace and culture.

The local NPO, the Okinawa Peace Assistance Centre (OPAC), took charge of the day-to-day running of the training. OPAC President Nakadomari Kazue, who had worked on JICA training for many years as an officer of the Japan International Cooperation Center (JICE), decided to join the NPO world 'because I thought it would be nice to work with JICA from the outside'. JICA Okinawa also has a section for citizen participation. She said that in Okinawa, 'NPOs don't necessarily know each other very well, so it's really helpful to have JICA as a bridge agent' [OKW 03].

6.4.4 Techniques to Communicate Tragedy

The collaboration between the two museums was carried out from 2009 to 2012 as the Okinawa-Cambodia 'Peace Museum' Cooperation Project under the JICA Partnership Program (Local Government Type). Since Sonohara, who was a key figure in designing the training, moved from the Peace Memorial Museum to the Okinawa Prefectural Museum,[29] the second phase was joined by both the Okinawa Prefectural Museum and Art Museum and the National Museum of Cambodia, and the new project for Okinawa-Cambodia 'Peace Culture' Museum Cooperation was implemented from 2012 to 2015. After inviting the director of the Tuol Sleng Genocide Museum as the first counterpart from Cambodia, groups of staff were accepted with

[29] Sonohara spoke of his dream of working with the Kyushu National Museum to organise an exhibition on the art of the Khmer Kingdom in the future. However, 'the stones are heavy and difficult to transport, and if they break, that would be a serious problem' [OKW 01].

a total of 21 participants excluding the director and his deputies (Sonohara 2016). Staff from the National Museum also participated in the second phase. 'We even accepted people from the Department of General Affairs. We also had counterpart departments in Okinawa, so I think they all learnt something from us' (OKW 01).

The topics of the training ranged from the museum's ideals, management, collecting and preserving materials, maintaining facilities, and creating exhibitions, to raising awareness through school and social education about peace, Okinawa's nature, history and culture, and presenting action plans to be implemented upon their return to Cambodia. The text was translated into Khmer and designed to be clear and concise. 'The Nago Museum is an open-air museum. It allows visitors to touch various exhibits and is visited by local schoolchildren. The trainees seemed to have found these aspects helpful.' [OKW 03]. The trainees also visited neighbouring schools and gave classes. A detailed report of the activities can be found in the Okinawa Prefectural Peace Memorial Museum (n.a.; 2011); the highlight of the month-long training was the 'Cambodian History and Culture Exhibition', a photo exhibition prepared by the trainees and held in the lobby of the museum during the very last week of the training. To follow up on the implementation of the action plan, the Okinawan staff visited Cambodia and made use of video conferencing.

Sakuma Ayumi, who was in charge of the training as JICA's citizen participation coordinator, said that not all the training went well. Some trainees perceived that they were 'made to work' on the action plan and did not want to put it into practice. Others thought Sonohara was too strict [OKW 02]. Nevertheless, one of the reasons for the success of the training, as agreed by all those involved, was that the staff at the Tuol Sleng Museum were not subject to a personnel reshuffle, and therefore the acquired skills and knowledge were accumulated in one place. 'Every time I went for a follow-up, the same people were there, so I saw the same faces over the six years. The bond was firmly established. I think they have also come to like Okinawa' [OKW 03]. 'The trainees brought their own spices and Cambodian foodstuffs. Apparently, they passed on various information to the trainees of the following year, so I think the stress was much eased for them' [OKW 02]. Nakadomari, who looked after the trainees on site, was loved by everyone.

The management of the Cambodian museum was surprised because the returned staff 'wanted to organise things spontaneously' [OKW 01]. The Tuol Sleng Museum began selling entrance tickets. In January and February 2015, the museum received about 1,000 visitors per day from 120 countries around the world. A museum logo was created, the uniform was designed, and flowers were planted for the emotional care of visitors, as witnessed by Sonohara (2016).[30]

[30] The materials stored in the Tuol Sleng Museum are on UNESCO's Memory of the World (MoW) Register, and the digitisation work was facilitated by funding from the Korea International Cooperation Agency (KOICA). https://archives.tuolsleng.gov.kh/About#.

6.4.5 *Okinawans in Cambodia*

The training is where settlers become temporary drifters, bringing new ideas and learning from each other. As Sakuma, who supported the JOCV activities in Okinawa, said, 'Okinawans are always light-footed. They are interested in the outside world and are used to travelling by air. There is no difference between going abroad and going to mainland Japan because both are outside Okinawa. Many people think now is the time to leave and go out, and after spending a few years there, they return to Okinawa. Okinawa is a more relaxed place. It's much easier to live here than in other places.' When Sakuma planned to send Okinawan high school students to Cambodia, her counterparts in Tuol Sleng always told her, 'If the party is from Okinawa, they can come to us any time. Please make them visit the museum!' For Okinawan high school students who are concerned about peace, a visit to the Tuol Sleng Museum is also an opportunity to reflect deeply on their own place. The same was true for the young trainees from Tuol Sleng. 'When they returned to Cambodia from Okinawa, they seemed to have realised that they needed to know more about their own place' [OKW 02].

There are things we can learn because we are different, and other things we can learn because we simply don't know. Oshiro Toroku, a storyteller at the Peace Memorial Museum, experienced the Battle of Okinawa. While hiding and preparing for battle, he witnessed US soldiers with their tops off firing their rifles in succession. Talking to trainees from Cambodia, he felt the experience was not the same. 'Here, it was a war with the US. The Cambodian people were fighting over ideology. Both are unfortunate, but I think there are aspects that cannot be compared' [OKW 06]. Kubota Satoru was a baby at the time of the Battle of Okinawa. 'My mother was running around with me and my brother on her back. She hid in a caldron in a sugar factory, and she was captured by the US military.' Kubota himself remembered nothing, so he told young visitors the stories his mother had told him [OKW 07].

Yoneda Miyuki, a social studies teacher at Yaeyama Commercial and Technical High School, was born and raised on Ishigaki Island. She found a call for applications for a visit to the Tuol Sleng Genocide Museum in a public announcement sent to her school from Okinawa Prefecture, and she decided to apply.[31] Yoneda, who had been to the Philippines for JICA's overseas teacher training, wanted to identify 'what Okinawa and Cambodia had in common.' She said:

> I didn't think about this when I was a student on the main island of Okinawa. But after I returned to Ishigaki Island and became a teacher, I began to wonder about the nature of war. The main island of Okinawa experienced a tragic ground war. On Ishigaki Island, there was hunger and malaria. Human relationships are sometimes very raw. During the war, they couldn't tell who took away what. They were keeping quiet for some time. And only later they all knew what had happened. [OKW 09]

---

[31] As part of the JICA Partnership Program (Support Type), Cambodia and Okinawa Museum-Initiated Promotion of Peace Education Project, which started in July 2016, a high school teacher was dispatched from Okinawa to Cambodia.

In August 2016, Yoneda visited Cambodia, where she prepared a lesson plan and facilitated a workshop for local high school students. She said, 'Some of the Cambodian students started to cry when they imagined what happened at Tuol Sleng. I thought they had the power to empathise with others.' Yoneda herself visited the site of the genocide and felt sick but decided not to be afraid. She thought that the piles of skulls 'express that humans were there, even after they died'.

> I don't think that simply teaching that war is horrifying and should be eliminated will work out. The structure of war is hierarchical. You can't challenge orders because if you don't kill, you will be killed. You have to think of where you are standing. The ground battle in Okinawa and the civil war in Cambodia took place in different countries at different times. But I realized that the nature of that structure was the same. [OKW 09]

So remarked Yoneda, who returned from Phnom Penh to her high school on Ishigaki Island. In December, she taught an open class on the subject of 'contemporary society'. She showed the students different images of wars and asked them to discuss their similarities. 'I asked them to consider whether they were on the side of giving orders or being given orders.' The approach was different from the usual one of peace education, and 'it was a big challenge for me to make it fit into the curriculum.'

Sonohara, who designed the training, stressed that Cambodians and Okinawans were all human beings and said, 'The fact that people lost their lives in battle remains the same. There would have been cases where those who killed were eventually killed. I think the Cambodian people empathised with the Okinawan experience when they felt it on the ground. It was when they got into dark *gama* [shelter caves]. It was when they walked into the mountains in Yaeyama and thought about those who died of malaria. I think the similarities between Cambodia and Okinawa, for example, in the natural vegetation, may have been one reason why it was easy for them to relate to the Okinawan experience' [OKW 01]. The training was accompanied by interpreters who spoke Japanese and English, and sometimes Khmer. A storyteller, Yasuda Kunishige, said that, when the interpreter had a disability, he and the trainees had to enter a *gama* where locals had evacuated, without knowing each other's language. Although there were no words, 'there was something we could feel together' [OKW 08].

The Tuol Sleng Genocide Museum attracts visitors from all over the world and seems to be the most popular destination after the ruins of Angkor and the Royal Palace in Phnom Penh. What did the young Cambodians who maintain displays in the museum and its garden every day think when they travelled to Okinawa? What did they feel when they closed their eyes in the darkness deep inside an enclosed *gama*? Nakadomari, who took care of the trainees, said that the Genocide Museum used to be 'a place where people were scared to go, because there were only skeletons. Ordinary visitors never wanted to go again. Now, the museum has become a place where people say, 'This place makes me very sad, but I am glad to be here. This is a necessary experience' [OKW 03].

After having conducted interviews in Okinawa in December 2019, I planned to visit the Tuol Sleng Genocide Museum myself, but I was not able to do so for several years due to the outbreak of the COVID 19 pandemic. It was only in August 2024 that I managed to travel to Cambodia to talk directly to those Cambodians who had attended the training in Okinawa. In the following two sections, let me present their voices to conclude the book.

6.4.6 Cambodians in Okinawa

Cambodians described what Tuol Sleng looked like before the collaboration began. Keo Monyroth, an exhibition professional who had been a local resident, said that the ground of Tuol Sleng used to be 'covered with grass. There were coconut trees but no flowers, and no decorations. The walls were crumbling, and the displays were stuck directly onto the walls. When it rained, the floor would be flooded with water' [CAM 08]. When the head of the administrators, Phal Kun, began working at the museum in 1994, 'the clothes worn by the prisoners were piled up, unwashed, and emitted a terrible odour' [CAM 12].

Concerning the Cambodian past, the interviewees had different memories and experiences depending on their age. Some had family members killed under the rule of Pol Pot, while others knew nothing about torture and mass killings until they started working at the museum. Both parents of Heng Sophara, the head of the education section, worked at the museum, making her a 'second-generation' staff member [CAM 03]. Oun Sokuntheavy, deputy director of the National Museum of Cambodia, grew up with memories of the war. She talked about her family.

> In 1975, I was two years old. On the night of 17 April, my mother and I were supposed to escape by helicopter and go to the United States, but the plan failed. We were relocated by the Khmer Rouge to a village in Battambang Province near the Thai border, where mass killings also took place. Someone we knew in Phnom Penh reported that my father was a police officer, so our family was interrogated. My brother was forced to confess and eventually killed. [CAM 05]

Cambodians remembered what they learnt in Okinawa. 'It was exciting to see people's lives displayed in a museum that looked like a farmhouse. I was impressed by how well the displays were sequenced in all museums.' [CAM 08; CAM 10]. The farmhouse-like museum would probably be the Nago Museum. The highlight of the training was the photo exhibition planned and executed by the trainees themselves. Chhabu Sopheara said, 'The exhibition we prepared for the last day was very successful. It was a great learning experience to think of the content of the final exhibition and cut out the panels' [CAM 06]. There was also professional technology transfer. One of the notable features of the Tuol Sleng Genocide Museum is the display of terrifying iron torture instruments, and Bun Korng, the deputy head of the administrators, learnt about the preservation of iron materials during the training. 'I learnt the technique of removing rust using chemical agents. Here, we perform iron maintenance every three months. We take meticulous care of items such as handcuffs, shackles, excrement disposal boxes, and those made of plastic' [CAM 10].

Even after the formal project period was over, Cambodians continued collaborating with Okinawans. Director of the Genocide Museum Hang Nisay said, 'Just yesterday, we accepted ten high school students from Okinawa. They stayed for about two hours, and we talked about various things. Some said they wanted to become schoolteachers' [CAM 01]. 'Local students who visit here without preparation would just feel scared. We created Khmer-language teaching materials together with specialists in Okinawa, so that students can view the exhibits while thinking about their meaning. We are currently working on revisions of the materials with people in Okinawa' [CAM 03].

Okinawans mused about the common and different aspects of war and violence. What were the thoughts of Cambodians on this question? While numerous human lives were lost in both places, Cambodians emphasised the unique backdrop of the Cold War. Tour guide Hor Chanleasksmy said that international politics influenced the Cambodian genocide by dividing the country into two ideological camps [CAM 14]. After World War II, Okinawa was reconstructed and developed, while Cambodia began to destroy itself after the end of the war in Indochina. Chhey Sophearith, who used to be a security guard and became a full-time archivist, said, 'In Hiroshima, someone pressed a button and slaughtered everyone, but in Cambodia, people killed each other, face to face, because they thought "this guy looks suspicious"' [CAM 11]. The museum management mentioned anger as an important factor. 'When the Vietnam War ended, the anger and fear were directed inward and accumulated in Cambodia. We are still addressing such emotions,' [CAM 01]. Ke Sophanaka, the chief legal document officer at the National Museum, concurred, 'People suffered, and anger accumulated, and this hindered the post-war development of the national economy,' [CAM 07]. On the other hand, the archivist Sdan Samrithpisey, who still remembers her visit to a shelter cave, *gama,* perceived that the war in Okinawa was yet to end. 'The war in Okinawa was supposed to be over. I wondered, if so, why was a US military base right next to the cave?' [CAM 02].

Phal Kun also visited a *gama.* 'We crawled down a narrow passage, but the interior was spacious. I heard a story about a mother covering her baby's mouth.... and suffocating it. I think I shared the feelings of the Okinawans.' [CAM 12]. Hang Nisay emphasised the importance of recording people's suffering:

> One of the things I learnt from Okinawa was the importance of listening to life stories of the survivors. Here, we started to conduct interviews with Cambodian survivors and carefully document what had happened to them in Khmer. Learning about their courage and the skills they used to survive can positively impact young people who will shape our future.... What stands out most in my memory of Okinawa is our visit to the cave. It was very dark and slippery. I could imagine the situation; Japanese soldiers were hiding inside, and American soldiers were patrolling outside, so no one was allowed to make a sound. [CAM 01]

Their training was also full of joyful moments, which the trainees vividly remembered. They sympathised with the lifestyle and culture of Okinawa and Fukuoka where the Kyushu National Museum is located. At the entrance to the Okinawa Peace Memorial Museum, there was a photograph of an elderly man playing *sanshin* (a snakeskin-covered instrument) with the background music of *Nada Soso,* which deeply moved Sdan Samrithpisey. She said, 'I felt it is essential to transform a place of sadness into a place of hope' [CAM 02]. There was also a remark that *Shisa* (guardian lions) were very cute [CAM 06]. Chhem Sokchamreoun, who took charge of education, recalled wearing traditional clothes and visiting the royal palace in Okinawa, as well as travelling by train and going to a public bathhouse in Fukuoka [CAM 04]. Those who encountered a typhoon remembered being confined to their lodgings. Living in Phnom Penh, many interviewees had few opportunities to go to the sea, so the Okinawa Churaumi Aquarium left a strong impression on them.

Both senior and junior staff members spoke about the 'action plans' that would ensure the real and lasting impact of the training. During the training in Okinawa, they discussed and decided what each trainee would do after they returned to Cambodia. These tasks were diverse and included the following: museum history exhibition; children's library; preparing lessons at school; booklets for visitors; improved museum management; scanning of materials; exhibitions on Okinawa's history and culture and museum cooperation; and preserving photographs and paintings. An archivist, Prak Sothy, worked with his colleagues on the mobile museum project, which continues to this day. 'I think it has become a good legacy. In Okinawa, I was impressed by having an exhibition on Ishigaki Island for several days' [CAM 09]. 'We work as a team here, so even if someone proposed a good action plan, it could not be implemented individually' [CAM 01]. Action plans were to be implemented with institutional support, and many plans now seem to have been incorporated in the daily activities of the Tuol Sleng Museum.

The Tuol Sleng Museum is expanding its network of partners. According to Sdan Samrithpisey, who is responsible for organising confession documents, biographies, microfilms, magazines, and registration records, the digitalisation process has made significant progress thanks to the support of the Korea International Cooperation Agency (KOICA) and UNESCO [CAM 02]. 'Our first partner was Okinawa. But in 2016, we also collaborated with people of GIZ (Deutsche Gesellschaft für Internationale Zusammenarbeit) from Germany to hold an exhibition on forced marriages' [CAM 01]. In the future, it will be necessary to repair the building and prepare for the possible disappearance of people who can give testimony [CAM 04; CAM 13].

The chief objective of peace museums is to make peace perpetual for the next generations, and many interviewees stressed the priority of reaching out to young people. While the genocide is not widely taught in Cambodian history education, the government discusses including the atrocities at S-21 in school textbooks [CAM 03; CAM 14]. Ny Samnang, the chief of the exhibition section, was impressed by the approach in Okinawa, where students were taught both the Japanese and American perspectives, enabling them to form their own opinions [CAM 13]. While the majority of Cambodians are Buddhists, there are also Muslim citizens, so the promotion of religious coexistence is becoming an appropriate theme for Cambodian museums [CAM 01; CAM 26].

In this context, it is noteworthy that cooperation between the National Museum of Cambodia and the Tuol Sleng Genocide Museum is progressing within Cambodia. Oun Sokuntheavy stated, 'If the Genocide Museum is the shadow, then the National Museum is the light. I feel the shadow and the light are closely interconnected' [CAM 05]. Museum officials said that the idea given by the Okinawan museums of holding special exhibitions in addition to permanent ones was helpful [CAM 01; CAM 05]. 'The same Cambodian student may visit our museum five times from elementary school to university. To avoid repeating the same content, we try to organise special exhibitions in both museums' [CAM 26].

The National Museum of Cambodia displays ancient objects, inscriptions, and dynamic sculptures. Under the subdued lighting, the stone figures appeared to me to be genuinely smiling. The charm of the space was extraordinary. After listening to the director of the museum, Chhay Visoth, I understood that this effect was brought by careful design.

> We tried to effectively spotlight the exhibits. Since direct sunlight from outside is inappropriate, we should keep the space dark, but completely blocking the room would prevent fresh air from entering and inhibit the natural feel. So we installed soft, semi-transparent curtains. From inside, the garden outside can be faintly seen. We wanted visitors to feel something special here. [CAM 26]

Chhay Visoth had taken the helm of the Genocide Museum for years. Although some claimed that Tuol Suleng had been used as propaganda for Vietnam, he refuted this, citing the existential truth left by one victim. 'People were chained in small cells and unable to stand up. One person carved numbers with fingernails into the wall near the floor. Day one, day two, day three, day four.... stopped. The person was executed. Many left only their initials as their identity' [CAM 26]. The remains of the Tuol Sleng are carefully preserved to convey the untold message of victims to the next generations.

6.4.7 Water for Human Security

Cambodia has a glorious past, a tragic recent history, and a future to come. For peace to take root, it is essential that people's lives gradually improve. To achieve this, a good socio-economic infrastructure must be in place, and such a system should be maintained by the people of that country. Since a major donor may abruptly decide to withdraw as we witnessed in the case of the dismantlement of the USAID in 2025, self-reliance is a *sine qua non* for successful nation-building and human security.

The case studies in this book began with the water management project in the Brantas River basin in Indonesia in Chap. 2. I would like to conclude this book by returning to the question of water to make both ends of the book meet. With the assistance from Japan, including the forward-looking contribution from Kitakyushu City, the water supply infrastructure of the capital city of Cambodia, Phnom Penh, has been rehabilitated and greatly improved (Chan 2009; Suzuki and Kuwajima 2015; Spencer and Meng 2019; Biswas et al. 2021). As the Pol Pot regime exterminated professional engineers, there were few professionals left to repair the infrastructure destroyed in the civil war, which included the water supply system. In 1993, only about 20% of the population of Phnom Penh had access to tap water. The rate of non-revenue water due to leakage, water theft, and the failure to collect fees amounted to 72% (Biswas et al. 2021: 22). In the same year, a man called Ek Sonn Chan was appointed director general of the Phnom Penh Water Supply Authority. Originally a physics teacher, Ek Sonn Chan had survived the Pol Pot era and was working tirelessly in the government for the reconstruction of Cambodia. His father was a soldier of the Khmer Rouge and was killed by the Khmer Rouge itself, and he nurtured a strong sense of independent justice (Leong 2010).

Japan, France, and the World Bank have provided support for the rehabilitation of Cambodia's water supply. In addition to the provision of yen loans, JICA was involved in technology transfer and took the lead in drawing up a master plan for the reconstruction of the water supply system in Phnom Penh. Ek Sonn Chan actively promoted young staff and in the 2000s installed second-hand telemeters (devices that electronically transmit the data of piped water flow to the information centre) with the support of Kitakyushu City to thoroughly eliminate water theft. Kitakyushu is a major industrial city in the northernmost part of Kyushu, and because of the past serious public pollution, the municipality has been keen to provide clean water to its citizens.

Ek Sonn Chan praised JICA, but what he emphasised was not the generosity of the assistance but the flexibility of its attitude. 'Donors want to stick to their original plans. They hate to deviate from them. But JICA did not follow such conventional methods but provided the necessary support according to the needs on the ground.' After the Standard Operating Procedures (SOPs) full of descriptions of 'specificity' necessary to maintain the system (Sect. 1.2.2) were established, Ek Sonn Chan and his team translated the document into Khmer and updated it with the spirit of Cambodians' ownership. Kitakyushu was involved in all processes. According to Mori Kazumasa, who initiated the collaboration, 'Kitakyushu City doesn't expect any major replacement of the water facilities in the next few decades. By helping Cambodia, we can test and preserve our technical expertise for the future generations. In this way, the project also benefits us, the citizens of Kitakyushu.'[32] By 2003, Cambodians began to disseminate the lessons learnt in Phnom Penh to other provinces in Cambodia. To date, the water supply coverage rate in Phnom Penh has reached almost 100%, and the ratio of the non-revenue water has dropped to less than 10%. The quality of tap water met the WHO standards in 2004 and is now safe for everyone to drink (Vanny et al. 2015). From 1993 to 2019, the number of customers of the Phnom Penh Water Supply Authority increased by 14.5 times, while the volume of treated water increased by 14.2 times (Biswas et al. 2021: 60, 109). The reform has been dubbed the 'Miracle of Phnom Penh' and has become a model for water infrastructure development in South Sudan and other developing countries. In the meantime, Kitakyushu is extending its collaborating partners to Asian nations including Vietnam.

The colleagues of Ek Sonn Chan also spoke out. Long Naro, who heads the Phnom Penh Water Supply Authority, studied mechanical engineering in East Germany, returned to Cambodia in 1989, and then worked for Oxfam for a while. 'Working with people from different countries has been beneficial for my career… I think the Japanese experts taught us in a thoughtful way. They didn't do things for us. They had things they wanted us to do, give advice to us, and waited for us to put them

[32] International development has served as capacity development for municipal governments. Based on the interview with Mr Mori in Kitakyushu on Monday, 29 July, 2024.

into practice' [CAM 23]. One of his deputies, Ma Noravin, 'studied water supply technology at Hokkaido University together with international students from around the world' [CAM 24]. Another deputy, Pheng Ty, said, 'In the first phase, we learnt from JICA, but now we serve as trainers for trainees of other provinces in the water sector' [CAM 25]. In Phnom Penh, I also spoke with several local citizens. While making lard in a big frying pan, a grocery shop owner said, 'I make lunch boxes for my husband's documentary film crew. I use a lot of water for my work' [CAM 22]. A garage owner said, 'Even on the third floor, the water pressure is strong enough' [CAM 21]. Both were happy with the quality of the water.

Many foreign visitors to museums in Phnom Penh visit Siem Reap as well. In this city, home to the ruins of Angkor, tourism requires a lot of water. Officers from the Siem Reap Water Supply Authority showed me around a brand new water treatment plant near Tonlé Sap Lake, the largest freshwater lake in Southeast Asia. Sam Senghan said that their job is stable and rewarding [CAM 15]. Van Sosamneang said that promoting competition was necessary between public utilities and private firms [CAM 16]. Kong Kun said, 'A friend from Kitakyushu came a long way to attend my wedding and flew back after the event' [CAM 17]. Citizens who recently gained access to tap water said, 'We used water from the well in the backyard, but it was muddy.' Some expressed regret, saying, 'Tap water is convenient, so we tend to use too much.' The citizens I encountered were enjoying their casual conversations with the field staff of the Water Supply Authority [CAM 18; CAM 19; CAM 20]. The benefit of urban infrastructure in Cambodia was obvious, but I did not have a chance to visit rural villages for interviews. Khut Vuthiarith, who was once dispatched by Ek Sonn Chan to solve problems in Siem Reap, wanted to advance guidance and facilitation for local private water companies. 'Urban customers use smartphone apps, but this hasn't penetrated rural areas. I want to prioritize rural areas in national water policies' [CAM 28].

There are two types of water. One is consumed directly by people, and the other is used indirectly by industry. Ek Sonn Chan argued that the former should be prioritised because supplying drinking water to everyone is a matter of 'security of society'. Tackling water theft was not just about financial self-reliance. It is a question of people's attitudes. He said:

> In the past, a lot of water was wasted. If people didn't pay water bills but used water for free as much as they wanted, we'd never nurture a sense of shared ownership. You should collect fees to recover costs. Otherwise, the system won't be sustainable. We need to foster a sense of responsibility. Think of it – if you save money to buy something, you'll take care of it. If you get it for free, you won't care. [CAM 27]

At the same time, water is the source of human life. A society in which the wealthy monopolise water is not a just society. He continued:

> We didn't stop providing water to poor people who didn't pay. Water bills are issued every two months. I was given a list of those who didn't pay, which was a very long list. My colleagues and I took the time to visit them door-to-door to find out why they didn't pay, why they couldn't afford even one dollar. Some had lost family members. Some had been ill, had been in accidents, or had been killed. There were people who had no means to pay. I told them, 'OK. I will pay for you. I will pay out of my purse.' And I explained to them

> that people in Japan are helping us. Even though the Japanese live far away, they think about the people of Cambodia. Cambodians who have learnt this become deeply grateful. What is important is to go to the people and explain everything honestly. [CAM 27]

When the conversation turned to families who had lost loved ones and been plunged into poverty, Ek Sonn Chan seemed to recall something, momentarily lost for words, and his eyes filled with tears in front of me. The primary motivation for development cooperation lies not in operating a machine-like, meticulously constructed institution, but in saving the life of each and every person in dire straits. And where there are dedicated leaders like Ek Sonn Chan, people will be eager to do something. The experts from Kitakyushu were not obtruding something but involved in the process initiated by such Cambodians.

The most significant feature of the currents of world history in the twentieth century has been the successive emergence of nation-states in the Global South. Within the framework of an emerging nation-state, substantial support was needed to make the feedback between the principals and the agents work. Consequently, much of this book, which describes the history of Japan's post-war development cooperation with other peoples, consists of narratives of nation-building through human (resources) development. However, as the world has become more interconnected, the destitution, deprivation, and suffering of people in other countries has begun to be perceived as 'our concerns', leading to a shift in the goal of development cooperation from nation-building to the security and well-being of every individual. This shift involves treating others not as means but as ends in themselves, so that all people, regardless of their conditions and social circumstances, are treated with dignity and respect and no one is left behind. Looking back on the case studies in each chapter from the perspective of this final chapter, it becomes clear that the goal of development cooperation has been to ensure that human dignity prevails everywhere in the world. Normatively, that was the case with the best part of Japan's experience, and I believe that the same applies to other donors.

Ultimately, the efforts towards nation-building and human security that Japan has supported can be regarded as a vital phase towards the realisation of a flourishing, equitable, and harmonious international society, the value of which must be revisited and constantly reaffirmed in our ongoing journey. The stories recounted in this volume, drawn from the experiences of Japan and its partners, are only a part of an ever-evolving corpus of narratives on international development. By leveraging spoken evidence, a richer and more inclusive global tapestry of oral histories of development cooperation will undoubtedly take shape, involving both emerging and traditional donors and their wider partners. I believe with the utmost confidence that this will happen.

List of Interviewees

The information in the list below is arranged in this order: [CODE] Name, Age, Gender. Position, Affiliation. Date of Interview, Place of Interview. The age, the position, and the affiliation of the interviewee are as of the time of the interview.

In the pre-arranged interviews, the significance of the research, the questions, and the intentions of these questions were explained in writing and verbally, and the interviewees were asked whether they wished their stories to remain anonymous. If this was the case, or if the interviews were arranged ad hoc *on the spot, or if the interviewees were minors without parental consent, the author anonymised them.*

[BRA 01] Maria Julia Tobase (飛瀬マリア・ジュリア), 22, F. Estudante de direito, Fundação Getulio Vargas. Segunda-feira 5 de agosto, 2019. Agência de Cooperação Internacional do Japão, Escritório em Brasília (JICA Brazil Office), São Paulo, Brasil.
[BRA 02] Jerson Hideaki Konishi (小西ジェルソン英明), 45, M. Departamento de vendas, Itaú Bank. Segunda-feira 5 de agosto, 2019. JICA Brazil Office, São Paulo, Brasil.
[BRA 03] Rumi Koroku Hisataka (高鹿久高ルミ), 14, F. Estudante, Colégio ETAPA. Segunda-feira 5 de agosto, 2019. JICA Brazil Office, São Paulo, Brasil.
[BRA 04] Daniel Akira Hashimoto (橋本ダニエル明), 20, M. Estudante, Instituto de Relações Internacionais da Universidade de São Paulo. Segunda-feira 5 de agosto, 2019. JICA Brazil Office, São Paulo, Brasil.
[BRA 05] Felipe Satoshi Takamura (高村フェリペ聡), 28, M. Banco de Sangue, Hospital Samaritano. Segunda-feira 5 de agosto, 2019. JICA Brazil Office, São Paulo, Brasil.
[BRA 06] Shizuo Abuno (鐙野獅珠雄), 24, M. Gerente de uma empresa agrícola. Terça-feira 6 de agosto, 2019. JICA Brazil Office, São Paulo, Brasil.
[BRA 07] Willian Kengo Tsukahara Ochi (塚原越智ウィリアン健吾), 18, M. Estudante de administração de empresas, Universidade Tecnológica Federal do Paraná. Terça-feira 6 de agosto, 2019. JICA Brazil Office, São Paulo, Brasil.

Y. Mine, *An Oral History of Development Cooperation*,
https://doi.org/10.1007/978-981-95-5479-9

[BRA 08] Eduardo Masao Tsukahara (塚原エドゥアルド正雄), 54, M. Diretor, Membro do comitê executivo, Cerâmica e Velas de Ignição NGK do Brasil ltda. Terça-feira 6 de agosto, 2019. JICA Brazil Office, São Paulo, Brasil.
[BRA 09] Isabel Satoko Ochi Ito, (越智伊藤イサベル諭子), 54, F. Professor de língua japonesa, Associação Cultural de Mogi das Cruzes. Terça-feira 6 de agosto, 2019. JICA Brazil Office, São Paulo, Brasil.
[BRA 10] Masayuki Mizuno (水野昌之), 95, M. Ex-repórter de jornal, editor e gerente de fazenda. Quarta-feira 7 de agosto, 2019. Perdizes, São Paulo, Brasil.
[BRA 11] Yoshio Leandro Maruoka (丸岡義雄レアンドロ), 22, M. Estudante de escola preparatória. Sábado 10 de agosto, 2019. Associação Pan Amazônia Nipo-Brasileira, São Brás, Belém, Brasil.
[BRA 12] Hiromi Hayashi (林寛美), 30, F. Professor de escola de língua japonesa. Sábado 10 de agosto, 2019. Associação Pan Amazônia Nipo-Brasileira, São Brás, Belém, Brasil.
[BRA 13] Daniel Sadayoshi Otsuki (大槻定芳ダニエル), 43, M. Gerente de incubatório. Domingo 11 de agosto, 2019. Radisson Hotel Belém, Belém, Brasil.
[BRA 14] Jonathas Hisamitsu (ジョナタス・ヒサミツ), 36, M. Designer de tecnologia da informação. Terça-feira 13 de agosto, 2019. Marco, Belém, Brasil.
[BRA 15] Jean Remy Davée Guimarães, 63, M. Professor Titular, Chefe do Laboratório de Traçadores, Instituto de Biofísica Carlos Chagas Filho, Universidade Federal do Rio de Janeiro. Quinta-feira 8 de agosto, 2019. Cidade Universitária, Rio de Janeiro, Brasil
[BRA 16] Olaf Malm, 62, M. Professor Titular, Chefe do Laboratório de Radioisótopos Eduardo Penna Franca, Instituto de Biofísica Carlos Chagas Filho, Universidade Federal do Rio de Janeiro. Quinta-feira 8 de agosto, 2019. Cidade Universitária, Rio de Janeiro, Brasil
[BRA 17] Zuleica C. Castilhos, 57, F. Pesquisador sênior. Centro de Tecnologia Mineral (CETEM), Ministério da Ciência, Tecnologia e Inovação. Quinta-feira 8 de agosto, 2019. Cidade Universitária, Rio de Janeiro, Brasil
[BRA 18] Patrícia Correia de Araújo, 49, F. Pesquisador de química, Centro de Tecnologia Mineral (CETEM), Ministério da Ciência, Tecnologia e Inovação. Quinta-feira 8 de agosto, 2019. Cidade Universitária, Rio de Janeiro, Brasil
[BRA 19] Elizabeth C. de O. Santos, 80, F. Ex-diretora, Instituto Evandro Chagas. Sábado 10 de agosto, 2019. Sua residência, Cremação, Belém, Brasil
[BRA 20] Terezinha Maria Cid de Souza, 61, F. Ex-coordenadora do Laboratório de Análises de Mercúrio, Departamento Nacional de Produção Mineral (DNPM). Segunda-feira 12 de agosto, 2019. Agência Nacional de Mineração, Marco, Belém, Brasil
[BRA 21] Maria da Conceição Nascimento Pinheiro, 66, F. Professora do curso de Medicina, Coordenadora do Laboratório de Toxicologia Humana e Ambiental, Universidade Federal do Pará – Núcleo de Medicina Tropical (UFPA-NMT). Segunda-feira 12 de agosto, 2019. UFPA-NMT, Umarizal, Belém, Brasil
[BRA 22] Marcelo de Oliveira Lima, 48, M. Coordenador do Laboratório de Mercúrio, Instituto Evandro Chagas. Terça-feira 13 de agosto, 2019. IEC, Ananindeua, Pará, Brasil

[BRA 23] Iracina Maura de Jesus, 54, F. Ex-chefe da Seção de Meio Ambiente, Instituto Evandro Chagas. Terça-feira 13 de agosto, 2019. IEC, Ananindeua, Pará, Brasil

[BRA 24] João Paulo Góes Pereira, 32, M. Técnico em pesquisa, Instituto Evandro Chagas. Terça-feira 13 de agosto, 2019. IEC, Ananindeua, Pará, Brasil

[BRA 25] Antonio Marcos Mota Miranda, 58, M. Pesquisador em Saúde Pública, Instituto Evandro Chagas. Terça-feira 13 de agosto, 2019. IEC, Ananindeua, Pará, Brasil

[BRA 26] Kleber Freitas Faial, 51, M. Pesquisador em Saúde Pública, Instituto Evandro Chagas. Terça-feira 13 de agosto, 2019. IEC, Ananindeua, Pará, Brasil

[CAM 01] Hang Nisay, 39, M. Director, Tuol Sleng Genocide Museum (TSGM). Thursday, 8 August 2024. TSGM, Boeung Keng Kang, Phnom Penh, Cambodia

[CAM 02] Sdan Samrithpisey, 50, F. Deputy Head, Archives Section, TSGM. Thursday, 8 August 2024. TSGM, Boeung Keng Kang, Phnom Penh, Cambodia

[CAM 03] Heng Sophara, 37, F. Head, Education Section, TSGM. Thursday, 8 August 2024. TSGM, Boeung Keng Kang, Phnom Penh, Cambodia

[CAM 04] Chhem Sokchamreoun, 39, M. Staff member, Education Section, TSGM. Thursday, 8 August 2024. TSGM, Boeung Keng Kang, Phnom Penh, Cambodia

[CAM 05] Oun Sokuntheavy, 50, F. Deputy Director in Charge of Education and Dissemination, National Museum of Cambodia (NMC). Friday, 9 August 2024. NMC, Chey Chumneah, Phnom Penh, Cambodia

[CAM 06] Chhab Sopheara, 43, F. Deputy Director in Charge of Conservation and Planning Projects, NMC. Friday, 9 August 2024. NMC, Chey Chumneah, Phnom Penh, Cambodia

[CAM 07] Ke Sophanaka, 53, M. Chief, Project and Legal Document Office, NMC. Friday, 9 August 2024. NMC, Chey Chumneah, Phnom Penh Cambodia

[CAM 08] Keo Monyroth, 50, M. Deputy Head, Project and Exhibition Section, TSGM. Friday, 9 August 2024. TSGM, Boeung Keng Kang, Phnom Penh, Cambodia

[CAM 09] Prak Sothy, 51, F. Deputy Head, Archives Section, TSGM. Friday, 9 August 2024. TSGM, Boeung Keng Kang, Phnom Penh, Cambodia

[CAM 10] Bun Korng, 51, M. Deputy Head, Administration, Cleaning and Security Section, TSGM. Friday, 9 August 2024. TSGM, Boeung Keng Kang, Phnom Penh, Cambodia

[CAM 11] Chhey Sophearith, 41, M. Staff member, Archives Section, TSGM. Friday, 9 August 2024. TSGM, Boeung Keng Kang, Phnom Penh, Cambodia

[CAM 12] Phal Kun, 54, M. Head, Administration Section, TSGM. Friday, 9 August 2024. TSGM, Boeung Keng Kang, Phnom Penh, Cambodia

[CAM 13] Ny Samnang, 42, M. Head, Exhibition Section, TSGM. Friday, 9 August 2024. TSGM, Boeung Keng Kang, Phnom Penh, Cambodia

[CAM 14] Hor Chanleasksmy, 36, F. Chief Tour Guide, TSGM. Friday, 9 August 2024. TSGM, Boeung Keng Kang, Phnom Penh, Cambodia

[CAM 15] Sam Senghan, 43, M. Director of Commercial Department, Chreav Water Supply Authority (SRWSA). Monday, 12 August 2024. Chreav Water Treatment Plant. Chreav, Siem Reap, Cambodia

[CAM 16] Van Sosamneang, 36, F. Director of Internal Audit, SRWSA. Monday, 12 August 2024. Chreav Water Treatment Plant. Chreav, Siem Reap, Cambodia

[CAM 17] Kong Kun, 37, M. Deputy Director of Commercial Department, SRWSA. Monday, 12 August 2024. Chreav Water Treatment Plant. Chreav, Siem Reap, Cambodia

[CAM 18] Anonymous. Monday, 12 August 2024. In front of their shops, Kantreang, Prasat Bakong, Siem Reap, Cambodia

[CAM 19] Anonymous. Shop owner. Monday, 12 August 2024. In front of her shop, Kantreang, Prasat Bakong, Siem Reap Province, Cambodia

[CAM 20] Anonymous. Shop owner. Monday, 12 August 2024. In front of his house, Roluos, Prasat Bakong, Siem Reap, Cambodia

[CAM 21] Anonymous. Garage owner. Tuesday, 13 August 2024. Sangkat Srah Chak, Phnom Penh, Cambodia

[CAM 22] Anonymous. Grocery shop owner. Tuesday, 13 August 2024. Sangkat Srah Chak, Phnom Penh, Cambodia

[CAM 23] Long Naro, 58, M. Director General, Phnom Penh Water Supply Authority (PPWSA). Tuesday, 13 August 2024. PPWSA, Sangkat Srah Chak, Phnom Penh, Cambodia

[CAM 24] Ma Noravin, 51, M. Deputy Director General, PPWSA. Tuesday, 13 August 2024. PPWSA, Sangkat Srah Chak, Phnom Penh, Cambodia

[CAM 25] Pheng Ty, 51, M. Deputy Director General, PPWSA. Tuesday, 13 August 2024. PPWSA, Sangkat Srah Chak, Phnom Penh, Cambodia

[CAM 26] Chhay Visoth, 46, M. Director, National Museum of Cambodia (NMC). Tuesday, 13 August 2024. NMC, Chey Chumneah, Phnom Penh, Cambodia

[CAM 27] Ek Sonn Chan, 74, M. Board Chair, PPWSA. Wednesday, 14 August 2024. PPWSA, Sangkat Srah Chak, Phnom Penh, Cambodia

[CAM 28] Khut Vuthiarith, 61, M. Under Secretary of State, Ministry of Industry, Science, Technology and Innovation (MISTI). Wednesday, 14 August 2024. MISTI, Sangkat Phsar, Thmey III, Phnom Penh, Cambodia

[CHL 01] Carlos Conley Milo, 74, M. Ex-Subdirector Nacional, Servicio Nacional de Pesca (SERNAP). Domingo 28 de julio, 2019. Sheraton Miramar Hotel & Convention Center, Viña del Mar, Chile

[CHL 02] Tulio Zuñiga, 71, M. Ex-Jefe de Área en Puerto Aguirre, SERNAP. Domingo 28 de julio, 2019. Sheraton Miramar Hotel & Convention Center, Viña del Mar, Chile

[CHL 03] Jorge Katz Sliapnik, 78, M. Profesor Titular, Universidad de Chile. Lunes 29 de julio, 2019. Departamento de Economía, Facultad Economía y Negocios, Universidad de Chile, Diagonal Paraguay, Santiago, Chile

[CHL 04] Pablo Aguilera Marín, 74, M. Ex-Director Regional de Aysén, Servicio Nacional de Pesca y Acuicultura (SERNAPESCA). Lunes 29 de julio, 2019. Su residencia, Las Condes, Santiago, Chile

[CHL 05] Pablo Martens, 66, M. Gerente, Jumbo Puente Alto. Lunes 29 de julio, 2019. Cafetería, Alto Las Condes, Santiago, Chile
[CHL 06] Mario Humberto Puchi Acuña, 68, M. Ex-Jefe Provincial de SERNAP Aysén. Martes 30 de julio, 2019. Inversiones El Pampino, Puerto Montt, Chile
[CHL 07] Hector Novoa, 71, M. Ex-funcionario SERNAP Coyhaique. Martes 30 de julio, 2019. Presidente Suites Puerto Montt, Puerto Montt, Chile
[CHL 08] Miriam Chávez, 44, F. Presidenta del Sindicato Número 3 Aguas Claras, AquaChile, y Elena Zuniga, 50, F. Tesorero del Sindicato Número 3 Aguas Claras, AquaChile. Martes 30 de julio, 2019. Cafetería, Calbuco, Chile
[CHL 09] Marcelo Guerra, 48, M. Jefe de Área, AquaChile Mañihuales, Puerto Aysén. Miércoles 31 de julio, 2019. Hotel Diego de Almagro, Coyhaique, Chile
[CHL 10] Anónimo. Jueves 1 de agosto, 2019. Fundación Chinquihue, Puerto Montt, Chile
[CHL 11] Anónimo. Jueves 1 de agosto, 2019. Fundación Chinquihue, Puerto Montt, Chile
[CHL 12] Javier Valencia Camp, 59, M. Subgerente de Desarrollo e Innovación. Jueves 1 de agosto, 2019. Fundación Chinquihue, Puerto Montt, Chile
[CHL 13] Rodolfo Aguirrebeña, 67, M. Ex- Jefe de Laboratorio en Coyhaique, Centro Piscicultura Dr. Yoshikazu Shiraishi, Servicio Nacional de Pesca (SERNAP). Jueves 1 de agosto, 2019. Presidente Suites Puerto Montt, Puerto Montt
[CHL 14] Eduardo Cárdenas, 65, M. Ex-funcionario de SERNAP Aysén. Viernes 2 de agosto, 2019. Cafetería, Dalcahue, Chiloé, Chile
[CHL 15] Mario Vargas González, 70, M. Ex-Jefe de Departamento Técnico, SERNAP. Viernes 2 de agosto, 2019. Cafetería, Castro, Chiloé, Chile
[CHL 16] Anónimo. Sábado 3 de agosto, 2019. Presidente Suites Puerto Montt, Puerto Montt, Chile
[CRI 01] José Arce Brenes, 45, M. Gestor de Políticas Públicas de PYME, Departamento de Empresariado, Dirección General de Apoyo a la Pequeña y Mediana Empresa (DIGEPYME), Ministerio de Economía, Industria y Comercio (MEIC). Lunes 22 de julio, 2019. MEIC, San José, Costa Rica
[CRI 02] Enrique González Villalobos, 57, M. Coordinador Programa de Gestión Ambiental para el Desarrollo Sostenible, Universidad Técnica Nacional (UTN). Lunes 22 de julio, 2019. UTN Sede Central, Villa Bonita, Alajuela, Costa Rica
[CRI 03] Arlette Jiménez Silva, 53, F. Coordinadora Técnico Superior Laboratorista Químico, Centro de Calidad y Productividad (CECAPRO), Universidad Técnica Nacional (UTN). Lunes 22 de julio, 2019. UTN Sede Central, Villa Bonita, Alajuela, Costa Rica
[CRI 04] Luigi Longhi Córdoba, 49, M. Coordinador Técnico Superior en Productividad y Calidad, Centro de Calidad y Productividad (CECAPRO), Universidad Técnica Nacional (UTN). Martes 23 de julio, 2019. UTN Sede Central, Villa Bonita, Alajuela, Costa Rica
[CRI 05] Zianno Ramírez Arias, 54, F. Consultora, Centro de Calidad y Productividad (CECAPRO), Universidad Técnica Nacional (UTN). Martes 23 de julio, 2019. UTN Sede Central, Villa Bonita, Alajuela, Costa Rica

[CRI 06] Gregorio Arce Gómez, 59, M. Coordinador Técnico Superior en Dirección de Proyectos, Centro de Calidad y Productividad (CECAPRO), Universidad Técnica Nacional (UTN). Martes 23 de julio, 2019. UTN Sede Central, Villa Bonita, Alajuela, Costa Rica

[CRI 07] Marvin Herrera García, 51, M. Consultor, Centro de Calidad y Productividad (CECAPRO), Universidad Técnica Nacional (UTN). Martes 23 de julio, 2019. UTN Sede Central, Villa Bonita, Alajuela, Costa Rica

[CRI 08] Marvin Herrera Araya, 79, M. Ex-Ministro de Educación Pública. Martes 23 de julio, 2019. Su residencia, Barrio El Carmen, Alajuela Centro, Costa Rica

[CRI 09] Hazel Rojas García, 54, F. Directora, Centro de Calidad y Productividad (CECAPRO), Universidad Técnica Nacional (UTN). Miércoles 24 de julio, 2019. Fábrica Irex, Concepción, Cartago, Costa Rica

[CRI 10] Anónimo. Miércoles 24 de julio, 2019. Fábrica Irex, Concepción, Cartago, Costa Rica

[CRI 11] Anónimo. Miércoles 24 de julio, 2019. Fábrica Irex, Concepción, Cartago, Costa Rica

[CRI 12] Anónimo. Miércoles 24 de julio, 2019. Fábrica Irex, Concepción, Cartago, Costa Rica

[CRI 13] Daniel Rodríguez Molina, 45, M. Gerente de Gestión de Calidad, Roma Prince, S.A. Viernes 26 de julio, 2019. Fábrica de Roma Prince, S.A., Villa Bonita, Alajuela, Costa Rica

[CRI 14] Giovanni Artavia Quesada, 40. M. Asistente de Manufactura, Roma Prince, S.A. Viernes 26 de julio, 2019. Fábrica de Roma Prince, S.A., Villa Bonita, Alajuela, Costa Rica

[CRI 15] Andrés Jiménez Quiros, 34, M. Técnico en Metrología, Roma Prince, S.A. Viernes 26 de julio, 2019. Fábrica de Roma Prince, S.A., Villa Bonita, Alajuela, Costa Rica

[GHA 01] Abraham Kwabena Anang, 58, M. Director, Noguchi Memorial Institute for Medical Research (NMIMR), University of Ghana. Monday, 25 February 2019. NMIMR, Legon, Accra, Ghana

[GHA 02] Mike Fransisco Ribeiro, 75, M. Former Register of College of Medical Sciences, University of Ghana. Monday, 25 February 2019. NMIMR, Legon, Accra, Ghana

[GHA 03] Maxwell Alexandar Appawu, 72, M. Associate Professor, Parasitology Division, NMIMR, University of Ghana. Tuesday, 26 February 2019. West African Centre for International Parasite Control (WACIPAC), NMIMR, Legon, Accra, Ghana

[GHA 04] George Armah, 63, M. Professor, Electron Microscopy Department, NMIMR, University of Ghana. Tuesday, 26 February 2019. NMIMR, Legon, Accra, Ghana

[GHA 05] Andrew Anthony Adjei, 63, M. Professor, Office of the Vice Chancellor, University of Ghana. Tuesday, 26 February 2019. Vice Chancellor's Strategic Office, University of Ghana, Legon, Accra, Ghana

[GHA 06] Richard Berko Biritwun, 73, M. Professor, Department of Public Health, University of Ghana Medical School. Wednesday, 27 February 2019. Teaching Hospital, University of Ghana, Korle Bu, Accra, Ghana
[GHA 07] Isabella Akyinbah Quakyi, 72, F. Professor, Foundation Dean, School of Public Health, College of Health Sciences, University of Ghana. Wednesday, 27 February 2019. NMIMR, Legon, Accra, Ghana
[GHA 08] Julius Mingle, 81, M. Professor, College of Medical Sciences, University of Ghana Medical School. Wednesday, 27 February 2019. Clinical Virology Laboratory, College of Health Sciences, University of Ghana, Korle Bu, Accra, Ghana
[GHA 09] Margaret Armar-Klemesu, 64, F. Professor, Nutrition Unit, NMIMR, University of Ghana. Thursday, 28 February 2019. NMIMR, Legon, Accra, Ghana
[GHA 10] Kwame Gabriel Attorkwe, 70, M. Former Chief Accounting Assistant, NMIMR, University of Ghana. Thursday, 28 February 2019. NMIMR, Legon, Accra, Ghana
[GHA 11] Badu Sarkodie, 58, M. Director, Public Health, Ghana Health Service. Friday, 1 March 2019. Ghana Health Service, Accra, Ghana
[GHA 12] George Amofah, 65, M. Former Deputy Director General, Ghana Health Service. Friday, 1 March 2019. National Malaria Control Programme Office, Accra, Ghana
[GHA 13] Alexander Nyarko, 65, M. Professor, School of Pharmacy, University of Ghana. Friday, 1 March 2019. School of Pharmacy, College of Health Sciences, University of Ghana, Legon, Accra, Ghana
[GHA 14] Michael David Wilson, 68, M. Department of Parasitology, NMIMR, University of Ghana. Friday, 1 March 2019. Lymphatic Filariasis Support Centre for Africa, NMIMR, University of Ghana, Legon, Accra, Ghana
[GHA 15] Anette Annan, 83, F. Chief's wife. Gomoa Fetteh. Saturday, 2 March 2019. Her Residence, Gomoa Fetteh, Central Region, Ghana
[GHA 16] Sampson A.K. Akyeh, 80, M. Former health inspector. Saturday, 2 March 2019. Residence of Chief, Gomoa Fetteh, Central Region, Ghana
[GHA 17] Zacharias Appah, 81, M. Former worker at Noguchi Clinic. Saturday, 2 March 2019. Residence of Chief, Gomoa Fetteh, Central Region, Ghana
[IDN 01] Anonymous. Monday, 27 August 2018. Ministry of Public Works and Public Housing, Jakarta, Indonesia
[IDN 02] Airlangga Mardjono, 47, M. Chief, Division of Dam for Western Region. Monday, 27 August 2018. Ministry of Public Works and Public Housing, Jakarta, Indonesia
[IDN 03] Fauzi Idris, 57, M. Director of Water Resource Management, Ministry of Public Works and Public Housing. Tuesday, 28 August 2018. Ministry of Public Works and Public Housing, Jakarta, Indonesia
[IDN 04] Muhammad Amir Hamzah, 59, M. Head of Center of Ground Water and Raw Water, Ministry of Public Works and Housing. Tuesday, 28 August 2018. Ministry of Public Works and Public Housing, Jakarta, Indonesia

[IDN 05] Almizan Abdullah, 84, M. Former President, PT Brantas Abipraya, and former Professor, Institut Teknologi Nasional Malang. Tuesday, 28 August 2018. His residence, Bintaro, Jakarta, Indonesia

[IDN 06] Anonymous. Wednesday, 29 August 2018. Jasa Tirta I Selorejo Office, Malang, East Java, Indonesia

[IDN 07] Anonymous. Wednesday, 29 August 2018. Jasa Tirta I Selorejo Office, Malang, East Java, Indonesia

[IDN 08] Hardiono, 67, M. Teacher, Professor Suryono Vocational High School. Thursday, 30 August 2018. Professor Suryono Vocational High School, Karangkates, Malang, East Java, Indonesia

[IDN 09] Bedjo Siswojo, 76, M. Principal, Intermediate Section, Professor Suryono Vocational High School. Thursday, 30 August 2018. Professor Suryono Vocational High School, Karangkates, Malang, East Java, Indonesia

[IDN 10] Mujianto, 58, M. Former radio announcer. Thursday, 30 August 2018. Jasa Tirta I South Tulungagung Tunnels Office, Tulungagung, East Java, Indonesia

[IDN 11] Sutomo, 66, M. Former officer, South Tulungagung Tunnels. Thursday, 30 August 2018. Jasa Tirta I South Tulungagung Tunnels Office, Tulungagung, East Java, Indonesia

[IDN 12] Abdul Aziz Hoesein, 72, M. Senior Lecturer, Department of Water Resources Engineering, Universitas Brawijaya. Friday, 31 August 2018. Universitas Brawijaya, Malang, East Java, Indonesia

[IDN 13] Rusfandi Usman, 77, M. Former President Director, Jasa Tirta I. Friday, 31 August 2018. His residence, Malang, East Java, Indonesia

[IDN 14] Siti Zubaidah, 72, F. Mr Rusfandi Usman's wife. Friday, 31 August 2018. Their residence, Malang, East Java, Indonesia

[IDN 15] Hasan Bisri, 66, M. Former President Director, Indra Karya. Friday, 31 August 2018. Indra Karya Malang Office, Malang, East Java, Indonesia

[IDN 16] Setyo Adiwidjono, 70, M. Chief Director, Sijanti Dinamika Teknika. Friday, 31 August 2018. Indra Karya Malang Office, Malang, East Java, Indonesia

[IDN 17] Tjoek Walujo Subijanto, 70, M. Former President Director of Jasa Tirta I. Saturday, 1 September 2018. Swissbel-Inn Malang, Malang, East Java, Indonesia

[IDN 18] Roedjito Dwidjomustopo, 77, M. Former President, Brantas River Basin Development Project Office, and Former President, Jasa Tirta I. Saturday, 1 September 2018. His residence, Malang, East Java, Indonesia

[JOR 01] Khawla Kawwa, 66, F. Former Head, Division of Family Planning and Reproductive Health, Ministry of Health, Jordan. Sunday, 26 January 2020. JICA Jordan Office, Amman, Jordan.

[JOR 02] Nuha Hanna Muhreiz, 62, F. Former Program Supervisor, Jordanian Hashemite Fund for Human Development (JOHUD). Sunday, 26 January 2020. JICA Jordan Office, Amman, Jordan

[JOR 03] Abdulmonim Malkawi, 54, M. Former Technical Expert, Higher Population Council (HPC). Sunday, 26 January 2020. JICA Jordan Office, Amman, Jordan

[JOR 04] Hiam Hamie, F. Former Head of Woman and Child Department, Karak Office, Ministry of Health. Monday, 27 January 2020. Karak Clinic, Institute for Family Health (IFH), Karak Governorate, Jordan
[JOR 05] Kittie Tawfig Jamil Hijazeen, 38. F. Health Educator, Ministry of Health. Monday, 27 January 2020. Al-Hmood Village Health Center, Karak Governorate, Jordan
[JOR 06] Anonymous. Housewife. Monday, 27 January 2020. Al-Hmood Village Health Center, Karak Governorate, Jordan
[JOR 07] Sahryeh Rawashdeh, 49, F. Housewife. Monday, 27 January 2020. Her residence, Musherfeh, Karak Governorate, Jordan
[JOR 08] Fawzieh Fahed Al-Zahran, 35, F. Health Educator, Ministry of Health. Tuesday, 28 January 2020. Al-Nake' Village Health Center, Karak Governorate, Jordan
[JOR 09] Anonymous. Housewife. Tuesday, 28 January 2020. Al-Nake' Village Health Center, Karak Governorate, Jordan
[JOR 10] Manal 'Mohammad said' Fares Al-Ghazawi, 55, F. Senior Researcher, Higher Population Council (HPC). Wednesday, 29 January 2020. JICA Jordan Office, Amman, Jordan
[KEN 01] Mabel Imbuga, 66, F. Vice Chancellor, Jomo Kenyatta University of Agriculture and Technology (JKUAT). Wednesday, 4 July 2018. JKUAT, Juja, Kiambu County, Kenya
[KEN 02] Glaston M. Kenji, 67, M. Director of Laboratories and Environmental Management, JKUAT. Wednesday, 4 July 2018. JKUAT, Juja, Kiambu County, Kenya
[KEN 03] Arnold N. Onyango, 44, M. Lecturer, Department of Food Science and Technology, JKUAT. Wednesday, 4 July 2018. JKUAT, Juja, Kiambu County, Kenya
[KEN 04] Paul Nyota Karanja, M. Chief Technologist–Laboratories, Department of Food Science and Technology, JKUAT. Thursday, 5 July 2018. JKUAT, Juja, Kiambu County, Kenya
[KEN 05] Daniel Ndaka Sila, 44, M. Lecturer, Department of Food Science and Technology, JKUAT. Thursday, 5 July 2018. JKUAT, Juja, Kiambu County, Kenya
[KEN 06] Bernard W. Ikua, 52, M. Principal, College of Engineering and Technology, JKUAT. Thursday, 5 July 2018. JKUAT, Juja, Kiambu County, Kenya
[KEN 07] Peter K. Kihato, 60, M. Manager, Engineering Workshops, JKUAT. Thursday, 5 July 2018. JKUAT, Juja, Kiambu County, Kenya
[KEN 08] Mwikamba Kaibui, 63, M. Linkages Directorate, JKUAT, Friday, 6 July 2018. JKUAT, Juja, Kiambu County, Kenya
[KEN 09] Naomi Nduhiu, 54, F. Senior Technologist in charge of Crop Production, Farm Department. Friday, 6 July 2018. JKUAT, Juja, Kiambu County, Kenya
[KEN 10] Johnson Muhara, 57, M. Chief Executive Officer, Afrimac. Friday, 6 July 2018. Afrimac Nut Company Ltd, Parklands, Nairobi, Kenya
[KEN 11] Ratemo W. Michieka, 67, M. Former Vice-Chancellor, Jomo Kenyatta University of Agriculture and Technology, and Professor, the University of Nairobi. Saturday, 7 July 2018. Sarova Panafric Hotel, Nairobi, Kenya

[KEN 12] Samuel K. Kibe, 78, M. Education Specialist, JICA Kenya Office. Monday, 9 July 2018. JICA Kenya Office, Nairobi, Kenya
[KEN 13] Bernard M. Njuguna, 60, M. Former Head, SMASSE In-Service Training Unit, KSTC (Kenya Science Teachers College). Monday, 9 July 2018. JICA Kenya Office, Nairobi, Kenya
[KEN 14] Simon Kariuki, 26, M. In-House Consultant, Education and Child Care Protection Sector, JICA Kenya Office. Monday, 9 July 2018. JICA Kenya Office, Nairobi, Kenya
[KEN 15] Stephen M. Njoroge, 60, M. Director, Centre for Mathematics, Science and Technology Education in Africa (CEMASTEA). Monday, 4 March 2019. CEMASTEA, Karen, Nairobi, Kenya
[KEN 16] Nchabira Lydia Muriithi, 54, F. Deputy Director, CEMASTEA. Monday, 4 March 2019. CEMASTEA, Karen, Nairobi, Kenya
[KEN 17] Muyanga B. Mutua, 55, M. National Trainer, CEMASTEA. Monday, 4 March 2019. CEMASTEA, Karen, Nairobi, Kenya
[KEN 18] Makoba Edmond Kizito, 51, M. National Trainer, CEMASTEA. Monday, 4 March 2019. CEMASTEA, Karen, Nairobi, Kenya
[KEN 19] Solomon Muina Mwangi, 57, M. Principal, Kiambu High School. Tuesday, 5 March 2019. Kiambu High School, Kiambu County, Kenya
[KEN 20] David Mwangi Kareri, 52, M. Chemistry teacher, Kiambu High School. Tuesday, 5 March 2019. Kiambu High School, Kiambu County, Kenya
[KEN 21] Robert Atsiaya Mukanzi, 43, M. Mathematics and physics teacher, Kiambu High School. Tuesday, 5 March 2019. Kiambu High School, Kiambu County, Kenya
[KEN 22] Kenneth Benson Muya, 35, M. Mathematics teacher, Loreto Kiambu Girls High School. Tuesday, 5 March 2019. Loreto Kiambu Girls High School, Kiambu County, Kenya
[KEN 23] Anonymous. Tuesday, 5 March 2019. Ngarariga Girls Secondary School, Kiambu County, Kenya
[KEN 24] Kenneth Mwaura Ng'ang'a, 48, M. Mathematics and physics teacher, Ngarariga Girls Secondary School. Tuesday, 5 March 2019. Ngarariga Girls Secondary School, Kiambu County, Kenya
[KEN 25] Jennifer Katumbi Mwiltea, 46, F. Principal, Ngarariga Girls Secondary School. Tuesday, 5 March 2019. Ngarariga Girls Secondary School, Kiambu County, Kenya
[KEN 26] A group discussion of lecturers mediated by Ongeri Z. Simon, 55, M. Deputy Principal, Thogoto Teachers Training College. Tuesday, 5 March 2019. Thogoto Teachers Training College, Kiambu County, Kenya
[KEN 27] Boniface Moses Wabuga, 56, M. Head of Science, Machakos Teachers Training College. Wednesday, 6 March 2019. Machakos Teachers Training College, Machakos County, Kenya
[KEN 28] Stephen Kasyoka, 55, M. Head of Mathematics, Machakos Teachers Training College. Wednesday, 6 March 2019. Machakos Teachers Training College, Machakos County, Kenya

[KEN 29] Samuel Thuku Chege, 42, M. Chemistry and physics teacher, Tala Girls High School. Wednesday, 6 March 2019. Tala Girls High School, Machakos County, Kenya

[MMT 01] Endo Kunio (遠藤邦夫), 69, M. Director, Soshisha, Supporting Centre for Minamata Disease. Nagano Michi(永野三智), 35, F. Director, Soshisha, Supporting Centre for Minamata Disease. Koizumi Hatsue(小泉初恵), 27, F. Staff member, Soshisha, Supporting Centre for Minamata Disease. Thursday, 6 June 2019. Soshisha Meeting and Accommodation Facility, Fukuro, Minamata City, Kumamoto Prefecture, Japan

[MMT 02] Akagi Hirokatsu (赤木洋勝), 77, M. Director and President, International Mercury Laboratory. Thursday, 6 June 2019. International Mercury Laboratory, Fukuro, Minamata City, Kumamoto Prefecture, Japan

[MMT 03] Yoshii Masazumi (吉井正澄), 88, M. Former Mayor of Minamata City. Thursday, 6 June 2019. Yoshii's House, Fukuro, Minamata City, Kumamoto Prefecture, Japan

[MMT 04] Ueno Eiko (上野エイ子), 91, F. Storyteller at the Minamata Disease Municipal Museum. Friday, 7 June 2019. Minamata Municipal Meisui-en, Minamata City, Kumamoto Prefecture, Japan

[MMT 05] Kagata Kiyoko (加賀田清子), 63, F. Minamata disease patient. Kaneko Yuji (金子勇二), 63, M. Minamata disease patient. Matsunaga Koichiro (松永孝一郎), 55, M. Minamata disease patient. Nagamoto Kenji (永本賢二), 59, M. Minamata disease patient. Nagai Isamu (長井勇), 62, M. Minamata disease patient. Kato Takeko (加藤タケ子), 68, F. Facility Staff, Hot House. Friday, 7 June 2019. Social Welfare Corporation Sakae no Mori Hotto Hausu, Hama-machi, Minamata City, Kumamoto Prefecture, Japan

[MMT 06] Ogata Masami (緒方正実), 61, M. Chairman, Minamata Disease Municipal Museum Storytellers' Association. Friday, 7 June 2019. Soshisha Meeting and Accommodation Facility, Fukuro, Minamata City, Kumamoto Prefecture, Japan

[MMT 07] Matsumoto Naomi (松本直美), 68, F. Farming. Saturday, 28 September 2019. Matsumoto's House, Fukuro, Minamata City, Kumamoto Prefecture, Japan

[MMT 08] Tashiro Hisako (田代久子), 61, F. Formerly an association staff member. Saturday, 28 September 2019. Naomi Matsumoto's House, Fukuro, Minamata City, Kumamoto Prefecture, Japan

[MMT 09] Ikeda Toshio (池田俊雄), 70, M. Former therapist. Sunday, 29 September 2019. Ikeda's House, Tatara-machi, Minamata City, Kumamoto Prefecture, Japan

[MMT 10] Ikeda Mitsuko (池田美津子), 79, F. Former therapist. Sunday, 29 September 2019. Ikeda's House, Tatara-machi, Minamata City, Kumamoto Prefecture, Japan

[MYS 01] Suraya Wang binti Abdullah. 70, F. Former Director, Economic Planning Unit, Prime Minister's Department. Monday, 3 September 2018. JICA Malaysia Office, Kuala Lumpur, Malaysia

[MYS 02] Zaihan bin Shukri, 56, M. Deputy Director General, Manpower Department, Ministry of Human Resources. Tuesday, 4 September, 2018. Ministry of Human Resources, Putrajaya, Malaysia
[MYS 03] Shamsida binti Zainal Abdin, 54, F. Deputy Director, Department of Skills Development, Ministry of Human Resources. Tuesday, 4 September 2018. Ministry of Human Resources, Putrajaya, Malaysia
[MYS 04] Ghazlan bin Ghazali, 56, M. Former Director, The Centre for Instructor and Advanced Skill Training (CIAST). Wednesday, 5 September 2018. CIAST, Shah Alam, Selangor, Malaysia
[MYS 05] Rahmat bin Ayop, 58, M. Former trainer. Wednesday, 5 September 2018. CIAST, Shah Alam, Selangor, Malaysia
[MYS 06] Azmi bin Ali, 68, M. Former technical advisor, Islamic Republic of Afghanistan. Wednesday, 5 September 2018. CIAST, Shah Alam, Selangor, Malaysia
[MYS 07] Norman bin Muhamad, 51, M. Undersecretary, International Cooperation and Development Division, Ministry of Foreign Affairs. Wednesday, 5 September 2018. Ministry of Foreign Affairs, Putrajaya, Malaysia
[MYS 08] Suimi bin Abd Majid, 57, M. Deputy Director General, Department of Skills Development, Ministry of Human Resources. Thursday, 6 September 2018. Ministry of Human Resources, Cyberjaya, Selangor, Malaysia
[MYS 09] Roslinda binti Daud, 54, F. Head of Electronics and Multi-Media Programme, CIAST. Thursday, 6 September 2018. CIAST, Shah Alam, Selangor, Malaysia
[MYS 10] Sayed Salim bin Sayed Mohd Nor, 55, M. Head of Unit (Instructor Skills Development and Human Capital). Thursday, 6 September 2018. CIAST, Shah Alam, Selangor, Malaysia
[MYS 11] Azhari bin Ibrahim, 54, M. Head of Program (Professional Skills Development), CIAST. Thursday, 6 September 2018. CIAST, Shah Alam, Selangor, Malaysia
[MYS 12] Mohd Noor bin Menhad, 55, M. Vocational Methodology Unit, CIAST. Thursday, 6 September 2018. CIAST, Shah Alam, Selangor, Malaysia
[MYS 13] Isrami bin Ismail, 42, M. Managing Director, I-Firm. Friday, 7 September 2018. Yamaguchi University International Collaboration Office, Malaysia Japan International Institute of Technology (MJIIT), Universiti Teknologi Malaysia (UTM), Kuala Lumpur, Malaysia
[MYS 14] A group discussion by former trainees at CIAST (8 participants. Current positions: 5 trainers at CIAST and 3 trainers at ADTEC). Friday, 7 September 2018. Library, CIAST, Shah Alam, Selangor, Malaysia
[OKW 01] Sonohara Ken (園原謙), 61, M. Senior Curator, Okinawa Prefectural Museum and Art Museum. Tuesday, 10 December 2019. Okinawa Prefectural Museum & Art Museum, Omoromachi, Naha City, Okinawa Prefecture, Japan
[OKW 02] Sakuma Ayumi (佐久間愛弓), 39, F. Staff member, Okinawa Office of Japan Overseas Cooperation Association (JOCA). Wednesday, 11 December 2019. JICA Okinawa Centre, Urasoe City, Okinawa Prefecture, Japan

[OKW 03] Nakadomari Kazue (仲泊和枝), 59, F. Director-General, Okinawa Peace Assistance Center (OPAC). Wednesday, 11 December 2019. OPAC office, Naha City, Okinawa Prefecture, Japan

[OKW 04] Hokama Hirotomo (外間裕朋), 58, M. Director, Okinawa Prefectural Peace Memorial Museum. Wednesday, 11 December 2019. Okinawa Prefectural Peace Memorial Museum, Itoman City, Okinawa Prefecture, Japan

[OKW 05] Hirata Mamoru (平田守), 59, M. Curator, Okinawa Prefectural Peace Memorial Museum. Wednesday, 11 December 2019. Okinawa Prefectural Peace Memorial Museum, Itoman City, Okinawa Prefecture, Japan

[OKW 06] Oshiro Toroku (大城藤六), 89, M. Advisor, Okinawa Prefectural Peace Memorial Museum. Wednesday, 11 December 2019. Okinawa Prefectural Peace Memorial Museum, Itoman City, Okinawa Prefecture, Japan

[OKW 07] Kubota Satoru (久保田暁), 74, M. Chairman of the Okinawa Peace Memorial Museum Fellowship, Okinawa Prefectural Peace Memorial Museum. Wednesday, 11 December 2019. Okinawa Prefectural Peace Memorial Museum, Itoman City, Okinawa Prefecture, Japan

[OKW 08] Yasuda Kunishige (安田國重), 78, M. Advisor, Okinawa Prefectural Peace Memorial Museum. Wednesday, 11 December 2019. Okinawa Prefectural Peace Memorial Museum, Itoman City, Okinawa Prefecture, Japan

[OKW 09] Yoneda Miyuki(米田美由紀), 42, F. Teacher of Geography, History and Civics, Okinawa Prefectural Yaeyama Commercial and Technical High School. Thursday, 12 December 2019. Yaeyama Commercial and Technical High School, Maezato, Ishigaki City, Okinawa Prefecture, Japan

[TAN 01] Eliakim Chitutu, 56, M. Acting Chief Executive Director, National Irrigation Commission (NAIC), Ministry of Water and Irrigation. Thursday, 28 June 2018. NAIC, Dar es Salaam, Tanzania

[TAN 02] Pascal J. Shayo, 59, M. Acting Director, Irrigation Infrastructure Development, NAIC, Ministry of Water and Irrigation. Thursday, 28 June 2018. NAIC, Dar es Salaam, Tanzania.

[TAN 03] Anne N. Assenga, 61, F. Retired Director of Training, Ministry of Agriculture. Thursday, 28 June 2018. Ministry of Agriculture, Dar es Salaam, Tanzania

[TAN 04] Eusebio M. Mlay, 67, M. Assistant Director of Training, Ministry of Agriculture. Thursday, 28 June 2018. Ministry of Agriculture, Dar es Salaam, Tanzania

[TAN 05] Maiko Marindo, 84, M. Farmer. Saturday, 30 June 2018. His homestead, Upper Mabogini, Lower Moshi, Kilimanjaro, Tanzania

[TAN 06] Atanasia (Mamangina), 78, F. Farmer. Saturday, 30 June 2018. Her homestead, Chekereni, Lower Moshi, Kilimanjaro, Tanzania

[TAN 07] Richard Kimicho, 63, M. Former staff member of KADC (Kilimanjaro Agricultural Development Centre) and KADP (Kilimanjaro Agricultural Development Project) and Former Coordinator of LMIS (Lower Moshi Irrigation Scheme). Saturday, 30 June 2018. Moshi, Kilimanjaro, Tanzania

[TAN 08] Godliving Moshi, 70, M. Former Director of KADC/KADP. Sunday, 1 July 2018. Parkview Inn, Moshi, Kilimanjaro, Tanzania

[TAN 09] Richard Shayo, 69, M. First Principal of KATC (Kilimanjaro Agricultural Training Centre). Sunday, 1 July 2018. Moshi, Kilimanjaro, Tanzania
[TAN 10] Beatus Nicolaus Macha, 62, M. Former staff member of KADP and Former coordinator of LMIS. Monday, 2 July 2018. KATC, Lower Moshi, Kilimanjaro, Tanzania
[TAN 11] A group discussion by local farmers and their representatives (29 participants including 5 women) conducted in Kiswahili (translated to English by Mr Fredrick Solomon Mawolle). Monday, 2 July 2018. KATC, Lower Moshi, Kilimanjaro, Tanzania
[TAN 12] Nicodemus N. Shauritanga, 56, M. Principal, KATC. Monday, 2 July 2018. KATC, Lower Moshi, Kilimanjaro, Tanzania
[TAN 13] Godwin Wilfred Chonjo, 63, M. Former staff member, KADP. Monday, 2 July 2018. KATC, Lower Moshi, Kilimanjaro, Tanzania
[TAN 14] Festus Joachim Kimaryo, 75, M. Former staff member, KADC. Monday, 2 July 2018. KATC, Lower Moshi, Kilimanjaro, Tanzania
[TAN 15] Zablon Sarakikya, 70, M. Former staff member, KADC/KADP. Monday, 2 July 2018. KATC, Lower Moshi, Kilimanjaro, Tanzania
[TAN 16] Mary Augustine Mtika, 57, F. Tutor, KATC and Fredrick Solomon Mawolle, 56, M. Coordinator, LMIS. Monday, 2 July 2018. KATC, Lower Moshi, Kilimanjaro, Tanzania
[THA 01] Ronnarong Thuamcharoen, 47, M. Farmer, originally from Rayong province. Friday, 3 September 2021. Telephone interview
[THA 02] Pinyo Srisutthi, 42, M. Farmer, originally from Rayong province. Wednesday, 8 September 2021. Wat Banlang (temple) in the suburb of Rayong city, Thailand
[THA 03] Bancherd Ruangpon, 67, M. Fisherman residing in the coastal area of Rayong city. Wednesday, 8 September 2021. Restaurant near his residence, Rayong city, Thailand
[THA 04] Bunyuen Sukmai, 52, M. Lawyer residing in Chon Buri province, originally from Nakhon Ratchasima province. Wednesday, 8 September 2021. Trade union office, Bo Win, Si Racha district, Chon Buri province, Thailand
[THA 05] Sitthisak Phiaia, 51, M. Company employee residing in Chon Buri province, originally from Nong Khai province. Wednesday, 8 September 2021. Trade union office, Bo Win, Si Racha district, Chon Buri province, Thailand
[THA 06] Chalermporn Klomkaew, 69, M. Retired; formerly an owner of a car service garage. Wednesday, 8 September 2021. His residence, Rayong city, Rayong province, Thailand
[THA 07] Sawat Thamkonkar, 66, M. Transport operator residing in Laem Chabang, originally from Ayutthaya province. Monday, 4 October 2021. Wat Laem Chabang (temple), Si Racha district, Chon Buri province, Thailand
[THA 08] Tawat Keethortet, 48, M. Company employee residing in Chon Buri province, originally from Phichit province. Monday, 4 October 2021. Laem Chabang Industrial Estate, Si Racha district, Chon Buri province, Thailand

[THA 09] Samroeng Thaiwee, 52, M. Company employee residing in Chon Buri province, originally from Sukhothai province. Monday, 4 October 2021. Laem Chabang Industrial Estate, Si Racha district, Chon Buri province, Thailand

[VOL 01] Koaze Hiroshi (小疇浩), 66, M. JICA Expert. Chief Advisor, Project for the Formation of an African-Style Innovation Promotion Network. The 3rd Batch of JOCV in 1980: From April 1981 to April 1984, Food Processing, JKCAT, Ministry of Higher Education, Kenya. Tuesday, 11 May 2021. Zoom interview

[VOL 02] Naganuma Keiichi (長沼啓一), 53, M. CEO, ILINK, Co. Ltd. The 2nd Batch of JOCV in 1996: From December 1996 to December 1998, Science and Mathematics Teacher, Zambia. Tuesday, 11 May 2021. Zoom interview

[VOL 03] Anonymous. JOCV in 1992. Thursday, 13 May 2021. Zoom interview

[VOL 04] Uchiyama Hazuki (内山葉月), F. The 1st Batch of JOCV in 1993: From July 1993 to July 1995, Science and Mathematics Teacher, Lukulu Secondary School, Zambia; JOCV Senior Volunteer, 2000: From August 2000 to August 2003, Science and Mathematics Teacher, Makueni County Education Office, Kenya. Monday, 17 May 2021. Zoom interview

[VOL 05] Baba Takuya (馬場卓也), 59, M. Professor, Graduate School of Humanities and Social Sciences, Hiroshima University. The 1st Batch of JOCV in 1984: From July 1984 to December 1986, Science and Mathematics Teacher, Special Science Secondary School attached to the Eulogio 'Amang' Rodriguez Institute of Science and Technology, Philippines. Tuesday, 18 May 2021. Zoom interview

[VOL 06] Nakai Kazuyoshi (中井一芳), 58, M. Specially Appointed Lecturer, Education Promotion Division (Centre for Research and Development of Higher Education), Osaka City University; Short-term Expert for Zambia. The 3rd Batch of JOCV in 1992: From April 1993 to June 1995, Science Teacher, Siota Provincial Secondary School, Central Province, Solomon Islands. Tuesday, 18 May 2021. Zoom interview

[VOL 07] Nishikata Norihiro (西方憲広), 60, M. JICA International Cooperation Specialist (Education). The 1st Batch of JOCV in 1987: From July 1987 to July 1990 (In-service dispatch from the Niigata Prefectural Board of Education), Primary School Teacher, Primary Education Bureau, Ministry of Education, Honduras. Thursday, 20 May 2021. Zoom interview

[VOL 08] Soma Takashi (相馬敬), 54, M. Executive Director, PADECO. The 1st Batch of JOCV in 1990: From July 1990 to August 1993, Science and Mathematics Teacher, Yendi Secondary School, Ghana; Short-Term Emergency Dispatch, 1995: From October 1995 to March 1996, Science and Mathematics Teacher, Amedjofe Teacher Training College, Ghana. Sekine Reiko (関根令子), 54, F. Associate, Education Development Department, PADECO. The 3rd Batch of JOCV in 2003: From January 2003 to February 2005, Early Childhood Education, Public Kindergarten (Hamadaniyeh Kindergarten), Syria; Short-term Senior Volunteer, 2012: From February 2012 to August 2012; Early Childhood Education, National Centre for Educational Resource Development, Guyana; The 2nd Batch of Senior Overseas Volunteer in 2013: From October 2013 to October 2015, Early Childhood Education, NGO-run Kindergarten (Children's House Kindergarten) Dominican Republic. Jibutsu Kenichi (持佛賢一), 51, M. Senior

Consultant, Education Development Department, PADECO. The 2nd Batch of JOCV in 1999: From December 1999 to December 2001, Science and Mathematics Teacher, Gesero Secondary School. Kenya. Sugiyama Ryuichi (杉山竜一) (Roundtable Discussion Coordinator), Director, Education Development Department, PADECO. The 1st Batch of JOCV in 1995: From July 1995 to August 1997, Science and Mathematics Teacher, Serenje Boys' Technical Secondary School, Zambia. Thursday, 27 May 2021. Zoom interview

[VOL 09] Miyazaki Atsumasa (宮崎充正), 29, M. Programme Coordinator in Kenya, AAR Japan (Association for Aid and Relief, Japan). The 3rd Batch of JOCV in 2015: From January 2016 to January 2018, Science Education, Mbenjere Secondary School, Malawi. Wednesday, 16 June 2021. Zoom interview

[VOL 10] Hoshino Masako (星野昌子), 89, F. Special Advisor, Japan International Volunteer Centre. The 1st Batch of JOCV in 1965: From December 1965 to December 1967, Japanese Language Teacher, Laos. Monday, 1 November 2021. Telephone interview

[VOL 11] Ogawa Akiko (小川晶子), 41, F. Staff member, Shapla Neer=Citizens' Committee in Japan for Overseas Support. The 3rd Batch of JOCV in 2011: From January 2012 to January 2014, Art Teacher, Valle de Angeles. Republic of Honduras. Saturday, 21 May 2022. Zoom interview

[ZAM 01] John Yabe, 43, M. Lecturer, Department of Para-Clinical Studies, Samora Machel School of Veterinary Medicine, the University of Zambia (UNZA). Wednesday, 11 July 2018. UNZA (Great East Road Campus), Lusaka, Zambia

[ZAM 02] Amoni Mwelwa, 30, M. Technologist, Samora Machel School of Veterinary Medicine, UNZA. Wednesday, 11 July 2018. UNZA (Great East Road Campus), Lusaka, Zambia

[ZAM 03] Edgar Simulundu, 41, M. Lecturer, Department of Disease Control, Samora Machel School of Veterinary Medicine, UNZA. Wednesday, 11 July 2018. UNZA (Great East Road Campus), Lusaka, Zambia

[ZAM 04] Henry Chimana, 60, M. Lecturer, School of Biomedical Science, UNZA. Thursday, 12 July 2018. UNZA (Ridgeway Campus), Lusaka, Zambia

[ZAM 05] Kennedy Choongo, 54, M. Lecturer, Samora Machel School of Veterinary Medicine, UNZA. Thursday, 12 July 2018. UNZA (Great East Road Campus), Lusaka, Zambia

[ZAM 06] Wilmot Benkele, 64, M. Former Chief Technician, Samora Machel School of Veterinary Medicine, UNZA. Thursday, 12 July 2018. Shimaiya Skills Training Centre, Lusaka Zambia

[ZAM 07] Girja Shanker Pandey, 70, M. Professor, Samora Machel School of Veterinary Medicine, UNZA. Thursday, 12 July 2018. UNZA (Great East Road Campus), Lusaka, Zambia

[ZAM 08] Katendi Changula, 40, F. Head of Para-Clinical Studies Department, Samora Machel School of Veterinary Medicine, UNZA. Thursday, 12 July 2018. UNZA (Great East Road Campus), Lusaka, Zambia

[ZAM 09] Mutale Mike Musonda, 64, M. Former Dean, Samora Machel School of Veterinary Medicine, UNZA Vice Chancellor, ZCAS University. Friday, 13 July 2018. ZCAS University, Dedan Kimathi Road, Lusaka, Zambia

[ZAM 10] Victor Zulu, 50, M. Senior Lecturer, Samora Machel School of Veterinary Medicine, UNZA. Friday, 13 July 2018. UNZA (Great East Road Campus), Lusaka, Zambia

[ZAM 11] Kenny L. Samui, 65, M. Former Dean, Lecturer, Samora Machel School of Veterinary Medicine, UNZA. Friday, 13 July 2018. UNZA (Great East Road Campus), Lusaka, Zambia

[ZAM 12] Danstan Mwiinga, 31, M. Veterinary surgeon, ZAMBEEF. Friday, 13 July 2018. Fringilla Farm, Chisamba, Zambia

[ZAM 13] Kasuka Muwauluka, 81, M. Former Vice-Chancellor, UNZA, Professor, School of Natural Sciences, UNZA. Friday, 13 July 2018. UNZA (Great East Road Campus), Lusaka, Zambia

References

For books and articles available only in Japanese, the original Japanese titles are given in parentheses for the convenience of readers searching the database. In this book, quotations from Japanese sources are my own translations.

Agosin, Manuel R., Christian Larrain, and Nicolas Grau. 2010. Industrial Policy in Chile. *IDB Working Paper No. 52* https://doi.org/10.2139/ssrn.1817286.

Akamatsu, Kaname. 1962. A Historical Pattern of Economic Growth in Developing Countries. *The Developing Economies* 1: 3–25 https://doi.org/10.1111/j.1746-1049.1962.tb01020.x.

Akashi, Yasushi. 2007. *Cambodia PKO Diary*: *December 1991 to September 1993*(Original in Japanese: 明石康『カンボジアPKO日記—1991年12月~1993年9月』岩波書店、2007年).

Akutagawa, Ryunosuke. 2006. *Rashōmon and Seventeen Other Stories,* trans. Jay Rubin. London: Penguin.

Alexander, Jocelyn, JoAnn McGregor, Blessing-Miles Tendi (eds). 2020. *Transnational Histories of Southern Africa's Liberation Movements.* Abingdon: Routledge.

Almizan, Abdullah. 2004a. Brantas River Development: Realization of a Dream. In *Semangat Brantas,* by Kerukunan Keluarga Eks Proyek Brantas di Jakarta & Sekitarnya, 61–67. Jakarta: PT Gramedia Pustaka Utama.

Almizan, Abdullah. 2004b. Transfer of Knowledge and Technology: From Management by Changes to Management of Changes. In *Semangat Brantas,* by Kerukunan Keluarga Eks Proyek Brantas di Jakarta & Sekitarnya, 85–90. Jakarta: PT Gramedia Pustaka Utama.

Ampiah, Kweku. 2022. The Political Economy of the TICAD Process: Bureaucratic Interests and the Immobility of the Japanese Private Sector. *International Journal of Afrasian Studies* 1 (1): 15–33 https://www.afrasia.org/_files/ugd/bb019d_9d614a2e67c44bab8f5b9a74a15bca49.pdf.

Anderson, Benedict R., and Ruth T. McVey. 1971. *A Preliminary Analysis of the October 1, 1965, Coup in Indonesia.* Ithaca, N.Y.: Modern Indonesia Project, Cornell University.

Anderson, Benedict. 1998. *The Spectre of Comparisons: Nationalism, Southeast Asia, and the World.* London: Verso.

Apter, David E. 2008. Ghana's Independence: Triumph and Paradox. *Transition* 98: 6–22 https://www.jstor.org/stable/20204242.

Araki, Mitsuya. 2014. *Samurais Who Created a University in Africa: The Story of Jomo Kenyatta University of Agriculture and Technology* (Original in Japanese: 荒木光弥『アフリカに大学をつくったサムライたち—ジョモ・ケニヤッタ農工大学物語』国際開発ジャーナル社、丸善出版、2014年).

Arendt, Hannah. 1963. *Eichmann in Jerusalem: A Report on the Banality of Evil.* New York: Viking Press.

Arimoto, Takafumi, Takeda Shinichi, Baba Osamu, and Yoshikawa Hisashi. 2017. Introduction of Fixed Fishing Nets by Villagers in Rayong Province, Thailand. In *Communities Are Born, Nurtured by Resources: The Practice of Area Capability,* eds. Ishikawa Satoshi and Watanabe

Y. Mine, *An Oral History of Development Cooperation*,
https://doi.org/10.1007/978-981-95-5479-9

Issei (Original in Japanese: 有元貴文、武田誠一、馬場治、吉川尚「タイ国ラヨーン県の村張り定置網導入」石川智士、渡辺一生編『地域が生まれる、資源が育てる—エリアケイパビリティーの実践』勉誠社、2017年、所収).

Asai, Makoto. 2025. *Kilimanjaro and the Waves of Rice Stalks: Half a Century of Rice Production in Tanzania.* Tokyo: JICA Ogata Sadako Research Institute for Peace and Development.

Assensoh, A.B. 1998. *African Political Leadership: Jomo Kenyatta, Kwame Nkrumah, and Julius K. Nyerere.* Malabar, Fla.: Krieger.

Azam, Jean-Paul, and Jean-Jacques Laffont. 2003. Contracting for Aid. *Journal of Development Economics* 70(1): 25–58 https://doi.org/10.1016/S0304-3878(02)00085-8.

Baba, Takuya. 2003. Toward the Endogenous Development of Mathematics Education in Developing Countries: A Case Study in Kenya. In *Development and Education in Africa: International Education Cooperation for Human Security,* ed. Sawamura Nobuhide (Original in Japanese: 馬場卓也「開発途上国における数学教育の内発的な展開に向けて—ケニアにおける事例をもとにして」澤村信英編『アフリカの開発と教育—人間の安全保障をめざす国際教育協力』明石書店、2003年、所収).

Baba, Takuya. 2007. Let's Work Together for the Future Society. In *International Volunteer Work: A Guide Based on Life Stories,* eds. Kubota Kenichi and Asano Eiichi (Original in Japanese: 馬場卓也「未来社会に向けてともに汗をかこう」久保田賢一・浅野英一編『ライフストーリーでつづる国際ボランティアの歩き方』国際協力出版会、2007年、所収).

Baba, Takuya and Nakai Kazuyoshi. 2009. The Potential of the Lesson Study Approach in International Education Cooperation: A Case Study in Zambia (Original in Japanese: 馬場卓也・中井一芳「国際教育協力における授業研究アプローチの可能性—ザンビアの事例をもとに」『国際教育協力論集』第12巻 第2号 (広島大学教育開発国際協力研究センター)、2009年、107–118頁).

Banerjee, Abhijit V., and Esther Duflo. 2011. *Poor Economics: A Radical Rethinking of the Way to Fight Global Poverty.* New York: PublicAffairs.

Bangura, Abdul Karim. 2012. *African Mathematics: From Bones to Computers.* Lanham: University Press of America.

Bauer, Peter T. 1981. *Equality, the Third World, and Economic Delusion.* Cambridge, Mass.: Harvard University Press.

Bauer, Peter T. 1984. *Reality and Rhetoric: Studies in the Economics of Development.* Cambridge, Mass.: Harvard University Press.

Bauer, Peter T. 2000. *From Subsistence to Exchange and Other Essays,* with an introduction by Amartya Sen. Princeton: Princeton University Press.

Beck, Ulrich. 1992. *Risk Society: Towards a New Modernity,* trans. Mark Ritter. London: Sage.

Bergson, Henri. 1911. *Creative Evolution,* trans. Arthur Mitchell. New York: H. Holt.

Bernard, Mitchell, and John Ravenhill. 1995. Beyond Product Cycles and Flying Geese: Regionalization, Hierarchy, and the Industrialization of East Asia. *World Politics* 47 (2): 171–209 https://doi.org/10.1017/S0043887100016075.

Bernstein, Peter L. 1998. *Against the Gods: The Remarkable Story of Risk.* New York: John Wiley & Sons.

Bertaux, Daniel. 1997. *Les récits de vie: Perspective ethnosociologique.* Paris: Editions Nathan.

Bevins, Vincent. 2020. *The Jakarta Method: Washington's Anticommunist Crusade and the Mass Murder Program That Shaped Our World.* New York: PublicAffairs.

Bierce, Ambrose. 1970. *The Complete Short Stories of Ambrose Bierce.* Garden City, N.Y.: Doubleday.

Bizot, François. 2000. *Le portail.* Paris: Table ronde.

Boccaletti, Giulio. 2021. *Water: A Biography.* New York: Pantheon Books.

Boholm, Åsa (eds). 2011. *New Perspectives on Risk Communication: Uncertainty in a Complex Society.* London: Routledge.

Boserup, Ester.1970. *Woman's Role in Economic Development.* London: Allen & Unwin.

Bourguignon, François, and Mark Sundberg. 2007. Aid Effectiveness: Opening the Black Box. *The American Economic Review* 97(2): 316–321 https://doi.org/10.1257/aer.97.2.316.

Brown, Graham K. 2005. *Balancing the Risks of Corrective Surgery: The Political Economy of Horizontal Inequalities and the End of the New Economic Policy in Malaysia.* CRISE (Centre for Research on Inequality, Human Security and Ethnicity), Queen Elizabeth House, University of Oxford

Brysk, Alison. 2005. Global Good Samaritans? Human Rights Foreign Policy in Costa Rica. *Global Governance* 11 (4): 445–466 https://www.jstor.org/stable/27800585.

Carr, Edward Hallett. 1987. *What Is History?: The George Macaulay Trevelyan Lectures Delivered in the University of Cambridge, January-March 1961.* 2nd ed. Harmondsworth: Penguin.

Cave, Mark, and Stephen M. Sloan. 2014. *Listening on the Edge: Oral History in the Aftermath of Crisis.* Oxford: Oxford University Press.

Chambers, Robert. 1983. *Rural Development: Putting the Last First.* Harlow: Longman Scientific & Technical.

Chan, Ek Sonn. 2009. Bringing Safe Water to Phnom Penh's City. *International Journal of Water Resources Development* 25(4): 597–609 https://doi.org/10.1080/07900620903306323.

Chandler, David P. 1992. *Brother Number One: A Political Biography of Pol Pot.* Boulder, CO: Westview Press.

Chandler, David P. 1999. *Voices from S-21: Terror and History in Pol Pot's Secret Prison.* Berkeley: University of California Press.

Chandy, Laurence, Hosono Akio, Homi Kharas, and Johannes Linn (eds). 2013. *Getting to Scale: How to Bring Development Solutions to Millions of Poor People.* Washington, D.C.: Brookings Institution Press.

Charlton, Thomas L., Lois E. Myers, and Rebecca Sharpless (eds). 2006. *Handbook of Oral History.* Lanham, Md.: Altamira Press.

Clastres, Pierre. 1974. *La société contre l'État: Recherches d'anthropologie politique.* Paris: Éditions de minuit.

Cleary, David. 1990. *Anatomy of the Amazon Gold Rush.* Iowa City: University of Iowa Press.

Comte, Auguste. 1822. *Plan des travaux scientifiques nécessaires pour réorganiser la société.* Présentation et notes par Angèle Kremer-Marietti. (Paris: L'Harmattan, 2001).

Cooper, Frederick. 1996. *Decolonization and African Society: The Labor Question in French and British Africa.* Cambridge: Cambridge University Press.

Daniel, Philip. 1979. *Africanisation, Nationalisation, and Inequality: Mining Labour and the Copperbelt in Zambian Development.* Cambridge: Cambridge University Press.

D'Ambrosio Ubiratan. 1985. *Socio-Cultural Bases for Mathematics Education.* Campinas, Brasil: UNICAMP.

D'Ambrosio Ubiratan. 2006. *Ethnomathematics: Link between Traditions and Modernity.* Rotterdam: Sense Publishers.

Dennis, Nyamwange Nyamari, Kyalo Benjamin Wambua, and Opakas Peter. 2017. The Effect of Smasse In-Service Training on Performance of Mathematics in Selected Secondary Schools in Kenya. *European Scientific Journal* 13(10): 169–185 https://doi.org/10.19044/esj.2017.v13n10p169.

Denzin, Norman K., Yvonna S. Lincoln, Michael Donald Giardina, and Gaile S. Cannella (eds). 2024. *The SAGE Handbook of Qualitative Research.* 6th edition. Thousand Oaks, Calif.: SAGE.

Dore, Ronald. 1990. *British Factory, Japanese Factory: The Origins of National Diversity in Industrial Relations,* with a new afterword by the author. Berkeley: University of California Press.

Dore, Ronald. 2000. *Stock Market Capitalism: Welfare Capitalism, Japan and Germany versus the Anglo-Saxons.* Tokyo: Oxford University Press.

Easterly, William. 2006. *The White Man's Burden: Why the West's Efforts to Aid the Rest Have Done So Much Ill and So Little Good.* New York: Penguin.

Eckstein, Gustav. 1931. *Noguchi.* New York: Harper & Bros.

Ehara, Yumi. 2007. The Current State and Issues of Japanese-Language Education in Brazil(Original in Japanese: 江原裕美「ブラジルにおける日本語教育の現状と課題」『帝京大学外国語外国文学論集』第13号、2007年、25–62頁).

Emerson, Robert M., Rachel I. Fretz, and Linda L. Shaw. 1995. *Writing Ethnographic Fieldnotes.* Chicago: University of Chicago Press.

Ende, Michael. 1984. *Ende,* translated by J. Maxwell Brownjohn. Harmondsworth: Penguin.

Estella, Antonio. 2002. *The EU Principle of Subsidiarity and Its Critique.* Oxford: Oxford University Press.

FAO: Food and Agriculture Organization. 2024. *Fishery and Aquaculture Statistics, Yearbook 2021.* Rome: FAO https://doi.org/10.4060/cc9523en.

Ferguson, James. 1990. *The Anti-Politics Machine: Development, Depoliticization, and Bureaucratic Power in Lesotho.* Cambridge: Cambridge University Press.

Ferguson, James. 2015. *Give a Man a Fish: Reflections on the New Politics of Distribution.* Durham: Duke University Press.

Fields-Black, Edda L. 2008. *Deep Roots: Rice Farmers in West Africa and the African Diaspora.* Bloomington: Indiana University Press.

Fischhoff, Baruch. 1995. Risk Perception and Communication Unplugged: Twenty Years of Process. *Risk Analysis* 15(2): 137–145 https://doi.org/10.1111/j.1539-6924.1995.tb00308.x.

Føllesdal, Andreas. 1998. Survey Article: Subsidiarity. *Journal of Political Philosophy* 6(2): 190–218 https://doi.org/10.1111/1467-9760.00052.

Føllesdal Andreas. 2025. *Subsidiarity.* Cambridge: Cambridge University Press.

Freire, Paulo. 1970. *Pedagogy of the Oppressed,* trans. Myra Bergman Ramos. New York: Continuum.

Frimpong-Ansha, Jonathan H. 1991. *The Vampire State in Africa: The Political Economy of Decline in Ghana.* London: James Currey.

Fujimoto, Koji. 2013. Brantas River Basin Development Plan of Indonesia. In *Aid as Handmaiden for the Development of Institutions: A New Comparative Perspective,* edited by Nissanke Machiko and Shimomura Yasutami, 161–194. Basingstoke: Palgrave Macmillan.

Fukuda-Parr, Sakiko, Carlos Lopes, Khalid Malik (eds). 2002. *Capacity for Development: New Solutions to Old Problems.* London: Earthscan, New York: UNDP.

Fukuda-Parr, Sakiko, and A.K. Shiva Kumar (eds). 2009. *Handbook of Human Development: Concepts, Measures, and Policies.* New Delhi: Oxford University Press.

Fukuyama, Francis. 2004. *State-Building: Governance and World Order in the Twenty-First Century.* London: Profile Books.

Funatsu, Tsuruyo. 2013. Industrial Pollution and Environmental Administration in Thailand in the 2000s: An Analysis of the Map Ta Phut Pollution Litigation in Rayong Province. In *The Formation Process of Environmental Policy: From the Perspective of 'Development and the Environment,'* edited by Terao Tadayoshi (Original in Japanese: 船津鶴代「2000年代タイの産業公害と環境行政—ラヨーン県マーッタープット公害訴訟の分析」(寺尾忠能編『環境政策の形成過程—「開発と環境」の視点から』アジア経済研究所、2013年、所収).

Gailmard, Sean. 2014. Accountability and Principal-Agent Theory. *The Oxford Handbook of Public Accountability,* eds. Mark Bovens, Robert E. Goodin, and Thomas Schillemans, 90-105. Oxford: Oxford University Press.

Gerschenkron, Alexander. 1962. *Economic Backwardness in Historical Perspective: A Book of Essays.* Cambridge, Mass.: Belknap Press of Harvard University Press.

Gomez, Edmund Terence. 2012. Targeting Horizontal Inequalities: Ethnicity, Equity, and Entrepreneurship in Malaysia. *Asian Economic Papers* 11(2): 31–57 https://doi.org/10.1162/ASEP_a_00140.

Goto, Kazumi. 1996. Beyond 'Structural Adjustment' and the 'East Asian Miracle': An Essay on the Nature of Development Management (Original in Japanese: 後藤一美「『構造調整』と『東アジアの奇跡』を超えて—開発運営のありかたに関する一試論」『国際協力論集』第4巻第1号、1996年、101–135頁).

Gulhati, Ravi. 1989. Impasse in Zambia: The Economics and Politics of Reform. *EDI Development Policy Case Series, Analytical Case Studies No. 2.* Washington, D.C.: World Bank https://documents1.worldbank.org/curated/en/340321468334477712/pdf/multi-page.pdf.

Haga, Shigeko. 1983. Survey Team Diary. In *The Revelation of Minamata: Comprehensive Survey Report on the Shiranui Sea, (Part 2)* edited by Irokawa Daikichi(Original in Japanese: 羽賀しげ子「調査団日誌」色川大吉編『水俣の啓示—不知火海総合調査報告(下)』筑摩書房、1983年、所収).

Hagiwara, Akiko, and Abdulmonem Malkawi. 2023. *Empowerment of Women through the Participatory Enter-Educate (PEE) Workshops: Report of Case Studies of Female Participants of PEE Workshops in Karak Governorate, Jordan.* Tokyo: Family Planning and Gender in Development Project, JICA.

Hamashita, Takeshi. 2008. *China, East Asia and the Global Economy: Regional and Historical Perspectives,* eds. Linda Grove and Mark Selden. Abingdon: Routledge.

Hamashita, Takeshi. 2011. From Tribute Trade to Migration Center: The Ryukyu and Hong Kong Maritime Networks within the East and South China Seas in a Long-Term Perspective. In *Connecting Seas and Connected Ocean Rims: Indian, Atlantic, and Pacific Oceans and China Seas Migrations from the 1830s to the 1930s,* edited by Donna R. Gabaccia and Dirk Hoerder, 172–197. Leiden: Brill.

Hancock, Graham. 1989. *Lords of Poverty: The Free-Wheeling Lifestyles, Power, Prestige and Corruption of the Multi-Billion Dollar Aid Business.* London: Macmillan.

Hanlon, Joseph. 1986. *Beggar Your Neighbours: Apartheid Power in Southern Africa.* London: Catholic Institute for International Relations.

Hanson, Jonathan K. 2015. Democracy and State Capacity: Complements or Substitutes? *Studies in Comparative International Development* 50: 304–330 https://doi.org/10.1007/s12116-014-9173-z.

Hashimoto, Ken. 2013. *The Unknown Endemic Disease in Central America: The Way to Overcoming Chagas Disease: An International Project to Eradicate the Insect Triatomine That Plagues Poor Villages* (Original in Japanese: 橋本謙『中米の知られざる風土病「シャーガス病」克服への道—貧困の村を襲う昆虫サシガメの駆除に挑んだ国際プロジェクト』ダイヤモンド社、2013年).

Hashimoto, Takehiko, and Kuriyama Shigehisa (eds). 2001. *The Birth of Tardiness: The Formation of Time Consciousness in Modern Japan* (Original in Japanese: 橋本毅彦、栗山茂久編『遅刻の誕生—近代日本における時間意識の形成』三元社、2001年).

Hardin, Garrett. 1968. The Tragedy of the Commons. *Science* 162/3859: 1243–1248 https://doi.org/10.1126/science.162.3859.1243.

Hardin, Garrett. 1994. The Tragedy of the Unmanaged Commons. *Trends in Ecology and Evolution* 9(5): 199 https://doi.org/10.1016/0169-5347(94)90097-3.

Hawkins, Darren G. Hawkins, David A. Lake, Daniel L. Nielson, and Michael J. Tierney (eds). 2006. *Delegation and Agency in International Organizations.* Cambridge: Cambridge University Press.

Hayner, Priscilla B. 2001. *Unspeakable Truths: Confronting State Terror and Atrocity.* New York: Routledge.

Hearman, Vannessa. 2018. *Unmarked Graves 2018: Death and Survival in the Anti-Communist Violence in East Java, Indonesia.* Singapore: NUS Press.

Hemingway, Ernest. 1987. *The Complete Short Stories of Ernest Hemingway.* New York: Scribner.

Heng, Pek Koon, 1997. The New Economic Policy and the Chinese Community in Peninsular Malaysia, *The Developing Economies* 35(3): 262–92 https://doi.org/10.1111/j.1746-1049.1997.tb00848.x.

Hill, Martin J.D. 1991. *The Harambee Movement in Kenya: Self-help, Development, and Education among the Kamba of Kitui District.* London: Athlone Press.

Hirschman, Albert O. 1958. *The Strategy of Economic Development.* New Haven: Yale University Press.

Hirschman, Albert O. 1967. *Development Projects Observed.* Washington, D.C.: Brookings Institution.

Hirschman, Albert O. 1970. *Exit, Voice, and Loyalty: Responses to Decline in Firms, Organizations, and States.* Cambridge, Mass.: Harvard University Press.

Hirschman, Albert O. 1981. *Essays in Trespassing: Economics to Politics and Beyond.* Cambridge: Cambridge University Press.

Hirschman, Albert O. 1984. *Getting Ahead Collectively: Grassroots Experiences in Latin America.* New York: Pergamon Press.

Historical Science Society of Japan (ed.). 1988a. *Oral History and Experiential History: On the Work of Honda Katsuichi* (Original in Japanese: 歴史学研究会編『オーラル・ヒストリーと体験史—本多勝一の仕事をめぐって』青木書店、1988年).

Historical Science Society of Japan (ed.). 1988b. *Verification of Facts and Oral History: On the Work of Sawachi Hisae* (Original in Japanese: 歴史学研究会編『事実の検証とオーラル・ヒストリー—澤地久枝の仕事をめぐって』青木書店、1988年).

Hobsbawm, Eric, and Terence Ranger (eds). 1983. *The Invention of Tradition.* Cambridge: Cambridge University Press.

Hokari, Minoru. 2011. *Gurindji Journey: A Japanese Historian in the Outback.* Sydney: University of New South Wales Press.

Honda, Katsuichi. 1984. *What Are the Facts?* (Original in Japanese: 本多勝一『事実とは何か』朝日文庫、1984年).

Honda, Kenji. 1983. *The Revival of Hideyo Noguchi's Spirit: A Medical Bridge Between Ghana and Japan* (Original in Japanese: 本多憲児『甦る野口英世の心—ガーナと日本を結ぶ医のかけ橋』本多憲児教授退官記念事業実行委員会、1983年).

Honda, Kenji. 1988. *Flying Emergency Medical Care: Human Love Beyond Borders (Volumes 1 and 2)* (Original in Japanese: 本多憲児『空翔ぶ救急医療—国境を超える人間愛』(上・下)毎日新聞社、1988年).

Hoopes, James. 1979. *Oral History: An Introduction for Students.* Chapel Hill: University of North Carolina Press.

Horn, Joshua S. 1969. *Away with All Pests: An English Surgeon in People's China, 1954–1969.* New York: Monthly Review Press.

Hosono, Akio. 1990. International Relations and the Central American Region at the Crossroads: The Structural Adjustment and International Cooperation. In *The Central American Region at the Crossroads: Analysis of the Crisis and Prospects*, edited by Kamo Yuzo, Hosono Akio, and Harada Kinichiro (Original in Japanese: 細野昭雄「転換期の国際関係と中米地域—構造調整と国際協力」加茂雄三、細野昭雄、原田金一郎編『転換期の中米地域—危機の分析と展望』大村書店、1990年、所収).

Hosono, Akio. 1995. *APEC and NAFTA: The Contradiction of Globalism and Regionalism* (Original in Japanese: 細野昭雄『APECとNAFTA—グローバリズムとリジョナリズムの相克』有斐閣、1995年).

Hosono, Akio. 2010. *The Japanese Who Turned Chile into a Salmon Export Powerhouse* (Original in Japanese: 細野昭雄『南米チリをサケ輸出大国に変えた日本人たち』ダイヤモンド社、2010年).

Hosono, Akio, Michiko Iizuka, and Jorge Katz (eds). 2016. *Chile's Salmon Industry: Policy Challenges in Managing Public Goods.* Tokyo: Springer.

Hudson, Derek. 2018. Quill Hermans' Role in the Development of Botswana Alongside Seretse Khama and Quett Masire. *Botswana Notes and Records* 50: 323–326 https://www.jstor.org/stable/90026923.

Huizinga, Johan. 1955. *Homo Ludens: A Study of the Play-Element in Culture.* Boston: Beacon Press.

Hussin, Mutalib. 1990. *Islam and Ethnicity in Malay Politics.* Singapore: Oxford University Press.

Hyden, Goran. 1980. *Beyond Ujamaa in Tanzania: Underdevelopment and an Uncaptured Peasantry.* London: Heinemann.

Ichikawa, Nobuko, Michael A. Cusumano, and Karen R. Polenske. 1991. Japanese Investment and Influence in Thai Development. *Technology in Society* 13(4): 447–469 https://doi.org/10.1016/0160-791X(91)90046-Y.

Iida, Tsuneo. 1988. *'Affluence' in the Mirror* (Original in Japanese: 飯田経夫『鏡のなかの「豊かさ」』ちくま文庫、1988年).

Iida, Tsuneo. 1992. On the World Bank's Structural Adjustment Approach (Original in Japanese: 飯田経夫「世界銀行の構造調整アプローチをめぐって」『国際協力研究』第8巻第2号、1992年、3–8頁).

Iizuka, Michiko. 2016. Transformation of Institutions: Crisis and Change in Institutions for Chilean Salmon Industry. In *Chile's Salmon Industry: Policy Challenges in Managing Public Goods,* eds. Hosono Akio, Iizuka Michiko, and Jorge Katz, 137–174. Tokyo: Springer.

Iizuka, Michiko, and Jorge Katz. 2011. Natural Resource Industries, 'Tragedy of the Commons' and the Case of Chilean Salmon Farming. *International Journal of Institutions and Economies* 3(2): 259–286.

Iizuka, Michiko, and Juan Pablo Zanlungo. 2016. Environmental Collapse and Institutional Restructuring: The Sanitary Crisis in the Chilean Salmon Industry. In *Chile's Salmon Industry: Policy Challenges in Managing Public Goods,* edited by Hosono Akio, Iizuka Michiko, and Jorge Katz, 109–135. Tokyo: Springer.

Iizuka, Michiko, Pedro Roje, and Valentina Vera. 2016. The Development of Salmon Aquaculture in Chile into an Internationally Competitive Industry: 1985-2007. In *Chile's Salmon Industry: Policy Challenges in Managing Public Goods,* edited by Hosono Akio, Iizuka Michiko, and Jorge Katz, 75–107. Tokyo: Springer.

Ikegami, Koichi. 2001. Changes in Food Production by Irrigated Paddy Cultivation in the Kilimanjaro Region. *Memoirs of the Faculty of Agriculture of Kindai University* 34: 55–69 https://kindai.repo.nii.ac.jp/records/4847.

Ikegami, Koichi. 2012. The Transformation of the Moral Economy in African Peasant Society: The Impact of Agricultural Development Projects and Fair Trade (Original in Japanese: 池上甲一「アフリカ小農社会におけるモラルエコノミーの変容—農業開発事業とフェアトレードによる影響」『農林業問題研究』第187号1、2012年、109–113頁).

Imai, Masaaki. 1986. *Kaizen: The Key to Japan's Competitive Success.* New York: McGraw-Hill.

Imai, Masaaki. 1997. *Gemba Kaizen: A Commonsense Low-cost Approach to Management.* New York: McGraw-Hill.

Indonesia, the Republic of, Ministry of Public Works and Housing. 2017. *The Project for Assessing and Integrating Climate Change Impacts into the Water Resources Management Plans for Brantas and Musi River Basins, Final Report.* Japan International Cooperation Agency, The University of Tokyo, and Nippon Koei Co., Ltd.

Infante Varas, Rodrigo, Magdalena Miller, and Matías Sanchez (n.a.) *Una Locura Llamada Salmón: Historias del Sur de Chile.* mimeo.

Inoue, Junji. 1984. Activities of the Tanzania Agricultural Development Centre (Original in Japanese: 井上淳二「タンザニア・農業開発センターの活動」『農業土木学会誌』第52巻第1号、1984年、27–30頁).

Iokibe, Makoto. 2020. *The Era of Great Disasters: Japan and Its Three Major Earthquakes,* translated by Tony Gonzalez. Ann Arbor: University of Michigan Press, 2020.

Iokibe, Makoto (supervising ed.), Inoue Masaya, Uenishi Akio, and Nagase Kanseki. 2021. *Biographical Essay on Takeo Fukuda – Seeking for Prosperity and Stability in Postwar Japan* (Original in Japanese: 五百旗頭真(監修)、井上正也、上西朗夫、長瀬要石『評伝福田赳夫—戦後日本の繁栄と安定を求めて』岩波書店、2021年).

Irokawa, Daikichi. 1980. *Minamata: The Climate and History of Discrimination*(Original in Japanese: 色川大吉『水俣—その差別の風土と歴史』反公害水俣共闘会議、1980年).

Irokawa, Daikichi. 2020. *History of the Shiranui Sea People (Vol. 2) – Oral History* (Original in Japanese: 色川大吉『不知火海民衆史(下)—聞き書き編』揺籃社、2020年).

Irungu, Mwangi Newton, and Mugambi Mercy. 2013. Evaluation of Strengthening of Mathematics and Science in Secondary Education (SMASSE) Program: A Case Study of Murang, a South District, Kenya. *International Journal of Education Learning and Development* 1(1): 46–60 https://doi.org/10.37745/ijeld.2013.

Ishihara, Shinichi. 2012. Network-Type Cooperation: Strengthening of Mathematics and Science Education in Western, Eastern, Central, and Southern Africa (SMASE-WECSA) Network. In

Scaling up South-South and Triangular Cooperation, edited by Kato Hiroshi, 83–106. Tokyo: JICA Research Institute.

Ishikawa, Satoshi and Watanabe Kazuo (eds). 2017. *Science in Dialogue with Communities: Area Capability Theory* (Original in Japanese: 石川智士、渡辺一生編『地域と対話するサイエンス—エリアケイパビリティー論』勉誠出版、2017年).

Ishikawa, Shigeru. 1990. *Principal Issues in Development Economics* (Original in Japanese: 石川滋『開発経済学の基本問題』岩波書店、1990年).

Ishikawa, Shigeru. 1994. Structural Adjustment: A Re-examination of the World Bank Method. *Asia Keizai* 35(11): 2–32 (Original in Japanese: 石川滋「構造調整—世銀方式の再検討」『アジア経済』第35巻第11号、1994年、2–32頁).

Ishikawa, Tatsuzo. 1951 (Original in Japanese: 石川達三『蒼氓』新潮文庫、1951年).

Ishikawa, Tomonori. 1979. Historical Factors of Overseas Emigration. In *In the Pursuit of the Meaning Overseas Emigration: Commemorating the 70th Anniversary of Japanese Emigration to Brazil – Symposium on Japanese Overseas Emigration* (Original in Japanese: 石川知紀「海外移住の歴史的要因」外務省『海外移住の意義を求めて≪ブラジル移住70周年記念≫—日本人の海外移住に関するシンポジウム』外務省、1979年、所収).

Ishimure, Michiko. 1969. *The Pure Land in the Sea of Suffering: My Minamata Disease* (Original in Japanese: 石牟礼道子『苦海浄土—わが水俣病』講談社、1969年).

Ishimure, Michiko. 1988. *Milky Currents* (Original in Japanese: 石牟礼道子『乳の潮』筑摩書房、1988年).

Israel, Arturo. 1987. *Institutional Development: Incentives to Performance.* Baltimore: Johns Hopkins University Press.

Jablonka, Ivan. 2012. *Histoire des grands-parents que je n'ai pas eus: Une enquête.* Paris: Seuil.

Japan Culture Forum (ed.). 1975. *Symposium: The Structure of Anti-Japanese Sentiment: Anti-Japanese Arguments in Asia*(日本文化フォーラム編『シンポジウム・反日感情の構造—アジアの反日論』自由社、1975年).

Japan Emigration Service. *Goals and Policy Directions for Overseas Emigration in the Age of Internationalisation*(Original in Japanese: 海外移住事業団『国際化時代における海外移住の目標と施策の方向』海外移住事業団、1973年).

Japan Institute for Labour Policy Training. 2005. Vocational Training Policies in Asian Countries: Focusing on the Youth Population(Original in Japanese: 労働政策研究・研修機構「アジア諸国における職業訓練政策-若年層を中心に」『労働政策研究報告書』No. 29、2005年5月).

Japanese Chamber of Commerce and Industry of Brazil. 1957. *Brazil Economic Yearbook*(Original in Japanese: ブラジル日本商業会議所編『ブラジル経済年鑑』ブラジル日本商業会議所、1957年).

Japanese Political Science Association (ed.). 2005. *Oral History (Annual Report on Political Science 2004)*(日本政治学会編『オーラル・ヒストリー(年報政治学2004年度)』岩波書店、2005年).

JBIC (Japan Bank for International Cooperation). 2000. *Ex-post Evaluation Report for ODA Loan Projects 2000.* Tokyo: JBIC https://www.jica.go.jp/Resource/english/our_work/evaluation/oda_loan/post/2000/pdf/intro_s.pdf.

Jensen, Michael C. 1998. *Foundations of Organizational Strategy.* Cambridge, Mass.: Harvard University Press.

Jensen, Michael C., and William H. Meckling. 1976. Theory of the Firm: Managerial Behavior, Agency Costs and Ownership Structure. *Journal of Financial Economics* 3(4): 305–360 https://doi.org/10.1016/0304-405X(76)90026-X.

JICA (Japan International Cooperation Agency). 1975. *Report of Japanese Planning Team for Kilimanjaro Integrated Regional Development*. Tokyo: JICA https://libopac.jica.go.jp/images/report/10634905.pdf

JICA. 1976a. *The Survey Report for Agricultural Cooperation Project in Kilimanjaro, Tanzania: Ground Water Survey*. Tokyo: JICA https://libopac.jica.go.jp/images/report/10636488.pdf

JICA. 1976b. *Basic Design Study Report on the Construction Plan for the Institute of Basic Medical Sciences, University of Ghana.* Tokyo: JICA https://libopac.jica.go.jp/images/report/P0000063437.html

JICA. 1978a. *Preliminary design for the Jomo Kenyatta College of Agriculture and Technology.* Tokyo: JICA https://openjicareport.jica.go.jp/807/807/807_407_10623932.html

JICA. 1978b. *Basic Design Study Report for the Construction Plan of the Jomo Kenyatta University of Agriculture and Technology, Republic of Kenya* (Original in Japanese:『ケニア共和国ジョモ・ケニヤッタ農工大学建設計画基本設計調査報告書』国際協力事業団、1978年).

JICA. 1979. *Preliminary Survey Report on the Chilean Aquaculture Project* (Original in Japanese:『チリ水産養殖プロジェクト事前調査報告書』国際協力事業団、1979年).

JICA. 1981a. *Annual Report: Chilean Aquaculture Project to Transfer Pacific Salmon to the Aisén Region of Chile* (Original in Japanese:『チリ水産養殖プロジェクト太平洋ザケのチリ・アイセン水域への移殖事業・年次報告』国際協力事業団、1981年).

JICA. 1981b. *Evaluation Study Report for ASEAN Rock Salt-Soda Ash Project in the Kingdom of Thailand.* Tokyo: JICA https://openjicareport.jica.go.jp/684/684/684_122_10500981.html.

JICA. 1981c. *Preliminary Design Survey Report for the Construction of the Eastern Seaboard Pipeline in Thailand* (Original in Japanese:『タイ王国東部海岸パイプライン建設実施設計事前調査報告書』国際協力事業団、1981年).

JICA. 1981d. *Jomo Kenyatta University of Agriculture and Technology Planning Consultation Team Report* (Original in Japanese:『ジョモ・ケニヤッタ農工大学計画打合せチーム報告書』国際協力事業団社会開発協力部、1981年).

JICA. 1982a. *Basic Design Study Report on the Establishment Project of the Centre for Instructor and Advanced Skill Training (CIAST) in Malaysia.* Tokyo: JICA https://openjicareport.jica.go.jp/213/213/213_113_10588101.html.

JICA. 1982b. *ASEAN Human Resources Development Project, Malaysia Project, Second Preliminary Survey Report: Centre for Instructor and Advanced Skill Training* (Original in Japanese:『ASEAN人造りプロジェクトマレイシア・プロジェクト第2次予備調査報告書—職業訓練指導員・上級技能訓練センター』国際協力事業団社会開発協力部、1982年).

JICA. 1982c. *Final Report: The Study on the Development Project of the Industrial Port on the Eastern Seaboard in the Kingdom of Thailand.* Tokyo: JICA https://openjicareport.jica.go.jp/728/728/728_122_10307346.html.

JICA. 1983. *Basic Design Study Report on the Construction Project for the School of Veterinary Medicine, University of Zambia, Republic of Zambia.* Tokyo: JICA https://openjicareport.jica.go.jp/pdf/11842101_01.pdf.

JICA. 1984a. *A Comprehensive Expert Report on Kilimanjaro Agricultural Development Project in Tanzania* (Original in Japanese:『タンザニア・キリマンジャロ農業開発計画専門家総合報告書』国際協力事業団、1984年).

JICA. 1984b. *10 Years of the Japan International Cooperation Agency* (Original in Japanese:『国際協力事業団10年の歩み』国際協力事業団、1984年).

JICA. 1984c. *Planning Consultation Team Report for the Centre for Instructor and Advanced Skill Training (CIAST) in Malaysia* (Original in Japanese:『マレイシア職業訓練指導員・上級技能訓練センター(CIAST)計画打合チーム報告書』国際協力事業団社会開発協力部、1984年).

JICA. 1985a. *Comprehensive Expert Report on Kilimanjaro Agricultural Development Project in Tanzania* (Original in Japanese:『タンザニア・キリマンジャロ農業開発計画専門家総合報告書(野坂治朗・鷹巣政男著)』国際協力事業団、1984年).

JICA. 1985b. *Introduction to CIAST* (Original in Japanese:『CIAST案内』国際協力事業団、1985年).

JICA. 1985c. *Final Report for the Study on the Development Project of Leam Chabang Coastal Area: Sectoral Report.* Tokyo: JICA https://openjicareport.jica.go.jp/617/617/617_122_10307379.html.

JICA. 1986. *Consultative Survey Team Report for the Centre for Instructor and Advanced Skill Training (CIAST) in Malaysia* (Original in Japanese:『マレイシア職業訓練指導員・上級

技能訓練センター(CIAST)計画打合せ調査団報告書』国際協力事業団社会協力事業部、1986年).

JICA. 1987a. *The Jomo Kenyatta University of Agriculture and Technology Project Evaluation Team Report* (Original in Japanese:『ジョモ・ケニヤッタ農工大学プロジェクトエバリュエーション調査団報告書』国際協力事業団社会開発協力部、1987年).

JICA. 1987b. *Comprehensive Report on the Centre for Instructor and Advanced Skill Training (CIAST) in Malaysia* (Original in Japanese:『マレイシア職業訓練指導員・上級技能訓練センター(CIAST)総合報告書』国際協力事業団、1987年).

JICA. 1988. *Seminar on Human Resources Development in Central America* (Original in Japanese:『中米人造りセミナー』国際協力事業団、1988年).

JICA. 1989a. *Comprehensive Expert Report on Kilimanjaro Agricultural Development Project in Tanzania,* authored by Seko Yoshikatsu (Original in Japanese『タンザニア連合共和国キリマンジャロ農業開発計画専門家総合報告書(瀬古良勝著)』国際協力事業団、1989年).

JICA. 1989b. *The Jomo Kenyatta University of Agriculture and Technology Project Evaluation Team Report* (Original in Japanese:『ジョモ・ケニヤッタ農工大学プロジェクト評価調査団報告書』国際協力事業団社会開発協力部、1989年).

JICA. 1990a. *Report on the Preliminary Study (First Phase) of the Project for the Promotion of Industrial Technology in Central America, Republic of Costa Rica* (Original in Japanese:『コスタ・リカ共和国中米域内産業技術育成計画事前調査(第一次)報告書』国際協力事業団、1990年).

JICA. 1990b. *Singapore Productivity Improvement Project, ASEAN Human Resources Development Project: Report on the Ideal and Practice of Technology Transfer* (Original in Japanese:『シンガポール生産性向上プロジェクト ASEAN人造りプロジェクト—技術移転の理念と実践に関する報告書』国際協力事業団、1990年).

JICA. 1990c. *Delegation Team Report on Noguchi Memorial Institute for Medical Research Project in Ghana* (Original in Japanese:『ガーナ国野口記念医学研究所プロジェクト巡回指導調査団報告書』国際協力事業団医療協力部、1990年).

JICA. 1991a. *Aquaculture (Chile) Project-Type Technical Cooperation Activity Series 48* (Original in Japanese:『水産養殖(チリ)プロジェクト方式技術協力活動事例シリーズ48』国際協力事業団国際協力総合研修所、1991年).

JICA. 1991b. *Comprehensive Expert Report on Kilimanjaro Agricultural Development Project in Tanzania* (Original in English and Japanese:『タンザニア連合共和国キリマンジャロ農業開発計画専門家総合報告書(冨高元徳著)』国際協力事業団、1991年).

JICA. 1991c. *Informe del estudio de diseño básico para el proyecto de construcción del centro de formación de formadores y de personal técnico para el desarrollo industrial de Centro America en la República de Costa Rica.* Tokyo: JICA https://libopac.jica.go.jp/images/report/P0000073190.html.

JICA. 1991d. *Jomo Kenyatta University of Agriculture and Technology Project (Kenya) Project-Type Technical Cooperation Case Study Series 46* (Original in Japanese:『ジョモ・ケニヤッタ農工大学プロジェクト(ケニア)プロジェクト方式技術協力活動事例シリーズ46』国際協力事業団国際協力総合研修所、1991年).

JICA. 1992. *Report on the Evaluation Study of Specific Themes: Vocational Training (Malaysia)* (Original in Japanese:『特定テーマ評価調査報告書—職業訓練分野(マレーシア)』国際協力事業団企画部評価監理課、1992年).

JICA. 1994a. *The Kilimanjaro Agricultural Development Centre Plan and the Kilimanjaro Agricultural Development Plan (Tanzania)* (Original in Japanese:『キリマンジャロ農業開発センター計画・キリマンジャロ農業開発計画(タンザニア)』国際協力事業団国際協力総合研修所、1994年).

JICA. 1994b. *Development and Cooperation: Sectoral Assistance Study Group Report* (Original in Japanese:『開発と協力—分野別援助研究会報告書』国際協力事業団、1994年).

JICA. 1994c. *Bachelor's Degree Completion Evaluation Report, Jomo Kenyatta University of Agriculture and Technology, Kenya* (Original in Japanese:『ケニア共和国ジョモ・ケニヤッタ農工大学学士課程終了時評価報告書』国際協力事業団社会開発協力部、1994年).

JICA. 1994d. *The 20 Years of Japan's International Cooperation and JICA: Human Development, National Development, and Heart-to-Heart Communications* (Original in Japanese: 国際協力事業団『日本の国際協力とJICAの20年—人づくり 国づくり 心のふれあい』国際協力事業団、1994年).

JICA. 1995a. *Impact Study on the ASEAN Human Resource Development Project: Case Studies in Malaysia (CIAST) and Indonesia (CEVEST)* (Original in Japanese:『ASEAN人造りプロジェクトにかかるインパクト調査—マレイシア(CIAST)、インドネシア(CEVEST)における事例研究』国際協力総合研修所、1995年).

JICA. 1995b. *An Overview of Okinawa International Centre: The 10th Anniversary of Its Establishment, 1995* (Original in Japanese:『平成7年度沖縄国際センター概要・設立10周年』国際協力事業団沖縄国際センター、1995年).

JICA. 1997a. *Costa Rica: Evaluation Report on the Completion of the Project for the Promotion of Industrial Technology in Central America* (Original in Japanese:『コスタ・リカ共和国中米域内産業技術育成協力事業終了時評価報告書』 国際協力事業団鉱工業開発協力部、1997年).

JICA. 1997b. *Report of the Baseline Survey Team for the Kenya Secondary Mathematics Education Strengthening Project* (Original in Japanese:『ケニア国中等理数科教育強化計画基礎調査団報告書』国際協力事業団社会開発協力部、1997年).

JICA. 1998a. *Development of the Brantas River Basin: Cooperation of Japan and Indonesia.* Tokyo: JICA https://openjicareport.jica.go.jp/pdf/11968989_01.pdf.

JICA. 1998b. *JICA-CIDA Joint Evaluation Study Report on the Kilimanjaro Agricultural Development Project (KADP) in Tanzania.* Tokyo: JICA https://libopac.jica.go.jp/images/report/11538394.pdf.

JICA. 1999a. *Republic of Kenya, Second Country Training Completion Evaluation Report: Agricultural Productivity Improvement Techniques for Rural Women* (Original in Japanese:『ケニア共和国第二国研修終了時評価報告書—農村女性のための農業生産性向上技術』国際協力事業団研修事業部、1999年).

JICA. 1999b. 25 *Years of the Japan International Cooperation Agency: Human Development, National Development, and Heart-to-Heart Communications* (Original in Japanese:『国際協力事業団25年史—人造り・国造り・心のふれあい』国際協力事業団、1999).

JICA. 2000a. *Final Evaluation Report on the Third Country Group Training Programme, Costa Rica: Productivity-Quality Improvement* (Original in Japanese:『コスタ・リカ共和国第三国集団研修終了時評価報告書：生産性—品質向上』国際協力事業団中南米部、2000年).

JICA. 2000b. *Completion Evaluation Report, Jomo Kenyatta University of Agriculture and Technology (Bachelor's Degree), Kenya* (Original in Japanese:『ケニア共和国ジョモ・ケニヤッタ農工大学(学士課程)終了時評価報告書』国際協力事業団社会開発協力部、2000年).

JICA. 2003. *Report by the Management Guidance Study Team for the Costa Rica Productivity Improvement Project (Interim Evaluation)* (Original in Japanese: 国際協力機構『コスタリカ共和国生産性向上プロジェクト運営指導調査団(中間評価)報告書』国際協力機構鉱工業開発協力部、2003年).

JICA. 2004a. *Capacity Development Handbook for JICA Staff: For Improving the Effectiveness and Sustainability of JICA's Assistance.* Tokyo: Task Force on Aid Approaches Japan International Cooperation Agency https://www.jica.go.jp/Resource/jica-ri/IFIC_and_JBICI-Studies/english/publications/reports/study/capacity/200403/pdf/200403.pdf.

JICA. 2004b. *An Effective Approach to Development Issues: Reproductive Health* (Original in Japanese:『開発課題に対する効果的アプローチ—リプロダクティブヘルス』国際協力機構国際協力総合研修所、2004年).

JICA. 2005. *Education in Japan: Thinking about Educational Development of Developing Countries* (Original in Japanese: JICA『日本の教育経験—途上国の教育開発を考える』東信堂、2005年).

JICA. 2006. *Informe de evaluation ex post: proyecto de desarrollo de la acuicultura de los recursos bentonicos en la Republica de Chile.* Santiago: JICA https://libopac.jica.go.jp/images/report/P0000172219.html.

JICA. 2007. *Case Study Report on Capacity Development: Analysis from a Capacity Development Perspective, Strengthening of Mathematics and Science in Secondary Education (SMASSE) Project in Kenya.* Tokyo : JICA https://libopac.jica.go.jp/images/report/11856432.pdf.

JICA. 2009a. *JICA Professional's Challenge – Series 7: Projects Related to the 'Strengthening of Mathematics and Science in Secondary Education (SMASSE)' in Kenya: ODA Transforming Education in Africa* (Original in Japanese:『JICAプロフェッショナルの挑戦シリーズ7—ケニア「中等理数科教育強化計画」関連プロジェクト—ODAがアフリカの教育を変える』国際協力機構国際協力人材部総合研修センター、2009年).

JICA. 2009b. *JICA Professional's Challenge – Series 8: Projects Related to the 'School of Veterinary Medicine, the University of Zambia': ODA Shaping the Future of Africa* (Original in Japanese:『JICAプロフェッショナルの挑戦—シリーズ8・ザンビア「ザンビア大学獣医学部」関連プロジェクト—ODAがアフリカの未来を創る』国際協力機構国際協力人材部総合研修センター、2009年).

JICA. 2012. *A Study on the Use of Maternal and Child Health Handbooks in Maternal and Child Health Projects: Findings, Lessons Learned, and Future Challenges* (Original in Japanese: 『母子保健事業における母子手帳活用に関する研究—知見・教訓・今後の課題』国際協力機構人間開発、2012年).

JICA. 2014. *Costa Rica: Project for Improving the Capacity of Facilitators for Quality and Productivity Improvement in Small and Medium-Sized Enterprises (Central America and the Caribbean) – Final Evaluation Report* (Original in Japanese: 国際協力機構『コスタリカ国中小企業の品質・生産性向上に係るファシリテーター能力向上プロジェクト(中米・カリブ広域)終了時評価報告書』国際協力機構産業開発・公共政策部、2014年).

JICA. 2016a. *Technical Cooperation on the Development of Basic Schemes for PRTR System in the Kingdom of Thailand: Final Report.* Tokyo: JICA https://libopac.jica.go.jp/images/report/12251039.pdf.

JICA. 2016b. *A Sustained Passion – The Miracle of 50 Years of the Japan Overseas Cooperation Volunteers (JOCVs)* (Original in Japanese: 国際協力機構『持続する情熱—青年海外協力隊50年の奇跡』万葉舎、2016年).

JICA. 2018. *The Study on Applying Development Experience on Third Country Training Programme in Malaysia: Final Report.* Kuala Lumpur: JICA and International Development Centre of Japan Inc. https://libopac.jica.go.jp/images/report/12319075.pdf.

JICA and Bureau of Water Resources, Ministry of Public Works, Republic of Indonesia. 1998. *The Study on Comprehensive Management Plan for the Water Resources of the Brantas River Basin in the Republic of Indonesia: Final Report Summary.* Nippon Koei and Japan Construction Consultants. Tokyo: JICA https://libopac.jica.go.jp/images/report/P0000098866.html.

JICA, IDCJ (International Development Centre of Japan) and IDJ (International Development Journal). 2013. *Final Report on Information Gathering and Confirmation Survey on Cooperation for Regional Human Resource Development in Africa* (Original in Japanese:『アフリカ地域人造り協力の在り方に係る情報収集・確認調査ファイナル・レポート』 国際協力機構、国際開発センター、国際開発ジャーナル社、2013年).

JICA and OECF (Overseas Economic Cooperation Fund). 1999. *JICA-OECF Joint Evaluation Survey: Coastal Development in the East of the Kingdom of Thailand* (Original in Japanese:『JICA-OECF合同評価調査—タイ王国東部臨海開発』国際協力事業団評価監理室、1999年).

JICA Kyushu. 2014. *Report on the Questionnaire Survey of Returning Trainees from the Environment Sector Training Course Conducted in Collaboration with Minamata City* (Original in Japanese: JICA九州『水俣市との協力による環境分野研修コース帰国研修員アンケート調査実施報告書』JICA九州研修業務課、2014年).

JICA ORI (JICA Ogata Sadako Research Institute for Peace and Development). 2022. *Revisiting Human Security: Human Security Today No.1: JICA Ogata Research Institute Report.* Tokyo: JICA ORI https://www.jica.go.jp/Resource/jica-ri/publication/booksandreports/jveaq800000071xq-att/Human_Security_Today_EN_20221031.pdf.

JICA ORI (JICA Ogata Sadako Research Institute for Peace and Development). 2024. *Human Security, Politics and Society under Compounded Crises: Human Security Today No.2: JICA Ogata Research Institute Report. Tokyo: JICA ORI* https://www.jica.go.jp/english/jica_ri/publication/booksandreports/20240801_01.html.

JICA Overseas Migration Center. 1989. *1988 Report on the Training of Japanese Language Students in Japan* (Original in Japanese:『昭和63年度日本語生徒本邦研修生研修報告書』国際協力事業団海外移住センター、1989年).

JKUAT. 2014. *JKUAT@20: A Pictorial History (1994-2014).* Nairobi: Jomo Kenyatta University of Agriculture and Technology.

JKUAT. 2018. *A Decade in Leadership 2008-2018.* Nairobi: Jomo Kenyatta University of Agriculture and Technology.

Jones, Michael D., and Mark K. McBeth. 2010. A Narrative Policy Framework: Clear Enough to Be Wrong?." *Policy Studies Journal* 38(2): 329–353 https://doi.org/10.1111/j.1541-0072.2010.00364.x.

Kaldor, Mary. 2007. *Human Security: Reflections on Globalization and Intervention.* Cambridge: Polity.

Kano, Masanao. 2018. *Okinawa's Abyss: Iha Fuyu and his Times* (Original in Japanese: 鹿野政直『沖縄の淵—伊波普猷とその時代』岩波現代文庫).

Kasahara, Shohei. 1991. *Cooperation for 'Self-Help': Experiences of Technical Cooperation in Malaysia* (Original in Japanese: 笠原昌平『「自助」への協力—マレイシア技術協力の経験から』国際協力出版会、1991年).

Kasahara, Shohei. 1998. *Cooperation for 'Human Resources Development'* (Original in Japanese: 笠原昌平『「人づくり」への協力』西田書店、1998年).

Kato, Hiroshi (ed.). 2012. *Scaling Up South-South and Triangular Cooperation.* Tokyo: JICA Research Institute.

Kato, Hiroshi, John Page, and Yasutami Shimomura (eds). 2016. *Japan's Development Assistance: Foreign Aid and the Post-2015 Agenda.* Basingstoke: Palgrave Macmillan.

Katsuki, Toshitaka. 1988. Development Assistance and the Transformation of Rural Society (Original in Japanese: 香月敏孝「開発援助と農村社会の変容」『アフリカレポート』No. 7(アジア経済研究所)、1988年).

Katsuki, Toshitaka. 2001. *Trends in Farm Household Economy under the Kilimanjaro Agricultural Development Project in Tanzania: Findings from a 1999 Farm Household Survey in the Lower Moshi Area* (Original in Japanese: 香月敏孝『タンザニア・キリマンジャロ農業開発計画下における農家経済の動向—ローア・モシ地域1999年農家調査から』国際農林水産業研究センター、2001年).

Katz, Jorge. 2006 Salmon Farming in Chile. In *Technology, Adaptation, and Exports: How Some Developing Countries Got It Right*, ed. Vandana Chandra, 193–223. Washington, D.C.: World Bank http://hdl.handle.net/10986/7118.

Katz, Jorge. 2016. Public Goods, Regulation and the Expansion of the Natural Resource Exploitation Frontier: The Future of Salmon Farming in Chile. In *Chile's Salmon Industry: Policy Challenges in Managing Public Goods,* edited by Hosono Akio, Iizuka Michiko, and Jorge Katz, 175-193. Tokyo: Springer.

Kawada, Junzo. 1998. *La voix: étude d'ethno-linguistique comparative,* traduit par Sylvie Jeanne. Paris: l'École des hautes études en sciences sociales.

Kayashima, Nobuko. 2019. *Internationalisation of Universities and Their Participation in ODA* (Original in Japanese: 萱島信子『大学の国際化とODA参加』玉川大学出版部、2019年).

Kayashima, Nobuko. 2022. Japan's ODA for the Development of Higher Education Institutions in Developing Countries: Supporting Leading Universities for Human Resource Development and Knowledge Creation and Diffusion. In *Japan's International Cooperation in Education: History and Prospects,* eds. Kayashima Nobuko, Kuroda Kazuo, and Kitamura Yuto, 197–216. Singapore: Springer.

Kayashima, Nobuko, Kuroda Kazuo, and Kitamura Yuto. 2022. Japan's International Cooperation in Education: An Overview. In *Japan's International Cooperation in Education: History and Prospects,* eds. Kayashima Nobuko, Kuroda Kazuo, and Kitamura Yuto, 1–26. Singapore: Springer.

Kayashima, Nobuko, Sugimura Miki, Kuroda Kazuo, and Kitamura Yuto (eds). 2024. *Impacts of Study Abroad on Higher Education Development: Examining the Experiences of Faculty at Leading Universities in Southeast Asia.* Singapore: Springer.

Kenyatta, Jomo. 1961. *Facing Mount Kenya: The Tribal Life of the Gikuyu.* London: Heinemann.

Kiernan, Ben. 1985. *How Pol Pot Came to Power: A History of Communism in Kampuchea, 1930–1975.* London: Verso.

Kiige, Mwangi James, and James Onywoki Atina. 2016. The Effectiveness of SMASSE Teacher Training Programme on KCSE Performance in Mathematics and Chemistry Subjects in Kikuyu District, Kenya. *Journal of Education and Practice* 7(6): 156–163.

Killick, Tony. 1978. *Development Economics in Action: A Study of Economic Policies in Ghana.* London: Heinemann.

Kimoto, Shoji. 1964. *The Sun of Kurobe: A Chronicle of Japanese* (木本正次『黒部の太陽—日本人の記録』毎日新聞社).

Kitahara, Atsushi, and Akagi Osamu (eds.) 1995. *Thailand: Industrialisation and Changes in Local Society* (Original in Japanese: 北原淳、赤木攻編『タイ—工業化と地域社会の変動』法律文化社、1995年).

Kitano, Koichi. 2011. Book Review: 'Hosono Akio, *The Japanese Who Turned Chile in South America into a Major Salmon-Exporting Country*' (Original in Japanese: 北野浩一「書評・細野昭雄著『南米チリをサケ輸出大国に変えた日本人たち』」『ラテンアメリカ論集』第45号, 2011年、75–79頁).

Koestler, Arthur. 1967. *The Ghost in the Machine.* London: Hutchinson.

Kojima, Kiyoshi. 2000. The 'Flying Geese' Model of Asian Economic Development: Origin, Theoretical Extensions, and Regional Policy Implications. *Journal of Asian Economics* 11 (4): 375–401 https://doi.org/10.1016/S1049-0078(00)00067-1.

Koizumi, Hajime. 2008. *Development as a Business: Learning from Kubota Yutaka about the Way Forward for Development Cooperation* (Original in Japanese: 小泉肇『開発は事業と捉えよ—久保田豊に学ぶ開発協力のあり方』DTP出版、2008年).

Koizumi, Makoto. 1939. *Noguchi Hideyo* (revised ed.) (Original in Japanese: 小泉丹『野口英世』(改稿版)岩波新書、1939年).

Komasawa, Makiko. 2005. *Jordan, Comprehensive Study of Family Planning and WID Projects: Analysis from the Perspective of Capacity Development* (Original in Japanese: 駒澤牧子『ヨルダン 家族計画・WIDプロジェクトの総合的研究—キャパシティ・ディベロップメントの視点による分析』国際協力機構国際協力総合研修所、2005年).

Konno, Toshihiko and Yukiharu Takahashi (eds.) 1993. *Migrants in Dominica Were Abandoned: The Trajectory of Post-War Japanese Emigrants* (Original in Japanese: 今野敏彦、高橋幸春編『ドミニカ移民は棄民だった—戦後日系移民の軌跡』明石書店、1993年).

Korten, David C. 1990. *Getting to the 21st Century: Voluntary Action and the Global Agenda.* West Hartford, Conn.: Kumarian Press.

Krugman, Paul. 1991. *Geography and Trade.* Cambridge, Mass.: MIT Press.

Kuranari, Tadashi. 1988. *Japanese Diplomacy in a Time of 'Crisis': Towards a Heartful Diplomacy* (Original in Japanese: 倉成正『"危うさ"の中の日本外交—「心の外交」をめざして』小学館、1988年).

Kurasawa, Aiko. 2014. *9.30, The Day that Shook the World: The Depth and Repercussions of the Indonesian Political Crisis* (Original in Japanese: 倉沢愛子『9・30世界を震撼させた日—インドネシア政変の深層と波紋』岩波書店、2014年).

Kuroda, Kazuo. 2023. *The Genealogy of International Educational Cooperation: Ideals, Policies, and Practices That Transcend Borders* (Original in Japanese: 黒田一雄『国際教育協力の系譜—越境する理念・政策・実践』東京大学出版会、2023年).

Langer, Arnim. 2013. The Contrasting Experiences of Ghana and Côte d'Ivoire: Horizontal Inequalities, Ethnic Politics and Violent Conflict. In *Preventing Violent Conflict in Africa: Inequalities, Perceptions and Institutions,* eds. Mine Yoichi, Frances Stewart, Sakiko Fukuda-Parr, and Thandika Mkandawire, 66–94. Basingstoke: Palgrave Macmillan.

Lee, Debbie, and Kathryn Newfont. 2017. *The Land Speaks: New Voices at the Intersection of Oral and Environmental History.* New York: Oxford University Press.

Leong, Ching. 2010. Ek Sonn Chan and the Transformation of the Phnom Penh Water Supply Authority. Available at SSRN 1588071 https://doi.org/10.2139/ssrn.1588071.

Lerise, Fred Simon. 2005. *Politics in Land and Water Use Management.* Dar es Salaam: Mkuki na Nyota Publishers.

Levi, Primo. 1982. *Il sistema periodico.* Torino: Einaudi.

Lilienthal, David E. 1944. *TVA: Democracy on the March.* New York: Penguin.

Lin, Justin Yifu. 2012. From Flying Geese To Leading Dragons: New Opportunities and Strategies for Structural Transformation in Developing Countries. *Global Policy* 3(4): 397–409 https://doi.org/10.1111/j.1758-5899.2012.00172.x.

Lipton, Judith Eve, and David P. Barash. 2019. *Strength through Peace: How Demilitarization Led to Peace and Happiness in Costa Rica, and What the Rest of the World Can Learn from a Tiny, Tropical Nation.* New York: Oxford University Press.

Lodge, Tom. 2011. *Sharpeville: An Apartheid Massacre and Its Consequences.* Oxford: Oxford University Press.

Lundgren, Regina E. and Andrea H. McMakin. 2018. *Risk Communication: A Handbook for Communicating Environmental, Safety, and Health Risks.* 6th ed. Hoboken, N.J.: Wiley.

Madjid, Abdul. 2004. Overcome with Discipline. In *Semangat Brantas,* by Kerukunan Keluarga Eks Proyek Brantas di Jakarta & Sekitarnya, 51–53. Jakarta: PT Gramedia Pustaka Utama.

Mahathir bin Mohamad. 1970. *The Malay Dilemma.* Singapore: TBI.

Mahuika, Nepia. 2019. *Rethinking Oral History and Tradition: An Indigenous Perspective* New York: Oxford University Press.

Mamdani, Mahmood. 2002. Amnesty or Impunity? A Preliminary Critique of the Report of the Truth and Reconciliation Commission of South Africa (TRC). *Diacritics* 32(3): 33–59 https://doi.org/10.1353/dia.2005.0005.

Martens, Bertin, Uwe Mummert, Peter Murrell, and Paul Seabright. 2002. *The Institutional Economics of Foreign Aid.* Cambridge: Cambridge University Press.

Martin, Mary, and Taylor Owen. 2014. *Routledge Handbook of Human Security.* London: Routledge.

Maruyama, Hideki. 2022. Civil Participation for 50 Years: Japanese Overseas Cooperation Volunteers. In *Japan's International Cooperation in Education: History and Prospects,* eds. Kayashima Nobuko, Kuroda Kazuo, and Kitamura Yuto, 317–333. Singapore: Springer.

Maruyama, Makoto. 2015. The Fukushima Disaster and Human Security in Japan: From 'Atoms for Peace' to People's Peace. In *Human Security, Changing States and Global Responses: Institutions and Practices,* eds. Sangmin Bae and Makoto Maruyama, 103–118. Abingdon: Routledge.

Matsunaga, Yasuzaemon. 1965. *Human Development and National Development* (Original in Japanese: 松永安左エ門『人づくり国づくり』実業之日本社、1965年).

Maura de Jesus, Iracina, Edilson da Silva Brabo, Marcelo de Oliveira Lima, Kleber Raimundo Freitas Faial, Lena Lillian Canto de Sá Moraes, Rosivaldo de Alcântara Mendes, Bruno Santana Carneiro, Vanessa Bandeira da Costa, Volney de Magalhães Câmara, Elisabeth Conceição de Oliveira Santos. 2016. Contribuição pioneira do Instituto Evandro Chagas para a saúde ambiental na Amazônia em 25 anos da Seção de Meio Ambiente. *Revista Pan-Amazônica de Saúde* 7: 83–92 https://doi.org/10.5123/S2176-62232016000500009.

McNeill, William H. 1998. *Plagues and Peoples.* New York: Anchor Books.

Meissner, Frank. 1988. *Technology Transfer in the Developing World: The Case of the Chile Foundation.* New York: Praeger.

Michieka, Ratemo W. 2012. *The Future of My Past.* Nairobi: Creative Publishing.

Mieno, Fumiharu. 2013. The Eastern Seaboard Development Plan and Industrial Cluster in Thailand: A Quantitative Overview. In *Aid as Handmaiden for the Development of Institutions: A New Comparative Perspective,* edited by Nissanke Machiko and Shimomura Yasutami, 81-105. Basingstoke: Palgrave Macmillan.

Mikami, Takeshi. 1987. *Current Situation of the Technical Cooperation Programme at the Faculty of Veterinary Medicine, University of Zambia, and My Views on Its Efficient and Effective Management.* mimeo (Original in Japanese: 見上彪『ザンビア大学獣医学部技術協力計画の現状と効率的効果的運営のための私見』非公式文書、1987年).

Mikuriya, Takashi. 2002. *Oral History: Oral Records for Contemporary History* (Original in Japanese: 御厨貴『オーラル・ヒストリー—現代史のための口述記録』中公新書、2002年).

Mikuriya, Takashi, and Nakamura Takafusa. 2015. *Politics and Power in 20th-Century Japan: The Reminiscences of Miyazawa Kiichi,* trans. Timothy S. George. London: Bloomsbury.

Miller, Sam. 2023. *Migrants: The Story of Us All.* London: Abacus.

Minami, Kazumori. 2004. Thinking about Dr. Hideyo Noguchi in Ghana. In *Noguchi Hideyo: Living in the 21st Century,* eds. Kogure Hamako and Tasaki Kimitsukasa (Original in Japanese: 南一守「ガーナで考えた野口英世博士」(小暮葉満子、田﨑公司編『野口英世—二一世紀に生きる』日本経済評論社、2004年、所収).

Mine, Yoichi, Frances Stewart, Sakiko Fukuda-Parr, and Thandika Mkandawire (eds). 2013. *Preventing Violent Conflict in Africa: Inequalities, Perceptions and Institutions.* Basingstoke: Palgrave Macmillan.

Mine, Yoichi. 2022. *Connecting Africa and Asia: Afrasia As a Benign Community.* London: Routledge.

Mine, Yoichi. 2023. The Global South and Human Security. *International Journal of Afrasian Studies* 2 (1): 1–11 https://www.afrasia.org/journal.

Miyagi, Taizo. 2004. *The Search for a Postwar Asian Order and Japan: The Postwar History of 'Asia of the Seas' 1957–1966* (Original in Japanese: 宮城大蔵『戦後アジア秩序の模索と日本—「海のアジア」の戦後史 1957~1966』創文社、2004年).

Miyamoto, Tsuneichi. 2010. *The Forgotten Japanese*: Encounters with Rural Life and Folklore, trans. Jeffrey S. Irish. Berkeley, Calif: Stone Bridge Press.

Miyoshi, Yasuhiko. 1999. *Third-Party Evaluation Report: Evaluation of Pollution Control Administration in the Map Ta Phut Industrial Park.* Tokyo Metropolitan Research Institute for Environmental Protection. In *Yen Loan Ex-post Evaluation Report 1999, Volume II,* edited by Research Institute of Development Assistance, Overseas Economic Cooperation Fund (Original in Japanese: 三好康彦『第三者評価報告書・マプタプット工業団地における公害対策行政に関する評価』東京都環境科学研究所(海外経済協力基金開発援助研究所編『1999年円借款事後評価報告書・下巻』海外経済協力基金開発援助研究所、1999年、所収).

Mizuhara, Yoshio. 1997. Deducting the Brantas River (Original in Japanese: 水原嘉男「ブランタス河を推理する」『砂防学会誌』第50巻第1号、1997年92–97頁).

Mlambo, Alois S., and Neil Parsons. 2019. *A History of Southern Africa.* London: Red Globe Press.

Monson, Jamie. 2009. *Africa's Freedom Railway: How a Chinese Development Project Changed Lives and Livelihoods in Tanzania.* Bloomington: Indiana University Press.

Moore, Aaron Stephen. 2013. *Constructing East Asia: Technology, Ideology, and Empire in Japan's Wartime Era, 1931–1945.* Stanford: Stanford University Press.

Moore, Aaron Stephen. 2020. Interrogating 'Comprehensive Development': The Colonial-Wartime Background to Japan's Development Cooperation. *Japan's Development Cooperation: A Historical Perspective, Background Paper* No. 10, September 2020 https://www.jica.go.jp/Resource/jica-ri/publication/other/sgjqgc0000007xp5-att/background_paper_No10.pdf.

Morisaki, Kazue. 1976. *Karayuki-san* (Original in Japanese: 森崎和江『からゆきさん』朝日新聞社、1976年).

Murai, Yoshinori. 1988. *Shrimp and the Japanese* (Original in Japanese: 村井吉敬『エビと日本人』岩波新書、1988年).

Murata, Aki, and Christine Kim-Eng Lee. 2021. *Stepping Up Lesson Study: An Educator's Guide to Deeper Learning.* Abingdon: Routledge.

Murotani, Ryutaro, and Mine Yoichi. 2015. Bridging State and Local Communities in Fragile States: Subnational Institutions as a Strategic Focus to Restore State Legitimacy. In *The Last Mile: In Ending Extreme Poverty,* eds. Laurence Chandy, Kato Hiroshi, and Homi Kharas, 76–94. Washington, D.C.: Brookings Institution.

Murphy, Craig N. 2006. *The United Nations Development Programme: A Better Way?* Cambridge: Cambridge University Press.

Nagai, Hiroshi. 1983. *Aid from the Perspective of the Recipients: Report from Thailand* (Original in Japanese: 永井浩『される側から見た「援助」—タイからの報告』勁草書房、1983年).

Nakachi, Shigeharu. 2009. Examination of Approaches to Community Development Compatible with Industrial Parks in the Map Ta Phut Industrial Region of Eastern Thailand and the Practice of Risk Communication (Original in Japanese: 中地重晴「タイ東部工業地域Map Ta Phutでの工業団地と共存できる地域づくりのあり方の検討とリスクコミュニケーションの実践」『水俣学通信』第18号、2009年、4頁).

Nakane, Chie. 1967. *Human Relations in a Vertical Society* (Original in Japanese: 中根千枝『タテ社会の人間関係』講談社、1967年).

Nakaoka, Tetsuro. 1970. *The Future of Humans and Labour: What Will Technological Progress Bring?* (Original in Japanese: 中岡哲郎『人間と労働の未来—技術進歩は何をもたらすか』中公新書、1970年).

Nakaoka, Tetsuro. 1971. *The Philosophy of the Factory: Organisation and Humans* (Original in Japanese: 中岡哲郎『工場の哲学—組織と人間』平凡社、1971年).

Nakayama, Mikiyasu, and Ryo Fujikura. 2013. Technology Transfer and Technology Development in post-World War II Japan Triggered by World Bank Projects. In *The Rise of Asian Donors: Japan's Impact on the Evolution of Emerging Donors,* ed. Jin Sato and Yasutami Shimomura, 49-65. Abingdon: Routledge.

Narayan, Deepa, Raj Patel, Kai Schafft, Anne Rademacher, and Sarah Koch-Schulte (eds). 2000. *Voices of the Poor: Can Anyone Hear Us?* New York: Oxford University Press for the World Bank.

Narayan, Deepa, Robert Chambers, Meera K. Shah, and Patti Petesch (eds). 2000. *Voices of the Poor: Crying Out for Change.* New York: Oxford University Press for the World Bank.

Narayan, Deepa, and Patti Petesch (eds). 2002. *Voices of the Poor: From Many Lands.* New York: Oxford University Press for the World Bank.

Ngau, Peter M. 1987. Tensions in Empowerment: The Experience of the 'Harambee' (Self-Help) Movement in Kenya. *Economic Development and Cultural Change* 35(3): 523–538 https://doi.org/10.1086/451602.

Ng'ethe, Njuguna. 1983. Politics, Ideology and the Underprivileged: The Origins and Nature of the Harambee Phenomenon in Kenya. *Journal of Eastern African Research and Development* 13: 150–70 http://www.jstor.org/stable/24325584.

Nishikata, Norihiro. 2017. *Improving Mathematical Literacy Among Children in Central America: The Miracle of 30 Years of International Cooperation Through Textbook Development* (Original in Japanese: 西方憲弘『中米の子どもたちに算数・数学の学力向上を—教科書開発を通じた国際協力30年の奇跡』佐伯印刷、2017年).

Nippon Koei. 1961. *Comprehensive Report on the Kali Brantas Overall Project.* Tokyo: Nippon Koei.

Nippon Koei and Koei Research Institute (eds.) 1997. *The Development of the Brantas River in Indonesia: Technology and Exchange between People* (Original in Japanese: 日本工営・コーエイ総合研究所編『インドネシア・ブランタス河の開発—技術と人々の交流』日本産業再建技術協会、1997年).

Nkrumah, Kwame. 1957. *Ghana: the Autobiography of Kwame Nkrumah.* Edinburgh: T. Nelson.

Nonaka, Ikujiro, and Hirotaka Takeuchi. 1995. *The Knowledge-Creating Company: How Japanese Companies Create the Dynamics of Innovation.* New York: Oxford University Press.

Nyerere, Julius K. 1968. *Ujamaa: Essays on Socialism.* Dar es Salaam: Oxford University Press.

O'Brien, Leslie. 1994. Some Characteristics of Work in the Manufacturing Sector. In *Transformation with Industrialization in Peninsular Malaysia,* ed. Harold Brookfield, 169-187. Kuala Lumpur: Oxford University Press.

Ogata, Masato. 2020. *Found Chisso Myself: The Thoughts of Minamata Disease* (Original in Japanese: 緒方正人『チッソは私であった—水俣病の思想』河出文庫、2020年).

Ogata, Masami. 2016. *Living in the Sea of Minamata and Meshima: My Life of Struggle with the Disease and the Patient Certification* (Original in Japanese: 緒方正実『水俣・女島の海に生きる—わが闘病と認定の半生』世織書房、2016年).

Ogino, Mizuho. 1989. *Outline of the Eastern Seaboard Development Project* (Original in Japanese: 荻野瑞『東部臨海開発計画の概要』バンコク日本人商工会議所、1989年).

Ohashi, Masaaki. 2016. NGOs and Japan's ODA: Critical Views and Advocacy. In *Japan's Development Assistance: Foreign Aid and the Post-2015 Agenda,* edited by Hiroshi Kato, John Page, and Yasutami Shimomura, 327–343. Basingstoke: Palgrave Macmillan.

Ohno, Izumi, Jin Kimiaki, Amatsu Kuniaki, and Mori Junichi (eds). 2024. *Introducing Foreign Models for Development: Japanese Experience and Cooperation in the Age of New Technology.* Singapore: Springer.

Okabe, Tatsumi. 1976. *The Future Paths of Southeast Asia and Japan: The Structure of Anti-Japanese Sentiment and the Role of China* (Original in Japanese: 岡部達味『東南アジアと日本の進路—「反日」の構造と中国の役割』日経新書、1976年).

Okabe, Yasunobu (ed.). 2024. *State-Managed International Voluntary Service: The Case of Japan Overseas Cooperation Volunteers.* Singapore: Springer

Okado, Masakatsu. 2017. *Speaking History, Listening to History: From the Field of Oral History.* Tokyo: Iwanami Shinsho (Original in Japanese: 大門正克『語る歴史、聞く歴史—オーラル・ヒストリーの現場から』岩波新書、2017年).

Okamoto, Tatsuaki (ed) 1978. *Records of the People in the Modern Age (7) Fishermen.* Tokyo: Shin Jinbutsu Oraisha (Original in Japanese: 岡本達明編『近代民衆の記録(7)漁民』新人物往来社、1978年).

Okamoto, Tatsuaki, Matsuzaki Tsuguo (eds.) 1990. *A History of Minamata People, Volume 5: The Colony Was a Paradise.* Tokyo: Sofukan 岡本達明、松崎次夫編『聞書水俣民衆史第五巻・植民地は天国だった』草風館、1990年.

Okinawa Prefectural Peace Memorial Museum. n.a. *Okinawa-Cambodia 'Peace Museum' Cooperation First Year Report: A Grassroots Technical Cooperation Project (Community Proposal Type)* (Original in Japanese: 沖縄県平和祈念資料館『草の根技術協力事業(地域提案型)沖縄・カンボジア「平和博物館」協力第1年次報告書』沖縄県平和祈念資料館、n.a.).

Okinawa Prefectural Peace Memorial Museum. 2011. *Okinawa-Cambodia 'Peace Museum' Cooperation Second Year Report: A Grassroots Technical Cooperation Project (Community Proposal Type)* (Original in Japanese: 沖縄県平和祈念資料館『草の根技術協力事業(地域提案型)沖縄・カンボジア「平和博物館」協力第2年次報告書』沖縄県平和祈念資料館、2011年).

Okumura, Tsurukichi. 1933. *Noguchi Hideyo* (Original in Japanese: 奥村鶴吉編『野口英世』岩波書店).

Olson, Mancur. 1993. Dictatorship, Democracy, and Development. *American Political Science Review* 87(3):567–576 https://doi.org/10.2307/2938736.

Omi, Kanako. 2024. Endogenous Development: Situating Kazuko Tsurumi's Work in International Development. In *The Semantics of Development in Asia: Exploring 'Untranslatable' Ideas through Japan,* eds. Jin Sato and Soyeun Kim, 93–112. Singapore: Springer.

Ostrom, Elinor. 1990. *Governing the Commons: The Evolution of Institutions for Collective Action.* Cambridge: Cambridge University Press.

Ota, Tsuneo. 1995. *'Japan Has Not Surrendered': The Ten-Year Conflict That Shook the Japanese-Brazilian Community in Brazil* (Original in Japanese: 太田恒夫『「日本は降伏していない」—ブラジル日系人社会を揺るがせた十年抗争』文藝春秋、1995年).

OECF (Overseas Economic Cooperation Fund). 1992. Issues Related to the World Bank's Approach to Structural Adjustment: Proposal from a Major Partner (OECF Occasional Paper No. 1, October 1991). *The OECF Research Quarterly* 73, 1992/2: 11–18.

OTCA (Overseas Technical Cooperation Agency). 1970. *Field Report on the Kilimanjaro Region of Tanzania* (Original in Japanese: 海外技術協力事業団『タンザニア国キリマンジャロ地域現地報告書』海外技術協力事業団、1970年).

OTCA. 1972. *Report on Brantas River Basin Development, Republic of Indonesia,* prepared for OTCA by Nippon Koei Co. Ltd. https://libopac.jica.go.jp/images/report/10549301.pdf.

OTCA. 1973a. *Report on the Brantas River Basin Development Plan, Government of Indonesia* https://libopac.jica.go.jp/images/report/10549368.pdf.

OTCA. 1973b. *Report of the Survey Team for Medical Cooperation at the Faculty of Medicine, University of Ghana* (Original in Japanese:『ガーナ国ガーナ大学医学部医療協力実施調査団報告書』海外技術協力事業団、1973年).

Perks, Robert, and Alistair Thomson 2016. *The Oral History Reader.* 3rd edition. London: Routledge.

Peycam, Philippe. 2020. *Cultural Renewal in Cambodia: Academic Activism in the Neoliberal Era.* Leiden: Brill.

Plesset, Isabel R. 1980. *Noguchi and His Patrons.* Rutherford, N.J.: Fairleigh Dickinson University Press.

Polanyi, Michael. 1966. *The Tacit Dimension.* Garden City, N.Y.: Doubleday.

Pritchett, Lant, and Michael Woolcock. 2004. Solutions When the Solution is the Problem: Arraying the Disarray in Development. *World Development* 32(2): 191–212 https://doi.org/10.1016/j.worlddev.2003.08.009.

Putnam, Robert D. et al. 1993. *Making Democracy Work: Civic Traditions in Modern Italy.* Princeton, N.J.: Princeton University Press.

Rackpanichamanee, Nicha, Dawan Chantarahasdee, and Kanis Pongnavin. 2016. Risk Communication and Chemical Accident Management: Case Study of BST Elastomers Factory Accident in Map Ta Phut Industrial Estate, Rayong, Thailand, translated by Miyakita Takashi (Original in Japanese: ラックパニチャマニー、ニチャ、ダワン・チャンタラハスディー、カニス・ポングナヴィン[宮北隆志監訳]「化学工場における爆発災害管理とリスクコミュニケーション―タイ・ラヨーン県マプタプット工業団地におけるBSTエラストマー工場の爆発災害」『水俣学研究』第7号、2016年、87–106頁).

Rasool, S. Ichtiaque. 1992. UNU Monitor. *Global Environmental Change* 2(1): 59–65 https://doi.org/10.1016/0959-3780(92)90036-7.

Ritchie, Donald A. 2015. *Doing Oral History.* 3rd ed. Oxford: Oxford University Press.

Ritchie, Donald A. (ed.). 2011. *The Oxford Handbook of Oral History.* New York: Oxford University Press.

Robins, Philip. 2019. *A History of Jordan,* 2nd ed. Cambridge: Cambridge University Press.

Robinson, Wayne. 1985. Imperialism, Dependency and Peripheral Industrialization: The Case of Japan in Indonesia. *Southeast Asia: Essays in the Political Economy of Structural Change,* edited by Richard Higgott and Richard Robison, 195–225. London: Routledge & Kegan Paul.

Roe, Emery. 1994. *Narrative Policy Analysis: Theory and Practice.* Durham: Duke University Press.

Roosa, John. 2006. *Pretext for Mass Murder: The September 30th Movement and Suharto's Coup d'État in Indonesia.* Madison, Wis.: University of Wisconsin Press.

Rostow, W.W. 1960. *The Stages of Economic Growth: A Non-Communist Manifesto.* London: Cambridge University Press.

Sachs, Jeffrey D. 2005. *The End of Poverty: Economic Possibilities for Our Time.* New York: Penguin.

Saint-Simon, Henri de. 1817. *L'industrie, ou, Discussions politiques, morales et philosophiques. Dans l'intérêt de tous les hommes livrés à des travaux utiles et indépendans.* Paris: Au Bureau de l'administration.

Sakai, Mitsuo. 1999. Overview of the Salmon Transplantation and Aquaculture Plans in Chile and the Activities of Dr. Shiraishi's Hatchery at IFOP: A Retrospective on the Chilean Aquaculture

Project Ten Years After Its Completion. In *Salmon Transplantation Plan.* JICA Chile Aquaculture, mimeo (Original in Japanese: 酒井光夫「チリにおけるサケ移植と養殖計画、およびIFOP白石博士ふ化場の活動概況—チリ水産養殖プロジェクト終了後10年を振り返って」JICAチリ水産養殖『サケ移植計画』、1999年).

Sakuma, Tomoko. 2007. *Report on a Survey of Salmon and Trout Farming in Southern Chile*(Original in Japanese: 佐久間智子『チリ南部におけるサケ・マス養殖に関する調査報告』アジア太平洋資料センター・水産資源研究会、2007年).

Salgado, Sebastião. 1999. *Serra pelada.* Paris: Nathan.

Salgado, Sebastião, et Isabelle Francq. 2013. *De ma terre à la terre.* Paris: Presses de la Renaissance.

Santhiago, Ricardo, and Miriam Hermeto (eds). 2022. *The Unexpected in Oral History.* Cham: Palgrave

Sato, Jin. 2008 Thailand's Environmental Policy and Decentralisation: The Multi-layered Nature of Planning and Administrative Incentives. In *Decentralisation and Environmental Policy in Asia,* eds. Terao Tadayoshi and Otsuka Kenji (Original in Japanese: 佐藤仁「タイの環境政策と地方分権—計画の重層性と行政のインセンティブ」寺尾忠能・大塚健司編『アジアにおける分権化と環境政策』アジア経済研究所、2008年、所収).

Sato, Jin. 2019. *The Reversal of the Environmental State: Beyond the 'Sustainability' Trap* (Original in Japanese: 佐藤仁『反転する環境国家—「持続可能性」の罠をこえて』名古屋大学出版会、2019年).

Sato, Jin. 2021. *The Making of Development Cooperation: Ecological History of Dependency and Self-Reliance* (Original in Japanese: 佐藤仁『開発協力のつくられ方—自立と依存の生態史』東京大学出版会、2021年).

Sato, Shigeru. 1994. *War, Nationalism, and Peasants: Java under the Japanese Occupation, 1942–1945.* Armonk, N.Y.: M.E. Sharpe.

Sato, Tokiko, Higher Population Council, and Japan International Cooperation Agency. 2008. *Integrating Health and Empowerment of Women in the South Region Project: Sharing Experiences and Learning from Good/Successful Practices in the Islamic Communities Workshop: JICA's Partnership for Reproductive Health Report: June 15th - 19th, 2008, Jordan.* JICA and Higher Population Council.

Sato, Tokiko. 2012. *Middle East Magazine: Jordan Report* (Original in Japanese: 佐藤都喜子『中東マガジン・ヨルダン報告』朝日新聞社(電子出版)、2012年).

Sato, Tokiko. 2021. *Contemporary Jordan Report: Arab Women Speak on Customs, Poverty, and Refugees* (Original in Japanese: 佐藤都喜子『現代ヨルダン・レポート—アラブの女性たちが語る慣習・貧困・難民』名古屋外国語大学出版会、2021年).

Sato, Yoshihiko. 1993. *Living in Zambia: A Veterinarian's Experience of the Wonders of Africa* (Original in Japanese: 佐藤良彦『住んでみたザンビア—獣医師のアフリカ不思議体験記』サイマル出版会、1993年).

Schlaufer, Caroline, Johanna Kuenzler, Michael D. Jones, and Elizabeth A. Shanahan. 2022. The Narrative Policy Framework: A Traveler's Guide to Policy Stories. *Politische Vierteljahresschr* 63: 249–273 https://doi.org/10.1007/s11615-022-00379-6.

Schmitt, Carl. 1997. *Land and Sea,* trans. Simona Draghici. Washington, D.C.: Plutarch Press

Schumpeter, Joseph A. 1942. *Capitalism, Socialism, and Democracy.* New York: Harper & Brothers.

Scott, James C. 1998. *Seeing Like a State: How Certain Schemes to Improve the Human Condition Have Failed.* New Haven: Yale University Press.

Sen, Amartya. 1999. *Development As Freedom.* New York: Alfred A. Knopf.

Shanahan, Elizabeth A., Michael D. Jones, and Mark K. McBeth. 2018. How to Conduct a Narrative Policy Framework Study. *The Social Science Journal* 55(3): 332–345 https://doi.org/10.1016/j.soscij.2017.12.002.

Sheftel, Anna, and Stacey Zembrzycki (eds). 2013. *Oral History Off the Record: Toward an Ethnography of Practice.* New York: Palgrave.

Shibahara, Tomoyo. 2016. The Current State and Issues of Japanese Language Education for Young People in Brazil (Original in Japanese: 柴原智代「ブラジルの年少者に対する日本語指導の現状と課題」『国際交流基金日本語教育紀要』、第12号、2016年、89–96頁).

Shimada, Go. 2018. The Strategy of U.S. Aid to Japan for Productivity Improvement, Labour Unions, and Expansion to Asia: Japan's Experience as an Aid Recipient (Original in Japanese: 島田剛「生産性向上のアメリカ対日援助の戦略と労働組合、アジアへの展開—被援助国としての日本の経験」『国際開発研究』第27巻第2号、2018年、69–84頁).

Shimada, Go, and Tetsushi Sonobe. 2018. Impacts of Kaizen Management on Workers: Evidence from Central America and the Caribbean Region. *JICA-RI Working Paper* 173 https://www.jica.go.jp/english/jica_ri/publication/workingpaper/wp_173.html.

Shimada, Go. 2024. Kaizen: Why Is It So Difficult to Understand? In *The Semantics of Development in Asia: Exploring 'Untranslatable' Ideas through Japan,* eds. Jin Sato and Soyeun Kim, 29–43. Singapore: Springer.

Shimomura, Yasutami. 2013. The Eastern Seaboard Development Plan of Thailand: Institutional Aspects of the Challenges and Responses. In *Aid as Handmaiden for the Development of Institutions: A New Comparative Perspective,* edited by Machiko Nissanke and Shimomura Yasutami, 106-123. Basingstoke: Palgrave Macmillan.

Shimomura, Yasutami, and Wang Ping. 2015. Chains of Knowledge Creation and Emerging Donors. *JICA-RI Working Paper* 88 https://www.jica.go.jp/english/jica_ri/publication/workingpaper/chains_of_knowledge_creation_and_emerging_donors.html.

Shimomura, Yasutami. 2017. *The Challenges of Opening New Horizons in Thailand: The Eastern Seaboard Development Plan and the Portraits Technocrats* (Original in Japanese: 下村恭民『タイの新しい地平を拓いた挑戦—東部臨海開発計画とテクノクラート群像』佐伯印刷、2017年).

Shimomura, Yasutami. 2020. *Evolution of the Japanese Model of Development Cooperation: Policy History I, 1945–1989* (Original in Japanese: 下村恭民『日本型開発協力の形成—政策史I・1980年代まで』東京大学出版会, 2020年).

Shimomura, Yasutami. 2022. *Japan's Rise to Top Donor and Its Aftermath: Policy History II, 1990s and Beyond* (Original in Japanese: 下村恭民『最大のドナーの登場とその後—政策史II・1990年代以降』東京大学出版会, 2022年).

Shirahata, Soichiro. 2015. Salmon Farming in Chile Was Initiated by the Daisui Investigation Team (Parts 1–3) (Original in Japanese: 白旗総一郎「チリのサケ養殖は大水調査団が契機だった(上・中・下)」『水産界』2015年8月号・9月号・10月号).

Shirato, Keiichi. 2022. Origin of the Tokyo International Conference on African Development (TICAD). *International Journal of Afrasian Studies* 1(1): 1–14 https://www.afrasia.org/_files/ugd/bb019d_c1feaf3e04024d09810cd6ea6b7e60df.pdf.

Shivji, Issa G., Saida Yahya-Othman, and Ng'wanza Kamata. 2020. *Development As Rebellion: A Biography of Julius Nyerere.* 3 vols. Dar es Salaam: Mkuki na Nyota Publishers.

Short, Philip. 2004. *Pol Pot: The History of a Nightmare.* London: J. Murray.

Sloan, Stephen M., and Mark Cave (eds). 2022. *Oral History and the Environment: Global Perspectives on Climate, Connection, and Catastrophe.* Oxford: Oxford University Press.

Simon, Herbert A. 1997. *Administrative Behavior: A Study of Decision-Making Processes in Administrative Organizations.* 4th edition. New York: Free Press.

Smiles, Samuel. 2002. *Self-Help, with Illustrations of Character, Conduct, and Perseverance.* Oxford: Oxford University Press.

Smith, Adam. 1999. *The Wealth of Nations: Books I-III.* London: Penguin.

Smith, Graham. 2017. *Oral History.* 4 vols. London: Routledge

Smith, W. Eugene, and Aileen M. Smith. 1975. *MINAMATA.* New York: Holt, Rinehart, and Winston.

Sonohara, Ken. 2016. International Cooperation for the Creation of a 'Culture of Peace' Originating from Okinawa: Cooperation between Okinawa and Cambodia in the Creation of a Museum of 'Culture of Peace' 2009–2014 (Original in Japanese: 園原謙「沖縄発の「平和文化」創造の国際協力について—沖縄・カンボジア「平和文化」創造の博物館づくり協力2009–2014」『沖縄県立博物館・美術館博物館紀要』第9号、2016年、111–128頁).

Spencer, Herbert. 1876. *The Principles of Sociology, Vol. 1.* London: Williams and Norgate.

Spencer, James H., and Bunnarith Meng. 2019. Resilient Urbanization and Infrastructure Governance: The Case of the Phnom Penh Water Supply Authority, 1993–2007. *Water Policy* 21(4): 848–864 https://doi.org/10.2166/wp.2019.211.

Stiglitz, Joseph E. 2024. *The Road to Freedom: Economics and the Good Society.* New York: W. W. Norton.

Subijanto, Tjeok Walujo. 2015. Toward Excellent River Basin Organization: Case of Brantas River Basin East Java – Indonesia. *India National Workshop on Integrated Water Resources Management,* New Delhi, 2–3 February, 2015

Subijanto, Tjeok Walujo, Harianto, Raymond Valiant Ruritan, and Fahmi Hidayat. 2013. Key Success Factors for Capacity Development in the Brantas River Basin Organizations in Indonesia. *Water Policy* 15: 183–205.

Sudo, Sueo. 1997. Japanese Diplomacy and Southeast Asia in the Volatile Age. In *Japanese Diplomacy in Crisis: The 1970s (Annual Report on Political Science, 1997),* ed. Japanese Political Science Association (Original in Japanese: 須藤季夫「変動期の日本外交と東南アジア」日本政治学会編『危機の日本外交—70年代(年報政治学1997年度)』岩波書店、1997年、43–58頁).

Sudo, Sueo. 2002. T*he International Relations of Japan and South East Asia: Forging a New Regionalism.* London: Routledge.

Suehiro, Akira. 2014. *Emerging Asian Economies: Beyond Catching Up* (Original in Japanese: 末廣昭『新興アジア経済論—キャッチアップを超えて』岩波書店、2014年).

Suehiro, Akira. 2018. Overcoming the 'Middle-Income Trap': 'Thailand 4.0' and the Adaptive Capacity of Thai Large Firms (Original in Japanese: 末廣昭「『中所得国の罠』の克服—『タイランド4.0』とタイ大企業の対応能力」『経済史林』第85号第4巻、2018年、67–128頁).

Suehiro, Akira and Yasuda Yasushi. 1987. *Industrialisation in Thailand: The Challenge of NAIC.* Chiba: Institute of Developing Economies (Original in Japanese: 末廣昭・安田靖編『タイの工業化—NAICへの挑戦』アジア経済研究所、1987年).

Sugihara, Kaoru. 2003 The East Asian Path of Economic Development: A Long-Term Perspective. In *The Resurgence of East Asia: 500, 150 and 50 Year Perspectives,* edited by Giovanni Arrighi, Hamashita, and Mark Selden, 78–123. London: Routledge.

Sugimura, Miki, and Kayashima Nobuko. 2022. Japan's ODA Scholarship Programs for International Students: Supporting Japan's Intellectual Contribution to the International Community. In *Japan's International Cooperation in Education: History and Prospects,* eds. Kayashima Nobuko, Kuroda Kazuo, and Kitamura Yuto, 217–238. Singapore: Springer.

Sugishita, Tsuneo. 2005. Aid Administration and Aid Policy. In *Japan's International Development Cooperation,* eds. Goto Kazumi, Ohno Izumi, and Watanabe Toshio (Original in Japanese: 杉下恒夫「援助行政・援助政策」後藤一美・大野泉・渡辺利夫編『日本の国際開発協力』日本評論社、2005年、所収).

Sumi, Kazuo. 1989. *ODA, the Reality of Aid* (Original in Japanese: 鷲見一夫『ODA援助の現実』岩波新書、1989年).

Suzuki, Kojiro and Kuwajima Kyoko. 2015. *The Miracle of Phnom Penh: Cambodia's Water Reform That Astonished the World* (Original in Japanese: 鈴木康次郎・桑島京子『プノンペンの奇跡—世界を驚かせたカンボジアの水道改革』佐伯印刷、2015年).

Suzuki, Ryo. 1988. The Method of Oral History for Historical Research. In *Oral History and Experiential History,* ed. the Historical Science Society of Japan (Original in Japanese: 鈴木良「歴史研究にとっての聞き取りの方法」歴史学研究会編『オーラル・ヒストリーと体験史』青木書店、1988年、所収).

Suzuki, Shizuo. 1991. The Logic of Anti-Japanese Sentiment in Southeast Asia in the Early 1970s. In *Southeast Asia and Japan,* ed. Yano Toru (Original in Japanese: 鈴木静夫「1970年代前半の東南アジアにおける反日の論理」矢野暢『東南アジアと日本』弘文堂、1991年、所収).

Syrpis, Phil. 2004. In Defense of Subsidiarity. *Oxford Journal of Legal Studies* 24: 323–334 https://www.jstor.org/stable/3600595.

Tadjbakhsh, Shahrbanou, and Anuradha Chenoy. 2009. *Human Security: Concepts and Implications.* London: Routledge.

Takara, Kurayoshi. 1993. *Ryukyu Kingdom* (Original in Japanese: 高良倉吉『琉球王国』岩波新書、1993年).

Takara, Kurayoshi. 1998. *The Ryukyu Kingdom in Asia* (Original in Japanese: 高良倉吉『アジアのなかの琉球王国』吉川弘文館、1998年).

Takara, Kurayoshi. 2012. *The Ryukyu Era: In Search of a Grand Historical Image* (Original in Japanese: 高良倉吉『琉球の時代—大いなる歴史像を求めて』ちくま学芸文庫、2012年).

Takemura, Shigekazu. 2008. *Educational Revolution: Through Science and Mathematics Education* (Original in Japanese: 武村重和『教育革命—理数教育を通して』理数教育研究所、2008年).

Taleb, Nassim Nicholas. 2001. *Fooled by Randomness: The Hidden Role of Chance in the Markets and in Life.* New York: Texere.

Taleb, Nassim Nicholas. 2007. *The Black Swan: The Impact of the Highly Improbable.* New York: Random House.

Tanaka, Akihiko. 2015. Toward a Theory of Human Security. *JICA-RI Working Paper* No. 91 https://www.jica.go.jp/english/jica_ri/publication/workingpaper/toward_a_theory_of_human_security.html

Tanaka, Takashi. 1997. *The Expansion of the Japanese Textile Industry into Central America* (Original in Japanese: 田中高『日本紡績業の中米進出』古今書院、1997年).

Tanaka, Yumiko. 2016. *How Did 'Modernisation' Change the Status of Women? Gender and Land Rights in Rural Tanzania* (Original in Japanese: 田中由美子『「近代化」は女性の地位をどう変えたか—タンザニア農村のジェンダーと土地権をめぐる変遷』新評論、2016年).

Tatara, Toshio. 1999. *Relief Supplies Crossing the Pacific: Postwar Japan and the Activities of Lara* (Original in Japanese: 多々良紀夫『救援物資は太平洋をこえて—戦後日本とララの活動』保健福祉広報協会、1999年).

Taylor, Charles. 2004. *Modern Social Imaginaries.* Durham: Duke University Press.

Taylor, Jean Gelman. 2003. *Indonesia: Peoples and Histories.* New Haven: Yale University Press.

Thomas, Caroline. 2000. *Global Governance, Development and Human Security: The Challenge of Poverty and Inequality.* London: Pluto Press.

Thompson, Paul. 2000. *The Voice of the Past: Oral History.* Oxford: Oxford University Press.

Toba, Kinichiro. 1973. *The Two Faces of the Japanese: In Southeast Asia*(Original in Japanese: 鳥羽欽一郎『二つの顔の日本人—東南アジアの中で』中公新書、1973年).

Tsuboi, Sakae. 1957. *Twenty-Four Eyes,* trans. Akira Miura. Tokyo: Kenkyusha.

Tsujimura, Hideyuki. 1999. *Rural Cooperatives in Southern Africa: Their Role and Development under Structural Adjustment Policies* (Original in Japanese: 辻村英之『南部アフリカの農村協同組合—構造調整政策下における役割と育成』日本経済評論社、1999年).

Tsurumi, Kazuko. 1996. *The Development of the Theory of Endogenous Development* (Original in Japanese: 鶴見和子『内発的発展論の展開』筑摩書房、1996年).

Tsurumi, Yoshiyuki. 1974. *Straight Talk from Asia* (Original in Japanese: 鶴見良行『アジアからの直言』講談社現代新書、1974年).

Uchio, Taichi. 2019. "A Comparative Study of Moai Tourism between Minami Sanriku Town and Easter Island," *Reitaku University Journal* 102: 54–61.

Umesao, Tadao. 1978. We Will Participate in the New World. In *We Will Participate in the New World: 70th Anniversary of Japanese Emigration to Brazil, International Symposium,* edited by Mainichi Shimbun (Original in Japanese: 梅棹忠夫「われら新世界に参加す」毎日新聞社編『われら新世界に参加す—ブラジル移住70周年国際シンポジウム』毎日新聞社、1978年、所収).

Umesao, Tadao. 1979. The Civilisational Significance of Emigration. In *In Search of the Significance of Overseas Migration: Commemorating the 70th Anniversary of Japanese Emigration to Brazil – Symposium on Japanese Overseas Emigration.* Ministry of Foreign Affairs of Japan (Original in Japanese: 梅棹忠夫「海外移住の文明史的意義」外務省『海外移住の意義

を求めて≪ブラジル移住70周年記念≫—日本人の海外移住に関するシンポジウム』外務省、1979年、所収).

Umesao, Tadao. 2003. *An Ecological View of History: Japanese Civilization in the World Context,* ed. Harumi Befu and trans. Beth Cary. Melbourne: Trans Pacific Press.

UNDP (United Nations Development Programme). 1990. *Human Development Report 1990.* New York: Oxford University Press.

UNDP. 2006. *Human Development Report 2006, Beyond Scarcity: Power, Poverty and the Global Water Crisis.* New York: UNDP.

UNDP. 2022. *New Threats to Human Security in the Anthropocene: Demanding Greater Solidarity, 2022 Special Report.* New York: UNDP https://www.undp.org/somalia/publications/new-threats-human-security-anthropocene-demanding-greater-solidarity.

UNICEF (United Nations Children's Fund). 2024. *The State of the World's Children 2024: The Future of Childhood in a Changing World.* New York: UNICEF https://www.unicef.org/reports/state-of-worlds-children/2024#downloads.

UNSG (United Nations Secretary-General). 2020. *Shared Responsibility, Global Solidarity: Responding to the Socio-Economic Impacts of COVID-19.* New York: United Nations https://unsdg.un.org/resources/shared-responsibility-global-solidarity-responding-socio-economic-impacts-covid-19.

Vanny, Leng, Ge Jiwen, and Hul Seingheng. 2015. Phnom Penh's Municipal Drinking Water Supply: Water Quality Assessment. *Sustainable Water Resources Management* 1: 27–39 https://doi.org/10.1007/s40899-015-0004-9.

Vogel, Ezra F. 1979. *Japan As Number One: Lessons for America.* Cambridge, Mass.: Harvard University Press.

Wanjala, Mukwabi Protus, Martin Wanjala, and Beatrice Shikuku. 2020. Influence of SMASSE Active Learning Techniques on Students Attitude towards Mathematics in Secondary Schools in Baringo County, Kenya. *European Journal of Education Studies* 6(11): 279–293.

Watanabe, Kyoji. 2020. *Remnants of Days Past: A Journey through Old Japan,* translated by Joseph Litsch. Tokyo: Japan Publishing Industry Foundation for Culture.

Wilson, Richard A. 2001. *The Politics of Truth and Reconciliation in South Africa: Legitmizing the Post-Apartheid State.* Cambridge: Cambridge University Press.

Wittfogel, Karl A. 1957. *Oriental Despotism: A Comparative Study of Total Power.* New Haven: Yale University Press.

World Bank. 1981. *Accelerated Development in Sub-Saharan Africa: An Agenda for Action.* Washington, D.C.: The World Bank.

World Bank. 1993. *The East Asian Miracle: Economic Growth and Public Policy.* New York: Oxford University Press.

Yamada, Junichi. 2021. *Japan's Cooperation to Infrastructure Development: Its History, Philosophy, and Contribution* (Original in Japanese: 山田順一『インフラ協力の歩み—自助努力支援というメッセージ』東京大学出版会、2021年).

Yanagita, Kunio. 1976. *A Study of Oral Literature History* (Original in Japanese: 柳田國男『口承文芸史考』講談社学術文庫、1976年).

Yano, Toru. 1975. *The Genealogy of the 'Southward Advance'.* (Original in Japanese: 矢野暢『「南進」の系譜』中公新書、1975年).

Yoshida, Masao. 1997. *Socio-Economic Theory of East Africa: Focusing on Tanzania* (Original in Japanese: 吉田昌夫『東アフリカ社会経済論—タンザニアを中心として』古今書院、1997年).

Yoshii, Masazumi. 2017. *'Janakashaba' The New Minamata* (Original in Japanese: 吉井正澄『「じゃなかしゃば」新しい水俣』藤原書店、2017年).

Yoshimoto, Tetsuro. 1995. *My Locality Studies: Messages from Minamata* (Original in Japanese: 吉本哲郎『わたしの地元学—水俣からの発信』NECクリエイティブ、1995年).

Yoshimoto, Tetsuro. 2008. *Let's Begin Local Studies* (Original in Japanese: 吉本哲郎『地元学をはじめよう』岩波ジュニア新書、2008年).

Yoshioka, Itsuo. 1998. *The True Face of the Japan Overseas Cooperation Volunteers* (Original in Japanese: 吉岡逸夫『青年海外協力隊の正体』三省堂、1998年).

UNZA Support Committee (Domestic Support Committee for the Technical Cooperation Project for the School of Veterinary Medicine, the University of Zambia). 1997. *The Technical Cooperation Project for the University of Zambia School of Veterinary Medicine: A Trajectory of Cooperation Over Twelve and a Half Years* (Original in Japanese: ザンビア大学獣医学部技術協力計画国内支援委員会『ザンビア大学獣医学部技術協力計画—二年半の協力の軌跡』国際協力事業団、1997年).

Name Index

Y. Mine, *An Oral History of Development Cooperation*,
https://doi.org/10.1007/978-981-95-5479-9

N

O

P

P

S

T

Y

Subject Index

Y. Mine, *An Oral History of Development Cooperation*,
https://doi.org/10.1007/978-981-95-5479-9

MIX
Papier aus verantwortungsvollen Quellen
Paper from responsible sources
FSC® C105338

If you have any concerns about our products,
you can contact us on
ProductSafety@springernature.com

In case Publisher is established outside the EU,
the EU authorized representative is:
Springer Nature Customer Service Center GmbH
Europaplatz 3, 69115 Heidelberg, Germany

Printed by Libri Plureos GmbH
in Hamburg, Germany